A Social and Cultural History of Republican Rome

Wiley Blackwell Social and Cultural Histories of the Ancient World

This series offers a fresh approach to the study of ancient history, seeking to illuminate the social and cultural history often obscured by political narratives. The books in the series will emphasize themes in social and cultural history, such as slavery, religion, gender, age, medicine, technology, and entertainment. Books in the series will be engaging, thought provoking accounts of the classical world, designed specifically for students and teachers in the classroom.

Published

A Social and Cultural History of Late Antiquity
Douglas Boin

Upcoming

A Social and Cultural History of Archaic Greece
Brian Lavelle

A Social and Cultural History of Classical Greece
Elizabeth Kosmetatou

A Social and Cultural History of the Hellenistic World
Gillian Ramsey

A Social and Cultural History of the Roman Empire
Jinyu Liu

A Social and Cultural History of Republican Rome

Eric M. Orlin
University of Puget Sound
Tacoma, Washington

WILEY Blackwell

This edition first published 2022
© 2022 John Wiley & Sons, Inc.

All rights reserved. No part of this publication may be reproduced, stored in a retrieval system, or transmitted, in any form or by any means, electronic, mechanical, photocopying, recording or otherwise, except as permitted by law. Advice on how to obtain permission to reuse material from this title is available at http://www.wiley.com/go/permissions.

The right of Eric M. Orlin to be identified as the author of this work has been asserted in accordance with law.

Registered Offices
John Wiley & Sons, Inc., 111 River Street, Hoboken, NJ 07030, USA

Editorial Office
111 River Street, Hoboken, NJ 07030, USA

For details of our global editorial offices, customer services, and more information about Wiley products visit us at www.wiley.com.

Wiley also publishes its books in a variety of electronic formats and by print-on-demand. Some content that appears in standard print versions of this book may not be available in other formats.

Limit of Liability/Disclaimer of Warranty
While the publisher and authors have used their best efforts in preparing this work, they make no representations or warranties with respect to the accuracy or completeness of the contents of this work and specifically disclaim all warranties, including without limitation any implied warranties of merchantability or fitness for a particular purpose. No warranty may be created or extended by sales representatives, written sales materials or promotional statements for this work. The fact that an organization, website, or product is referred to in this work as a citation and/or potential source of further information does not mean that the publisher and authors endorse the information or services the organization, website, or product may provide or recommendations it may make. This work is sold with the understanding that the publisher is not engaged in rendering professional services. The advice and strategies contained herein may not be suitable for your situation. You should consult with a specialist where appropriate. Further, readers should be aware that websites listed in this work may have changed or disappeared between when this work was written and when it is read. Neither the publisher nor authors shall be liable for any loss of profit or any other commercial damages, including but not limited to special, incidental, consequential, or other damages.

Library of Congress Cataloging-in-Publication Data
Names: Orlin, Eric M., author. | John Wiley & Sons, publisher.
Title: A social and cultural history of Republican Rome / Eric M. Orlin, University of Puget Sound, Tacoma, Washington.
Other titles: Wiley Blackwell social and cultural histories of the ancient world
Description: Hoboken, NJ : John Wiley & Sons, Inc., 2022. | Series: Wiley Blackwell social and cultural histories of the ancient world | Series information from ECIP data view. | Includes bibliographical references and index.
Identifiers: LCCN 2021008935 (print) | LCCN 2021008936 (ebook) | ISBN 9781118357118 (paperback) | ISBN 9781118359495 (pdf) | ISBN 9781118359501 (epub)
Subjects: LCSH: Rome--History--Republic, 510–30 B.C.
Classification: LCC DG231 .O748 2022 (print) | LCC DG231 (ebook) | DDC 937/.02--dc23
LC record available at https://lccn.loc.gov/2021008935
LC ebook record available at https://lccn.loc.gov/2021008936

Cover image: Wall painting - Actor and two muses - Herculaneum (insula orientalis II - palaestra - room III) National Archaeological Museum in Naples; (background) © ke77kz/Getty Images
Cover design by Wiley

Set in 10.5 on 12.5 pt Plantin Std by Integra Software Services, Pondicherry, India
Printed and bound by CPI Group (UK) Ltd, Croydon, CR0 4YY

C055884_061021

Table of Contents

Acknowledgments viii

Timeline of Roman History x

Introduction: We Are All Historians 1
A Note on the Text 3

1 What Is Historical Thinking? 5
   Literary Sources 9
   Material Culture 15
   Conclusion 22
   Discussion Questions 23

2 How Do We Tell the Story? 25
   An Outline History of the Roman Republic 28
   Marking Time 41
   Conclusion: Historical Narratives 43
   Discussion Questions 45

3 The Building Blocks of Roman Society 47
   Rome as a City-state 50
   Rome as a Mediterranean Empire 61
   Conclusion 65
   Discussion Questions 65

4 The Practice of Politics — 67
- What Was the Roman Republic? — 68
- The Late Republic — 79
- Julius Caesar and the End of the Republic — 84
- Discussion Questions — 85

5 The Roman Family — 87
- An Overview of the Roman Family — 89
- Changes in the Roman Family — 98
- Conclusion: Family Values — 104
- Discussion Questions — 104

6 Gender and Sexuality — 106
- Sex and Gender — 107
- Sexuality — 109
- Gender Roles — 117
- Conclusions — 122
- Discussion Questions — 123

7 Outsiders — 125
- Rome and Italy: The Early Republic — 126
- The Impact of Expansion — 131
- Conclusion — 142
- Discussion Questions — 143

8 Religion — 145
- What Is Roman Religion? — 146
- Changes in Roman Religion — 154
- The Late Republic — 161
- Conclusion — 162
- Discussion Questions — 163

9 Law — 165
- The Twelve Tables — 166
- The Effects of Expansion on Roman Law — 173
- The Late Republic — 178
- Conclusion — 181
- Discussion Questions — 181

10 The Military — 183
- The Army in Early Rome — 184
- The Beginnings of an Imperial Army — 195
- Conclusion — 199
- Discussion Questions — 200

11	The Economy	202
	The Agricultural Basis of the Early Roman Economy	203
	Changes in the Roman Economy	212
	Conclusion	219
	Discussion Questions	219
12	The City of Rome	221
	The Beginnings of the City	222
	Archaic Rome	224
	The Late Republican Transformation	239
	Conclusion	242
	Discussion Questions	242
13	Roman Arts and Letters	244
	The Early and Middle Republic	245
	On the World Stage	250
	Conclusion	259
	Discussion Questions	262

Ancient Authors   264

Notable Figures from Roman History   266

Glossary   269

Index   273

Acknowledgments

The idea of writing a textbook on Roman history began on a long drive from Calgary, Alberta back to Berkeley, California, after attending the Annual Meeting of the Association of Ancient Historians. Fired up by presentations at the conference, two graduate school friends, Judy Gaughan and Beth Severy, and I brainstormed what we might do if we ever decided to write a textbook.

Thankfully this book is not the crazy text that three sleep-deprived students conjured out of the midnight air as we crisscrossed the Pacific Northwest. However, that night did plant the seed, of what parts of the story are often omitted or of how one might try to tell the story of the Roman Republic differently. As I taught courses over the past twenty years, I tried to include as many of those parts as I could, always looking for different ways to tell the story. My courses always involved a significant focus on religion, the family, social structure, arts and letters, and the economy, and I often found myself frustrated that even the new wave of excellent Roman history textbooks did not devote the space I wanted to these topics. When Wiley informed me that they were developing a series of textbooks for the ancient world focused on social and cultural history, I felt I had to say yes, even as I felt there had to be people more qualified than I to write it.

A book such as this does not stand on its own: it rests on the work of many scholars who have written in greater depth on various subjects covered in this book. Indeed, one of the great challenges of this book has been to take brilliant ideas of others expressed in a book of 80 000 words and try to shrink them down to 500 words. Most of these books can be found in the Further Readings section, but I want to acknowledge my debt also to those authors whom space prevented me from listing. I want to express particular appreciation to colleagues and friends who took the time to read chapters and try to save me from as many mistakes as possible: Bill Barry, Douglas Boin, Lee Brice, Judy Gaughan, Matthew Loar, Carolyn MacDonald, Carlos Noreña, Andrew Riggsby, Brett Rogers, Nate Rosenstein, Beth Severy-Hoven, and Jesse Weiner. Special thanks go to Nandini Pandey, who not only read chapters multiple times, but also offered encouragement at critical moments. The mistakes that remain, however egregious, are my own fault.

Words cannot begin to express my appreciation to my colleagues in the Department of Classics and Ancient Mediterranean Studies at the University of Puget Sound: Bill Barry, Aislinn Melchior, and Brett Rogers, as well as colleagues who have spent time with us including Megan Daniels, Matthew Gorey, Kyle Helms, and Megan O'Donald. They have all been excellent companions on my journey and have expanded my horizons as I worked through different elements of teaching the Roman Republic. The Provost at the University of Puget Sound, Kristine Bartanen, offered invaluable support in the form of both time and treasure. My wife and boys deserve special mention for putting up with my rants on topics from the Romans to racism and everything in between.

Appreciation is also due to many generations of students at the University of Puget Sound, who tolerated me as I led them through these topics year after year and who taught me more about the texts and teaching them. That is doubly true for the past two generations of students who allowed me to inflict early drafts of several chapters on them. I also wish to thank the students in HIST 491 at CSU Pueblo in the fall of 2020, who read the chapter on Law and allowed me to Zoom into their class for discussion and critique. Finally I want to thank my two partners on that long overnight drive many years ago, Judy Gaughan and Beth Severy-Hoven, who have continued to put up with me after all these years, to support and correct me even when I go wrong, and to open up new vistas of understanding for me. I have learned more in the process of writing this book than I ever would have imagined, and I am grateful to all those who taught me along the way.

Timeline of Roman History
Parentheses indicate an approximate date

Period	Date	Military	Political	Social	Cultural	Religious
Monarchy	753 BCE		Traditional date for Foundation of City of Rome	(Romulus creates patricians, plebeians, and patron–client relationships)		(Cult of Hercules arrives in Rome)
Early Republic	509		Traditional date for Foundation of Roman Republic		Etruscan terracotta statues	Temple of Jupiter Capitolinus
	494	Local skirmishes	Traditional date for First Secession of Plebs	Struggle of Orders (Traditional dates 494–287 BCE)		Temple of Castor and Pollux
	451–50				Twelve Tables written	
	431					Temple of Apollo
	396	Conquest of Veii				*Evocatio* of Juno Regina
	390	Gallic Sack of Rome			Destruction (?) of City	
	367		Creation of praetor	Plebeians eligible for consulship	(Construction of "Servian" wall)	
	341–338	War vs. Latin League	Settlement of 338		(Manipular Organization of Army)	
	326			Abolition of *Nexum* slavery		

(*Continued*)

(Continued)

Period	Date	Military	Political	Social	Cultural	Religious
	312				Aqua Appia and Via Appia constructed	
	304				Publication of *legis actio*	
	290	Conquest of Samnium complete			(Capitoline Brutus)	Temple C of Largo Argentina
Middle Republic	280–275	Wars vs. Pyrrhus in S. Italy			(Introduction of Roman coinage)	
	270			Death of Scipio Barbatus		
	264–241	First Punic War			(Livius Andronicus)	
	218–202	Second Punic War				
	218	Hannibal crosses Alps into Italy				
	216	Hannibal destroys 100 000 Roman soldiers			(Naevius)	
	212				Marcellus brings Greek art from Sicily	
	204				(Fabius Pictor)	Magna Mater brought to Rome
	202	Scipio invades N. Africa; victory over Carthage			(Plautus)	
	200–146	Conquest of Greece and Asia Minor		(Massive Influx of enslaved persons)	(development of formulary procedure)	

Year			
195		Repeal of *lex Oppia*	
186			(Ennius) Bacchanalia incident
184	Censorship of Cato the Elder		(Terence)
			Basilica Porcia
177		Italian recruitment difficulties	
171		Spurius Ligustinus	
169		*lex Voconia*	
167	Triumph of Aemilius Paullus		Polybius arrives in Rome
161		*lex Fannia* sumptuary legislation	
160		(Cornelia raises the Gracchi brothers)	(Cato's *On Agriculture*)
154			Stone theater in Rome destroyed
149			Creation of first permanent court
149–146	Third Punic War		
147	Victory in Greece		First marble temple in Rome
146	Destruction of Carthage and Corinth		

(Continued)

(Continued)

Period	Date	Military	Political	Social	Cultural	Religious
	139		Introduction of Secret Ballot		(Lucilius)	
Late Republic	133		Tiberius Gracchus			
	122		Gaius Gracchus	(Tombstone of Claudia)		
	107	(Army reforms)	First consulship of Marius			
	104				First election for *Pontifex maximus*	
	91–89	Social War		Italians gain full citizenship	(Jurist Mucius Scaevola)	
	88	War vs. Mithridates	Sulla marches on Rome	Massacre of Italians in Asia		
	82–79		Sulla's dictatorship		(Appearance of Dressel amphorae)	
	80			Cicero and Terentia marry	First surviving amphitheater at Pompeii	
	70		Cicero's prosecution of Verres		(Veristic portraits, e.g. statue of general from Tivoli)	
	67–63	Pompey the Great conquers East				
	60		"First Triumvirate" formed		(Catullus)	

59	Caesar's Campaigns in Gaul	Consulship of Julius Caesar	
55			Pompey marries Julia
			Theater of Pompey built
53			Tiro gains free status (Cicero)
49	Civil War between Pompey and Caesar	Caesar crosses Rubicon	
48–44		Dictatorship of Caesar	
46			Cicero and Terentia divorce
			Dedication of Forum of Caesar
45			Death of Tullia
44		Caesar assassinated	
			Caesar deified after his death
31	Battle of Actium		
27		Octavian becomes Augustus, first Roman Emperor	
25			Livy publishes first five books of history
20			(Horace, Ovid, Sulpicia active)

(Continued)

(Continued)

Period	Date	Military	Political	Social	Cultural	Religious
	19 BCE				Vergil dies; *Aeneid* published after death	
	79 CE				Eruption of Vesuvius buries Pompeii	
	450				(Oldest surviving manuscript of Terence)	
	529				Justinian's *Digest* published	
	1748				Rediscovery of Pompeii	
	1764				Winckelmann argues that white statuary is ideal	
	1789		Authors of Federalist Papers use Roman pseudonyms			
	2020				White supremacists deploy SPQR as symbol	

Introduction: We Are All Historians

Most of us do things that historians do every day.

Almost one hundred years ago, Carl Becker delivered a speech to the national gathering of professional historians titled "Everyman His Own Historian." In it he told the story of a figure whom he called Mr. Everyman who had stumbled across a handwritten note at home reminding him to "Pay Smith for a coal delivery." Even though Mr. Everyman did not recall actually seeing Smith deliver the coal, the helpful note, combined with the 20 tons of coal in his house, led him to believe that the coal actually had been delivered, and off he went to pay the bill. When he got to Smith's office, however, Smith reminded him that his operation had been unexpectedly out of coal that day and so he had passed the delivery job to Brown. Mr. Everyman dutifully went to Brown's office and paid his invoice for $1,017.20. After returning home from his country club that night, Mr. Everyman went through his records. Sure enough he found the invoice from Brown, and so went to bed secure in the knowledge of what happened.

Becker's point was that Mr. Everyman models historical behavior: he uses his memory and consults written records to determine what happened, and when the records do not match up, he continues investigating until he has a clearer and more certain picture of the past.

This book is about the Roman Republic, but it is also about this process of historical thinking: each reader is invited to consider themselves a historian and ask: how do we know what we know (or think we know) about ancient Rome?

The process can be a challenge: the Romans often seem so familiar to us, especially since so many aspects of their society have been incorporated into modern societies, and especially American society. The United States Senate is explicitly modelled on the Roman Senate, and our system of checks and balances derives from ideas about the Roman government. Roman law is the basis for our legal

A Social and Cultural History of Republican Rome, First Edition. Eric M. Orlin.
© 2022 John Wiley & Sons, Inc. Published 2022 by John Wiley & Sons, Inc.

system. Roman architecture is all around us in our public buildings, and Latin literature has been a touchstone for many authors. Yet we need to remember that the Romans are far distant from us in time and space.

In 2009, eighty years after Carl Becker delivered his lessons about Everyman to a gathering of historians, Laurel Thatcher Ulrich stood up before the same professional setting and reflected on the distance between Becker's distant time and her own. People no longer heated their houses with coal, nor did most people physically show up in an office to pay a bill. More significantly, a twenty-first century audience may not immediately recognize just how much 20 tons of coal really is: it is 10 times larger than the equivalent amount of heating oil that until last week I used to heat my house. Nor do we recognize that the fictional Mr. Everyman paid almost *four times* the going rate for coal in 1931, or that the $1,000 he paid represented the median salary for an entire year in 1931, equivalent to about $40,000 today. That is, Mr. Everyman paid a year's salary to purchase an overpriced delivery of coal that would have heated his house for four years.

Ulrich's point was that context matters in understanding a text. Becker's audience surely knew these things immediately, which means they knew Mr. Everyman was no everyman; perhaps the detail of Mr. Everyman returning from his country club was meant as a clue. As she concluded her speech, "it is easy enough to figure out the price of coal, hard to capture the contexts that give events their meaning." Historians do not just recount facts, they have to work to generate meaning from events.

This book is built around these two intertwined ideas: that we are all historians and that we need context to understand the past. Historians need to ask questions of a text, as Ulrich did: who says what, and when, and why, matters. And often the most important part of a document is not what it says on the page, but what it *does*: what argument or image is the author trying to advance through the text on the page? Often this means following a maze of sometimes unintended clues to uncover just what the author is up to. If the story of Mr. Everyman's coal reminds us vividly of how different the United States was in 1931 and 2009, how different must Rome be, separated by thousands of miles and thousands of years? One of the aims of this book is to help readers recognize that distance and the difference it makes. Each chapter in this book offers examples of questions that could be asked, inviting readers to join in the journey of trying to understand the Romans by inquiring about both facts and meaning.

One of the themes of Roman history is the Romans' encounter with other peoples, first their neighbors in central Italy, then the rest of the peninsula, and eventually the entire Mediterranean basin as they built a multi-ethnic society. One might ask how they managed the conquest of the Mediterranean, but an even more interesting question is how these encounters changed the Romans and how those encounters helped the Romans understand what was distinctive about their own society. We might view our own encounter with the Romans in the same way, as an opportunity not only to learn about the Romans but to reflect upon our own society and the choices we have made and are making as we build our own multi-ethnic societies.

I completed work on this book in the summer and fall of 2020, after the killings of George Floyd, Breonna Taylor, and many other Black Americans laid bare how much work needs to be done for America to build an equitable multi-ethnic society. It would be foolish to claim those events had no impact on the text that has emerged. Just as many citizens have become more aware of the breadth and depth of the problem of white supremacy, scholars have become more aware of the particular role played by the field of Classics in the flourishing of white supremacy. Most scholars in the discipline continue to be Euro-American, and the study of Greek and Latin has often served as a gatekeeper, meant to advance some (elite white) people into the upper reaches of society while excluding (Black and brown) others. Research into the ancient world has often placed the Romans and Greeks as the ancestors of European nations as a means to project the superiority of European culture, and the symbolism of the ancient world has often been explicitly adopted by white supremacist groups in the twenty-first century. As a white male who has benefitted from the structures of both Classics and broader society, it felt important to emphasize the ways in which ancient Rome was not a pure white European world: it was not "pure," it was not "white" (a word that had no racial meaning in ancient Rome), and it was not only "European."

While the context of this era may have led me to emphasize these points, the facts have not changed. It simply took some of us, myself included, until this summer to ask these types of questions. My hope is that readers of this book will develop the ability to ask their own questions of Roman history, of me, and of others.

A Note on the Text

The story of the Roman Republic is a remarkable one. Most histories choose to focus on how Rome grew from a small village located at a marshy crossing of a river that flooded seasonally to become the dominant military power in the Mediterranean basin, and then how the Roman Republic "fell" into one-man rule. These military and political questions are important to be sure, but they only tell a portion of the story, and perhaps not the most important one. They pay insufficient attention to the way people lived their lives in the Roman Republic, to the structures that organized their lives: family, religion, economy, and law, to name only a few. This book reverses that emphasis, telling the story of Rome's political and military growth in only a few chapters and devoting most of its energy to understanding the institutions of Roman life and how they were changed by the growth into an imperial power.

This book is therefore organized thematically after the first two chapters that offer a chronological introduction. These thematic chapters generally employ a two-part structure. The first part of the chapter attempts to identify the key elements of Roman practices in each area, and the second half tries to understand the impact of Roman conquest on that particular area of life. Some readers or instructors may prefer to operate thematically and make connections across the chapters, and the book tries to offer frequent call-backs to assist with these connections. Others may prefer to read the first half of related chapters (for instance on the family and sex/

gender) together and then read the second halves of these chapters, to better see how the changes in family life connect to changes in sex/gender behavior. Readers are invited to use the book in whatever way is most useful to them.

A final note. Since the book lacks a formal conclusion, the last two paragraphs of the final chapter might be seen as a conclusion, not just to that chapter, but to the entire work. They pose the question whether the Roman adoption of practices from other cultures should be viewed in a positive light, as an openness to cultural exchange with others, or in a negative light, as appropriation of another culture. Readers might ask themselves the same question about our own adoption of Roman practices. The answers may vary from practice to practice, and from person to person. Good historians raise their own questions and come to their own conclusions.

1
What Is Historical Thinking?

The Roman historian **Livy** (Titus Livius, 59 BCE–17 CE) offers the following narrative about the life of **Romulus**, the founder of Rome. Rhea Silvia was made a Vestal Virgin in the hopes of preventing her from having children; she became pregnant, by the god Mars according to her account. When she gave birth to the twins Romulus and Remus, the king ordered the babies to be exposed by the Tiber River, but they were miraculously nourished by a she-wolf and then discovered by a farmer (**Figure 1.1**).

After they grew up, they overthrew their evil grandfather and decided to found a new city on the spot where they had been exposed, but the brothers could not agree who should be the ruler of the new city. They decided to hold a contest by looking out for birds; Remus saw six, but a moment later Romulus saw twelve. The conflicting result led to an argument in which Remus was killed. Romulus then offered his new settlement as a place of refuge for fugitives and other dispossessed people. His men then kidnaped women from a neighboring community in order to get wives, and the city prospered. Finally, one day as Romulus was reviewing the Roman army, a sudden thunderstorm arose, with clouds so thick that no one could see him and "from that moment Romulus was no longer seen on earth." A few men took the initiative and began to say that Romulus had been swept up into the heavens and soon the entire people were calling Romulus a god and the son of a god and praying that he might forever protect his children, the people of Rome. However, even then, says Livy, there were some who quietly claimed that the king had been torn to pieces at the hands of the senators (Bk. 1, Ch. 3–16).

Few historians today would accept the details of these stories, and fewer still would be willing to stake their reputation even on Romulus being a historical person, but these stories are still the place where we must start our work of understanding the Romans. At the very least, they represent the stories that the Romans

A Social and Cultural History of Republican Rome, First Edition. Eric M. Orlin.
© 2022 John Wiley & Sons, Inc. Published 2022 by John Wiley & Sons, Inc.

Figure 1.1 Bronze statue of a she-wolf suckling Romulus and Remus. Musei Capitolini, Rome. The wolf was originally considered to be Etruscan, but is now thought to date to the tenth century CE. The twins definitely date to the fifteenth century CE.

themselves told about the foundation of their city. As historians, we can only work with the material that we have; we cannot create stories out of thin air, but parts of the narrative – the she-wolf nourishing infant twins, the ascension of Romulus into heaven – seem too fanciful to believe. Sometimes we can use our common sense to decide what to accept, but sometimes our assumptions about what is possible are not reliable. The story of Romulus' ascension may seem unbelievable, but the story of Jesus' ascension into heaven has billions of believers around the world, and in principle is no different from Romulus. So how do we, as people living twenty centuries or more after the Romans, handle these stories? That is our task as practitioners of historical thinking.

The most important element to understand about a historical source is not its date, or the identity of its author, or the bias of the author, although those are all important. *It is understanding what the author is trying to do and what their purpose is in writing.* The first question we should ask about Livy's account is: what is he trying to accomplish with these stories about Romulus?

Fortunately, Livy, like most ancient and many modern historians, reveals his purpose at the very beginning of his text. He indicates that he will concern himself with:

> the life and morals of the community; the men and the qualities by which through domestic policy and foreign war dominion was won and extended… so that you see, set in the clear light of historical truth, examples of every possible type. From these you may select for yourself and your country what to imitate, and also what, being disgraceful in its origin and disgraceful in its conclusion, you are to avoid (Livy, *Preface*).

How might the knowledge that Livy wants to use Romulus to suggest something of the "life and morals of the community" help us understand his stories? For one it helps make sense both of the she-wolf story and of Romulus becoming a god. Livy wants us to know that the Romans viewed Romulus as someone so special that he must have had a direct link to divinity. Ancient texts are full of stories of the miraculous rescue of infants exposed to a premature death: Oedipus from Greek mythology or Moses from the Bible are similar examples. All of these stories are meant to tell the reader that an individual was destined for greatness, and in some way connected to the divine. If we read the story as Livy's attempt to make us understand the greatness of Romulus rather than as a literal description of facts, the text becomes more understandable.

We can go further with our analysis. In the story about the death of Remus, the brother of Romulus, Livy actually offers two versions. He first describes how Romulus and Remus engaged in a battle of words over the founding of the city: the verbal fighting led to physical fighting where Remus was killed. But Livy goes on to tell another version in which Remus leaped over the walls of the new city as a way to mock his brother, leading his brother to strike him dead with the words "So perish all who leap over my walls!" Livy here makes the morals of Rome's founder clear: Romulus placed the honor and protection of the city above the ties of family, a character trait that reappears frequently in episodes from Roman history. It might be seen as a part of Roman morality. However, we have to grapple with the fact that Livy tells us two stories, and seems to tell us this second story only because it was "more frequently told." Did Livy not believe the second story? Does he want us not to believe it? Is the lesson really that Rome's founder placed civic ties above family ties, or was it that he killed his brother out of anger? Perhaps Romulus is not an example to be imitated after all, but an example to be avoided. Note that once we know that Livy wants us to draw moral lessons from Roman history, we can start asking different questions rather than asking whether it really happened that way.

In the story of Romulus' own death Livy again gives us two versions, and again forces us to confront a series of problems. On the one hand is the miraculous disappearance of Romulus, which is clearly intended to indicate divine intervention; in this version Romulus is never said to have died, only that he was no longer seen. On the other hand, Livy notes that some people claimed that Romulus was torn to pieces by senators. To Livy's readers, the second story must have sounded an awful lot like the death of **Julius Caesar**, which occurred when Livy was around 15 years old. Caesar was stabbed 23 times by a group of senators as he conducted a meeting of the Senate. Again Livy presents an example that might well be worthy of imitation immediately alongside an example to be avoided. In this instance, Livy's purpose seems more directly relevant to his own day: is the lesson that Romans should avoid being ruled by a dictator or that they should avoid the habit of assassinating people? Livy again does not give us a clear answer: he asks us to think for ourselves.

This habit of retrojecting current history into the past – of explaining past events according to present circumstances, as if history never changes – is widespread among all historians and even other writers. Often this is simply a product of being shaped by our own experiences: if I think the world works in a certain way, then I am more likely to think that events in the past happened that way.

Key Debates: *How Do We Tell the Story of the Past?*

For many people, one of the frustrations of studying the past is that there often seems to be no clear answer, no story that scholars can agree on. William Cronon, an environmental historian, in an article titled "A Place for Stories" (1992), once noted that two books, published in the very same year, looked at the same materials drawn from the same past and reached almost completely opposite conclusions. How can this be? Are there no answers in history?

Not exactly. History is a humanistic discipline: that is, it deals with human beings. Human beings often have fundamentally different views about the world. What makes a person good or evil? What makes a person happy? Does nature or nurture shape human character? These questions do not admit of a single answer that can be found scientifically.

Cronon, in analyzing the two books mentioned above, suggested that most historians tell one of two types of stories: either that the world today is better than it was yesterday or that the world was better before. Cronon says that "the one group of plots might be called 'progressive,' given their historical dependence on eighteenth-century Enlightenment notions of progress; the other might be called 'tragic' or 'declensionist,' tracing their historical roots to romantic and antimodernist reactions against progress"(Cronon, 1992, p. 1352).

Roman historians also participated in these types of debates. For the most part, they subscribed to the tragic narrative. For instance, Livy wrote that "as our standard of morality gradually lowers, let my reader follow the decay of the national character, observing how at first it slowly sinks, then slips downward more and more rapidly, and finally begins to plunge into headlong ruin" (Livy, *Preface*). There's no beating around the bush here: the arrival of wealth corrupted the good morals of the Roman people, making people of his own day unable to bear either the diseases or their remedies. However, others saw Roman society differently: the very wealth that Livy criticized allowed the first emperor Augustus to famously claim that he found Rome a city of brick but left it a city of marble, a place with all the amenities that an imperial capital should have. Clearly Augustus felt that Rome of his day was better than earlier generations.

Discussions like these continue to this day. We have probably all heard stories about how our parents had to walk three miles to school in the snow (mine used to say uphill both ways!): is the point of the story that today's world is better because I did not have to do that, or that today is worse because I lack the character and strength built over the course of those journeys? These questions depend on what we consider to be the key factor in making a judgment: is having a house filled with the latest gadgets more important than spending time with one's grandparents? Each person needs to decide for themselves: there is no one answer, just as there is no one answer to our historical questions.

Think of the hit musical *Hamilton*: it suggests that politicians in the eighteenth century were, just like politicians today, making deals in back rooms and engaging in brutal partisan politics. It even presents a character approving of a Presidential candidate because "it seems like you could have a beer with him," a comment often made about George W. Bush during his campaign. In some ways this habit helps us understand the past better, as *Hamilton* surely does, but it can also make us believe the past was just like the present when it may have been dramatically different. No historian today believes that Romulus might have been assassinated by senators. Once we see that the historian is shaped by their own experiences, we can ask more productive questions rather than simply discarding a text as inaccurate or biased. In the end, that is our task as historians when we confront a source: to find out what the source may be telling us rather than discarding it because it does not meet our expectations.

Using Livy as an example has opened a window onto how historians deal with sources. Livy does not provide an eyewitness account, but eyewitnesses have disadvantages as well as the advantage of being present at a particular event. Eyewitnesses see only a portion of the action, and so may not be able to gain as complete an understanding of an event as others. The ability to gather a wide variety of evidence and to consider what each piece might be telling us is critical to good historical thinking. In the case of the Roman society and culture, we are both blessed and cursed in this regard. The blessing is that we have a wide variety of source material on which to draw, as the Roman Republic, and especially its last 200 years, is one of the best attested periods in the ancient Mediterranean world. We have multiple texts from both Roman and Greek authors on which to draw. We also have what scholars call **material culture**: physical remains of both monumental public buildings and private dwellings uncovered in archaeological excavations, as well as inscriptions left on stone and coins minted by the Roman state and others. All of these sources assist us in reconstructing a picture of Roman life. The curse is that this material is widely scattered like pieces of a puzzle, since most of it was created for purposes other than helping us tell a history of Roman social and cultural life. Our task then is first, to find the information that is relevant to our story and second, to understand the original purpose of the evidence so that we can put it in the proper place in our puzzle. The discussion that follows examines the major sources of information and then discusses how we might use these sources throughout this book to understand Roman society at any given point in time.

Literary Sources

One of the primary issues we must confront in approaching the literary sources from Roman history is to recognize that fundamentally Rome was an **oral** society. Although the alphabet had been invented as early as the eighth century BCE, Rome did not develop a written literary tradition until the middle of the third century BCE. For comparison's sake, Homer's *Iliad* and *Odyssey* seem to have been committed to writing in the eighth century, and the great Athenian tragedies were composed over the course of the fifth century. Mass literacy is a relatively recent phenomenon and it remains unclear how many Romans could read and write.

Exploring Culture: *Could the Average Roman Read?*

"Stronius knows nothing!" "Vote for Popidius Ampliatus and Vedius Nummianus!" "Rufus loves Cornelia." The walls of Pompeii are covered with graffiti written by residents and visitors to the town, but how many people could read them?

Some scholars have suggested that the percentage of inhabitants of the Roman empire who were literate was as low as 10%. If we are interested in those who had formal training and could read and especially write Roman history or poetry, that number might not be far off. Our written texts clearly come from this segment of the population.

There is reason to believe that literacy was more widespread from an early period in Roman history. Rome possessed a written law code from the middle of the fifth century BCE and it seems to have been a point of importance to the lower classes to have important public documents made available publicly in writing. It is possible that relatively limited numbers of the lower classes could read these documents for themselves, but clearly some outside of the elite circles possessed this ability and could either share it with others or read when need be. At the same time, the language of the early law codes suggests that many agreements were verbal and that witnesses might be crucial to establishing them. Written contracts for transactions were not the norm.

The graffiti from Pompeii falls further out on the literacy spectrum. For one thing, this evidence dates to 79 CE, two hundred or more years after Rome had established itself as the dominant city in the Mediterranean, and it is likely that literacy rates had improved as more money flowed into Rome from her conquests. However, it also suggests a more widespread picture of literacy: it would make little sense to go to the trouble and expense of expressing oneself on the walls of the city if only a small percentage of the city's population could read them. Some of the graffiti even engage in conversation with other messages, indicating that the author of the second graffiti, or perhaps a friend, had read the first post. The graffiti at Pompeii might be seen as the social media of its day, which certainly implies a higher level of literacy than 10% if one is willing to count composing tweets on subjects ranging from politics to sports to sex.

Further down the literacy spectrum, it seems likely that the majority of Romans could at least recognize the letters of the alphabet. Individual letters have been found on building blocks and roof tiles, suggesting that manual laborers could recognize these for use in construction projects. The letters SPQR (the abbreviation, still used, for "the Senate and People of Rome") appear frequently, apparently familiar enough that recognizing these four letters would be enough to indicate the involvement of the Roman state.

Like other non-literate societies, most communication in Rome, including stories about the past, was handed on orally from one person to another. Adding to the challenge, whatever written texts might have existed prior to 390 BCE were probably destroyed when the Gauls sacked Rome in that year. This situation means that Roman historians face particular challenges: we lack contemporary texts for the first 600 years of Rome's history and we have only scattered contemporary texts for the next hundred. The vast majority of surviving Latin texts date from after 80 BCE, and our copies of them come from many centuries after that (**Figure 1.2**).

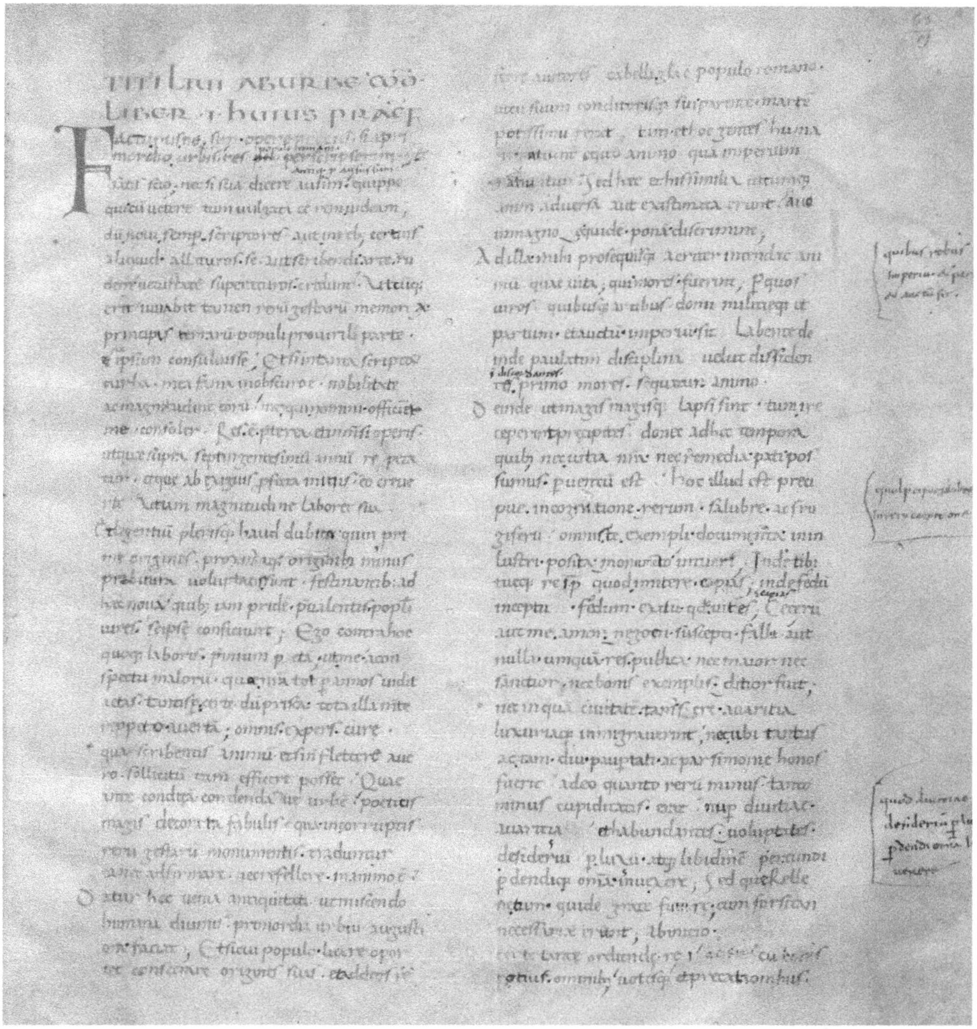

Figure 1.2 Fol. 1r from ms Plutei 63.19, a tenth century CE manuscript of Livy, originally copied in Verona and now in the Biblioteca Medicea-Laurenziana in Florence.

On the one hand, the absence of texts from the earliest years of Rome's history might appear to be a serious problem: the distance between Livy and the death of Romulus is greater than that from us to Christopher Columbus, but as we have discussed, later texts do not mean that they have no valuable information about early Rome. It means that we have to ask different questions about someone like Livy, who drew on earlier written material that we no longer have, than we would about other authors. Knowing when authors were writing is important because we can use that knowledge to ask questions more appropriate to that historian and therefore more useful to us in attempting to understand Roman society.

The abundance of sources dating after 80 BCE means that a Roman historian does have plentiful eyewitnesses for the Late Republic (133–31 BCE; see Chapter 2 for an outline history of the Roman Republic). Chief among these are the texts of the Roman orator and statesman **Marcus Tullius Cicero** (106–43 BCE). Cicero provides us with three different types of texts: speeches written and delivered primarily in the law courts, philosophical treatises, and personal letters to family and friends. Because Cicero apparently did **not** intend for his letters to be made public, they are often the most revealing source. His correspondents ranged from leading politicians of his day to his wife and daughter and his best friend Atticus, and the letters range over a wide set of topics, from politics to personal matters such as the death of his daughter in childbirth. Not only do they allow us to see his unpolished opinions about affairs of state or others in the Roman elite, but we get glimpses into his actual day-to-day activities and his family life. No other source can compare to Cicero, which sometimes has the consequence of giving too much weight to the evidence we get from him.

Indeed, Cicero's writings suffer from a flaw common to almost all literary sources from antiquity: they give us a slice of life for the upper class only. The texts we have usually emerged from elite society, the top 1% of the Roman world, and we have no historical texts authored by a woman, restricting us to one-half of that 1%. Compounding the problem, the elite tended not to be interested in the lives and concerns of the non-elite and so rarely wrote about them. Cicero's correspondents are almost entirely other members of the elite; in the surviving collection are only four letters to his wife and four letters to his secretary Tiro. One challenge we will have to take up in this book is how to make the silence speak: how to learn something about the lives of women and the other 99% of Rome's inhabitants despite the nature of our sources.

One way that modern historians try to fill the gaps in our picture is through comparative history. While recognizing that every society is unique in its details, anthropologists and other specialists have often been able to identify features that can be found in multiple societies. For instance Rome, as we will see, was a heavily agrarian society, dependent on farming for the majority of its economic output. As such, it likely shared certain features with other agrarian societies, such as the seasonal nature of the cycle of work: manufacturing societies are less dependent on the sun and rain for survival. Similarly, almost all pre-modern societies, because they lacked modern medical knowledge and equipment, suffered from very high infant mortality rates and shorter life spans than today. By looking to other societies and considering the ways in which they might compare to Rome, a Roman historian can get a better overall picture of Roman society, even if that picture remains fuzzy around the edges.

Another tool that Roman historians use to get around the problem of sources is to consider a much wider collection of texts than are normally considered "historical". To some extent, all literary creations might be considered historical. Even if they were not written for the purpose of recounting historical events, they reveal critical elements of their society. Think of movies in our own society: the story may be fictional, but the movie shows us how people dressed at the time, what cars they drove, and how they lived. Sometimes a movie can tell us something of the values of the people at the time: how men and women related to each other or to their jobs. Theater played this role for the Romans. Among the earliest written Latin texts are comedies by **Plautus** (c. 250–184 BCE) and **Terence** (c. 190–160 BCE), both of whom came from outside the elite class. The depiction of women and enslaved persons upon the stage provides some useful material, even if the representations may be exaggerated or distorted for comic effect. In a later period, the love poetry of poets such as **Catullus** (87–54 BCE), **Propertius** (c. 50–16 BCE), and **Ovid** (43 BCE–17 CE) can suggest something of how Roman men conceived of relationships and how they expected women to behave. These texts, which drew on Greek predecessors, are also an essential resource for understanding how the Romans responded to Greek culture, which in turn helps us understand how the Romans thought about their own place in the world. For that reason, we will return repeatedly to the Roman response to Greek culture in learning about the Roman Republic.

Not only did the Romans have to respond to Greek culture, but the Greeks eventually had to learn to live in a world dominated by Roman power, and several Greeks left us valuable sources. Chief among these is the historian **Polybius** (c. 200–120 BCE). Polybius was an aristocratic Greek who was sent to Rome to serve as a hostage to ensure the good behavior of the defeated Greeks following a Roman military victory in 167 BCE. As an upper-class Greek, Polybius was accepted into Roman aristocratic circles. Far from being angry at the Romans for their treatment of him, Polybius grew to respect and admire the Romans, to the extent that he chose to stay in Rome even when the Romans allowed him and the other hostages to return home. Polybius took advantage of his time in Rome and of his connections to compose a history of the rise of Roman power, with an eye toward explaining to his countrymen how this upstart city to the west had become the dominant power in the Mediterranean.

Polybius' account strikes most readers as evenhanded, but his dependence on some Roman families forces us to examine in each incident how far Polybius might have been attempting to flatter particular individuals. As we have already discussed, Polybius' purpose in writing is also critical to understanding his text, and he tells us the following in that regard:

> to discover, in the first place, the words actually spoken, whatever they were, and next to ascertain the reason why what was done or spoken led to failure or success. For the mere statement of a fact may interest us but is of no benefit to us: but when we add the cause of it, study of history becomes fruitful (*Histories*, 12.25).

Historians trained in North America and Europe have mostly adopted these principles – to understand causes and not just list facts – so Polybius is often held in high regard today.

Polybius' greatest value to the social and cultural historian may actually lie in the fact that he often appears as what we might call a cultural anthropologist. As a Greek living in Rome, Polybius found himself confronted with customs and behaviors that seemed strange to him. In his concern to explain the Romans to his countrymen, he took the time to describe things that Roman authors took for granted. For instance, our best description of a Roman funeral comes from Polybius, and he also left us a detailed discussion of the Roman government. We still need to ask questions of Polybius; as a Greek, he often used his Greek experience to understand Roman customs, and on occasion seems to have misunderstood Roman behavior because of that perspective. However, he often provides us with crucial data missing from Roman sources, and the fact that he was present in Rome during a crucial period in Rome's expansion makes him an invaluable resource.

Another Greek deserves mention in this regard: the biographer and moralist **Plutarch** (45–127 CE). Although he wrote substantially later than the people he described, Plutarch was able to draw upon many sources contemporary with those individuals that no longer survive for us. Among his numerous writings, Plutarch wrote a series of *Parallel Lives*, matching a figure from Roman history with one from Greece. Perhaps the greatest value for our study lies in the fact that he included many details about the private or personal lives of the people involved, allowing us to learn something of the practices of the Roman upper class. At the same time, we need again to ask about Plutarch's purpose in writing: in most cases he aimed to provide a moral lesson from these lives and he explicitly matched his pairs in order to draw moral comparisons between the Greek and the Roman.

Plutarch's treatment of Romulus provides an example of his method and a good contrast to Livy. Plutarch's version of the fateful clash between Romulus and Remus states that Romulus lied about the number of birds that he saw. It was this deceit that led Remus to make fun of the walls and jump over them, which is when Romulus killed him. Plutarch's story thus presents Romulus in a much less flattering light than Livy does. Indeed, Greek texts are often less sympathetic to the Romans, perhaps because they had no interest in celebrating Roman greatness.

Working with Sources
Vae Victis!

In 390 BCE, a tribe of Gauls (modern France) made their way south across the Alps toward Rome. They put the Romans to flight at the River Allia, 11 miles from Rome, and laid siege to the city. The Romans sent their women, children, and religious items out of the city for safekeeping, while the men of military age took up a position on the Capitoline hill, the highest and most easily defended of Rome's seven hills. Eventually the defenders ran short on food and negotiated surrender terms with the Gauls: in exchange for an agreed sum of gold, the Gauls would depart from the city.

To add insult to injury, the Gauls used unequal weights as the gold was being measured, so that the Romans would end up paying more than the agreed sum. When the Romans objected, the Gallic leader threw his sword on the weights, making the Romans add extra gold to cover its weight as well. As he did so, he uttered the words "*Vae victis* (Woe to the conquered)!" reminding the Romans that those defeated in war have no bargaining power.

> Livy describes what happened next:
>
> By good fortune it happened that before the infamous ransom was completed and all the gold weighed out, the Dictator [Camillus] appeared on the scene and ordered the gold to be carried away and the Gauls to move off.... Fortune now turned, divine aid and human skill were on the side of Rome. At the very first encounter the Gauls were routed as easily as they had conquered at the Allia (Livy, 5.49).
>
> Diodorus Siculus, a Greek contemporary of Livy, tells a different story however:
>
> [when] the Romans sent ambassadors to negotiate a peace, they [the Gauls] were persuaded to leave the city and to withdraw from Roman territory in exchange for one thousand pounds of gold (Diodorus, 14.116).
>
> Diodorus knows nothing of the miraculous arrival of the Roman dictator, and neither does the very brief mention of Polybius, another Greek who is our earliest surviving source on this episode. And even Roman sources, including Livy, acknowledge the devastation to the city caused by the Gauls. The image that emerges from all of our sources is more consistent with the notion of the Gauls plundering the city and then moving off.
> Even if the Greek accounts provide a useful corrective, Livy's account is still valuable. It reveals an attempt to save face, to avoid having to admit that Rome had once paid bribes to secure its survival. More than that, Livy's account helps us understand Roman imperialism. The story of *Vae victis* became an important part of the Roman mentality: if losers have no bargaining rights, the Romans resolved never to suffer this fate again and so developed a stronger military that they used to engage anyone who even remotely threatened their security.

That does not automatically make Greek sources more reliable. Plutarch had his own purposes in writing. In his commentary on the character of Romulus, Plutarch made clear that he saw Romulus as a tyrant, guilty "of unreasoning anger or hasty and senseless wrath," but he also includes the unlikely account of Romulus' assassination. His version seems less concerned with Caesar, perhaps because he was writing 200 years later. Instead his text serves to reinforce his moralizing critique: Romulus was deservedly killed because he was a tyrant. Moralizing aims can affect a historian's account as much as contemporary politics or a desire to paint a founder in a positive light.

Material Culture

Now that we have begun to develop a list of questions that we might ask of our literary sources, it is time to turn to the other major source of information for the Roman Republic: the material evidence. For a number of topics (visual arts and architecture, the city of Rome, the economy) the main source of evidence is not literary but physical. First and foremost, there is information that has been gathered through the practice of **archaeology**, the systematic uncovering of ancient remains in the earth, including private houses, cemeteries, roads, and large public structures such as temples and grain warehouses. The Roman state and individual Romans also left writings on stone or bronze, from public decrees to private tombstones; **epigraphy**, which is the analysis of these inscriptions, provides another key source of information. **Numismatics**, or the study of ancient coins, provides a third key primary source, not just for the economic information that can be derived but from the messages that Romans sent through the design on their coins. Each will be discussed more fully in the section below, to understand the questions we should ask of each source.

Archaeology

When archaeology is mentioned, we might think first of the remains of major cities and monuments: the city of Pompeii, the Colosseum, and the Forum in Rome. These monuments offer the most visible clues to understanding the growth of cities such as Rome. The development of new architectural forms, often by adapting them from other societies, can also tell us about the relationship between Rome and foreign cultures. For instance, several early Roman temples clearly follow the design of earlier temples in Etruria, suggesting a high degree of Etruscan influence in early Rome. For monuments such as these, we can ask questions about broad cultural trends and the development of city life over a long span of time. However, for questions such as what people ate, what they wore, or what their daily lives were like, major monuments have no answers.

For those questions, it is the small and often fragmentary remains that offer the most information. Archaeology is, in fact, one of our primary sources of information for non-elites in the ancient world. If Cicero has very little to say about the non-elite, we must recover that information by other means, and archaeology is tops on that list. The humble garbage dump turns out to be a tremendous source of information, as specialists can recognize plant and animal remains, household goods, and other items that tell us what people ate or used on a daily basis. We can ask about how the diet of the lower classes compares to that of the wealthy, but we can also ask questions such as the origins of either natural or manufactured products, which can tell us about contact with other regions and trade practices. As historians have begun to pay proper attention to the non-elite, excavations have increasingly focused not on the grand houses of the elite, but on the homes of the less fortunate. For example, at Ostia, the port city of Rome, multi-story apartment buildings have been uncovered, offering a glimpse into the one or two room dwelling places in which an entire family might live (**Figure 1.3**). Excavation of cemeteries sheds light on family structure, demographic trends, and even the kinds of affectionate language used by family members to commemorate their deceased, offering insight into how Roman family members felt about each other. The deliberate disposal of items in garbage dumps and cemeteries not only does a better job preserving items than items left out in the open, but forces us to ask questions about why a particular item might have

Figure 1.3 Insula of Diana, Ostia Antica, second century CE.

been discarded. The lives of individual Roman men, women, and children are illuminated more by archaeology than by any other source.

Archaeological evidence cannot answer every question we might have. One challenge is simply the availability of archaeological data for our time period, which is generally less abundant than for the Empire. **Pompeii** provides a good example (**Figure 1.4**). The city has a long history and was refounded as a colony by the Romans in 80 BCE, but the city owes its fame and its preservation to the eruption of Mt. Vesuvius in 79 CE, a full hundred years after the end of the Republic, and of course the years closest to the eruption are the best preserved. Sometimes we do have evidence for an earlier period; for example, many houses in Pompeii have rooms that can be dated to the Republican period. The vast majority of the material from Pompeii, however, dates to the period of the Empire. Historians must then decide how much the evidence from the later period can be used to understand practices of a century or more earlier. While Pompeii offers unparalleled evidence on issues such what Roman houses looked like, religious practices of the household, and town planning, it also vividly demonstrates some of the challenges of using archaeological evidence.

Pompeii also reminds us of the seemingly random nature of archaeology: archaeologists find what they happen to find. A volcano happened to erupt five miles from Pompeii that almost perfectly preserved the city, which happened to be discovered when the King of Naples wanted a new summer palace, but other cities elsewhere in

Figure 1.4 Aerial view of Pompeii. Mt. Vesuvius is in the background.

Italy remain completely undiscovered by archaeologists. This phenomenon presents challenges for the historian; our questions have to be tailored to the information that has been randomly provided, and we always wonder what evidence we are missing that might either confirm or refute the answers we develop. Certain time periods may be over-represented (or under-represented), not because there actually was more (or less) material produced in a given period, but because archaeologists happened to find more or less of it. Historians constantly question how far the practices of any one city represent Roman culture as a whole: what happens in Seattle may be very different from what happens in Dallas or in smaller cities like Pueblo, Colorado. Nor should we automatically assume that the larger cities were more "civilized": we know that by 60 BCE Pompeii was home to several theaters as well as Italy's first surviving stone amphitheater, but at that time Rome itself had none of these buildings. The smaller the sample size, the harder it is to know what might be typical; with a larger data set – a collection of cities or many acres of countryside – archaeologists are able to compare data across sites and look for general patterns that are true across the spectrum.

Inscriptions

Inscriptions left on permanent materials (generally stone or bronze), many of which turned up in the course of archaeological excavations, provide a second crucial source from material culture. Some inscriptions offer information about the practice of politics in Rome and Italy: electoral graffiti on the walls of Pompeii gives glimpses into the ways in which political campaigns were waged. Similarly, two town charters apparently drawn up by Julius Caesar and published shortly after his death offer insight into government structures, from magistrates to the grain dole. One of the most famous Republican inscriptions, the so-called Senatorial decree *de Bacchanalibus* ("on the Bacchanalians") (**Figure 1.5**) is of interest not only for information about certain religious behaviors but also because it was found in southern Italy and so can tell us something about the relationship of the Roman **Senate** to the cities of Italy. In addition, the *fasti*, Roman calendars inscribed on stone, not only help us order the Roman year with its festivals and other holidays but also provide chronological information about magistrates and triumphs. As with any source, we need to ask questions about why a given document was published: why did the Roman state feel the need to tell everyone in Italy about their treatment of a particular religious practice? Why was it felt necessary to start posting calendars in different towns across Italy? However, these documents are invaluable because they provide direct evidence for contemporary Roman behavior.

Just as with archaeology, the less impressive inscriptions often have a greater impact on our understanding of Roman society. Two types in particular stand out: dedications (usually to one or more divinities) and burial epitaphs, both of which give us insight into the behavior of the non-elites that would otherwise be missing. Dedications can help us understand actual rather than idealized religious behavior, showing us to which gods people expressed their gratitude and for what purposes. On occasion they present a picture that never would have been evident from the literary sources. For instance, the literary sources pay little attention to the god Faunus, but his popularity is attested by numerous dedications far beyond anything we would have imagined from the literary evidence. That discovery forces us to ask both what made Faunus so popular, and with whom, and why he did not

Figure 1.5 Bronze tablet recording the Senatorial decree on the worship of Bacchus, 186 BCE. Kunsthistorisches Museum Vienna.

attract the attention of the elites. It thus raises new questions for the historian: a history of religious behavior at Rome simply cannot be written without inscriptional evidence.

In a similar fashion burial epitaphs can tell us a great deal about Roman life among both the elite and non-elite. We are fortunate to possess some epitaphs of famous Romans known from the literary sources, such as members of the Scipiones who conquered Carthage. These materials not only deepen the understanding gained from the literary sources but also allow us to see how the family members wished to be perceived. Ordinary Romans also wanted to be commemorated after death and we can look at their tombstones to compare their practices to the elite and ask in what ways they shared in a common understanding of death, the afterlife, or even family relationships. In addition to these monuments, we have large numbers of simpler tombstones bearing minimal text but which attest to the desire of the lower classes to leave a memorial behind even with their limited resources. The large number of tombstones allows us to ask questions about which members felt a duty to erect a monument and which family members they felt they needed to remember. We can also explore the language and images used on these tombstones to understand the nature of relationships within the family or the values that ordinary Romans held dear. These inscriptions often offer an intimate look into the lives of Romans that cannot be matched by other sources.

Coins

Coins provide a third type of primary source, an object that was actually used by the people of the Roman world. In terms of sheer volume of evidence, coins are the most numerous of any surviving source. The Romans began minting coins in the third century BCE; already one might ask why the Romans did not start minting coins before this point: coins were in use in other parts of the Mediterranean long before. What did they use in the marketplace before this time and why did they start now? Once the Romans start minting, coinage contributes greatly to our understanding of Roman economic history, but coins in the ancient world served other functions beyond just a medium of exchange. While the Roman state guaranteed the value of the coinage minted under its authority, it provided no standard imagery. Rather, it delegated the physical task of minting coins to individuals, sometimes to relatively minor functionaries, and so coinage design thus might change according to a variety of factors: historical events or family ties could play a large role. We might think of how designs on postage stamps today reflect the values and interests of the countries that produce them: a stamp with Elvis on it can tell us about the importance of rock-and-roll in the United States. In Rome, some minters placed designs intended to further their own political ambitions or those of a political ally, while other coins revealed the shared values of the Romans (**Figure 1.6**). Because of their large number and the fact that they can usually be dated with great precision, coins provide a chronological means to understand both the Roman economy and a range of political and social issues.

WHAT IS HISTORICAL THINKING? 21

Figure 1.6 Silver denarius, minted 43 or 42 BCE.

Political Issues: *Using Coins to Tell Your Story*

In 2011, a Roman coin, similar to the one shown in Figure 1.6, sold for over $500,000 at auction in Long Beach, California. What could make an old chunk of silver so valuable?

This coin provides a unique view into the debate among Roman politicians in the years following the death of Julius Caesar in 44 BCE. When Brutus and Cassius led a group of senators to kill Caesar in the Senate house, was it an act of unwarranted murder or the legitimate removal of a would-be tyrant? Did it undermine the foundations of a civil society or was it necessary to protect the Roman state? The coin reveals the argument for the latter.

On the obverse, or front of the coin, we find the head of Brutus, identified by the abbreviation *BRUT IMP*, or Brutus Imperator. Around the lower left side of the coin we find the name L. (for Lucius) Plaetorius Cestianus. This coin was thus minted by Plaetorius, a middling Roman politician who clearly supported Brutus, whom he identifies as a successful military general; at this point in Roman history *imperator* had not yet come to mean "emperor." The family of Plaetorius is known to have minted coins during this period, and here Plaetorius uses his position to advocate for a political cause.

The reverse, or back of the coin, depicts two daggers along with the inscription EID MAR; specifying the Ides of March makes clear that the daggers are meant to symbolize the weapons used to kill Caesar. Between the daggers is an image of a cap, known to the Romans as a *pileus*. In Roman society, when an enslaved person was given their freedom, a part of the ceremony involved placing this cap on the head of the newly freed citizen. The coin thus suggests that by killing Caesar with the daggers, the entire Roman state had been freed from slavery. Brutus was killed in battle in 42 BCE, so we can date this coin with precision between 44 and 42 BCE. Because Brutus' side lost the war, we do not have many sources offering their viewpoint in Caesar's death; in fact we have very few of these coins

> because the victors melted down all the ones they could find, which explains why a single coin could be worth a half million dollars. The coin is valuable both to historians and to collectors.
>
> We also have coins showing the views of Brutus' opponents, Mark Antony and the young Octavian. In the summer of 44 BCE a comet appeared in the skies over Rome, and Caesar's supporters argued that this comet represented the ascension of Caesar to the heavens, and that Caesar should thus be worshipped as a god, much as Romulus was worshipped as a god. After the conclusion of the Roman civil wars, Octavian, now known as Augustus, issued a series of coins referencing this star with the legend *DIVUS IULIUS*, or "the deified Julius." These coins thus made the claim for Caesar's divinity and, by association, Augustus' own descent from a god. In a world of limited communication, these coins served as perhaps the best way to share a message.

Conclusion

The sources for Roman social and cultural history are thus numerous and impressively varied, but not without challenges. One issue that will crop up repeatedly throughout this book is the balance between **synchronic** history and **diachronic** history.

Synchronic history means taking pieces from different times (*chronos*) and putting them together (*syn*) to form a single picture. Roman historians are often to forced to write synchronic accounts because of the nature of our evidence. For example, we may learn about Roman fathers from a document in one period and about Roman mothers from a slightly different period, and historians combine the two to provide a picture of "the Roman family." The problem, which sharp-eyed readers might have noticed, is that there may never have been a single time when the Roman family looked exactly like our picture. Synchronic history offers a composite image that can help us understand a subject broadly but sometimes the image remains fuzzy as the details do not match up fully.

Diachronic history goes through (*dia*) time (*chronos*) and so focuses more attention on documenting change. Tracing the rise and fall of an empire is a good example of diachronic history. Our evidence for military affairs often allows us to know the specific battles and the dates that allowed an empire such as Rome to grow, and so we can describe the steps by which Rome grew into an imperial power.

As we embark on our exploration of Roman social and cultural history, we thus face two challenges. One is to combine the literary and material culture sources into a single picture, and the second is to employ both synchronic and diachronic history to understand Roman society. Each historian will find a different balance for these two challenges, which explains why each historian's picture of Roman society looks slightly different.

Let us close this chapter by taking the Roman family as an example of how we might proceed. We could start with the stories about Romulus and note that some literary sources suggest that the Roman family may have been dysfunctional by our standards. At the same time, we have to note that this story concerns the elite – the founder of Rome! – and we might wonder whether all families felt this way. Plautus and Terence left us comedies from the second century that feature fictional families with stereotyped relationships: a doddering father, a shrewish wife, and a young man mooning over the girl next door, and we might wonder how much truth lies in these stereotypes. Funerary inscriptions written by a husband for his wife or vice versa offer a different kind of evidence and suggest a type of devotion that looks different from the comedic picture. Cicero's letters offer another type of evidence from the first century BCE and show us his personal devastation when his daughter died as a result of childbirth. The houses from Pompeii and elsewhere show that Roman houses, both rich and poor, had few spaces that family members might consider their own private space, and so raise questions about what family life looked like on a day-to-day basis. Each isolated piece of evidence by itself can give us only a partial or even misleading picture. Taken together, however, as we will do in the pages that follow, these sources will allow us to develop a rich picture of Roman life, a life that was both like and quite unlike modern Western experiences.

Discussion Questions

1. If the most important element of historical thinking is understanding the author's purpose in writing, what do you think is the purpose of the author of this textbook? of your professor?
2. Given the absence of female voices from antiquity, how can a historian learn anything about that half of the population of the ancient world?
3. What challenges can you foresee in trying to mingle both archaeological and textual evidence?
4. What subjects do you think will be the most difficult to handle for a cultural historian of Rome? What subjects might be the easiest? Why?
5. What value might there be in developing comparisons between the Romans and modern Western peoples, or peoples living in other times or places?

Further Reading

Ancient Authors (Cicero, Livy, Plutarch, et al.)
    Often the best place to find the texts of ancient authors is within the Loeb Classical Library series, with each author listed by name; translations in the Penguin Classics or Oxford World Classics are also usually reliable. While translations do exist on the Internet, many of these are very old-fashioned, occasionally misleading (as early twentieth-century translators often shied away from taboo topics), and sometimes even incorrect.
Chaplin, Jane (2000). *Livy's Exemplary History*. Oxford: Oxford University Press.
    Chaplin's book is one of a number of recent books that offer new ways of thinking about Livy, whose text provides the foundation for the history of Rome down to the early second century CE. She focuses on how Livy's use of examples was intended to make history relevant for his Roman audience, even as the meaning of those examples might shift over time.

Feldherr, Andrew (Ed.) (2009). *The Cambridge Companion to the Roman Historians.* Cambridge: Cambridge University Press.

Contains essays on a variety of topics, with attention paid both to texts that survive only in fragments as well as sources for history that remained unwritten. Good focus on themes (religion, space, the setting of examples) rather than merely a historian-by-historian description.

Keppie, Lawrence (2001). *Understanding Roman Inscriptions.* London: Routledge.

A book designed for the non-specialist, Keppie's book covers a range of issues, from how the stone-cutter did his work to how to read and date inscriptions. No knowledge of Latin is necessary; Keppie provides all terms needed. Later chapters in the book cover thematic topics such as government, the army, and religion.

Laurence, Ray (2012). *Roman Archaeology for Historians.* London: Routledge.

A recent introduction specifically aimed an integrating the study of archaeology and Roman history. The complexity of archaeological data sometimes makes the book's language difficult, and examples tend to be drawn from Roman Britain (the author's home country), but the range of topics covered is especially valuable.

Lintott, Andrew (2008). *Cicero as Evidence: A Historian's Companion.* Oxford: Oxford University Press.

A recent concise work focused precisely on using Cicero as a source for Roman history, rather than on the politician or his views. Superbly organized into four sections, on Reading Cicero, Reading Oratory, History in Speeches and Letters, and History and Ideas. A must-read for this topic.

Yarrow, Liv M. (2021). *The Roman Republic to 49 BCE: Using Coins as Sources.* Cambridge: Cambridge University Press.

Yarrow's book introduces students of ancient history to the ways in which coins provide information about the history of the Roman republic. She uses coins to offer insights on early Roman-Italian relations, Roman imperialism, urban politics, and constitutional history, among other topics. This book helps take the mystery out of numismatics, with over 200 illustrations and a guide to research for non-specialists.

2
How Do We Tell the Story?

In 509 BCE according to the Roman historians, **Sextus Tarquinius** developed a lust for **Lucretia**, the noble wife of one of his friends (Livy 1.58–60). Sextus's family was originally **Etruscan**, from the territory just north of Rome, and his father Tarquin the Proud was then king of Rome and leading an army against a neighboring town. One evening while the Roman men were still away on this campaign, Sextus snuck into her house late at night and forced her to have sex with him. After he left, Lucretia sent for her husband Collatinus and her father. When they arrived with a few friends, she explained what had happened, then pulled a knife from under her dress and plunged it into her heart, falling dead on the ground in front of them. **Brutus**, one of the friends, drew the dripping knife out of Lucretia's body and held it in front of him, swearing that he would drive the king and his family from Rome and not allow them or anyone else to rule as a king in Rome. The others joined with him, and together they aroused the anger of the people against the king and proceeded to drive him out of Rome. In place of the monarchy that had ruled Rome for the past two hundred and forty-two years, the Roman people created a new form of government, which we know today as the Roman Republic. Brutus was chosen to serve as one of the first two consuls, the chief magistrate of the new Republic and set the standard for later generations of Romans.

A Social and Cultural History of Republican Rome, First Edition. Eric M. Orlin.
© 2022 John Wiley & Sons, Inc. Published 2022 by John Wiley & Sons, Inc.

Working with Sources
Brutus in Bronze?

A bronze head found in the sixteenth century (**Figure 2.1**) tells us as much about how people have wanted to view the Romans as it does about the Romans themselves. From a purely aesthetic standpoint, we can appreciate the quality of the work and gain an insight into Roman art. The inlaid glass and bone eyes are original and can help us visualize the appearance of other statues where these materials no longer survive. The style bears similarities to Etruscan bronzes in technique and appearance, an indication of artistic links between the two cultures, while the seriousness of expression becomes a regular feature of Roman portraits. It is certainly one of the finest bronze sculptures to have survived from ancient Rome and a highlight of many visits to Rome.

Figure 2.1 So-called Capitoline Brutus, dated to the fourth or third century BCE, found in the sixteenth century CE. Musei Capitolini, Rome.

> Problems arise when we try to ask questions about the statue, such as who it represents or when it was made, because do not know the exact provenance (find spot) of the head and so lack crucial information about it. The sculpture is known as the Capitoline Brutus because it was given to the Capitoline Museum in Rome in 1564. Already in the sixteenth century the head was already being identified as Brutus. The high cheekbones, beard, and stern expression were felt appropriate for a statesman, and the antiquarian aristocrats of the sixteenth century felt there was no better example of a Roman statesman than the founder of the Roman Republic. In a short time the statue became a symbol of liberty: it was actually carried off to Paris by Napoleon and then returned to Rome following Napoleon's downfall.
>
> There is, however, no firm evidence linking this portrait head to Brutus. Not knowing where the statue was found means we can only guess based on its appearance. Arguments about its identification as Brutus are based on comparisons to other objects such as coin portraits that have labels, but these assessments are often inconclusive. We do not even know whether the statue presented the figure as engaged in civic or military business; the togate chest and shoulders (known as the "bust") suggest a civilian, but these were added to the head in the sixteenth century. Such reconstructions are common and often give a misleading impression of the original artwork, which is another problem that a modern scholar must confront.
>
> Even the date of manufacture is uncertain. Most scholars believe that it dates from around 300 BCE, which would make it one of the oldest surviving bronze statues from Rome, but some have argued that certain features suggest it was made in the late second century and intentionally designed to have a "retro" look. These arguments again depend on subjective impressions. Knowing the archaeological context might enable us to answer this question. For instance, if it was found in a building dating to the third century, it cannot have been made 200 years later.
>
> The information we can get from the Capitoline Brutus is thus highly limited. More than anything else, the bronze head illustrates the need for proper archeological excavation and documentation of ancient objects if we are to understand them and not just appreciate their beauty.

Using the dates traditionally assigned by Roman authors, the Republic began in 509 BCE and lasted for nearly five hundred years. We will have occasion to study this story, known as the Rape of Lucretia, more closely later (see Chapter 6), but even this brief summary is sufficient to reveal many themes that are important to understanding the Roman Republic:

- An almost obsessive hatred of one-man rule. Kingship was viewed by the Romans as a form of slavery, because as absolute rulers, kings could order others to do their bidding. Furthermore, because kings made the laws, there was no recourse when they committed misdeeds. The Roman elite wanted to promote the notion that they were all equal and that government was a public thing, not a private possession.

- An emphasis on honor. Men believed that their honor was connected both to their military accomplishments and to the chastity of the females in the family, though we should note that women's own views are harder to detect.
- An openness but also a wariness about foreigners. The Romans were more generous with citizenship than many other ancient societies and frequently integrated foreign customs into their own behavior, but they could also display a violent xenophobia.
- Frequent military warfare. Roman men of all social classes were frequently away from home on campaign, leaving women at home to manage their households on their own.

With these themes in the front of our minds, we are ready to embark on a brief tour of Roman history, to gain a familiarity with key figures and an understanding of the key events that shaped social and cultural developments throughout the Republic.

An Outline History of the Roman Republic

The First Hundred Years

We are so accustomed to think of Rome as the massive empire it became, dominating the Mediterranean, that we do not often think about how Rome began. The lack of contemporary sources makes it difficult to know much about this period with any precision, and later Romans were inclined to exaggerate Rome's early accomplishments. Yet even the stories that the Romans themselves told suggest that at first Rome was just an ordinary city on the Italian peninsula, and not a particularly strong one either. The first hundred years of the Republic are marked by constant border skirmishes with their neighbors without significant territorial gains. The first major conquest of the Roman state as they saw it was the town of **Veii**, around 396 BCE. Roman accounts of this campaign bear a strong resemblance to the epic narrative of the Trojan War: a ten-year long campaign, a heroic commander, and a victory assured only when the chief deity left the besieged state. Yet Veii lies merely ten miles from Rome – in one hundred years the Romans had expanded only ten miles to the north. Certainly the pace of conquest picked up over the following centuries, but in her early years Rome was merely one city out of many, fighting for her very existence.

Rome's weakness is further demonstrated by a massive defeat that she suffered a mere six years after the conquest of Veii. Around 390 BCE, a nomadic tribe of **Gauls** (modern day France) made its way down the Italian peninsula. Although the Romans marched out to defend their territory, they were badly beaten at a battle on the Allia river; the defeat was so bad that the date was remembered as a *dies ater*, a "black day", on the Roman calendar. The Gauls proceeded to sack the city of Rome and could easily have uprooted and destroyed the entire Roman state. Fortunately for the Romans, the Gauls were a nomadic people more interested in collecting as much money as they could and then moving on to a new target (see Textbox in

Chapter 1). Following their departure, the Romans quickly rebuilt their city and recovered the territory they had lost, so the Gallic sack had only a minimal impact on Roman expansion. The impact on the Roman mindset, however, was enormous: throughout the Republic the Romans had an almost irrational fear of the Gauls, and they engaged in warfare almost constantly for the next four hundred years, seemingly never satisfied that they were safe from potential invaders.

Part of Rome's weakness may be traceable to internal dissension, though it is difficult to trace through the layers of later exaggeration. Roman sources paint this period as one of conflict between two hereditary orders, or groupings: **patricians**, who were generally wealthier and were viewed as Rome's aristocracy, and **plebeians**, the lower classes who comprised the great mass of the populace. Stories from this period revolve around the plebeians' struggle to gain a measure of political power from which they were initially excluded; modern historians call this the **Struggle of the Orders**. Their standard technique was known as the **Secession of the Plebs**: the plebeians would abandon the city of Rome and take up residence outside the city, sometimes even on the Aventine hill just across the valley where the Circus Maximus would one day be (**Figure 2.2**). Because the plebeians made up the bulk of the fighting men in the army, a war with one of Rome's neighbors would force the patricians to recognize how much they needed the plebeians, and so they would make some concession to their demands. At first the concessions involved the creation of ten **Tribunes of the Plebs**, who were given the authority to intervene in deliberations of the patrician Senate and prevent any proposal from even being discussed, let alone becoming law. Later secessions brought the plebeians the right to have one of the two consuls come from the plebeian class, and eventually all political offices were opened to the plebeians. Modern historians typically place the end of the Struggle of the Orders in 287 BCE, when the *lex Hortensia* declared that any proposal passed by the assembly comprised of the plebeians alone would be binding upon all Romans, plebeian and patrician alike. More recent studies have seen this process not as the gradual empowerment of the entire plebeian class, but as the gradual empowerment of rich and successful plebeian individuals, who had previously been barred from political influence no matter how rich and successful they became.

One milestone that the Romans often connected with the Struggle of the Orders was their first written legal code, known as the **Twelve Tables**. It was passed, according to Roman tradition, in 451 and 450 BCE. This lawcode, despite its early date, remained the basis of Roman law all the way through the Republic and into the Empire (see further Chapter 10). The stories surrounding the creation of the legal code bear a similarity to other stories whose moral is to restrain abuses committed by the powerful members of society; one story bears a remarkable resemblance to the sexual assault of Lucretia described above. However, most of the surviving provisions of the Twelve Tables are heavily weighted towards the preservation of property rights, which clearly benefits the wealthy, causing many modern historians to doubt whether the creation of this law code should be seen as a victory for the lower classes. One might see the Twelve Tables as a step forward for the plebeians in the simple fact of engraving laws; in a society without mass communication, it is likely

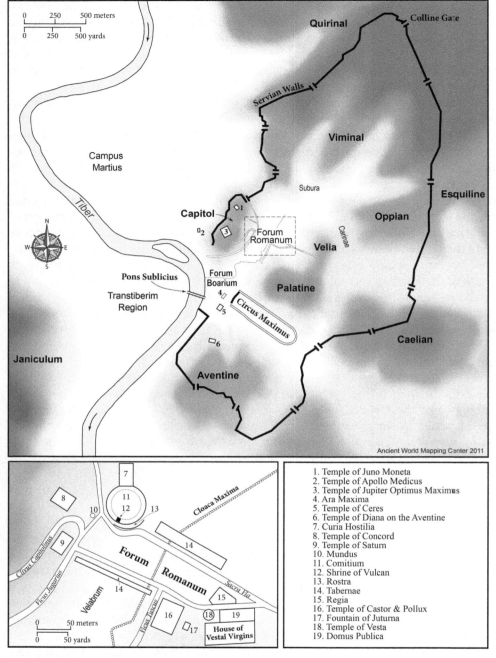

Figure 2.2 Map of Republican Rome.

that only the elites would have known what the laws were, making it difficult for plebeians to challenge legal judgments against them. If we understand the Struggle of the Orders as wealthy plebeians fighting for inclusion into the ruling elite of Rome rather than for the rights of the mass of plebeians, provisions benefitting the wealthy make more sense. Wealthy plebeians had no desire to help the poor any more than wealthy patricians did. By the end of the fourth century BCE, the formation of a mixed patrician–plebeian aristocracy based primarily on wealth and family connections had temporarily resolved much of the internal conflict.

The Growth of Rome

Following the Gallic sack, the Romans picked up right where they left off, bringing Italy south of the Po River under their control by the early third century BCE. Two key milestones in the conquest of Italy are worth noting.

In 338 BCE, Rome imposed a settlement on a group of former allies in central Italy who had broken treaty obligations with Rome and banded together to fight the growing power in their midst. In the aftermath of the Latin Revolt, as it is known, different cities received different treatments: some were destroyed or depopulated, some were given Roman citizenship, and some were given ***civitas sine suffragio***, "citizenship without the right to vote." As citizens, these people had access to the Roman legal system, which enabled them to marry and trade with Roman citizens, but they were not allowed to vote in Rome. This structure became the blueprint for future conquests, with two important consequences: (1) each community, and especially the elites within them, was given incentives for cooperating with Rome, in the hopes that they might earn better privileges in the future and therefore (2) Rome thus did not have to garrison or provide bureaucratic oversight, but left the control of the local population to local elites. These communities were tied directly to Rome with obligations to provide manpower in times of war, and this continual supply of manpower served as one of the strengths of the Roman army through the subsequent years of expansion.

The second milestone came as a result of the first war that Rome fought against an overseas foe. In 280 BCE, King Pyrrhus of Epirus (western Greece), invaded Italy and defeated the Romans in several battles, though in one battle he lost so many soldiers that he remarked: "if we are victorious again, we shall be utterly ruined" (the origin of the phrase "Pyrrhic victory"). Eventually the Romans did defeat Pyrrhus, which gave them control of southern Italy and completed their conquest of the peninsula of Italy. The conquest of southern Italy is significant because the area had previously been settled by colonists from Greece, so many that it was known as **Magna Graecia** ("Great Greece") (**Figure 2.3**). While elements of Greek culture can be found in Rome as far back as c. 500 BCE, this sequence of battles increased the amount of exchange with Greek culture, and also began to acquaint the Romans with the Greek kingdoms that ruled the eastern Mediterranean following the death of Alexander the Great in 323 BCE.

Figure 2.3 Map of southern Italy, including Magna Graecia and Sicily.

Key Debates: *How Did the Romans Come to Rule the Mediterranean?*

In 390 BCE, the Roman state suffered a massive defeat to a marauding band of Gauls, leaving the city in a shambles and perhaps at its lowest point in terms of power. The Romans destroyed the cities of Carthage and Corinth 250 years later, wiping out the only challenge to her power in the western Mediterranean, and cementing her control of the eastern Mediterranean. The rise from nowhere to the sole superpower of the ancient Mediterranean is as remarkable as it was surprising. How did it happen?

One theory has become known to modern historians as "defensive imperialism." In an effort to avoid a repeat of the Gallic sack, the Romans went to great lengths to protect themselves. As a result, they pushed back on any bordering state that they felt presented a possible threat. By claiming a defensive posture, they could also assure themselves that each war was a just war fought against an aggressor, and therefore they might earn the sanction of the gods for their war effort.

In the 1970s, William Harris began to push back against the theory of defensive imperialism promoted by the Romans and accepted by many modern historians. He argued that the military ethos that ran through Roman society continually led the Romans into new wars. Valor in war was a key sign of being a true Roman man, and military success was seen as the be-all and end-all of a successful politician. The way to electoral success was through success in war, not social programs or just application of the law. Thus almost every member of the elite wanted to see Rome in a state of war that would give them a chance of political advancement.

A third theory, perhaps driven by thinking about modern wars, suggests that Rome's conquests were driven by economic concerns. There is limited evidence that the Romans fought in order to acquire trade routes and natural resources to exploit. Rather, the Romans may have been driven by individual desires. Since Roman generals both kept a share of captured treasure for themselves and distributed some to their soldiers, individuals stood to benefit economically from conquest. This notion of economic motivation makes sense of the First Punic War where Polybius claims the Romans only went to war when their generals "pointed out the great benefit in terms of plunder that each and everyone would receive from it." In other words, personal greed may have led the Romans into war.

All of these answers are likely to have some element of truth to them. Indeed, each conquest brought with it new territory and thus a world that became increasingly complex, and Roman motives must surely have shifted over time.

The Roman conquest of Magna Graecia also brought them into contact with the island of Sicily, just off the toe of Italy. The western part of the island had also been settled by Greeks in the eighth century BCE, but the remainder was controlled by the city-state of Carthage (located in modern day Tunisia). Over the next century, Rome fought a series of three wars against Carthage, known as the **Punic Wars**, which made Rome the sole power in the western Mediterranean. The First Punic War (264–241 BCE) centered on control of Sicily and required Rome to develop a navy for the first time. The Second Punic War (218–202 BCE) represented undoubtedly the greatest threat to Rome's survival. The Carthaginian general **Hannibal** crossed the Alps with an army of 30,000 infantry, 10,000 cavalry, and 38 elephants, and won three consecutive battles in Italy, killing over 100,000 men in the process. This casualty rate represents about one-third of the Roman adult male population at the time. While some of the soldiers killed came from allied towns in Italy, the losses were so severe that Hannibal was able to march his troops to the very gates of Rome without opposition. However, Hannibal was not equipped for siege warfare, and the Romans managed to rally enough allies to resist. They then employed guerrilla warfare to avoid another massive defeat in battle, and by weakening Hannibal's supply lines, the Romans were able to force him to return to Africa. In 202 BCE, **Scipio Africanus** (236–183 BCE) led Roman troops to a victory at the battle of Zama (202 BCE) and brought the war to a successful conclusion for the Romans. The war gave Rome control of coastal Spain and so catapulted the Romans to the world stage as a major power. But the Romans maintained a constant, possibly irrational fear, of a Carthaginian revival. Forty years later, the Roman statesman **Cato the Elder** (234–149 BCE) took to ending every speech in the Senate with the words "*Carthago delenda est!*" (Carthage must be destroyed!). Eventually the Romans listened and launched the Third Punic War (149–146 BCE). After a short siege they captured Carthage, destroyed the city completely and, according to legend, sowed salt in the ground as a sign that the land would never again be inhabited.

Just as the war against Pyrrhus brought Rome into conflict with Carthage, the Punic Wars brought Rome into conflict with the Greek kingdoms of the Hellenistic world: Macedonia, Asia, and Egypt (**Figure 2.4**). The Romans had actually fought an indecisive war against King Philip V of Macedon simultaneously with the Second Punic War, and immediately upon the conclusion of the war with Carthage they turned their attention back to Philip. Using the slogan "freedom of the Greeks", they defeated Philip in 197 BCE and then defeated his son and successor Perseus more decisively in 167 BCE. These wars in turn brought them into contact with the Seleucid kingdom in Asia Minor and the Ptolemaic kingdom in Egypt, and Rome soon launched attacks on these areas as well that brought them under Roman control. Roman domination is symbolized best by an episode at Eleusis in Egypt in 168 BCE, told by both Livy (45.12) and Polybius (29.27). The Syrian king Antiochus was marching on Alexandria when the Roman ambassador Popilius Laenas caught up with him. Popilius offered the king a choice: withdraw from Egypt immediately

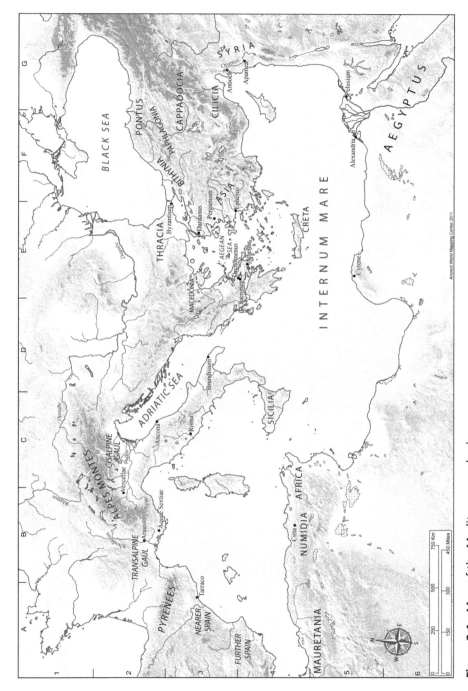

Figure 2.4 Map of the Mediterranean basin.

and remain a friend of Rome, or continue and become an enemy. Antiochus asked for time to think and Popilius agreed: he drew a circle in the sand around Antiochus and told him to decide before he stepped outside it. Antiochus, recognizing the power of Rome, chose to withdraw his forces.

In the eastern Mediterranean, the Romans adopted some of the same principles they had used during their subjugation of Italy: they generally chose not to govern these areas directly, but signed treaties spelling out the obligations of the defeated kingdom and proclaimed that they were giving them freedom, even allowing the defeated ruler to remain in power on occasion. "Freedom" turned out to mean freedom to act in ways that Rome approved, as Antiochus found on the outskirts of Egypt. This practice proved less successful in Greece and Syria than in Italy, since the greater distance encouraged the local kingdoms to attempt to assert their independence on several occasions. The Romans ended up having to return to these areas for further fighting, and eventually in 146 BCE, the same year in which Rome eradicated Carthage, the Romans completely destroyed Corinth, the most prosperous city in Greece. From this time forward, Rome was the undisputed master of the Mediterranean basin.

The Growth of Political Discord

The overseas wars of the third and second centuries and the Roman conquests of additional territory began to stress the political system that had been worked out in the earlier periods of the Republic. As we will see further in Chapter 4, this system relied on two principles apparently designed to avoid a return to a monarchy: collegiality and annuality. Each magistrate had a colleague who was his equal in office, and each magistrate only served in office for a single year. The only exception to this practice came during military emergencies, when they appointed a dictator for a period of no more than six months. In the second century, however, magistrates on military campaigns served further and further away from Rome. This distance reduced the ability of those in Rome to oversee their choices and so gave them tremendous flexibility as commander in chief in choosing a course of action. The distance from Rome also made it inefficient and even counterproductive to replace troops and commanders every twelve months. Many generals thus remained in military command beyond a single year, and many citizen-soldiers remained on overseas campaign for multiple years at a time.

Exploring Culture: *Cincinnatus, the Model Roman*

The Roman government was built on the principle that no man should have more power than any other man, in order to avoid the possibility of one man becoming king. Under most circumstances this system worked fine, but what happened if the two leading magistrates could not agree on what to do in an emergency? Their powers would cancel each other out, and leave the state vulnerable to an attack.

In these situations, the Romans resorted to the appointment of a dictator. The dictator possessed sole authority in the state, but the trick was that his appointment could last for a maximum of six months. This amount of time was felt to be enough to handle a crisis while still minimizing the chances of someone turning the dictatorship into a tyranny.

For the ideal model of a dictator, the Romans always thought of Lucius Quinctius **Cincinnatus**. Livy (3.26–29) tells us that he was working on his farm one day when a delegation from the Roman Senate showed up. He put down his plow and put on his toga so that he could talk with them, and they saluted him as Dictator and explained the desperate situation of the Roman army, currently fighting the Aequi. Cincinnatus followed them to Rome and immediately put Rome on a war footing: he suspended all public business, closed shops throughout the city, and ordered all men of military age to appear fully armed in the Campus Martius before sunset. By midnight of the next day the newly raised army had reached the war front. Upon arrival the dictator surveyed battle lines and immediately began a battle against the enemy. By dawn the enemy had been completely surrounded and agreed to surrender their arms and depart. Cincinnatus returned to Rome in triumph, carrying the spoils of war before him. Having completed his mission, he resigned his office on the sixteenth day and returned to his farm.

This story has had a profound impact not just on the image of an ideal Roman leader, but ideal American leaders as well: George Washington has often been compared to Cincinnatus, even in his own lifetime. Like Cincinnatus, he was called out of retirement to lead the Continental army, then resigned his commission in 1783 and returned to his farm at Mount Vernon. Washington then came out of retirement again to serve as President in 1789, before retiring to Mount Vernon for good after serving two terms as President. Jean-Antoine Houdon's statue (see **Figure 2.5**) of Washington, erected in 1796, made the comparison clear: Washington stands in front of a plow and rests his left hand on a bundle of rods known as the *fasces*, the Roman symbol of power. Americans no less than Romans mythologize their leaders so that they have the values that we want them to have.

Figure 2.5 Statue of George Washington as Cincinnatus. Jean-Antoine Houdon, 1792. Note the fasces that represent Roman military authority under his left arm and the plow behind his feet.

These features allowed individual generals to gain popularity and stature beyond what earlier generals had seen. Scipio Africanus, the conqueror of Carthage, provides a good example. The Roman difficulties in the war against Hannibal led the Romans to appoint him to a military command at an earlier age that was normal, and despite the fact that he had at the time held no office above that of **aedile**, a minor city management position. Scipio spent four years campaigning successfully in Spain before being elected to the office of **consul**, the highest Roman magistracy, and then spent the next four years campaigning in Africa where he finally defeated Hannibal. On his return he celebrated a lavish triumph and became the single most prominent politician in Rome. Legends grew up around him that he talked with Jupiter in the god's temple late at night, and even that he was the son of Jupiter, who had appeared in his mother's bed in the form of a snake; a similar story had circulated about Alexander the Great. In turn, these stories created concerns that Scipio could assume sole authority in Rome, always a fear of the Romans as we mentioned with the Lucretia story. Other leading Romans launched lawsuits against his family to weaken his influence and, although Scipio was able to avoid conviction, his influence faded and he died on his farm in 183 BCE. Already in the early second century, Scipio's experience showed the limits of Roman unity: less than twenty years after every ounce of energy was required to defeat Hannibal, the general responsible for that great victory died in solitude and disgrace.

The next fifty years saw a tremendous influx of money into the Roman state. Some arrived as a direct result of military conquest, as generals returned from campaigns against wealthy eastern kings loaded with captured treasure. A portion of this money would be distributed to the soldiery or set aside for public building projects, but most of it went directly to the general and his friends. Money also came directly to the Roman state as a result of peace treaties that obligated the defeated party to make cash payments to Rome, and even more came from Roman exploitation of the natural resources of the lands they captured. This money began to reshape the entire Roman state, not just the Roman economy (on which, see further in Chapter 11). It upset the balance between the rich and the poor, and also the balance between different members of the Roman aristocracy, as the controversies around Scipio Africanus suggest. The problems that arose beginning in the late second century BCE came as a direct result of the successes of the Roman military system, and the inability of the Roman political system to cope with them.

The tribunate of **Tiberius Gracchus** (c. 170–133 BCE) in 133 BCE is often viewed as a turning point in the disintegration of the Republican system. Plutarch and Appian make clear that Tiberius was a well-connected member of the Roman aristocracy; his grandfather was Scipio Africanus and his father-in-law was the most respected legal scholar of his day. During his term in office, Tiberius decided to sponsor land reform legislation to address some of the economic, social, and military issues that had arisen. His legislation was opposed by the bulk of the upper classes, which led Tiberius to employ unorthodox strategies in order to pass his legislation. Tiberius' decision to run for re-election, contrary to Roman custom that depended on the annual transition of office, was seen by some as a step on the way to one-man rule, so they moved to confront Tiberius just as Scipio had been confronted. In this case, however, Tiberius and 300 of his supporters were killed in a violent confrontation. Eleven years later Tiberius' brother Gaius Gracchus (154–121 BCE) was also killed in a premeditated riot after proposing a revolutionary set of reforms. The use of violence as a tool for settling political disputes became normalized over the next one hundred years. While initially the use of violence allowed the aristocracy to maintain control of Roman society, the recourse to violence would eventually play a major role in their complete loss of power.

Even while the Romans battled these internal problems, they were faced with a significant challenge from the inhabitants of Italy. Ever since the settlement of 338 BCE, most inhabitants of Italy had lacked full Roman citizenship, even though they provided much of the manpower that had enabled Rome to conquer the Mediterranean. Over the years these Italians had become increasingly unhappy with their second-class status, and finally in 90 BCE, these resentments boiled over into outright revolt. This war, known as the **Social War** (after the Latin word *socius*, "ally"), was perhaps the most fierce the Romans ever fought, in part because their opponents had the same training, techniques, and equipment as the Romans themselves, and in part because the Italians were fighting for their independence. The Romans suffered significant losses in the first two years of the war, which forced them to grant most of the concessions sought, including the right to full citizenship for any communities that had not revolted. Only then were the Romans able to defeat the remnant that held out for full independence. However, once the threat was past, the Romans found loopholes to reduce the influence of the Italians, such as limiting them to only 4 out of 35 voting blocs, so the Italian question remained an issue for the next sixty years.

During these episodes, the Roman aristocracy had found itself mostly unified in their response to the Gracchi and to the demands of the Italians, but even this unity shortly broke down. Lucius Cornelius **Sulla** (138–78 BCE) had come to prominence by serving as a lieutenant to Gaius **Marius** (157–86 BCE) during a war against King Jugurtha of north Africa; Sulla had in fact been the key player in arranging for the capture of Jugurtha that ended the war. In 89 BCE, Sulla was elected to the consulship in order to pursue a war against King Mithridates of Pontus (modern Turkey), in part because of his success in the Social War. His rival Marius found a legal loophole to transfer the military command to himself as a private citizen, contrary to Roman custom but reminiscent of Scipio Africanus. When Sulla heard the news, he took six of the legions that had been preparing for war against Mithridates and marched on Rome to regain his command. This event marked the first time that a Roman commander had marched his troops against Rome; in theory a Roman general's command expired as soon as he entered the city, but Sulla's troops followed him anyway, lured by the promise of loot from the campaign. As soon as Sulla left the city again for his campaign, Marius returned and slaughtered his political opponents; he had their heads placed on spears around the Roman Forum. Marius died only seventeen days after returning to Rome, but not before Sulla was declared an exile and Sulla's actions invalid. Thus when Sulla returned to Italy after a successful campaign, he was considered an outlaw and needed to fight a second civil war to regain his position within the state. After defeating his opponents in 82 BCE, Sulla had himself appointed dictator, typically an office reserved for a military emergency and limited to a six-month term. Sulla spent two years in office passing legislation that he hoped would restore unity and Rome's traditional way of governing, and then resigned shortly before dying at his farm south of Rome.

Sulla's reform package proved to be short-lived; the example he had set by his behavior – using military authority to ignore unfriendly legislation – proved stronger than the legislation itself. Within ten years, two individuals who rose to prominence through military commands, **Marcus Licinius Crassus** (115–53 BCE) and Gnaeus Pompey, better known as **Pompey the Great** (106–48 BCE), joined forces to undo much of Sulla's legislation, which was viewed as too friendly to the traditionalists in the Senate. Pompey gained the consulship despite the fact that he was below the minimum age requirement for the office and over the next ten years, he conducted successful military campaigns throughout the entire Mediterranean, adding Syria, Lebanon, and Judaea to Roman holdings. Crassus meanwhile remained in Rome and built both his wealth and his connections. They were joined in the top ranks of Roman leadership by **Julius Caesar** (100–44 BCE), who in 63 BCE surprised almost everyone by winning election as *pontifex maximus*, the head of the college of **pontiffs**, a symbolically important office though with little real power.

When the traditionalist members of the Senate decided that the time had come to reassert their authority, they assigned Caesar to drain swamps in Italy during his consulship and refused to ratify Pompey's treaty settlements from his campaigns. In response, the three politicians banded together in a loose alliance known as the **First Triumvirate**, which dominated Roman politics for the next ten years. As a result of the alliance, Caesar spent the next ten years conquering Gaul, even crossing briefly into Britain, while Pompey and Crassus were left to arrange matters in Rome, mostly to their liking, which included Crassus taking a command in 55 BCE to fight against the Parthian Empire on Rome's eastern frontier. In 53 BCE, Crassus suffered a major defeat against the Parthians and was killed during an attempt to negotiate a surrender, thus ending the three-person alliance. The year before, Pompey's wife Julia, the daughter of Caesar, had died during childbirth, leaving the alliance between Pompey and Caesar without any direct ties. The traditionalists in the Senate saw Crassus' death as an opportunity to separate Pompey from Caesar, and they gradually won Pompey over to their side. Conflict between Pompey and Caesar became inevitable, though to this day scholars debate the reasons for the conflict and which of the parties was more responsible for its outbreak.

Caesar had much the better of the civil war that followed: crossing the Rubicon River, which marked the boundary of his province, he became the second Roman (after Sulla) to march on Rome. Pompey was unable to defend the city and moved first south and then across to Greece, where Caesar followed him and defeated him at the battle of Pharsalus (48 BCE). Returning to Rome, Caesar became dictator as Sulla had done and instituted many reforms to make for the smoother functioning of the Roman state (including a calendar reform that remains in use today).

However, when Caesar became dictator for life, a small group of Senators formed a conspiracy, believing that Caesar was aiming to be king (or worse in Roman eyes, a god), and assassinated him in the Senate house on the Ides of March (March 15) in 44 BCE. His murder was, perhaps contrary to the expectations of the assassins, not met with support from the populace of Rome, and the assassins had to flee the city, leaving Caesar's most trusted commander, **Mark Antony** (83–30 BCE), and Caesar's heir, his 19-year-old grand-nephew **Octavian** (63 BCE–14 CE) to vie for power within the city.

The 13 years from 44 to 31 BCE were among the most unsettled periods in all of Rome's history. Antony and Octavian maneuvered for the backing of Caesar's supporters, while the traditionalists in the Senate, such as the orator Cicero, tried to influence the direction of affairs, and the assassins Brutus and Cassius gathered military resources in Greece. In 42 BCE, Antony and Octavian came to a formal agreement known as the **Second Triumvirate** (the third member, Marcus Lepidus ended up not playing a significant role in events), in which they gave themselves supreme power in Rome. They then turned their joint attention to eliminating Senatorial opposition – Cicero was among the first to go – and to defeating the assassins of Caesar in battle, which they accomplished at the battle of Philippi in 42 BCE. From there, Antony moved on to the East, where he attempted another attack on Parthia and developed a relationship with Cleopatra VII of Egypt (69–30 BCE). In the meantime Octavian had to fight off the navy of Sextus Pompey, the son of Pompey the Great, and reorganize affairs in Italy. The alliance between Octavian and Antony was inherently unstable, and although they agreed once to renew the Triumvirate, when the second five-year term ended in 32 BCE, Antony and Octavian quickly came to war. On September 2, 31 BCE, in a sea battle at **Actium** off the coast of Greece, Antony's forces were decisively defeated; Octavian followed him to Alexandria, the capital of Egypt, and after a short siege overwhelmed the remnants of Antony's forces. As immortalized by Shakespeare, Antony and Cleopatra committed suicide, leaving Octavian, soon to rename himself Augustus, as the sole ruler of the Mediterranean basin and marking (for modern historians) the end of the Roman Republic.

Marking Time

In placing the end of the Republic in 31 BCE, we have performed one of a historian's most characteristic activities: dividing history into periods. Typically these divisions are based on characteristics that historians believe are common to this period. For instance, the medieval period, lying between the Roman Empire on the one side and the Renaissance on the other, is often characterized as having significant authority vested in religious officials. Larger periods, such as the Roman Republic that lasted for 500 years, are often divided into smaller units as well, and the process of deciding where to place the breaks forces us to think about larger trends in Roman history rather than the details of individual episodes.

Historians of ancient Rome have tended to divide its history into three broad phases based on the form of its government: the Monarchy (753–509 BCE) from Romulus to Tarquin; the Republic (509–31 BCE), when power was vested in magistrates elected by the citizen body; and the Empire (31 BCE–476 CE) following the battle of Actium, where power was again vested in one man. Other divisions are possible: one could use territorial control as the criterion and divide Rome's history into an early period as a city-state (753–338 BCE); a middle period as a world power (338 BCE–260 CE), lasting until the emperor Valerian was captured in battle; and a late period when Rome's power was in decline (260–410 CE or 546 CE), ending with the sack of Rome by a foreign army. For simplicity's sake we will stay with the traditional divisions in order to keep our focus on the period of the Republic.

When we try to divide the Republic into smaller periods, we run into problems similar to those just mentioned. Modern historians have generally divided the Republic into three periods – historians seem to like the Early, Middle, and Late formula. The challenge has been that it is not always easy to find unifying characteristics or agreed end-points for all three periods, such that new divisions have been proposed. For instance, Harriet Flower has kept the idea of using political systems as the criterion for defining periods, but suggested that the period from 509 to 33 BCE should be divided not into three, but into *thirteen* separate periods. She identifies five different forms of government between 450 and 88 BCE, each using the principle of government shared by leading citizens but operating in a slightly different fashion. She identifies a further four "transitional" periods with no clear government principles, two periods of Triumvirates (rule by three men), and a period of one-man rule in the dictatorship of Julius Caesar. In this book we will stick for simplicity's sake with the traditional division into an Early Republic (509–287 BCE), Middle Republic (287–133 BCE), and Late Republic (133–31 BCE), but we should recognize that these periods are defined by historians and that some of the markers may be more useful for conversation than reflective of real changes in the Roman state.

Early, Middle, and Late Republics

The beginning of the Early Republic seems clear enough – it begins with the downfall of the monarchy in 509 BCE – but there is no clear end-point. Historians focused on internal developments see the unifying characteristic as the conflict between the patricians and plebeians and place the end-point at 287 BCE. This is the date assigned to the *lex Hortensia*, the Roman law that on this view ended the Struggle of the Orders. Others use a military perspective and prefer to end the Early Republic in 264 BCE. In this year the Romans sacked the Etruscan town of Volsinii and eliminated the last challenge to their power over the Italian peninsula. In the same year they launched an attack on Sicily that marked the beginning of the First Punic War,

Rome's first overseas military conflict and thus the first step in her acquisition of a territorial empire and control over the Mediterranean basin. The fact that historians have difficulty agreeing on a unifying characteristic suggests that perhaps there was not one, although we should also acknowledge that our evidence for this period is so limited that we may not be able to see it clearly.

The Middle Republic begins in the third century, wherever one chooses to end the Early Republic, and is generally agreed to end in 133 BCE with the tribunate of Tiberius Gracchus. This period is the one that might be referred to as the "classical Roman Republic," when the Roman government operated in the way that the elite Romans thought it should operate. That meant that power was shared among the elite of Rome, an elite that included wealthy persons of plebeian birth as well as noble-born patricians, and that the lower classes of Rome generally followed the lead of the elites. Externally the period was marked by Roman imperialism and the dramatic increase in the amount of territory subject to Roman power. In this period Rome conquered what is now Italy north of the Po River, Carthage, Spain, Greece, and Asia Minor, culminating with the twin sacks of Carthage and Corinth in 146 BCE. In 133 BCE, the Romans could justly refer to the Mediterranean Sea as *mare nostrum*, our sea.

The Late Republic is considered to run from 133 BCE to the battle of Actium in 31 BCE, and its unifying feature was the erosion of governmental institutions and the use of violence to resolve internal political matters, as described above. From the Gracchi to the Social War to Marius and Sulla to Caesar and Pompey to Antony and Octavian, this period was marked by a series of civil wars, whether in the civic spaces of Rome or on battlefields in Italy and overseas. We might even view this entire period as one approaching anarchy, as whatever written and unwritten rules that governed Roman society changed with such frequency that stability was hard to find. The triumph of Octavian/Augustus at Actium placed him in a position of sole military authority over the Roman state, just as Caesar had been after his victory over Pompey. Augustus, however, proved more successful in creating a stable system of government, inaugurating the period we know as the Roman Empire that lasted into the fifth century CE.

Conclusion: Historical Narratives

It has been common among historians, both ancient Roman historians and modern ones, to use the narrative of decline to paint a picture of the Late Republic in terms of a descent from an ordered government to chaos, as we saw Livy did (see Chapter 1). This perspective is especially popular when people want to compare modern governments to the Roman Republic.

Political Issues: *Are We Rome?*

Blog posts and newspaper columns love to dangle the comparison of current politics to Rome. There is almost always a parallel one can find, but these almost always say more about the witty point the writer wants to make about our own problems than they do about Rome.

Comparisons to the end of the Republic have always provided one of the most popular versions of this exercise. The thinking is that if we could understand why the republican system of government gave way to a system of one-man rule, we might better understand how to avoid a similar problem in the future.

Some modern historians argue that the personal ambitions of individual Romans brought about the civil wars that ended the Republic. Certainly some Romans looking back on the era saw it in these terms: the poet Lucan (39–65 CE) wrote that "Caesar could bear no superior, Pompey could bear no equal" and this conflict drove them to battle. From Sulla all the way through to Octavian/Augustus we have plenty of examples of individual Romans placing their own good above that of the state, and these have provided ample fodder for modern scolding.

Another group of scholars has focused on the intransigence of the Roman aristocracy. Beginning in the second century BCE they opposed efforts to address the growing wealth inequality within Roman society, highlighted by the opposition to Tiberius Gracchus. In the first century the conservatives continually opposed proposals benefitting the populace of Rome. They worked to drive a wedge between Caesar and Pompey and fought against any compromise, precipitating a civil war that may have been avoidable. The clearest sign that the aristocracy had come to serve their own interests rather than the state comes in 44 BCE when they led the assassination of Caesar: the lower classes of Rome did not approve of this action and the surprise of the Roman elite at the lack of support betrays how out of touch they were. Modern commentators who want to rail against the dangers of wealth inequality can again look to the Roman experience.

Rather than assigning individual blame, a third group of scholars focuses on the larger forces at play in the last hundred years of the Republic. The Roman system of government developed in order to govern a small city-state in central Italy; it was not designed to govern a far-flung empire where it took a month to travel from one end to the other. The Romans simply failed to adapt republican institutions to the changing world, until Octavian/Augustus changed the system entirely. Many institutions of the United States developed in the eighteenth century can seem out of place in the twenty-first century, and those who want to critique them can also use Rome as their historical example.

"Rome" thus means many things to many people. Perhaps the question is not "are we Rome?" but "what does it mean to be Rome?" What are we praising or condemning when we compare ourselves to Rome? It may be true that those who ignore the lessons of history are condemned to repeat it, but the end of the Roman Republic suggests that everyone sees those lessons differently.

Using that narrative assumes the perspectives of the elite; the transition from a republican form of government to one-man rule resulted in a loss of power for these members of society, who naturally saw it as a worse form of government. Adopting different perspectives allows for different narratives to emerge. For example, non-elites living in Italy gained opportunities for advancement that were closed to them under the Republic, such that they might have seen the rise of one-man rule as a mark of progress. To name one such person, an Italian writer named Velleius Paterculus wrote that he found himself unable to count the blessings that the battle of Actium conferred upon the world. The provinces, territories outside Italy ruled by Rome, also saw an improvement in their status under imperial rule; these areas had been subject to governmental abuse and corruption during the Republic, which the new system of government was able to minimize or eliminate.

It is part of our job as historians to make judgments based on the evidence that we find. As we proceed to explore the social and cultural history of the Republic, we need to observe whose perspective we are adopting, what other perspectives might exist, and what conclusions we might draw if we consider the view from other perspectives.

Discussion Questions

1. How would you personally apply the ideas of "progressive" and "declensionist" narratives discussed in Chapter 1 to the history of the Roman Republic as presented here?
2. What themes throughout the course of the Republic can you identify?
3. What differences can you see between the Early Republic and the Late Republic? How might you imagine the acquisition of a territorial empire might affect other aspects of Roman life (aspects that we will explore in the following chapters)?
4. How might the history of Rome and the growth of Rome be seen differently from the perspective of an elite leader of Roman society (for instance, a Senator) and an ordinary Roman (for instance, a foot soldier)?

Further Reading

Cornell, Tim (1995). *The Beginnings of Rome: Italy and Rome from the Bronze Age to the Punic Wars (c.1000–264 BC)*. London: Routledge.
   Although this book only provides discussion of the Roman Republic up to the beginning of the Punic Wars, it offers a tremendous synthesis of archaeological and literary material to provide a fundamental rethinking of the Early Republic. The relative lack of sources makes this period one of the most challenging to understand, and Cornell's book provides useful clarity, even if some hypotheses must remain conjectural.

Flower, Harriet I. (2010). *Roman Republics*. Princeton, NJ: Princeton University Press.

Flower offers a new analysis of the different periods of Roman Republican history. Rather than dividing the Republic into only three phases, she argues instead for a series of six distinct Republican forms of government, along with several transitional periods too brief to be considered a stable system of government. Her approach has the virtue of helping us recognize the tremendous degree of change that must have occurred over a nearly 500 year period.

Rosenstein, Nathan (2012). *Rome and the Mediterranean 290 to 146 BC: The Imperial Republic*. Edinburgh: Edinburgh University Press.

Part of a series, Rosenstein focuses on the Middle Republic, the period when Rome acquired its territorial empire. He offers analysis of key historical problems, contained within an engaging overall text. His treatment of the Punic Wars is particularly detailed and offers insight into the reasons why the Romans went to war and how they acquired an empire.

Steel, Catherine E. W. (2013). *The End of the Roman Republic, 146 to 44 BC: Conquest and Crisis*. Edinburgh: Edinburgh University Press.

Part of the same series as Rosenstein, Steel focuses on the Late Republic. She focuses especially on key issues such as freedom and honor, and power, greed and ambition, and explores the processes that transformed Rome from a republic to a monarchy. She depicts Rome as a dynamic and evolving system reflecting continuous changes in citizenship and in the elite classes.

Woolf, Greg (2012). *Rome: An Empire's Story*. Oxford: Oxford University Press.

Woolf offers a concise history of both the Roman Republic and the Roman Empire that followed the accession of Augustus. His focus is to consider Rome as an empire in theoretical terms and he often compares Rome to other world empires (China, for example), which helps show both the ways in which Rome behaved like other empires and ways in which it was unique.

3
The Building Blocks of Roman Society

Livy relates that in 494 BCE the plebeians of Rome, complaining about crushing burdens of debt, marched out to the Sacred Mount, three miles outside the city (2.32–33). The Roman Senate, now deprived of the soldiers on whom the state depended, sent ambassadors out to the people. They chose Agrippa Menenius because he was a plebeian and they thought he might have more success. When Menenius reached the plebeians' camp, he told them a fable about the body: once upon a time the other parts of the body complained that they did all the work and the stomach did nothing, so they decided not to provide food to the stomach any longer. The result, of course, was that the entire body was weakened. Menenius compared this situation to the plebeians' anger against the patricians, and prevailed upon the plebeians to accept the compromise that resulted in the creation of the Tribunes of the Plebs. Further secessions of the plebs led to further political concessions to the lower classes: the publication of a law code, the ability of plebeians to run for the higher political offices, and eventually that decisions of the plebeians were accepted as binding on the entire state.

Even if we do not believe all the facts of this episode, the story – like the stories about Romulus – offers valuable clues to understanding Roman society. It suggests that the plebs were willing to accept a certain degree of inequality: that they (like the hands) should do the hard work as long as the patricians (the stomach) returned an appropriate amount to them. It also raises questions about what degree of inequality is acceptable. Is representation in government sufficient? The publication of a law code? The eligibility to run for office? The Struggle of the Orders might have us questioning what equality might have meant to a Roman.

In abstract terms, the fable of the stomach revolves around the concepts of dominance and dependence: the stomach, the hands, and the mouth all depend on each other, even if one has more power than the others. Dominance and dependence are

A Social and Cultural History of Republican Rome, First Edition. Eric M. Orlin.
© 2022 John Wiley & Sons, Inc. Published 2022 by John Wiley & Sons, Inc.

the twin poles around which all of Roman society revolved. The Secession of the Plebs highlights this point: while the patricians dominated positions of power within the state, they were nonetheless dependent on the plebeians for military manpower. At the same time, while the plebeians were numerically dominant, their lack of resources often made them dependent on wealthy patricians for survival. This situation should makes us think more carefully about what is meant by dominance and dependence. Most often we are talking about power, and almost all relationships in Roman society were structured around the powerful and the less powerful: patrician and plebeian, but also patron and client, male and female, free and enslaved and restored to free status. As we explore these relationships, we will see the themes of dominance and dependence repeated in different ways.

Another significant point is that Menenius, a plebeian, agreed to serve as an ambassador representing the interests of the Senate. Menenius's action suggests that plebeian identity could be complicated, and that we should not assume that all plebeians behaved in the same way or shared the same interests. Different plebeians might see different paths to advancement for themselves, especially as the definition of plebeian changed over time. Originally the distinction between patrician and plebeian was based on birth: according to Roman tradition, the patricians were the descendants of the first group of Senators created by Romulus, who called them *patres* ("fathers"), and the plebeians were everyone else. At first being a patrician was hereditary and only patricians could become Senators. As wealthy plebeians began to serve in the Senate, distinctions based on birth became less important than those based on wealth, though the Romans always retained a recognition of the hereditary aspect; in the Late Republic it could even become an advantage to claim membership as a plebeian. Menenius' role reminds us that identity is complicated and shifts over time, and that we will have to pay careful attention to the evolution of Roman social structure.

Political Issues: *Senatus Populusque Romanus*

SPQR, the abbreviation indicating the "Senate and the Roman People," is everywhere in Rome today: on the sides of buildings, on fountains, even on manhole covers (**Figure 3.1**). Where does it come from?

The "Senate and the Roman people" was the ancient Roman phrase used to describe the entire state. The Romans therefore understood these as two separate entities. The original distinction between the Senate and the people was by birth: only descendants of Romulus' original Senate of 100 *patres* – the origin of the term "patricians" – could serve in the Senate. The remainder of the population could be referred to as the *populus Romanus*, the Roman people. The phrase highlights that in the beginning the patrician Senate was not actually a subset of the people, but an entirely separate body.

Figure 3.1 Manhole Cover, Rome.

The distinction between patricians and plebeians became more complicated after the conclusion of the Struggle of the Orders. One of the key outcomes of the Struggle was the ability of some plebeians to serve in the Senate, but a plebeian serving in the Senate upsets the neat categories just described: a plebeian Senator was no longer a member of the *populus* and the Senate was no longer comprised theoretically only of patricians. Roman authors often further complicate clarify our understanding: sometimes they use patricians and plebeians to refer to the Senate and the *populus*, sometimes they use patrician and plebeian to refer to a hereditary legal distinction, and sometimes there seems to be an economic sense with patrician meaning rich and plebeian poor. Some Roman authors even use *populus* in a negative way to refer to "the mob" without a precise political, legal, or economic meaning. The meaning of the phrase continued to change.

Despite these changes, Roman politicians remained very aware of the distinctions between patrician and plebeian and tried to use them to their advantage. Publius Clodius built a political career by presenting himself as the champion of the people. To do so, he had to overcome the obstacle of his patrician birth. Therefore he changed the spelling of his name from Claudius to the more plebeian-sounding Clodius, and had himself adopted into a plebeian family. As a plebeian, he was then able to serve as tribune of the plebs, the traditional magistracy that championed the rights of the people; that is, while still a member of the Senate, he successfully made himself part of the people of Rome, a bold feat that outraged many conservatives of his day.

> Curiously, the actual phrase *Senatus Populusque Romanus* is most frequently found during the time of the Roman Empire, a time when neither the Senate nor the People still had any power. It thus has more connections to autocracy than to republican or democratic norms. Its adoption by Mussolini and his fascist party in the 1930s only deepened this connection. This relationship to autocratic rule may be part of the reason that white supremacists today have often adopted SPQR as a symbol. The meaning of the symbol, just like the meaning of the phrase "the people" continues to change.

Because the information we have for the Romans is hopelessly biased towards the powerful, we will need to develop our own categories to describe Roman society. To take one example, the Romans often divided themselves into three orders (from Latin *ordo*), or classes, based on wealth: the Senatorial *ordo*, the Equestrian *ordo*, and the rest of Roman society fell into the third *ordo*. Using modern categories, we might consider the equestrians to be the "middle class", but in reality they were a subset of the aristocracy. To be an equestrian originally meant that you had enough wealth to provide your own horse for the Roman cavalry: any horse-lover can tell you that owning and caring for a horse is an expensive proposition. It is difficult to estimate wealth in the ancient world, but a reasonable guess is that the Senatorial *ordo* contained the top 0.1% of Roman society, and the equestrian *ordo* represented perhaps the top 10%. The lower classes of Rome therefore comprised 90% of the population. Some might have been able to make ends meet, but many individuals struggled simply to feed themselves and their families. Roman authors did not discuss this basic demographic fact often, but it highlights the dominance of the wealthy and the degree of dependence felt by the common people of Rome.

Rome as a City-state

Patrons and Clients

Perhaps the most important relationship structuring Roman society was the bond that linked a **patron** and a **client**. The patron–client relationship has been described by Jeremy Boissevain as "an asymmetrical, quasi-moral relationship between a person (*the patron*) who directly provides protection and assistance (*patronage*) ... to persons (*clients*) who depend on him for such assistance. Clients, in turn, provide loyalty and support when called upon to do so." The elements of this definition can thus be broken down as follows:

- Patronage is a relationship between unequals (it is "asymmetrical").
- Patrons are superior and provide needed assistance to people of lower social standing.
- Clients are inferior and provide political support to people of higher social standing.
- Both sides have some moral obligation ("quasi-moral") to fulfill in the relationship.

The patron thus dominated certain aspects of a client's life: he could summon the client to attend him as a show of support at a moment's notice, and may have been able to draw upon them for additional labor, during harvest season for instance. The client depended on the patron for essential services: protection against violence or threats of violence, financial support in hard times, or legal support if the client found himself in court. Cicero also suggests that patrons "used to make their counsel available to all citizens...not only with questions about the law but even about the marriage of a daughter, about buying a farm or cultivating a field, in a word about every kind of obligation or business affair" (*On Oratory*, 3.133–4). Cicero's words make clear that the relationship was not merely transactional, where each party acted in the hope of a tangible future benefit and could jettison the other simply to meet the needs of the moment, but was a long-term relationship. The failure of either party to live up to their obligations was seen as a serious moral failing.

The importance of this relationship in Roman society can be understood from the fact that the Romans traced the origins of the patron–client relationship to Romulus, the founder of Rome. According to Cicero's outline of Roman history, Romulus "distributed the plebeians among the prominent citizens who were to be their patrons" (*On the Republic*, 2.16). Each plebeian was thus placed in an unequal relationship with a single patrician, and this relationship was hereditary just as the status of plebeian or patrician was. The historical accuracy of this action is less important than what it says about the importance of patronage: the same person who founded Rome also founded the institution of patronage. It was literally impossible for the Romans to imagine a time when Rome existed and patronage did not.

The moral element in the patron–client relationship becomes clear when we consider the phrases that the Romans used when they referred to it. They did not in fact use the terms patron and client frequently, but rather said that someone had been committed "into the trust" of another person. The Latin word used in this context, ***fides***, is often translated as "sworn faith" and is one of the highest of the Roman moral values. To violate *fides* was among the most serious offenses a Roman could commit. The earliest law code in Roman history, the Twelve Tables, demonstrates how seriously the Romans believed in the importance of *fides*. A special punishment was set aside for patrons who committed fraud against a client, highlighting that the Romans placed obligations on the powerful and not just on the weaker party.

For clients, the relationship with their patron may have been most visible when they were involved in a legal proceeding. The patron was supposed to show up and provide legal assistance, which could range from offering advice to appearing in court as a supporter or even a witness. The patron's assistance might even have been necessary to protect oneself from being physically dispossessed without even a court hearing. The dependence of the client on the patron was especially pronounced in these circumstances. It is possible than many clients were illiterate, and even those that could read might not have known how to use the Roman legal system. If we think about our own legal system, we know that there are very specific actions and words that are required at just the right moment. The assistance of someone experienced in the courts was therefore essential, whether one was an illiterate farmer or an inexperienced politician in Rome.

These examples describe relationships of dominance and dependence between the rich and the poor, but clients were also drawn from members of the elite. An aspiring politician clearly had different needs than a poor farmer, but both might need the support of a patron. Plebeians who had become wealthy were often clients of patrician Senators and might need the support of their patron to become part of the ruling class. The Romans called an individual who had no ancestors who had previously held high political office a ***novus homo*** ("new man"), and these individuals often needed the support of a more powerful aristocrat to advance their careers. The same might be true of an individual from a lesser known family. To take one example, we might consider the relationship between Cicero and Gnaeus Plancius. Plancius' family came from a town in southern Latium and his father had moved to Rome after service as an equestrian in the Roman army. Plancius therefore did not have many friends he could count on; he depended on Cicero for political assistance and especially for a defense against an accusation of bribery. Cicero in turn was a *novus homo*, and early in his career had depended on other Roman aristocrats in a similar fashion. Cicero was thus building his own network of clients even as he still owed obligations to the patrons who had enabled his career. This example demonstrates how the Roman aristocracy consisted of a web of interconnected patron–client relationships, and navigating conflicts that might occur between patrons and clients and one's personal objectives was a central challenge for all but a handful of individuals.

Patronage appears to have been an inherited relationship, creating a lasting dependent status for the client's family. This fact is suggested by the early stories about Romulus and is confirmed by actions in later historical periods. When a patron died, his son inherited the responsibility for his father's clients, and similarly a client's son would assume his deceased father's obligations towards the patron. This arrangement certainly benefited a young patron: he instantly gained a group of loyal supporters as he set out to make a political name for himself. Young clients might also benefit, especially those that were not yet old enough to manage affairs on their own. Knowing that there was a powerful person to whom one could turn in efforts to keep his family afloat may have been a huge benefit to someone who was not yet an adult. Inherited patronage could benefit both parties as individuals.

At the broader societal level, however, patronage played a significant role in maintaining the dominance of the ruling elite. Patronage seems to have been more about prestige than elections; it does not seem that clients were obligated to vote in accordance with their patron's wishes and so patronage did not directly lead to the aristocracy's control of the state. Collectively patronage benefited the elite by maintaining relationships of dominance and dependence across the generations. Inheriting a position of inferiority presented significant hurdles if one wanted to climb the social ladder, and especially the political ladder. Until the Late Republic, moving into the ruling elite needed the active aid of a powerful patron. Other forms of status offered more avenues for social mobility.

Key Debates: *Did Patronage Determine Roman Elections?*

It was long argued that patronage played the crucial role in electoral politics. Many scholars viewed the obligation to vote for one's patron as the single most important obligation for a client. Since some aristocrats could be both patrons of members of lower class *and* clients of elites at the top end of the ladder, Roman elections could be seen as contests of political networks. A person running for office in theory could count on the vote not only of his direct clients but also of the clients of those clients, and so on. Until the introduction of the secret ballot in 139 BCE, Roman elections were conducted publicly so a patron could ensure that a client voted as directed. In this view, therefore, elections were primarily a question of alliances and networks.

Recently several arguments have been raised to challenge the traditional interpretation of Roman patronage and elections. Roman sources are very clear about the obligations of patrons towards their clients: support in legal and financial matters. They are much less clear on the obligations of clients. Clients were clearly expected to support their patrons in political and public life. Roman authors describe elite Romans going to the Forum attended by throngs of followers. A larger throng brought more prestige to the elite individual, and a client was certainly expected to perform this type of duty. However, the votes of poorer clients were of little value in the Roman electoral system, so it may not have made sense to the Romans to extend the obligation to the ballot. Certainly Roman sources never specify that a client was expected to vote for a patron under all circumstances, and we hear of no accusations against clients that they failed to vote for their patron.

Other scholars have pointed to the unpredictable nature of Roman elections to suggest that clients had no specific obligation to vote for their patron. We know of many occasions where the Romans seem to have been genuinely surprised by the results of elections. If the elites could control elections by directing blocs of voters to vote in a particular way, surprises should have occurred only rarely. Furthermore, we have numerous stories of candidates frantically canvassing for votes: going around the Forum on a regular basis, meeting with and talking to potential voters from all classes. This type of political activity seems inconsistent with elections that were predetermined by amassing blocs of clients.

A final point comes by considering the point of view of the clients themselves. It is difficult to imagine clients being constantly ordered to vote against their own interests – to vote for someone whose approach or ideas ran completely opposite to their own, or perhaps someone who had become a personal enemy. A rigid system that forced clients to vote for someone not of their own choosing might have a short lifespan.

For all of these reasons many scholars have come to believe that the patron–client relationship was simply one factor out of many that a Roman voter considered when making his choice.

Rich and Poor

Wealth is a marker of social status in almost every society, and Rome was no different. We noted earlier the vast gap between the top and the bottom. There was very little economic middle class in Rome, certainly not when compared to modern societies. The previous discussion, however, raises questions in this regard: if social mobility was limited by inherited status, how far could the acquisition of wealth change one's place in Roman society? On the one hand, wealthy plebeians who began as clients could pose problems within the Roman social system, since their position as a client was out of sync with their wealth. On the other hand, this problem might not have happened as often as we might think. Increased wealth alone is often not enough to gain access to the ruling elite. In addition, wealth is also inherited, and so patrons who had large fortunes were likely to pass both the fortune and the clients on to their heirs.

This observation is even more true for heavily agricultural societies such as Rome: significant wealth was generally held in the form of land and created by the produce of that land. It was therefore difficult for an individual to make a sudden fortune through entrepreneurial means. Roman values reinforced those difficulties: to be a member of the elite, money had to be made in the right way. Cicero offers a good representation of Roman attitudes: he belittled those engaged in the market economy while praising agriculture as the proper occupation of a free man. Since ownership of land defined who belonged to the dominant class and land is a finite quantity, acquisition of wealth in a socially acceptable manner had to be drawn out into several generations of a family. Social mobility based on wealth thus operated at a snail's pace.

Exploring Culture: *Roman Oratory and Values*

The natural historian Pliny the Elder (23–79 CE), in a discussion of human happiness, noted that Quintus Metellus had eulogized his father who died in 221 BCE by claiming that "his father had achieved the ten greatest and highest objects in the pursuit of which wise men pass their lives: for he had made it his aim to be the best warrior, the best public speaker and the bravest general, for the most important matters to be conducted under his authority, to enjoy the greatest honor, to be supremely wise, to be judged the most eminent senator, to obtain great wealth in an honorable way, to leave behind many children, and to be the most famous man in the state" (*Natural History* 7.139).

As always, a historian needs to ask questions of the source. While speeches can be a tremendous source of information, since they are contemporary first-hand accounts, we might suspect that Metellus has exaggerated his father's accomplishments. But the text is useful nonetheless: it indicates what Metellus believed were the top ten accomplishments for a Roman of the late third century. Half of these goals tie closely to military service, which should not be surprising in a society such as Rome where military conquest was a constant feature of the Roman Republic. In that regard, it is important to note that acquiring wealth is only one small part of happiness as defined by Metellus and that it is the eighth out of the ten items listed.

Perhaps even more important than the lack of emphasis on wealth are the specific words that Metellus used to describe his father's achievement. The father obtained "great wealth" in an "honorable way" and both parts are important. On all of the previous accomplishments, Metellus was the "best," the "bravest," in charge of the "most important" matters. For wealth, "great" was enough: Metellus did not have to have the greatest wealth. It was also important for the son to note that his father had obtained such wealth honorably: for the Romans this could be a combination of land ownership as well as wealth taken from a defeated city after a military conquest.

There may be some special pleading here: the Metelli were not the richest family in Rome. However, while some Romans might have quibbled with aspects of the list or the order of Roman values – what group ever agrees on a Top Ten list? – the relative importance of military glory and wealth seems to have been broadly accepted by the Roman elite until well into the first century BCE.

Cicero's attitude of course represents that of the "gentleman class." We have good reasons to believe that the lower classes saw things differently. The tombstones of many people of the lower classes, especially freedpeople but also enslaved persons, make a point to indicate the individual's profession, whether craftswoman, fishmonger, baker, or hairdresser (**Figure 3.2**). These people did not see anything vulgar in their behavior, but saw honor and dignity in these professions. Many working individuals also joined associations known as ***collegia***, usually organized by trade. These organizations both provided a space where they could feel that they belonged and also allowed them to achieve distinction within their own community. Cicero's dismissive attitude may also hide his recognition of a certain dependence on those very

Figure 3.2 Tomb of Eurysaces the Baker, Rome, late first century BCE. The frieze at the top depicts scenes from his daily work.

professions: a society needs the services provided by bakers, fishmongers, and craftspeople. We can again observe the twin poles of dominance and dependence: Roman society depended on the lower classes, but wealth was always unequally distributed in Rome and the lower classes remained economically dependent on the rich throughout the entire history of Rome.

Working with Sources
Dead People Do Tell Tales

Tombstones offer a crucial source of information for Roman historians. People of all social classes choose to commemorate themselves or be commemorated by others: rich, poor, and even enslaved. No other source speaks so broadly from the non-elite level, and this information is crucial to learning about how they understood their lives. At the same time, tombstones need the same careful attention as all other sources.

One challenge comes simply from the fact of commemoration. Not everyone could afford to pay for even a humble tombstone and not everyone with the resources wanted to spend it on a monument for a deceased person. Erecting a tombstone is a choice, and people might make different choices for different reasons. The habit of commemorating young children falls into this category. The percentage of young children commemorated is much higher than it should be: no society with a child mortality rate as high as the tombstones indicate could survive. The large numbers of tombstones can often help us spot these imbalances, but we still have to recognize that we are only hearing voices that chose to memorialize the deceased in this way.

We also do not always know whose voice we are hearing. It is possible that a deceased person left instructions for their tombstone. That would enable us to hear from them about how they wanted to be remembered. Other monuments may have been erected by family members or by colleagues in work. These stones might then tell us how those friends wanted to remember the individual. Modern historians are therefore careful about using this information to develop conclusions about the individual. We are more comfortable using it to develop overall impressions of societal values, on the assumption that anything on a tombstone, whether written by the deceased or a friend, must be a positive value.

A third challenge is trying to determine social status from a short inscription. Sometimes individuals might indicate whether they were a citizen or a freedperson, but some freedpersons might try to hide the fact that they had once been held in servitude. Roman names followed certain predictable rules, so sometimes a name can help us supply missing information. At the same time it can be misleading to make assumptions based on information that a person chose to include or not include, or even from the size and quality of a tombstone. People have all sorts of reasons for the choices that they make, and accounting for individual choice can be complicated.

The typical strategy for resolving these problems is to draw conclusions from a large number of these tombstones. In this way, a single unusual example does not distort the entire sample. As long as we maintain an awareness of the margin of error, statistical analyses or networking software programs can help uncover previously unseen conclusions about Roman life.

Men and Women

Another expression of dominance and dependence can be seen in the relationship between men and women in ancient Rome. We will have the opportunity to discuss the relationship between husbands and wives in Chapter 5, but here we want to focus on men and women in Roman society at large. As a rule, with some notable exceptions that we will explore below, the dichotomy between a public space inhabited by men and a private sphere to which women were restricted is a useful model for Rome. For instance, women could not hold office or vote in Roman elections. Since women had no formal political rights, men dominated the public sphere.

In the private sphere, however, we can see a greater degree of mutual dependence just as we saw with patrons and clients. Roman men recognized their dependence on women for reproductive purposes: without children their family line would die out. Indeed, a good portion of the effort to dominate Roman women stemmed from their desire to control women's childbearing capacity and thus to manage this dependence. Although women clearly held an inferior position to men in Roman society, there are reasons to believe in a degree of mutual dependence between men and women in Rome. Women attended dinner parties with their husbands, and we know of a number of women who were quite educated: able to read, write, and to conduct business.

More importantly, women were allowed to own property in their own name, a right that was not granted in the United States until 1839 and in the United Kingdom until 1870. This point is no small matter: husbands or brothers might well need funds to advance their political or economic interests. In the case of divorce, the dowry that the woman had brought into the marriage returned with her, which might leave her husband in an awkward financial position. Cicero's letters, although from a later period, reveal clearly the financial situation of an elite male whose wife owned more assets than he did, and the challenges he faced when the couple divorced.

The Vestal Virgins offer another example of the dominance and dependence of Roman women, this time in the sphere of religion. The Vestals were the most prominent, though not the only, public priestesses of the Roman state (**Figure 3.3**). Their primary religious tasks were to maintain the hearth fire in the temple of Vesta and to make *mola salsa*, a special grain that was used in sacrificial rites. If the hearth fire was to go out, it was viewed symbolically as a bad religious omen for the Roman state. In a world without recourse to matchbooks or lighters, the hearth fire also served a practical purpose, available to all citizens of Rome for their personal use. In many ways it could be said that the wellbeing of the entire Roman state depended on the work of the Vestal Virgins, just as the wellbeing of an individual household depended on the work of the women in the house. In recognition of their importance, the Vestals possessed several rights that other women lacked: they were released from the guardianship of their father and they could make wills and give testimony in court without having to swear an oath. They were also among the most visible women in Rome and given special seats at public games. Some Vestals became quite wealthy: one named Licinia owned "a pleasant villa in the suburbs" that the powerful Marcus Crassus tried for years to purchase before finally convincing her to sell.

Figure 3.3 Portrait of a Vestal Virgin, Rome, first to second century CE. Museo Nazionale Romano, Rome.

These privileges carried with them certain costs that reinforced the dominance of the male-centered state. Vestals were chosen for service when they were between six and ten years old, and they served for a minimum of thirty years, during which time they lived in a special house next to the temple and had to abstain from sexual activity. The term of service was such that child-bearing years had passed before they were released, making it difficult if not impossible to marry once the minimum term of service was up. Many Vestals therefore chose to remain in that role, and Roman texts contain several stories of Vestals who did leave the service and came to regret it. Although they were freed from the obligations of their father, they came under the control of the *pontifex maximus*; in essence, he assumed the role of father. Plutarch (*Numa* 10) notes that "If the Vestals commit any minor fault, they are punishable by the high-priest only, who scourges the offender" in the way that a father might in the home. Most famously, in a case where a Vestal was judged to have been unchaste, she was buried alive in a special tomb. The Roman state thus dominated control of the Vestals' bodies: for all their privileges, we might question whether they actually enjoyed more freedom than other Roman women.

The position of women within non-elite households was of course quite different in many ways. With smaller estates, or even no estates at all, these families had fewer reasons to be concerned about legitimate heirs to carry on the family name, and concerns about property often took second place to survival. We have a great deal of evidence for working women, often alongside the men of the household on the family farm or elsewhere, but also outside of the house. Some worked as prostitutes or actresses, but many worked in respectable professions, including scribes and secretaries. We even know of a small number of female painters and poets. We also have evidence that women worked outside the home, either running a shop on their own or working side-by-side with their husbands in a butcher's shop or fullery, the ancient equivalent of a laundry (**Figure 3.4**). These families were far from the ideological concerns of the upper classes with male dominance, though they likely did not approach modern notions of shared responsibilities or equality.

Figure 3.4 Funerary relief of a butcher and his wife, Ostia, early second century CE. Ostia Archaeological Museum.

Free and Enslaved and Freed

The practice of slavery is perhaps the most obvious example of a relationship of dominance and dependence among human beings. One human being exercises complete dominance over the body of another human being, and that other human depends on the first for virtually everything: food, clothing, housing, even one's life. Slavery is known in the Twelve Tables, indicating that the practice goes back at least to the fifth century, before Rome had even begun to exercise control over Italy. A critical difference between slavery in the Roman world and slavery in the United States is the lack of a distinction based on skin color. Men, women, and children were enslaved largely as a result of a defeat in war: the sale of captured enemy combatants and civilians was standard practice in the ancient Mediterranean, recognized and accepted by defeated parties as well as victorious ones. Subsequently children of enslaved mothers were born into slave status. As a result, people from any society might be enslaved, such that no ideological attempt was made to justify the seizure and sale of any one ethnic or racial group: the enslaved looked much like the enslavers. That fact does not make Roman slavery "better" than American or European slavery: slavery still enacts the desire of some people to completely dominate another. However, because it was not race-based, the ideology of slavery did not have the same impact on Roman society as it has on the United States.

The Roman habit of restoring enslaved persons to free status also changed the impact of slavery on their society. The Romans practiced **manumission** (from *manus* "hand" and *mitto* "to send" – elements in the ceremony that conferred free status on an individual) with greater frequency than many other slave societies (**Figure 3.5**). Urban enslaved persons, who might earn money with which they could purchase free status, or those with direct interaction within the enslaver's household, seem to have obtained free status more frequently than those whose stolen labor was put to use on farms. A person restored to free status, known as a **freedperson,** automatically became a client of their former enslaver and owed the patron additional legal and financial obligations over and above the normal deference of a client. Thus a freedperson was not removed entirely from the relationship of dominance and dependence with their former enslaver, but they did exchange a form that insisted upon total domination for one that had some mutual obligations.

Freedpersons in Rome also became citizens upon manumission, which further changed the nature of their dependence. As we will see in Chapter 7, most members of the aristocracy in Italian towns were excluded from Roman citizenship for many years, so for an individual to go from the least privileged legal status to a highly privileged status in a single step, leapfrogging longtime allies of the Roman elite, is remarkable. It is not clear why the Romans chose this path, though it likely served their own purposes rather than being a sign of generosity. Restoration to free status needed to create significant privileges to be meaningful as a carrot to dangle in front of enslaved persons. In addition, formerly enslaved persons faced certain legal

Figure 3.5 Relief showing two freedpersons, on the left and at the bottom. 1st century BCE. Musée Royal de Mariemont inv. B.26. The pileus on their heads was an element in the manumission ceremony and so became a visual representation of freed status and liberty more generally.

disabilities in addition to the duties they owed their patrons: they were not permitted to run for political office, for example, allowing the ruling elite to maintain its dominant hold on politics. The children of formerly enslaved persons carried no such political disability and became undifferentiated members of the Roman population, with the same social mobility as other dependents in Roman society.

Rome as a Mediterranean Empire

As might be imagined, Rome's rise to the position as the dominant state in the Mediterranean basin brought changes in the social status of everyone connected to the Roman state. Wealth poured into the Roman state, altering notions of rich and poor, and changing the bonds between patrons and clients. Women's roles and legal capacities changed, perhaps because Roman men were engaged in more and longer overseas campaigns. Rome's conquests also resulted in a dramatic increase in the number and variety of enslaved persons present in Roman society. These changes all contributed to the turmoil of the Late Republic. The relationships of dominance and dependence that had structured Roman society had occasionally been challenged earlier by individuals who did not fit easily into the rigid categories. In the Late Republic, however, this structure almost ceased to function entirely.

Patronage and Wealth

At the political level, the model of patronage became the means of managing relationships with the leaders of Rome's overseas conquests. Kings defeated by the Romans in battle needed powerful persons in Rome to advocate for themselves and their territory, and individual Roman generals were only too happy to acquire clients with this type of wealth and power. As a result. conflict over military commands became more intense: the civil war between Marius and Sulla revolved around which of them would assume control of the campaign against Mithridates of Pontus. The increasing importance of these commands weakened the traditional bonds between members of the aristocracy: even earlier, Marius had decided that he could achieve his aims more easily through obtaining a military command rather than waiting for his patrons to act on his behalf. These challenges to the traditional social structure contributed to the political disunity that resulted in the civil wars described in Chapter 2.

The increasingly globalized world brought new economic opportunities for trade and led to the emergence of new groups within the Roman aristocracy. Despite Cicero's criticisms, some members of the Roman upper classes chose to engage primarily in economic matters, including trade. The existence of powerful individuals who had vested interests in political policies but who deliberately took no formal part in politics created new pressures on Roman society. These people sought the economic advantages of Rome's imperial holdings but took no responsibility for maintaining a stable and sustainable system of government. The arrival of wealth and possibilities for even more further destabilized traditional notions of dominance and dependence. The aristocracy itself was thus not as unified as it once was, and its division presented one set of challenges to Roman society.

Women

The impact of the Roman conquest of the Mediterranean was also felt far outside the aristocracy. Although Roman women continued to face many legal disabilities, a number of stories from the second and first centuries BCE show us that they took a more visible role in both public and private life at this time. Women appeared in public advocating repeal of the Oppian Law in 195 BCE, an affair we will discuss further in Chapter 4. Around the same time and perhaps in response, Cato the Elder complained about women exercising more authority than he thought was proper:

the woman brought you a big dowry; next, she retains a large sum of money which she does not entrust to her husband's control but gives to him as a loan; finally, when she is annoyed with him, she orders a "reclaimable enslaved person" to chase him about and pester him for it (quoted in Aulus Gellius, *Attic Nights* 17.6.8).

Women in his view were beginning to exercise greater economic power, causing inconvenience and more to men. As the earlier laws limiting women's economic power of women became less effective, Roman men devised a number of new strategies. In 169 BCE, they passed a law that banned the richest Romans from making daughters heir to more than half of their estate (on this law, see further in Chapter 5). If we ask why the law was passed at this time, we may suspect that the increasing wealth in Rome from the overseas military conquests was leading to increasingly large amounts of property in the hands of women. Male dominance in economic matters was no longer as strong as it had once been.

The most famous woman of this period must be **Cornelia** (195–115 BCE), and elements of her life might illustrate the increasingly less dependent position of elite women after Rome's rise to empire. As is typical for women in the ancient world, she is identified by the men in her life. She was the daughter of Scipio Africanus, the conqueror of Carthage, and is best known as the mother of Tiberius and Gaius Gracchus whose tribunates created such controversy. Even her name derives from men: her name is simply the feminine form of the family name Cornelius. Her marriage was arranged by her relatives in order to create a political alliance with a prominent family, but on the death of her husband, she chose not to remarry. Roman authors hold her up as the Roman ideal of a woman loyal to a single man throughout her life, but we might also note that she had sufficient wealth and education to be able to manage her own affairs after her husband's death. Plutarch notes that after her husband's death she "took charge of the children and of the estate," managing the finances with no apparent difficulty and educating her children such that "they were thought to owe their virtues more to education than to nature." Some authors suggest that she even declined an offer of marriage from the Ptolemaic king of Egypt: though the story may have been exaggerated in order to highlight her devotion to her husband's memory, it suggests both her high status as well as her desire for independence. Cornelia's experience and long life – she died when she was around 80 years old! – suggests that at the top of the social order, women in the Late Republic could establish a certain degree of autonomy.

Enslaved and Freed Persons

Rome's conquests also resulted in a dramatic increase in the number and variety of enslaved persons present in Roman society. The available evidence suggests that ten times as many enslaved persons were brought to Rome after Rome's conquests than before. The impacts were felt throughout Roman society: larger households had more enslaved persons than before, and even less wealthy Romans might own several enslaved individuals. The number of freedpersons grew as a result, adding more complexity to the Roman social structure. Inscriptions suggest that enslaved persons frequently noted their relationships within their enslaver's household as well as to other enslaved persons. Perhaps these relationships gave them some small sense of social belonging, even as they were subject to complete domination. In contrast, freedpersons often omitted notice of relationships forced on them by their previously enslaved status, preferring to focus attention on the relationships they had chosen to build rather than those that had been forced upon them.

As Roman conquests led to an increase in economic activity in the second century BCE, some of the more oppressive restrictions on freedpersons were modified, and they were more easily able to enter the mainstream of Roman society. Since individuals became Roman citizens when they regained free status, these developments raise questions about the impact on Roman society of a growing population of new Roman citizens, especially since many of these people had been born not only outside Rome but outside Italy as well. Such questions are not easy to answer: we lack reliable quantitative data and we lack personal accounts from these individuals, but perhaps we can get at some of these questions by exploring the life of one of the best-known enslaved persons in the Roman world.

Marcus Tullius Tiro (103–4 BCE) is known to us primarily through the letters of Cicero, who had held Tiro in slavery and eventually restored him to free status. Tiro not only worked with Cicero on the orator's writings, but handled financial affairs for Cicero and often served as a sounding board or confidant. It is through Tiro that many of Cicero's vast literary writings became public, for Tiro organized and published Cicero's correspondence as well as a number of speeches. Tiro was therefore clearly well-educated: he seems to have been born into servile status and was given an education for reasons no longer known, though it is possible he was educated prior to being forced into slavery. When Cicero moved from Arpinum to Rome, Tiro would have gone with him; as an enslaved person he had no choice in the matter, but the apparently good relationship between himself and Cicero may have made him willing to go. Tiro regained free status in 53 BCE and accompanied Cicero to Cilicia in 52 BCE, even though he was no longer enslaved. Cicero's brother Quintus praised Cicero for recognizing that Tiro's "former condition [was] below his worth and preferring to have him as a friend rather than an enslaved person" and several letters of Cicero to Tiro express concern for Tiro's health. The evidence from the Roman side thus offers an ideal picture of the potential relationship between enslaver and enslaved: the former expressing care and concern for the other and restoring him to freedom, and the latter acting with as much devotion as a free person as he had as an enslaved person. This image allowed the Romans to believe that the difference in status made no difference to the relationship.

Of course we have no evidence about what Tiro thought of these arrangements, for we seldom hear about the perspective of the weaker person in this relation of dominance. As an enslaved person he was required to take Cicero's family name so that all of Roman society knew that he had once been enslaved to Cicero. His continued appearance in Cicero's letters indicates that the relationship continued even after his manumission, but since Tiro owed Cicero additional duties even as a free person, it is difficult to tell how willingly Tiro maintained this relationship. Did he feel that he had no choice but to accompany Cicero to Cilicia in order to fulfill his obligations or because he lacked other options? We might note that Cicero apparently continued to think of Tiro as an inferior rather than a friend as his brother suggested: Cicero's letters continue to use language more appropriate to a superior. For example, just after Caesar's assassination in 44 BCE, Cicero wrote that he had charged Tiro to handle some important financial matters while he himself prepared to leave Italy: a friend or an equal might have made a request rather than giving a command.

Cicero and the rest of Roman society never fully credited Tiro for his contributions simply because he had at one time been enslaved, and often we continue that trend today. Tiro is known to have developed a system of shorthand that was used first by Roman emperors and later in the Catholic church hierarchy. Indeed, Tiro may well be said to be the inventor of shorthand, but he gets little notice for this invention. It is certain that if any of Tiro's own writing had survived, we would have a different picture of Tiro the man and of his relationship to Cicero. Enslaved persons could challenge the dominance of their former owners once returned to free status, but they could never fully escape the relationship of dependence.

Conclusion

Perhaps it should not be surprising that a society whose growth was based on dominating other people developed a society based around relationships of dominance and dependence. Many ancient societies, and modern ones as well, have formalized unequal relationships between free and unfree or between men and women and operated on this basis. The Romans, however, extended this model to include relationships between free adult male citizens in a variety of aspects. As a set of governing principles, they were reminded that physical dominance was not the only issue: the physically dominant still depended on others in a number of other ways, and while they controlled others through force, they nonetheless recognized obligations to those dependent on them in these ways. This understanding helped them structure the entire world, and we will see that once they had established these types of relationships among themselves, it was natural to extend them to other areas of life: the family (Chapter 5), gender relationships (Chapter 6), foreigners (Chapter 7), and others. But first, let us explore how the Roman political system worked.

Discussion Questions

1. What are the key aspects of the Roman social structure? You might think in terms of how people were grouped and how easy or difficult it was to move from one social group to another. How do these work in your own community or country? What might account for any differences between the Romans and yourself?
2. Did the concepts of dominance and dependence apply in the same way to the different social groups in Rome, or how did the balance shift according to which groups of people were involved? What might those shifting balances reveal about Roman society?

3. What techniques could Romans use to resist or evade the limitations of the social structure in the world? What techniques are available to you?
4. What do the stories of your own community (true or not) reveal about the values of your community?
5. In what ways, if at all, does the Roman institution of patronage differ from how networking works today?

Further Reading

Bradley, Keith R. (1994). *Slavery and Society at Rome.* Cambridge: Cambridge University Press.
Bradley's book has been a fundamental starting place for understanding not just the impact of slavery on Roman society, but also what it was like to be an enslaved person in the classical Roman world. It discusses the work roles enslaved persons fulfilled, conditions under which they spent their lives, and the way in which slavery was an integral part of Roman civilization.

Gardner, Jane F. (1990). *Women in Roman Law & Society.* London: Routledge.
Gardner uses both literary and legal evidence to discuss the status of women in ancient Rome. She explores the ways laws affected women throughout their lives: as daughters, wives, and parents; as heiresses; as owners and controllers of property; and as workers. A central point is laws themselves tell us much about the economic situation of women and the range of opportunities available to them outside the home.

Joshel, Sandra R. (1992). *Work, Identity, and Legal Status at Rome: A Study of the Occupational Inscriptions.* Norman, OK: University of Oklahoma Press.
Joshel uses tombstone inscriptions to explore how the lower classes shaped their identities through their occupations. She highlights work as a source of community, as a way to reframe their legal status, and as a way to base their position on economic achievement rather than birth.

Raaflaub, Kurt A. (2005). *Social Struggles in Archaic Rome: New Perspectives on the Conflict of the Orders.* Malden, MA: Blackwell Publishers.
This collection of essays offers analyses of the social conflicts between the patrician elite and the plebeians in the first centuries of the Roman republic. Different chapters focus on the definition of patricians and plebeians, the reliability of the historical narratives, and different ways of understanding the Conflict of the Orders.

Wallace-Hadrill, Andrew (1989). *Patronage in Ancient Society.* London: Routledge.
This volume offers a collection of essays on patronage in the ancient world, with the majority of essays focused on Rome. Wallace-Hadrill's chapter on personal patronage in Rome is especially helpful. Other chapters focus on patronage in literary circles and patronage as a means of conducting foreign policy.

4
The Practice of Politics

In 200 BCE, the Romans had barely stopped celebrating their triumph over Hannibal in the Second Punic War when the consul Publius Sulpicius Galba proposed that they should go to war with Philip V, the ruler of Macedonia. The reason given was that during the war against Hannibal, Philip had attacked Rome's allies in Greece and in so doing had aided and abetted the Carthaginian war effort. The proposal was almost unanimously rejected by the Centuriate Assembly. As Livy says (31.6), "the length and exhausting demands of the recent war had made men weary of fighting and they shrank from incurring further toils and dangers." The ruling class was angry with this result, and "each of the senators in turn [urged] the consul to call another meeting of the Assembly to consider the proposal afresh and at the same time to rebuke the people for their want of spirit and show them what loss and disgrace would be entailed by the postponement of that war." Sulpicius made a dramatic speech in front of the people, stressing that war with Philip was coming and Rome could only choose whether to fight in Greece or in Italy. He then took a second vote, and this time the result was in favor of war.

Several players appear in the story above. There is the Sulpicius, the consul, the highest magistrate of the Roman state, who would lead troops into war and who puts the question before the assembly. There is the Senate, a body of former magistrates, which advises the consul to renew his efforts to get the people to declare war but apparently can not declare war on its own. Then there is the Centuriate Assembly, the assembled citizenry of Rome whose approval was, as the story makes clear, necessary for a declaration of war. Analyzing the roles of these three players – magistrates, a Senate composed of former and future magistrates, and the mass of the populace – is crucial to understanding the formal structures of the Roman government.

At the same time, every political system is also shaped by informal structures, and these also need attention if we are to understand Roman politics. What are informal

A Social and Cultural History of Republican Rome, First Edition. Eric M. Orlin.
© 2022 John Wiley & Sons, Inc. Published 2022 by John Wiley & Sons, Inc.

structures as opposed to formal structures? The United States offers a useful comparison. On the one hand, there have been relatively few changes to the formal structures in 230 years; there still is a President, a Congress, and a Supreme Court. In the era of social media and 24-hour cable news networks, however, power is exercised in different ways: for example, Twitter has replaced smoke-filled cloakrooms as a means of influencing decision-makers. The system still operates, but not in the same way. The challenge of understanding politics in Rome is even harder than for the USA: Rome had no written Constitution that laid out the formal political structures, and at this distance in time it is even harder to understand the informal factors. Yet these are the questions we must answer if we want to know what was really going on in Roman politics.

What Was the Roman Republic?

The Romans made no effort to define the rules that governed their political system in the way that modern political scientists might, and very little effort even to define the principles. The English word "republic" comes from the Latin **res publica**, which literally means "public thing." The state was the thing that concerned itself with the welfare of the public, but it did not necessarily refer to any specific form of government. As we discussed in Chapter 2, it has recently been suggested that there were six different Republics, if "Republic" refers to a specific form of government. Modern scholars have devoted countless hours to observing the operations of the Roman government and trying to deduce its rules in various periods, but in simple fact there appear to have been very few rules and for many years they were rarely written down. If a Roman could convince a majority of his fellow Romans that an action was legal, then it was.

Often these claims were grounded in an appeal to an earlier precedent: the Romans generally looked to the **mos maiorum** ("custom of the ancestors") for guidance and less frequently to **ius** ("law"). One major challenge for historians is therefore that changes were frequently disguised as continuity with an imagined past, making it difficult today to see where and when a custom changed. So we will start our study with a synchronic view of how the system operated in its idealized form, perhaps in the third and second centuries BCE. Where we can observe specific historical changes, we will note them to explore the impact of Rome's growing empire on the practice of politics.

The Roman System: Formal Structures

The Roman Republic has often been cited as an example of a government displaying a healthy balance of powers, with a system of checks and balances that enabled it to function smoothly. James Madison drew inspiration for the US Constitution from this feature (for an example, see *Federalist Papers*, no. 47). The Founding Fathers looked to balance the executive, legislative, and judicial branches, but thinkers in the ancient world used other terms. Especially in Greece, they thought in terms of monarchy, oligarchy, and democracy – that is, rule of the one, rule of the few, and rule of the many. The Greek historian Polybius, who came to Rome as a war captive in the second century BCE, described the operation of the Roman government in these terms and argued that "the whole state had been regulated with such a scrupulous regard to equality and equilibrium, that no one could say for certain whether the constitution as a whole were an aristocracy or democracy or monarchy" (Polybius, 6.11). Polybius is thus our starting point for analyzing the Roman government, though as always we need to ask critical questions of his account.

Polybius noted that the consuls were chief magistrates while they were in Rome and that they served as military commanders leading troops during their year in office. Consuls and **praetors**, the magistrates primarily responsible for the judicial system, were invested with *imperium* (**Figure 4.1**). The term, often translated as "power" or "rule," is a designation that meant that those who wielded it could command others and, if necessary, put a Roman citizen to death for disobedience. Once elected these magistrates could act according to their own sense of the right thing to do. They might need legislative approval for certain actions – remember that Sulpicius needed to obtain the approval of the assembly for a declaration of war

Name	Number of Magistrates	Possessed *imperium*	Election	Main Duties
CONSULS	2	YES	Centuriate Assembly	Lead armies
PRAETORS	2, rising to 8	YES	Centuriate Assembly	Military governors, administration of law
CENSORS	2	NO	Centuriate Assembly (every 5 years)	conduct census; enroll new citizens; most highly respected office
QUAESTORS	2, rising to 40	NO	Tribal Assembly	financial officers both civilian and military
AEDILES	4	NO	2 by Tribal Assembly 2 by Plebeian Council	upkeep of the city; public games
DICTATOR	1	YES	chosen in emergency by Senate and approved by Assembly	term limited to six months; sole head of state with primarily military focus
TRIBUNES* of the PLEBS	2, then rising to 10	NO	Plebeian Council	power of veto; personal body inviolable; could take votes in Plebeian Council with force of law

*Technically the Tribunes were merely representatives of the plebeians who elected them and not magistrates of the state. In practice they did form a part of the Roman government.

Figure 4.1 Public Officials of the *Res Publica*.

against Philip – and they could on rare occasions face a trial for misconduct. However, the most remarkable thing about Roman magistrates is how little formal oversight there was, and thus how much influence a single person could theoretically have in setting Roman policy. Polybius noted that "they have all but absolute power" so that a review of their powers "would in fact justify describing the constitution as despotic – a clear case of royal government." Of course, as we discussed in Chapter 2, the Romans had a deep fear of royal government and so they attempted to protect the system in two ways: each magistrate served for only one year at a time and each had at least one colleague with the same rank who therefore could not be commanded by his colleague and could block undesirable actions. The Romans thus developed a system of checks and balances even with the part of the government that exercised monarchical power.

Polybius next describes the role of the Senate, which also features in Livy's account of the war debate in 200 BCE. He notes that the Senate controlled the treasury and had responsibility for what we today would call foreign policy. Embassies from allies in Italy or from foreign powers outside Italy were received in the Senate and the Senate gave responses that set the direction of policy. Polybius writes that "with such business the people have nothing to do. As a result, if one were staying at Rome when the consuls were not in town, one would imagine the constitution to be a complete aristocracy: and this has been the idea entertained by many Greeks, and by many kings as well, since nearly all the business they had with Rome was settled by the Senate" (Polybius 6.13).

Livy's narrative of the war debate in 200 BCE should make us think carefully about the account of Polybius. Recall that Livy gives the Senate only a background role in this debate. The Senate does not make the decision nor even express an opinion prior to the first vote. The Senate gets involved to urge the consul to raise the question a second time only after the initial proposal was defeated. Even then they had no authority to act on their own. Other accounts match what we see in Livy: the Senate's formal role was purely advisory. At the same time its advice was often crucial in decisions taken by both magistrates and the people, and the Senate, as in the war debate of 200 BCE, usually got the result it wanted.

This episode suggests that Polybius might have overstated the formal role of the Senate, perhaps out of a desire to fit the Roman government into his theory of monarchy, aristocracy, and democracy. The Senate's lack of formal power does not fit neatly into his categories, but he also might have been closer to the truth if our question includes understanding the informal structures of how political decisions were really made during the Middle Republic. In many ways the Senate was the primary political power in the Roman government. A consul served only one year as a magistrate, but might be a member of the Senate for thirty years or more, and so even as consul he had an incentive to make sure that the Senate played a significant role in decision-making. The issues of dominance and dependence discussed in Chapter 3 are useful here: the Senate was the dominant force but it also depended both on its magistrates and on the assemblies of the people.

Further questions about Polybius' account arise when we turn our attention to his discussion of the role of the people, which he saw as the democratic component of the Roman government. He noted that the people elect magistrates to their offices and that they had the power of passing or repealing laws and of declaring peace or war. Polybius claims that "these considerations would lead one to say that the chief power in the state was the people's, and that the constitution was a democracy." From the formal perspective, the claims of Polybius are supported here by the war debate of 200 BCE: the failure of the first vote in the assembly prevented the consul from mobilizing for battle, and he was forced to gain their approval at a second meeting. As we just saw, however, the consul and the Senate were often able to gain approval for the actions they wanted to take. We might consider some other factors that should force us to question how much decision-making authority the people actually held.

One factor is the method of voting in the assemblies. Rome actually possessed four different assemblies, each organized according to a different principle. In this case the consul sought approval from the Centuriate Assembly (***Comitia Centuriata***), with the people divided into groups according to wealth. Since Romans were expected to provide their own equipment when called for military service, a person's wealth reflected the role they played in the army: wealthier people served as fully armed infantry or even cavalry (horses are expensive!), while poorer citizens provided support. This feature explains why the most important decisions and most important elections, those relating to war and peace, were placed before the Centuriate Assembly – it was the citizen body assembled as the army (see further, Chapter 9). The primary other assemblies were the Tribal Assembly (***Comitia Tributa***) and the Plebeian Council (***Concilium Plebis***), both organized by geographical distribution: one's "tribe" depended on where one's father had held land. Even if your family no longer possessed land in that tribal area, you maintained your membership in that tribe.

The key factor overlooked by Polybius is that citizens were not evenly distributed in the assemblies. Each century or each tribe possessed one vote on the question: the majority vote of that group would count as one vote in the assembly. Because there are always fewer rich people than poor people in any society, there were naturally fewer people in the centuries of the rich. As a result the votes of the rich counted proportionately more: your vote is more important if it is one of a hundred rather than one of a thousand. Even more, the Romans doubled down on this approach: there were actually more centuries devoted to the first and second wealth classifications than to any other. The Tribal Assembly possessed a similar imbalance: only four tribes were devoted to the city of Rome, despite the fact that urban populations are almost always larger than rural populations. The Electoral College in the USA might offer a good comparison, as it is similarly weighted towards rural states rather than those with large urban populations. Therefore, on any issue where the upper classes were in broad general agreement, they had enough votes to carry the day. Indeed, once an absolute majority was reached the Romans actually stopped the voting, so while in principle every citizen had the right to vote, those in the lower centuries who made up the majority of Roman citizens might not even get a chance to exercise this right on every occasion. The issue of whether voting should be seen as a "democratic" feature is a complicated question for Roman society no less than for our own.

Polybius only briefly mentions what modern historians have often seen as the most significant power of the people: the right of the tribunes of the plebs to prevent any action by a magistrate or any vote in the Senate or assembly. This power, known as *intercessio* in Latin, has come to be known in English as a veto, from the Latin word meaning "I forbid." The tribunes were elected by the plebeians and in theory their power came originally from an oath of the plebeians to defend their persons, though eventually the tribunes came to be considered as part of the system rather than an outside check on the system. Early Roman history is filled with stories of the tribunes rising to defend the interests of the lower classes. Polybius' omission of the tribunes in his account of Roman government is a prime example of the dangers to any historian of developing a hypothesis in advance of exploring the evidence: the tribunes do not fit neatly into Polybius' system of monarchy, aristocracy, or democracy, and so they simply do not appear as a major factor in his account.

Understanding these aspects of the formal structures of Roman power enables us to see the remarkable elements in Livy's account of the war debate in 200 BCE. While the narrow group of the upper class that sat in the Senate was entirely in favor of the war, they clearly misread the feelings of the rest of the upper class, something that did not happen very often. At the same time, while the tribune was opposed to the motion, he did not veto the motion to propose a war. This incident thus provides fertile ground for questioning whether Rome can be called democratic in a meaningful sense.

Key Debates: *Democracy in Rome?*

The framers of the United States Constitution explicitly drew upon Roman models both in designing the system of checks and balances and in defending their new system in the Federalist Papers. Because the United States is viewed as one of the world's leading democracies, many people have assumed that Rome must also have operated as a democracy. This question has actually been one of the most challenging to resolve, and scholars are still not agreed on an answer.

For many years, the main line of argument suggested that Rome was *not* a democracy. This view acknowledged that the Romans did conduct elections on a regular basis and that the assemblies did have to approve every piece of legislation, including decisions to go to war. However, scholars pointed to the dominance of the elite classes in Roman politics. The same names appear over and over in the lists of magistrates, suggesting that people from the lower classes did not really have an opportunity to serve as a magistrate or a Senator. They pointed out that legislation originated with the Senate and the Senate could generally get the assemblies to approve their decisions, so that the people did not have a chance to pass or create laws on their own. And even the assemblies were weighted towards the wealthy classes: there was no principle of one man, one vote (and women did not vote in Rome, just as they did not until the twentieth century in the US). The only voice of the people was a negative one: the tribunes could veto legislation that they did not like. However, this

> lone voice seems hardly enough to make a democracy.
>   Recently Fergus Millar argued that the role of the crowd in Rome has been underestimated, especially for the last 50 years of the Republic. He referred not to mob rule, but to the public and active role played by the people in the Forum, both listening and responding to speeches made by the leading politicians on crucial issues of the day. He also argued that by the Late Republic, most legislation passed through the assembly organized geographically rather than by wealth, the *comitia tributa* rather than the *comitia centuriata*. That assembly did approximate a one man, one vote system. Both in theory and in practice, therefore, the people did in fact possess the decisive power in the Late Republic.
>   Many scholars have accepted Millar's views, though some have sought a middle ground. These individuals have suggested that both the picture of Rome as an oligarchy and Rome as a democracy have been overstated. Perhaps we might consider the United States government of our own day, in which we have free and fair elections but wealthy individuals and corporations appear to have more influence than ordinary citizens. Strict definitions of democracy and oligarchy may not be sufficient to properly analyze these systems.

The System: Informal Structures

As important as it may be to understand the formal structures of the Roman state, we have already noted in our discussion of the Senate how the informal structures may reveal a truer picture of Roman politics. For Roman politicians, these informal actions may have been even more critical to their success than they are for modern politicians. Political parties with defined and long-term ideological programs – people who might be counted on to serve as a base of support – did not exist in the Roman Republic. Roman politicians therefore needed to build support out of personal loyalties and individual needs in each moment. Even more than today, Roman politics was process-oriented and performance-oriented: that is, individuals needed to build alliances with people of higher, equal, and lower social rank, and they needed to craft a public persona through carefully staged behaviors that might influence others to support them.

Working with Sources
How to Win an Election Campaign

The *Commentariolum Petitionis* (literally a "Little Handbook on Running for Office") may be the best source for understanding how to obtain public office in Rome. The document claims to have been written by Quintus Cicero, the younger brother of the famous orator. It offers advice to Marcus, who ran for, and won, the consulship in 64 BCE.

The first challenge in dealing with this source is establishing its authenticity. The document is missing from the oldest medieval collection of Cicero's works, and there are some words and phrases that some scholars believe were not used in Cicero's day. These scholars suggest that the document may have been a schoolboy exercise from 50 to 100 years after Cicero's death. Since the evidence against authenticity is circumstantial, most scholars have continued to believe it is a genuine work of Quintus. Even if not, the author shows a detailed understanding of Roman politics at the time of Cicero, so the document may still be useful for us today.

The document contains three main sections. The first is a long discussion on overcoming the disadvantages of being a *novus homo* (a "new man"). Roman politics was notoriously conservative. Office-holders in Rome, particularly the more important magistrates, were overwhelmingly drawn from a relatively small number of prestigious families. The same names recur over and over again, so much that modern scholars often have difficulty distinguishing different members of the same family (a grandfather from a grandson, for example). A man who had no ancestors who had served in the Senate was labeled a *novus homo*: his family was new to the consulship. The Romans generally distrusted anything that was labelled "new." Cicero was a *novus homo* and so the document well applies to his situation, but we may wonder how applicable the advice might be for someone with a long history of Senatorial ancestors.

Most scholars find the second section most useful; the third is just a short digression on what to do if your opponent resorts to bribery. The second section focuses on two primary means of building support. The first is through networking among the elite. Quintus encourages his brother to make friends with people of every class and background. The idea was to create relationships where people might feel personally obligated to vote for you, perhaps in exchange for a promise to vote for them in the future. This personal element may partly explain the success of more established families; they had developed these relationships over a long period of time and had wide networks on which to draw. Quintus' second suggestion revolves around canvassing among the common people. Here he encourages Cicero to be visible in the Forum every day and to make himself known to as many voters as possible.

Curiously to modern eyes, Quintus makes no mention of promoting issues or policies that Cicero might pursue once in office. Scholars have taken this to be a sign that elections in Rome did not revolve around issues, even at the very end of the Republic when there were clearly burning issues at stake. It is possible or even likely that Roman voters would have been aware of a politician's general political views, but the absence of political issues from this pamphlet has usually suggested that, even more than today, Roman elections were personal.

One regular activity that generated support drew on the patron–client relationship discussed in Chapter 3. While Romans do not appear to have demanded that their clients vote in certain ways (see Textbox in Chapter 3), patrons did draw on their networks in order to create public displays of support. Clients were expected to call upon their patrons daily and accompany them to the Forum where public business was conducted (**Figure 4.2**). The throng of individuals crowded around a patron

Figure 4.2 Roman Forum, looking towards the Palatine hill.

provided visible evidence of the number of Romans who had received benefits from a single individual: the larger the crowd, the more important the person. In an era without mass communication, public displays like this were essential: they allowed Romans to demonstrate the good works they had done both for individual Romans and for the community as a whole.

Women and Roman Politics

Women possessed no formal political power in Rome, just as in every pre-modern state and most modern states until the twentieth century. They did possess certain legal rights and could play significant roles in Roman society, as discussed elsewhere in this book, but they could not vote in any of the Roman assemblies. That does not mean, however, that women could not influence Roman politics, as seen in a famous example from 195 BCE.

During the Second Punic War (218–202 BCE), a law known as the *lex Oppia* had been passed limiting the amount of gold a woman could own and forbidding her from certain luxuries, such as wearing a multi-colored garment. In theory this law was an economic response to the crisis of the early defeats suffered by Rome during the war, and so at war's end the tribunes of the people proposed repealing the law. Women came out into the streets to demonstrate in support of this repeal. Opposition came from some of the most powerful statesmen of the day and it looked for a moment as if the repeal might be blocked. Livy relates what happened next: "after these speeches in support of and against the law, women poured out into the streets the next day in much greater force, nor would they desist" until repeal of the law was assured (Livy, 34.8).

On the one hand, it is likely that Livy selected this example because it was unique. We know of no other episodes in which women proved to be the decisive voice. This episode might then be viewed as a criticism of women's priorities: the one issue on which they chose to make their voices heard concerned what the Roman (male) elite viewed as stereotypical women's issues (and, we might observe, elite women only): jewelry and expensive clothing. At the same time, we do know of occasions, especially in the Late Republic, where individual women appeared in public and altered political debates. These examples indicate that even if men controlled the formal mechanisms of the Roman state and dominated the informal mechanisms, Roman women had ways of making their voices heard.

Exploring Culture: *Hortensia and the Women of Rome*

In one of the most famous instances of female power in the Roman Republic, a woman named Hortensia stood up to the three most powerful men in Rome.

In 42 BCE, Octavian, Mark Antony, and Lepidus had banded together, forming the Second Triumvirate to pursue a war against the assassins of Julius Caesar. Because the state treasury had been raided repeatedly during the civil wars, they needed to raise funds for their armies. One method they chose was to tax the 1400 wealthiest women in Rome. These women chose Hortensia to articulate their complaints at paying a special tax for a war that did not concern them. Hortensia was the daughter of Quintus Hortensius (114–50 BCE), one of the most famous orators and lawyers of the period, and a rival of Cicero.

The women of Rome marched together to the Roman Forum, where Hortensia addressed the triumvirs. According to the historian Appian (*Civil Wars*, 4.32–33), Hortensia began by noting that the three leaders had already killed many of their fathers, sons, husbands, and brothers and taken their property. If triumvirs were to take away the women's property as well, it would reduce them to a condition unbecoming their birth and their sex. She went on:

> Why should we pay taxes when we have no part in the honors for which you contend against each other with such harmful results? Our mothers in the past rose above their sex and made contributions when you were in danger of losing the whole empire and the city itself through war with the Carthaginians. But then they contributed voluntarily, not from their landed property, their fields, their dowries, or their houses, without which life is not possible to free women. And they did so not under fear of informers or accusers, not by force and violence, but what they themselves were willing to give. If war with the Gauls come, we shall not be inferior to our mothers; but for civil wars may we never contribute.

The next day, the tax was changed to affect only 400 women.

Hortensia was clearly an extraordinary woman. We should remember that as the daughter of Hortensius, she had access to an education available only to some Roman women **(Figure 4.3)**, but her speech impressed not only the triumvirs, but subsequent generations of Romans. The orator Quintilian, who wrote a handbook on rhetoric 100 years later, noted that the oration of Hortensia "is still read and not merely as a compliment to her sex." He even used her example to argue that it was important for the raising of children that both fathers and mothers should be as educated as possible.

Hortensia's example suggests several key points. One is that the male authors of our surviving historical texts rarely chose to include the stories of powerful women. Clearly, however, some women in Rome were not only well-educated but they could have a significant impact on public policy.

Figure 4.3 Fresco of woman with wax tablets and stylus (so-called "Sappho") from Pompeii, c. 50 BCE. National Archaeological Museum of Naples (inv. 9084).

Limitations on Politicians

If we have given some thought to how Romans might build support for themselves, we should also consider the impact of the absence of a written constitution in the Roman Republic. In a system that ran on personal networks and without clear rules, a Roman might be able to do anything he could convince a majority of fellow-citizens that he was allowed to do. So what, in practice, limited the behaviors or policies of Roman politicians?

For the Romans, a key limitation on behavior was the notion of the *mos maiorum*, discussed earlier. Like other pre-literate and traditional societies, the Romans were frequently guided in making decisions by their sense of what they had done in the past. The Romans had a general distrust of anything "new" – indeed, the Latin *res nova*, "new thing," could be used to describe anything revolutionary. Thus Roman politicians rarely claimed that change was necessary, and when they did it was often poorly received. A politician named Laelius was given the nickname "the Wise" when he abandoned a program of political reform in the middle of the second century. Of course, since the Romans generally lacked written texts about the distant past, it was often difficult to determine exactly what the custom of the ancestors had been, and this provided the flexibility for the Romans to enact change: one just needed to be able to make a plausible case that one was acting according to custom. For example, a Roman politician could argue that a proposal which appeared to mark a departure from past practice was actually a return to an old custom that had been forgotten. They might make this argument even if no such custom had ever existed. By forcing politicians to work in this manner, the *mos maiorum* acted as a check on Roman behavior and marked Rome as a conservative society and slow, though not impossible, to change.

Another limitation prominent in the Middle Republic was the amount of cooperation that the Roman system required. To some extent, cooperation is essential to the smooth functioning of any political system; while politicians clearly compete with each other for position, they are also invested in a system that gives them power over other citizens. Cooperating to ensure the continuation of the system itself is often a high priority. In Rome, the relationship of the Senate to individual magistrates in Rome reveals how they attempted to balance these two ingredients. As a magistrate a Roman politician would often seek and listen to the advice of the Senate while in the city, while outside of Rome he might act on his own authority in pursuit of military glory. As a member of the Senate, he might choose to allow other magistrates a free rein with their command, knowing that he himself would have that freedom when his turn came. Thus individuals aimed for accomplishments that would set them apart in the competition to be first among peers, but recognized that their competitive needs could often best be met by working with the Senate as a governing body. This factor highlights again the enormous influence of the Senate despite its limited formal authority: as the place where the collective will of the aristocracy was debated and expressed, it provided a means of limiting the competitive drive of individuals.

One might question how effective these limitations were in checking the ambitions of Roman politicians. The answer, for a good chunk of the Republic, is "quite well." As best we can tell, the system stayed in balance down to the beginning of the second century, with occasional self-corrections. However, with the advent of territorial empire, these informal mechanisms no longer sufficed to maintain the equilibrium between one elite and another, between elites and non-elites, and between magistrates and the Senate. In the early second century, the Romans passed several laws – formal mechanisms – in an apparent effort to keep competition among the elite under control. For instance, the *lex Villia* passed in 180 BCE set minimum ages for higher offices, setting the age for different offices three years apart. It thus required a Roman politician to spend two years out of office following each successful election. However, even these measures proved inadequate to the challenges posed to the system by Rome's imperial expansion.

The Late Republic

As discussed in Chapter 2, political developments have traditionally been used to divide Roman history (or all history) into periods, so it follows that the Late Republic must have been marked by significant changes in the practice of politics. The most obvious change is the frequent recourse to violence by politicians and factions of all stripes. Indeed, this is usually considered to be *the* defining feature of the Late Republic. However, we must be careful not to ignore the other significant changes of the period: structural changes such as the introduction of the secret ballot; modifications in the way soldiers were recruited for the army; the granting of multi-year commands to outstanding generals; and the appearance of factions where politicians might identify themselves with an approach to politics and not just with individuals. As we proceed we should consider two questions about these changes: (1) what is the relationship of these other changes to the violence and did they cause the violence or were they a response to it? and (2) what happened in the years preceding the Late Republic that brought about all of these changes?

The violence that is the most visible sign of change appeared for the first time in connection with the tribunate of Tiberius Gracchus in 133 BCE and that of his brother Gaius eleven years later. Let us briefly note a few features of the violence without entering into the debates about the goals, behavior, and justifications of either the Gracchi or their opponents, although these continue to be hotly debated. Plutarch noted in his account that these episodes mark the first time in the history of the Republic that the Romans were not able to resolve their internal political differences without recourse to large-scale violence. The government mechanisms clearly did not function in the way they were supposed to function: one group of citizens (or perhaps both sides) viewed the actions of the other as illegitimate and so resorted to violence in order to overturn what they viewed as illegal actions.

Naturally this response raises the question of why the system could no longer cope with this challenge. Most answers are tied in some fashion to the rapid growth of Rome into a world empire during the previous 75 years. One line of thinking sees the problem in the refusal of the wealthy class to share some of the spoils of the

Political Issues: *Who Was Tiberius Gracchus?*

The tribunate of Tiberius Gracchus remains one of the most controversial episodes in Roman politics. We have two fairly complete narratives of this event, a biography by Plutarch and a narrative by Appian, but these accounts have generated multiple interpretations. Each of these interpretations relies on the same set of facts, but sees different motivations at play.

One line of thinking sees Tiberius as seeking personal power. He noticed the problems of small farmers and promised a reform program in order to gain their support. When a tribune vetoed his program, he appealed to the people and had them vote to remove the tribune from office. This action effectively demonstrated that tribunes could not block his power. He then decided to run for re-election, against all Roman custom. This action suggested to other Romans that Tiberius wanted to become sole ruler of Rome: a magistrate who remained in office forever and who was superior to all others was more like a king than a Roman. Thus a group of magistrates banded together, attacked the supporters of Tiberius in the Forum, and killed Tiberius. Their action was justified to preserve the balance of power essential to the Roman Republic.

This version has seemed far-fetched to most scholars, who generally see Tiberius as legitimately concerned with the welfare of small farmers, but there is still room for disagreement. One group argues that Tiberius served as the champion of the poor in Rome. His proposal aimed squarely at redistributing wealth in Roman society to address the wealth inequality that had widened over the past fifty years. The rich naturally objected and tried to block Tiberius through the political system, but Tiberius found ways to get around these obstacles. Seeing no other way to stop Tiberius, the greedy members of the Roman elite joined together and killed Tiberius before his program could take full effect. This interpretation of Tiberius has been especially popular with those who see the class struggle as the primary motivator for political events.

The interpretation most favorable to Tiberius believes that he was genuinely concerned for the welfare of the state. Since small farmers made up the backbone of the Roman army, their decline was an issue of public concern. Tiberius consulted with many leading aristocrats before proposing moderate reforms to aid recruitment for the army. This effort was blocked by people who refused to make a sacrifice for the good of the state. Tiberius thus felt that he had no choice but to break with custom in order to help the state. The Senate was divided, but some Senators felt Tiberius had broken the laws and went to confront him in the Forum. Misunderstandings led to a violent scuffle and in the melee Tiberius was killed. This interpretation was favored by the Greek historian Appian, who summarized Tiberius' career by saying that "he lost his life as a result of an excellent plan which he pursued too violently."

Each of these interpretations contains a different lesson about Roman history. Accepting that each interpretation contains some element of truth might not only be the best we can do as historians, but might give us the most to think about as we contemplate our own behavior.

success with the lower classes, while an alternative locates the problem in a handful of individuals who saw greater gains in acting outside of the system than within it; that is, they no longer saw cooperation as a viable means to achieve their goals. A broader view avoids placing blame with any individual actors, noting instead that the Roman system was not designed to handle the kinds of economic and social changes that running an empire created. In this view, the Roman tendency toward conservatism left them unable to respond sufficiently when the situation demanded it. Remember that Laelius' abortive reform effort came less than 10 years before the tribunate of Tiberius. Perhaps a reform at that moment might have avoided the violence, but reform may have been as impossible then as it proved 10 years later. The violence of the Late Republic might have been the outcome of a situation in which it was the only way to make necessary changes to the political system, much like the American or French Revolutions depended on violence to change their systems.

Violence, however, can move in unexpected directions. The initial instances of violence within the Roman state seem to have been based to some degree in policy disputes. Examples include Senators opposed to the policies of the Gracchi or supporters of a grain bill put forward by the tribune Saturninus in 100 CE. However, in the course of the next decade the focus of violence shifted more strongly toward personal struggles for supremacy: Sulla's decision to march on Rome rather than accept the transfer of his command to Marius provides the first such example, followed later in the century by individuals such as Pompey, Julius Caesar, and others. Violence, or the threat of violence, seems to have become more commonplace as well. In the case of the Gracchi, violence appears as an extraordinary outcome of an apparently insoluble dispute, but by the middle of the first century it had become part of the practice of politics itself. Political leaders would gather around themselves a group of armed thugs whom they could use to scare off opposition voters rather than a group of leading politicians or a coalition of influential clients as in earlier periods. Elections and other votes in the assemblies depended as much on whose gang managed to control the voting area on the day of the vote as on political support. The Late Republic thus appears as a classic example of violence begetting more violence: if one's political opponents are using violence to intimidate your supporters, the obvious recourse is to defend yourself by resorting to violence as well.

The Roman aristocracy, and Roman politics in general, continued to become more and more divided. Two loose groupings become visible, though it is important to note these were not political parties in the modern sense, which have a clear organization, hierarchy, and defined ideological platforms. One group was called **optimates** (*optimus* means "best" in Latin), who generally believed that authority should be invested in the "best men" in the state; in practice this meant relying on the Senate and traditional aristocratic privileges. The other group were known as **populares**. Although they themselves were aristocrats, they presented themselves as supporting the interests of the general populace (or in the "popular" interest) and relied more on the assemblies of the people for their power. For instance, a *popularis* politician might support policies such as land reform or free grain distribution or he might show himself as willing to challenge traditional procedures, such as bypassing the Senate's opinion in favor of one of the assemblies. These terms could be loosely used: politicians could adopt them for themselves and might even present themselves as a *popularis* at one moment and an *optimate* as another, depending on his political needs at the moment. Identification with these groups was thus fluid. *Popularis* politicians such as Julius Caesar and Publius Clodius came from long-established families of the Roman aristocracy, while the *optimate* Cicero was born outside Rome and was the first in his family to reach the consulship. Although Roman politics continued to be organized around individual politicians, the appearance of political groupings around a set of habits as a supplement to personal charisma marks another change from the earlier period.

The appearance of these groupings may be tied to the more general breakdown in the Late Republic of the principles on which the Roman system of government had been based. One of those principles was the notion that magistrates should only hold office for one year and should always have a colleague with equal authority in office. This principle came under fire primarily from the opponents of the traditional aristocracy; for instance, Marius was elected consul five years consecutively. We also see individual Romans assigned to multi-year military commands with little or no oversight. Later in the first century, the Senate even consented to having Pompey elected as sole consul, a position without precedent in Roman practice. While these actions may have been responses to immediate crises, such as the need to fight a multi-year campaign at a great distance from Rome, earlier periods had met these challenges without resorting to these solutions.

This fact highlights the difficulty in answering the question about the relationship of the growth of Roman power, violence, and these decisions: was there a "tipping point" beyond which these violations of Roman norms was inevitable, or were they simply poor choices made by the politicians of the time that led to further problems with no good answers? However one answers the question, breaking with established protocols clearly undermined the proper functioning of the system.

In addition to the violation of the underlying principles of Roman government, this period also saw the loss of the balance between competition and cooperation that marked the Middle Republic. Rather than accept the authority of the Senate as the binding factor, many politicians – Marius, Sulla, Pompey, Crassus, Caesar, to name only the most well-known – sought ways to overcome the will of the Senate. Sometimes they appealed directly to the people for support, but sometimes, as with Sulla's march on Rome, they resorted to violence. These politicians may have genuinely believed that their behavior was in the best interests of the people and not merely in their own personal interest, but again the net result was to shift authority away from the Senate and towards individuals.

The shift towards individuals can also be seen in the decline in authority of the leading aristocratic families. The clearest example comes from Caecilii Metelli, a family whose members are frequently found among Rome's magistrates in the second century, including a 15-year stretch where one member was always a magistrate. Marius began his career thanks to support from this family, but turned against the Metelli in order to campaign for, and win, the consulship on his own. Personal ambition began to replace cooperation or loyalty to longtime friends.

A structural change in the Roman government of this period reveals how some of these pressures and changes played out in practice: the introduction of the secret

Figure 4.4 Silver denarius, minted 63 BCE by L.C. Longinus, depicting a voter casting a ballot.

ballot. In 139 BCE, just prior to the tribunate of Tiberius Gracchus, a law was passed providing for a secret ballot for elections. Over the next 20 years a series of laws were passed guaranteeing greater privacy in all meaningful votes (**Figure 4.4**). There is some debate as to how much of a practical difference the secret ballot made, as some scholars have asserted that the nobility found ways to circumvent the intent of the secret ballot and thus to maintain control of the voting process. However, secret ballots do seem to have been important to *populares* politicians as well as a focus of aristocratic discontent, suggesting that both sides felt they had made an impact.

All of these changes present us with a chicken and egg dilemma: did the structural changes lead to the disintegration of the system, or are they a sign that the system was already disintegrating and the changes were a failed effort to save the system? We see many more accusations of bribery in this period; this might be a sign of disintegration, but it is difficult to know how to interpret these accusations. Politicians may have found it useful to level a charge of bribery against an opponent, so the actual degree of bribery could be overstated. However, it is also possible that more members of the aristocracy resorted to this method of influencing the vote once they realized that the traditional means of gaining support no longer worked.

The question of the impact of the secret ballot is tied closely to the broader question of the nature of Roman politics during the Late Republic, and whether the power base had shifted away from the aristocracy and towards the lower classes. The structural changes may not have directly benefited the lower classes, but they certainly did not take power away from them. The rise of *populares* politicians does suggest that a politician could build a successful power base by appealing to the people. We also see more policies enacted that benefit the lower classes, either because they held more power or because elite politicians now felt the need to cater to their desires.

There also seem to be more "new men" who reached the consulship in this period, again suggesting a loosening of aristocratic control. It is certainly possible that the Roman political system became more friendly to the lower classes at this time. Even in the late Republic, however, the needs of the upper classes, or of individual members of the upper classes, remained the primary object of consideration.

Julius Caesar and the End of the Republic

The life of Julius Caesar (100–44 BCE) marks the end of the period known as the Roman Republic, so it is fitting to conclude this chapter with a consideration of what his career might mean for an analysis of Roman politics. Caesar began his career in a fairly straightforward fashion: a charismatic figure born into a noble family, he developed alliances with numerous elements of Roman society and embarked on a military career (**Figure 4.5**). He gained particular prominence when he surprisingly won the election for *pontifex maximus* in 63 BCE; charges that Caesar bribed his way to the office were widespread. In 60 BCE he formed a working alliance with the two

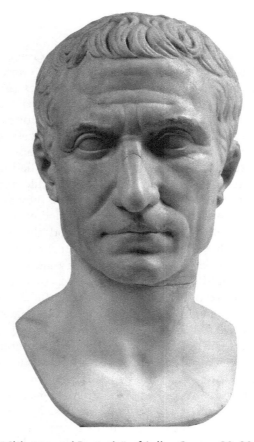

Figure 4.5 So-called "Chiaramonti Portrait" of Julius Caesar, 30–20 BCE. Vatican Museums, Rome.

other leading politicians of the day – the so-called First Triumvirate with Pompey and Crassus – that enabled him both to win the consulship for 59 BCE and to gain an extended military command in Gaul. Over the course of the next 10 years this alliance fell apart. For both Caesar and for his opponents the competition for supremacy outweighed cooperation, which eventually led to Caesar's fateful decision to cross the Rubicon River and to civil war. In the famous words of the first century CE Roman poet Lucan, "Caesar could not tolerate a superior, nor Pompey an equal."

It is worth considering what precisely was different about Caesar's career, at least up until the point when competition finally overwhelmed cooperation and the Rubicon was crossed. *Popularis* politics, bribery, shifting alliances, extended military campaigns, special treatment of leading figures: these are all features of the Late Republic. It has become common to assert that Caesar aimed at supremacy in the state and that he cared more about his own ambition than the society itself, but those same accusations can be levelled against Caesar's opponents among the traditional aristocracy as well. Senators bemoaned Caesar's failure to respect precedent and mourned the loss of *libertas*, but the lower classes did not share in this "freedom" that the upper classes claimed to value. The fact that the assassins of Caesar seem to have been genuinely surprised that the people at large did not support the murder of Caesar demonstrates that their politics were not the politics of the people. The freedom they claimed to seek was not the freedom that the people sought, reminding us that words such as freedom can mean very different things, even to people living in the same society.

Viewed in that way, one could argue that Caesar's success represented a triumph of power for the people, not the demise of the state. However, there are a great many hints that Caesar used the unpopularity of the wealthy class as a means to vault himself into power, and that he did not care much for the needs of his supporters, either. History is filled with examples of demagogues who have done the very same thing. In the end, our picture of Caesar's actions, and indeed of the Roman Republic itself, is like a Rorschach test: we see what our experience has taught us to see. As with most historical analysis, our answers to the questions raised in this chapter – about the nature of Caesar's actions, the Roman state, or governments in general – depend more on our own values than on the subject we are considering.

Discussion Questions

1. What criteria do you think are most important to determine whether a political system is a democracy, an oligarchy, or something else?
2. Do you think that formal or informal power was more valuable in the Roman system? What about in your system?
3. What are the advantages of using formal or informal means to limit a politician's power? What options does one have in each case if these methods fail to limit their power?
4. Are there circumstances when violence can be justified as a means of resolving internal political disputes? Based on the Roman experience, can you suggest some of the unintended consequences of using violence to resolve political disputes?

Further Reading

Flower, Harriet (2010). *Roman Republics*. Princeton, NJ: Princeton University Press.
    Flower argues that instead of speaking of the Roman Republic as a single unit, we should speak of six separate Republics, divided by a series of transitional periods. She uses a political science approach to analyze the surviving texts and identify different features of the Roman political system.

Hodgson, Louise (2017). *Res Publica and the Roman Republic: "Without Body or Form"*. Oxford: Oxford University Press.
    Hodgson analyzes the phrase *res publica* (public thing) and its shifting meaning as the key to understanding politics at Rome. She focuses primarily on incidents from the Gracchi onward, but her understanding of these events has implications for understanding the earlier periods as well.

Millar, Fergus (1998). *The Crowd in Rome in the Late Republic*. Ann Arbor, MI: University of Michigan Press.
    This small volume brings together many of Millar's ideas to argue that the Late Republic in particular should be seen as a time of popular control. He focuses not so much on the mob violence that the crowd could employ, but their ability to control the terms of the debate and to control decisions through voting in the assemblies.

Patterson, John R. (2000). *Political Life in the City of Rome*. London: Bristol Classical.
    Patterson offers a terrific introduction to both formal and informal politics in the city of Rome, including discussions of aristocratic competition, client/patron relationships, and the changes in the Late Republic. His discussion of how the physical layout of the city of Rome played a role in Roman politics is especially valuable.

Rosenstein, Nathan and Robert Morstein-Marx (2006). *A Companion to the Roman Republic*. Malden, MA: Blackwell Publishers.
    This collection of essays provides an overview of current thinking on the Roman Republic. It includes chapters that focus on the narrative of Roman history and also chapters that focus on particular aspects such as values, civic structures, and the creation of a Roman identity. It uses both literary and archaeological evidence and highlights key controversies in the study of the Roman Republic.

5
The Roman Family

Livy tells us the following story about the first marriages in Rome. Seeing that none of their neighbors would allow their daughters to intermarry with inhabitants of the upstart city in their midst, Rome's first king Romulus invited all of Rome's neighbors to celebrate a festival in Rome. When everyone had settled in for the spectacle, Roman men dashed through the crowd and kidnapped the young women who were present, marking them off as wives for themselves or for others (**Figure 5.1**). The Sabines, both men and women, were furious. Romulus tried to point out the advantages to the Sabine women of being married to Romans, and urged them to "soften their anger and give their hearts to those whom fortune had given their bodies." According to Livy (1.9), these pleas were effective above all others in appealing to "a woman's nature." Not so with the Sabine men, who launched an attack against the Romans. In the midst of the battle, the Sabine women "throwing off their womanish fears" ran on to the battlefield between the two armies and begged them to stop fighting, since the war would result in the death of either their fathers or their husbands. The two sides heard their plea: not only did they make peace on the spot, but they agreed to unite the two communities into one state.

We will have occasion to come back to this story again: so many elements of Roman ideology can be seen in this legend, including attitudes about women and about foreigners. Here let us simply ask what the story might reveal about Roman family structures. In this story the women served as bridge-builders between the different communities: as daughters and as wives, women served to forge relationships between powerful and otherwise unrelated men. Often, as in the story, women were given little choice but to accept their new husbands. Yet the women do exercise some agency in rushing the battlefield and demanding an end to the fighting. The story itself seems to recognize that the ideology of women as passive recipients of men's actions did not always match the reality of women taking steps in their own

A Social and Cultural History of Republican Rome, First Edition. Eric M. Orlin.
© 2022 John Wiley & Sons, Inc. Published 2022 by John Wiley & Sons, Inc.

Figure 5.1 *The Abduction of the Sabine Women*. Nicolas Poussin, 1633–1634. Metropolitan Museum of Art, NY. Poussin is one of the few artists to portray the Sabine women as struggling against the Roman men.

interests. As we proceed to explore the Roman family we must continue to ask what values might be represented by certain practices and to what degree the reality of the Romans' lives matched that ideal picture.

The first question to ask in talking about the family is what precisely we mean by the word family. Is it just mother, father, and children, the so-called "nuclear family"? Are grandparents included? Cousins and nieces or nephews? The answers to these questions vary from person to person and even from country to country today: understanding how the Romans might have answered them is critical to understanding their family life. Although the English word family derives from the Latin word *familia*, the similarity of language does not mean that the family structures were the same. As we proceed, we will see that a Roman *familia* included many people who were not related to the head of the household, including enslaved and formerly enslaved persons who lived under the same roof. It could also include the adult (especially male) children who lived in a separate house entirely.

Our first task is therefore to attempt an outline of the basic framework of the Roman family, and then consider how the Roman conquest of the Mediterranean brought changes to the family structure. The task is complicated by the fact that our literary sources rarely speak directly about the family, and where they do they are almost exclusively focused on the families of elite Romans. For the bulk of the Roman population, we will have to rely on archaeology as well as a comparison to other agrarian societies with pre-modern medical practices. Perhaps we cannot answer all of our questions with certainty, but we can sketch a range of possibilities that help us to understand the relationships and obligations of the Roman family.

An Overview of the Roman Family

Patria Potestas

Perhaps the most discussed feature about the Roman family is the legal power granted to the family patriarch. In Latin this power is known as **patria potestas** ("paternal power") and among other things it gave the oldest living male member of the family the power of life and death over every other member of the household: he was within his legal rights to put to death any family member at any time. These people included his wife, as long as she had become a legal part of his *familia* (see section on marriage); his legitimate children, both male and female, no matter their age; nieces and nephews for whom he might be responsible, such as when a brother had died; as well as enslaved persons. In theory, the **paterfamilias** as head of the family owned all of the property of the family, including that of his adult male children who might have moved out of his physical house and begun to set up a household of their own. *Patria potestas* might in fact be one useful way to define the Roman family: all those who fell within its scope might be considered members of his *familia*, whether or not they actually lived in the same house. As odd as it may seem to us, this could result in his adult children living elsewhere and their children being considered a part of his *familia*, but not his wife living in the same house. In turn, this situation might lead us to question whether the legally defined *familia* is the most useful way of thinking about the Roman family.

The authoritarian nature of *patria potestas* has made many modern observers uncomfortable. The notion that a father could kill even his grown children at any time for any reason raises questions about the relationships between parents and children in ancient Rome. To take one example, it placed children on the same legal level as enslaved persons: both groups were subject to punishment up to death upon the sole authority of the head of household, and both groups were unable to own anything in their own name. Of course, in reality sons and enslaved persons were not treated the same even if they held the same legal status, a fact that should alert us to the limitation of using legal sources as a guide to understanding Roman life. In this instance, other sources help us see these relationships more clearly. For instance, a wide variety of literary texts indicate that corporal punishment – beating or even whipping – was not a punishment used on free children in ancient Rome, unlike in other societies, even modern ones. Bodily integrity was one of the signs of a free man (see Chapter 6), and so this type of punishment was reserved for enslaved persons. These concerns about distinguishing between free children and enslaved persons may also have been a primary concern only to some families: those that had enslaved persons. These facts should cause us to question how far the legal institution of *patria potestas* actually affected the relationships between fathers and their children.

Another factor that may have limited the impact of *patria potestas* is the demographic makeup of Roman households. Comparison with other pre-modern societies suggests that by age 25 only about half of the males would have a father who was still alive, and by age 40 only 20% would still have a living father. Roman society may have differed in some small ways, but the actual numbers are likely to be within a few percentage points of these figures. Thus, the situation of a grown son, married and starting his own family but legally still under the authority of his father and subject to death as a punishment for misbehavior, likely did not occur as frequently as the legal sources would have us believe. That conclusion points to an important point about legal commentaries: these texts often concerned themselves with unusual situations where a law needed to be applied to resolve a dispute rather than with more typical situations. It is thus hardly surprising if they contain proportionally more examples of grown children still in the *potestas* of their father than actually occurred.

In practice, Roman fathers do not seem to have executed their children very often. Livy records only a handful of examples, and they all raise more questions than answers. For instance, in a battle against the Latins in 340 BCE, Manlius Torquatus disobeyed an order not to engage the enemy in single combat. Even though he was victorious in the battle, his father, who was in command of the army, ordered him executed for disobeying the order. In this example, although it was the father who ordered the death, he seems to have been acting in his capacity as consul to punish a soldier rather than a father punishing a son. The one legendary example of a father killing his own daughter also suggests the uniqueness of the practice: Verginius killed his daughter Verginia to prevent her from being sexually assaulted by a corrupt magistrate. There are real questions about whether these incidents actually occurred, but more importantly they are clearly designed as object lessons in how a Roman should behave (or not behave) in extraordinary circumstances. While they may not be representative of typical parental behavior, they show where the limits of the family were and suggest ways in which family life might replicate Roman society on a smaller scale.

Considering all of this evidence, we might conclude that *patria potestas* served an ideological purpose rather than playing a role in daily life: it set down the limits of the *familia* and highlighted the dominance of the patriarch of the household and the dependence of the family on him as an introduction to the hierarchies of Roman society. The power reflected the authority of the Roman state, where the Roman consuls held the highest authority and had the ability to put soldiers (but not civilians) to death without a trial.

Marriage

Why did people get married in Rome, and what do their marriage practices tell us about the Roman family? These are not easy questions to answer at such a distance, and the answers must have differed according to social class and especially from person to person, but we should attempt to draw some overall conclusions. We might begin by noting that both marriage and divorce were straightforward processes in Rome. The legal sources make clear that the only requirement was that the couple should desire to be married. Marriages could of course be celebrated with elaborate rituals, but there were no licensing or registration requirements, and divorce could be as simple as moving out of the husband's house. The ease of marriage and divorce suggests that as a rule the Romans did not view marriage as a partnership for life, but one that could be terminated at any time for any reason: poor behavior by a partner might be a reason, but also better prospects elsewhere. This observation should force us to dig deeper into the reasons Romans got married.

One reason seems to be reproductive: a family and indeed a society needs children in order to reproduce itself, and Roman men clearly viewed one of women's primary roles as the bearer of children. We can see this concern appear in the age of women at marriage. Evidence from Roman texts as well as comparative evidence from other societies suggests that women, and upper class women in particular, appear to have married in their mid-teens, close to the time when they reached childbearing age. Upper-class men, on the other hand, married only in their mid-twenties. One reason that women tended to marry at such a young age was the need to produce multiple children. In view of the mortality rates in ancient Rome, where about half of young children are likely to have died before age 5 (see section on children), each woman needed to give birth to four or five children simply in order for the family to reproduce itself. We should pause here to note clearly the danger that this burden posed to women: childbirth was likely the single greatest cause of premature death for Roman women, even among the elites with the best access to medical care. Cicero's daughter **Tullia** died one month after giving birth to her second son, and Julius Caesar's daughter also died in childbirth: being rich and powerful provided no advantages when it came to the dangers of childbirth (**Figure 5.2**). The necessity to undertake a pregnancy four or five

Figure 5.2 Funerary relief of a midwife depicting a birth scene; Ostia, first century CE.

times simply worsened the odds of survival for women, and likely shaped their day to day existence during the childbearing years, whether rich or poor.

Of course, marriage is not necessary for procreation itself, and we have many examples of children in Rome born outside of marriage. Marriage was, however, necessary for the children to be considered legitimate members of the *familia*. The primary purpose of marriage may in fact have been to define the legitimate members of the family. For the upper classes, the successful birth of a son created an heir to the family estate and thus enabled property to be handed from one generation to the next, which placed special emphasis on the birth of male children. Concerns with the transfer of property, and with status more broadly, meant that for the upper classes almost all marriages were arranged with a view towards these ends. Many marriages were arranged with a view towards creating a personal relationship among the males, a relationship that might then be used for networking in the political arena. Transfer of property or political advancement would have been less of a concern for the lower echelons of Roman society. Rather, the addition of an able-bodied worker available to help the family make ends meet would have been a more important concern, and there is reason to believe that female children in the lower classes engaged in work along with their brothers. For both classes, therefore, marriage created an economically viable and legally recognized unit within Roman society.

We have reason to think that women might have been involved in discussions about appropriate grooms and alliances for the family. Livy (38.57) tells the (perhaps fictional) story of Scipio Africanus, the conqueror of Carthage, who betrothed his daughter Cornelia to Tiberius Gracchus the Elder, the most eligible bachelor in Rome at the time. On returning home, his wife was furious, saying she should have been consulted "even if you were to promise her to Tiberius Gracchus!" The fact that Scipio had done exactly that enabled him to restore peace in his home, but the lesson of the story is clearly that Scipio's wife expected that she should have a role in choosing a husband for her daughter. The ease of marriage and divorce may have taken some pressure off the initial choice: marriages that were designed as political alliances as much as personal ones might be altered when a new political alliance was needed.

In addition to creating family relationships, marriages might involve transfers of money: a bride often brought a significant dowry with her. The dowry may have represented a daughter's share of the estate, especially if a daughter married into her husband's family, and thus was no longer a natural heir of her father. A marriage could thus bring a significant infusion of cash to the groom, but the husband needed to consider expenditure from this sum carefully. In Roman law, a dowry needed to be paid back in case of divorce, and so a woman's return to her father's house could have threatened the husband's financial and social position. The relative ease of divorce thus may have improved the position of women, especially where she had brought a large dowry into her new household and could wield significant economic clout. Thus marriage and divorce in the upper classes often involved a calculation of both status and money: the issues of dominance and dependence discussed in Chapter 3 were complicated. These considerations were likely to be less important for those lower down the social and economic scale. Non-elites would not have had sizable dowries and may have been less concerned with legal niceties about paternal control, property, or social status, but the lack of evidence prevents us from knowing much about how marriage bonds were formed for the vast majority of Romans.

This discussion of arranged marriages for political and/or economic gain raises an important question: what kind of affection did Roman husbands and wives have for each other? On the one hand, there was often a significant gap in age between upper class males and females at the time of their first marriage. Since the husbands were generally about 10 years older than their wives in elite households, it is possible that they may have initially appeared more as a father-figure than a life-partner, especially since these were arranged marriages. The age gap may have been smaller among the lower classes, where men may have married earlier since they were more consumed with establishing a viable economic household than with launching a political or military career. Nor should we automatically assume that an arranged marriage could not involve affection. Pompey the Great married Caesar's daughter Julia to cement their political alliance in 59 BCE: at the time he was 59 and she was 17, but all the evidence suggests that the pair cared deeply for each other and that Pompey was legitimately grieved when Julia died in 54 BCE giving birth to their child.

Archaeological sources may be more useful than literary sources in trying to answer the question about affection between husbands and wives. We have no letters from women, and the letters that have survived from Cicero do not give us much glimpse into the nature of the relationship with his wife **Terentia**. However, we do have numerous inscriptions on tombstones that can provide another window. One famous epitaph (*CIL* 6.9499) erected by Lucius Aurelius describes his wife Aurelia Philematio as "my one and only – a loving woman who possessed my heart, she lived as a faithful wife to a faithful husband with affection equal to my own" (**Figure 5.3**). These sentiments sound quite similar to a modern eulogy; they might be merely the stock phrases one says at a funeral. Perhaps more useful are the numerous less elaborate tombstones which speak of a "darling" or a "dear one," or describe the sorrow of the person erecting the tombstone. While the act of erecting a memorial

Figure 5.3 Funerary relief of L. Aurelius Hermia and his wife Aurelia Philematio; Rome, circa 80 BCE. British Museum, London. Although both had been enslaved during their lives, they are here shown after they had been restored to free and citizen status.

to the deceased and preserving their name for posterity may not be noteworthy itself, the language used implies a depth of feeling for the dead. Most of these tombstones are of lesser quality, suggesting that they were erected by individuals of modest wealth. These gravestones suggest that Romans of all social classes did in fact care deeply for their partners and that, just as in modern relationships, the degree of caring might vary from person to person as much as from class to class.

Children

We have touched on some elements of children and child raising already, but pulling all of the pieces together will give us a better understanding of their place in the family. Perhaps the most critical piece of information to absorb is the extremely high infant mortality rate in ancient Rome, as in most societies with pre-modern medicine. Estimates vary since hard data is very difficult to come by; the gravestones we have do not offer a representative sample allowing us to calculate an average age of death. However, using the gravestones and skeletal remains alongside models derived from other societies with better evidence suggests that perhaps one-third of all infants would not have survived the first year and a full one-half would not have lived to see their fifth birthday. This impact of this basic demographic point on marriage practices was discussed in the section on marriage, but it has also figured in arguments about the affection that Roman parents may have felt for their children.

Key Debates: *Did Romans Love Their Children?*

One of the persistent debates about the Roman family is whether they felt the same affection for their children as modern parents feel. Of course this question is nearly impossible to answer definitively: how are we to judge what counts as affection? And how are we to know for certain how parents two thousand years ago felt about their children, given the types of evidence available to us? Because the structures of the Roman family are so different from our own, and because so many of them initially appear to suggest unfeeling parents (*patria potestas*, exposure, wet nurses), it has often been suggested that the harshness of ancient life, including the high infant mortality rate, led to a situation where parents did not develop the same affectionate bonds with the children as today. Some texts from ancient Rome appear to support this view: Cicero (*Tusculan Disputations* 1.93) wrote that "if a child dies young, one should console himself easily; if he dies in the cradle, one doesn't even pay attention." Authors supporting this view generally suggest an evolutionary model, where primitive early societies lacked certain essential features and over the centuries civilization has progressed to the point where we value every child.

Leaving aside the question of whether this ideal picture of modern society is accurate, there is evidence to suggest that there was a great deal of affection in Roman families. This evidence comes from a variety of sources. Toys and other such items associated with childhood have been found in many places, clearly given as presents from adults to children (**Figure 5.4**). Poetry, including epic poetry of warriors and battles, often depicts parents bemoaning the loss of a child. Gravestones often reveal these sentiments, suggesting that such feelings were not confined

Figure 5.4 Coin Bank shaped as a beggar girl, circa 50 CE. Getty Villa, Los Angeles. Note that the girl is not portrayed as impoverished even as she stretches out her hand for money.

to the elite classes. The following inscription (*CIL* 6.37412) dates from the early Empire, but likely reflects earlier attitudes:

> Lo, under/behind this marker are placed the bones of Soteris;
> she lies buried, devoured by pitiless death.
> She had not yet filled up twice three years when she was bidden to enter the house of black Dis.
> The lamentations which the mother ought to have bequeathed to her daughter, these the daughter suddenly bequeathed to her mother.

Noteworthy here is that the inscription commemorates the experience of the females in the family.

Even Cicero famously manages *not* to follow his own advice; upon the death of his daughter Tullia, he was so wracked with grief that he withdrew from Rome to solitude at his country estate, where he spent hours walking in the woods. His experience suggests that perhaps the very act of writing to others that they should not grieve the loss of a child is an indication that grief might overwhelm some parents. Grieving over a lost child is of course only one way of measuring affection, but pulling all the different pieces together suggests that while the Romans may have expressed their emotional attachment to their children in different ways, there is no reason to believe that they felt this attachment less than we do.

Related to the issue of affection are questions about the exposure of children. Exposure refers to the conscious decision of the head of the household to not raise a child, but rather to "expose" it by setting it outside the door of the house or in some other public place. We might recall that the foundation myth of Rome involves such a scenario: Romulus and Remus were exposed near the Tiber river, only to be saved by a wolf. In this legendary case, the exposure was a deliberate attempt of an evil king to rid himself of potential threats to his power. It is worth noting that the story already indicates that exposed children did not always die, but could be raised by any passersby. The practice of exposure was clearly known in Rome, though in real life reasons for exposure more likely included the birth of sickly children, whose low odds of survival in an already difficult environment might have led to a decision not to use precious family resources on a seemingly lost cause. Evidence that Romans used exposure on a large scale or simply as a means of family-planning is lacking. Contraceptives and abortion were both known in the ancient world, and it appears that Roman family planning, such as it was, utilized these techniques more than the exposure of healthy children, whether male or female. While the practice of exposure is one of the more uncomfortable elements of Roman family life, it seems to reflect the difficult decisions about family resources in a pre-modern world.

Exploring Culture: *Family Planning in Rome*

Almost every ancient text – legal, literary, medical – makes clear that its author believed it was possible for Romans to control the size of their families. The legal and literary texts, to be sure, do not view this as a positive development. The poet Ovid, who lived just after the Republic, devoted an entire poem to a complaint about his girlfriend who apparently had just had an abortion:

> Can it be possible that, simply to avoid a few stretch-marks,
> you'd make your womb a bloody battleground?
> ...if Ilia, her belly swollen big,
> had terminated her twins in utero, who would have founded
> the City that was bound to rule the world?
> If Venus, in her audacity, had aborted fetal Aeneas
> the Caesars never would have graced our land.
> Even you (though you were meant to be born a beauty) would have died
> if your mother had attempted what you've tried.
> I myself (though personally I plan to die of love) would not
> have seen the light of day, had mother killed me
> (*Amores*, 2.16).

The Romans, though perhaps not Ovid, also distinguished between contraception as an effort to prevent conception in the first place, and abortion as the termination of the embryo.

> Roman medical texts, primarily dating from a later period, indicate a preference for contraception over abortion, and a preference for non-surgical efforts at abortion such as baths or acidic suppositories. Soranus of Ephesos, a second century CE writer, notes in his *Gynecology* (65) that one must beware "of detaching the embryo with some sharp instrument, for there is danger that the surrounding tissues may be injured," indicating clearly that surgical abortion was at least known in his day.
>
> Soranus offers a number of different contraceptive methods, ranging from the superstitious (and thus likely ineffective) to ones that likely did have an impact. For instance, he advised that the woman could get up immediately after having sex, squat, and try to sneeze, and perhaps have something cold to drink. We might wonder if this technique ever worked! On the other hand, he also suggested something similar to the birth control sponge: a piece of wool, which especially when soaked in various mixtures of acidic liquids may have had some success in limiting conception. Soranus also suggested smearing the genitals with olive oil or honey, both of which would have acted to reduce the ability of the semen to reach the woman's uterus. The Romans apparently also attempted to track a woman's cycle in order to have sex at the least fertile times of the month; unfortunately they believed that a woman was most fertile immediately after her period, so reliance on this technique was likely to be less successful.
>
> The mix of effective and ineffective techniques contained in Roman sources means that any individual couple attempting to limit procreation might not have been successful. The discussion of abortion by Ovid and in other texts indicates that these efforts likely failed a fair amount of the time, and even attempts at abortion may have only been moderately successful, leading to the exposure of children discussed in the main text. At the same time, these efforts did succeed often enough to provide some ability for women to avoid the challenges and dangers of an unwanted pregnancy.

These questions and relationships with children in general were different for elite Romans than for poorer citizens, as is true for most societies. Upper class Romans gave responsibility for the raising of children to enslaved persons or other servants in the household from a very early age. Despite some complaints from moralizing writers, most elite Roman households employed a *nutrix* (wet nurse) to feed infants in order to free the mother from this task. Wet nurses might be drawn from the enslaved persons of the household or the family might employ someone from the lower classes, often a formerly enslaved person, in this role. Frequently the *nutrix* continued to care for the child past the point at which the child had been weaned; at this stage her role might be considered similar to that of an English governess or an *au pair*. An elite family might also employ other enslaved persons as teachers or in other roles; in non-elite families, children likely received much less formal schooling but began to work with their parents when it became practicable. While the father might undertake to introduce his sons to politics or business, mothers were expected to have a role in shaping their children's moral character and urging them to bring distinction to the family, and they assumed primary responsibility for raising daughters. Gravestones and other testimony show that the relationships between family members, including the *nutrix* and children, was often warm and long-lasting. On the one hand this fact should not be too surprising since the nurse likely spent more time with the child than the parents during the child's early years, but it may be surprising that the *nutrix* often remained a valued member of the *familia* long after she had ceased to perform duties for the household. This observation thus reminds us of the place from which we started: that the Roman *familia* encompassed a much wider sphere of individuals than the modern family, even if its concerns were still built around the nuclear family unit.

Changes in the Roman Family

The picture of the Roman family as described above might be considered the synchronic image, but we might question whether the "standard" family ever existed at any point in Roman history. Family structures and practices are constantly changing, and this is true for the Romans no less than for us. Certainly by the Late Republic, the period for which we have the most evidence, the picture painted above had changed significantly. In light of the broader changes to Roman society as a result of Rome's growth from a single city in Italy to the dominant power in the Mediterranean basin, this observation can hardly be surprising. The challenge for us in this section is to identify those changes as well as the reasons for them. Often the changes have been connected to the changing nature of Roman warfare and increasing Roman conquests overseas. In the earlier period Roman armies mostly engaged in campaigns in Italy: men could be drafted into the army, head off for a summer of fighting, and return home in time to finish the harvest and get ready for the next planting season. As Roman conquests moved further afield, Roman armies might stay in the field for several years at a time, and we need to consider what impact might this have had on family life. These campaigns also brought large amounts of money into the city, unequally distributed between rich and poor but benefiting everyone, and this newfound wealth likely affected family structures as well. Our sources for family in the 2nd and 1st centuries BCE are more robust, so we can explore some of these changes in detail.

Changes in Women's Position

The influx of wealth into Rome as a result of Roman expansion altered the position of elite women both within the family and within society more broadly. Women brought larger dowries into a marriage and/or became the owners of large amounts of property. At the same time, marriages *sine manu* (literally, "without the hand"), where the wife remained legally a part of her father's family, became more common at this time, limiting the amount of control a husband could exercise over his wife. Both of these developments improved the position of women within the household and perhaps made the relationship more like a partnership. Husbands and wives in a marriage *sine manu* had entirely separate financial lives: there was no notion of joint ownership. Spouses could not even give gifts to each other over a certain value.

Cicero's letters make it apparent that women were not merely passive agents, but that they often understood their importance and could exercise their own authority. For instance, we know that Tullia's third marriage, to Publius Cornelius Dolabella, was arranged entirely by Tullia and her mother Terentia, since Cicero was away from Rome serving as governor in Cilicia. Cicero's letters indicate that the match that did not thrill him; he would have preferred marriage to another politician. It is unclear whether the women actively disregarded his advice or simply didn't receive his advice in time to act upon it; either way they were able to take the lead in arranging the marriage. What emerges most clearly from Cicero's letters is that both husband and wife recognized a need to work for the financial future of their children and that they used their separate financial resources to work together towards this goal. When we compare this episode with the story of Cornelia and Tiberius Gracchus, we can see clearly the difference in women's agency: Cornelia was offended not to be consulted, while Terentia took a leading role in making arrangements for her daughter. The advent of wealth shifted the balance of dominance and dependence within the household: although women did not approach full equality with men, they were able to exercise more authority.

Roman imperial expansion also affected women's roles in Roman society more broadly. Not only did elite women have more financial resources at their disposal, but they seem to have engaged more often in business. A woman in a *sine manu* marriage became legally independent when her father died, offering her greater opportunities for action. Although Roman law insisted that she still have a guardian to approve any business transactions, the Romans found ways around these restrictions as women became increasingly involved in business. For instance, it became possible for the woman choose her guardian, and even to change her guardian if she desired, thus enabling her to carry out whatever transaction she wished. These evasions suggest that again that the legal situation reflects the needs of Roman ideology rather than actual practice: the legal code insisted on the fiction of male control, even while providing numerous avenues for women to behave independently.

Working With Sources: The *Lex Voconia*

One way to judge the increasing position of elite women at least is through the legislation passed at this time. In 169 BCE, as the Romans were about to conclude 30 years of warfare in the Greek eastern Mediterranean, the tribune Q. Voconius pushed a law through the assembly; the law is thus known as the *lex Voconia* (Voconian law). The law stipulated that individuals in the top census class could not make a woman their heir, and furthermore no one could leave a legacy in an amount greater than the portion left to the heirs.

The law is primarily known from the *Institutes* of Gaius, a jurist who lived during the middle of the second century CE. He wrote, among other commentaries, a textbook on Roman law in four books for students of his own day. Because Gaius lived 300 years after the law in question, and because his concern focused on legal issues, we have work to do in order to understand the purpose for this law.

At first glance, there seems to be a concern with too much money concentrated in the hands of women. It has been suggested that the Romans may have worried that women would not spend their money on the military or other masculine priorities. This analysis, however, says more about the misogyny of modern male scholars than it does about the Romans, for it ignores critical evidence that suggests otherwise. Gaius himself points out a loophole in the law: Romans were still allowed to direct the executor of the estate to transfer part or even all of it to a person of their choosing, including a woman. Cicero indicates that this trick was known much earlier in the Republic, saying that Voconius "did not by his law take away her inheritance from any female." The law may have been more concerned to reaffirm what Roman men saw as proper gender roles than to actually limit money in the hands of women.

Whatever the purpose of the law, social historians find great value in reading legal codes for the information that they contain. For example, laws tend to be passed in response to a perceived problem: there is no point in passing a law that does not affect people's lives. The very fact that the Romans decided to pass a law limiting women's inheritance suggests that over the previous decades women *had* been inheriting large sums of money. The fact that some males saw this as a problem is hardly surprising, but it perhaps is surprising that they apparently did not care enough about women's ownership of property to close the loopholes. The *lex Voconia* thus confirms what one often sees with legal prescriptions: they may be useful as statements of ideology, but in many cases their practical day-to-day impact is limited or nonexistent.

Enslaved Persons in the familia

The increasing wealth of Roman women is but one way in which the money coming into Rome from its Mediterranean conquests affected the Roman household. The household changed at a more structural level as well, for Rome's conquests brought not only hard cash into the city, but human capital in the form of enslaved persons as well. Slavery was known in Rome from an early period (see Chapter 11), but the campaigns against Carthage and then the Hellenistic kingdoms in the second century BCE led to a massive influx of enslaved persons. This development profoundly changed the nature not just of wealthy households that owned many enslaved persons, but even of modest households with small numbers of enslaved persons. Many enslaved persons were forced to perform agricultural work on large estates, sometimes displacing small farmers in the process. Many others worked smaller properties, while others were put to work as domestic servants – cooking, serving, cleaning – allowing the enslavers and their wives to engage in other activities. Some of the newly enslaved persons were well educated and found themselves employed in households: as nurses or teachers for aristocratic children, or even as the personal family doctor, and these enslaved persons clearly became part of the *familia*. Gravestones and other evidence indicate that bonds of affection often existed between an enslaved nurse or a teacher and their charges, as well as between enslaver and enslaved (or freedperson if they had been restored to free status). From the middle of the second century BCE forward, the presence of enslaved and freed persons became a regular feature of a wider proportion of Roman households.

Changes in Marriage Practices

Marriage practices appear to have changed as well, though it is difficult to assess the degree of change. As noted earlier in the chapter, aristocratic Romans had always arranged marriages with an eye towards social and political connections; the story of Scipio and Tiberius Gracchus narrated earlier was not unusual. It seems that this process accelerated in the late Republic. What we might call "serial monogamy" – repeated marriages and divorces – became more common as prominent Romans shifted political allegiances in response to the increased competition for glory and power. Pompey the Great, Julius Caesar's great competitor for power and authority at the end of the Republic, is a prime example. Indeed, the death of Julia in childbirth, daughter of Julius Caesar and wife of Pompey, has often been seen as one factor that severed the bonds between these former allies. At the same time, we should not assume that marriages made for political reasons lacked feeling; as noted earlier, Pompey and Julia had deep affection for each other and her death affected both her husband and her father.

Political Issues: *The Marriages of Pompey the Great*

During the late Republic elite Roman men practiced what we might call serial monogamy: many men married and divorced a number of women sometimes in quick succession and often for political reasons. Pompey the Great, one of the leading figures of the period, offers perhaps the best example of this phenomenon, as he was married five times over the course of his life. Pompey came from a wealthy but relatively undistinguished family; his father had been the first member of the family to become a Roman senator. Pompey therefore had need of alliances if he was to build a successful career.

His first marriage was to Antistia, the daughter of a praetor whom Pompey had impressed in court and a member of a family that could trace its origins back to the earliest days of Rome.

After Sulla's victory in the civil war of the 80s BCE, the dictator suggested that Pompey divorce Antistia (whose family was connected to Sulla's enemy Marius) and marry his stepdaughter Aemilia instead. Aemilia was actually pregnant at the time from her existing marriage, but Pompey accepted the offer no doubt as a way to demonstrate his loyalty and support for Sulla. Aemilia soon died in childbirth.

Pompey then married Mucia, daughter of Quintus Mucius Scaevola, who had served as consul and also pontifex (and coincidentally was an important authority on Roman law), and so was at the very center of Roman public life. Scaevola had actually been killed in the

> struggle between Sulla and Marius for refusing to take sides, so the marriage may represent an attempt by Pompey to move past this conflict. This marriage lasted for 17 years and produced a daughter and two sons before Pompey divorced Mucia.
>
> In 59 BCE Pompey married Julia, the daughter of Julius Caesar, in a clear effort to strengthen the bonds between two members of the so-called First Triumvirate. Julia miscarried in 55 BCE and then died in 54 BCE giving birth to a daughter who survived only a few days.
>
> In 52 BCE Pompey married Cornelia Metella, daughter of Metellus Scipio, a powerful aristocrat who was one of the leading voices against Julius Caesar. Pompey's marriage to Cornelia has thus been taken as one of the signs of Pompey's shifting allegiance away from Caesar.
>
> Although several of these marriages seem clearly to have been arranged for political purposes, we should not assume that there was no emotional attachment between Pompey and his wives. He and Julia seem to have been devoted to each other, and he is reported to have been distressed at her death. Cornelia seems to have been devoted to Pompey, following him to Greece and to Egypt following his defeat at the hands of Caesar, and then returning to Italy to live alone on Pompey's estates after his assassination in Egypt. The story of Pompey and his wives thus suggests that arranged marriages in Rome could be affectionate, just as the ideal in our modern world.

Just as we should be wary of reading too much political meaning into marriage, the same is true of divorce. Thanks to Cicero's letters, we know more about the marriages of his daughter Tullia than about any other Roman woman, and his experience indicates that families could remain on amicable terms despite a divorce. Tullia was married three times, each time to families who had long been prominent in Rome. Such connections may have been particularly important to Cicero since he came from Arpinum, approximately three days journey away from Rome, and so was a relative newcomer to Roman politics and society. Cicero's letters make clear that he remained on good terms with Tullia's former husbands even after the divorces, even in the case of her last husband Dolabella, whom Cicero frequently criticized in private for his treatment of Tullia. Nor did marriage imply close political alliance, as Cicero and Dolabella were generally not in the same political camp at this highly charged time. Cicero's experience may be different in detail from other elite men, but he likely illustrates the general pattern. No doubt many marriages were arranged with an eye towards political connections, but we should not overstate the importance of this factor or its effectiveness.

Blended Families

As a result of the shifting relationships and multiple remarriages that became more frequent in elite Roman households at this time, most elite Roman families were what we would today describe as "blended families" and we might ask about the impact of these relationships on the individuals involved. It would have been normal for a Roman child to have had either half-siblings (who shared one parent but not both with them) or step-siblings (who were brought into the family via remarriage). For example, Pompey's daughter Pompeia had two children with her first husband Faustus Sulla and then after his death in battle she married Lucius Cinna by whom she had two additional children, forming a single family with four siblings. Typically the children would follow the father in cases of divorce, forming part of his *familia*; our surviving sources give little indication of the amount of visitation by a biological mother.

The Romans did develop a stereotype of the stepmother that was every bit as unflattering as Cinderella's, concerned for her natural children rather than her husband's. As in fairytales and other societies, however, the stereotype seems to be more a product of cultural fears than of reality. The few historical cases that we know, involving Cato the Elder and Cicero, involve grown sons objecting to their father remarrying a woman who was actually younger than the sons themselves – something that seems awkward to us and was apparently no less awkward for the Romans. Fears about stepmothers stealing parts of the family inheritance again seem to reflect the Roman ideology of the family as a means of transmitting property rather than reality.

Strategies for transmitting property complicated the Roman family structure in other ways, since the Roman elite often employed adoption to ensure a smooth inheritance. As noted earlier, many Romans lost their father before they reached age 25, but the reverse is also true: many Roman fathers outlived their children, due to the high infant mortality rate and young men dying as a result of Rome's constant warfare. Of course, daughters could inherit property, and a high casualty rate in the early second century BCE may have been a factor in the passage of the *lex Voconia* that restricted the wealthiest families from leaving daughters as sole heirs, as discussed in the textbox on Women and Wealth: The *Lex Voconia* above. Roman men wanted to ensure the continuation of their line and the smooth handover of the family's property. Therefore Romans often adopted an adult son from another branch of the family tree, and this practice seems to have increased in the second and first centuries BCE.

Scipio Aemilianus, the successful commander in the Third Punic War (146 BCE) provides a good example. His birth father was Aemilius Paullus, the conqueror of Macedon in 168 BCE, but Aemilius ended up with four male children from two marriages, too many to support both financially and politically. When a cousin from the prominent Scipionic family had no natural children, the families arranged for him to adopt Aemilianus, thus preserving that branch of the Scipionic family line. Aemilianus' full brother was adopted by a different family, while two half-brothers survived to carry on the family of Aemilius Paullus. The four brothers would thus have become heads of households in three different families, but unfortunately Paullus' two sons did not survive beyond age 15. As a result, the family of Aemilius Paullus came to an end; since his other natural born children had already become members of other families, they could not carry on his family name. Paullus even had to specifically bequeath his property to them in his will. Nor was the experience of Paullus unusual. Elite Romans attempting to manage their property and their family name faced disruptions to the family structure on a regular basis.

Conclusion: Family Values

The chaotic situation of the Late Republic has often been seen as a time of weakened family bonds. This interpretation has been fostered by the picture painted by Roman authors, especially of the Augustan period, who argued that a decline in family values had been one of the contributing factors to the civil wars that had pitted brother versus brother (sometimes literally). For example, Horace (*Ode* 3.6) suggested that "our age, fertile of blame, first defiled the marriage bed, our offspring, and our homes; coming from this source, disaster has flowed over our people and country." The poetry of Catullus from the Late Republic, which revels in the affair of the poet with a married woman, has been taken as a representative example of this behavior. Yet complaints about the breakdown of family life are not new to this period; among the writings of the earliest Roman authors such as Cato and Plautus can be found moralizing concerns about the state of the family. Hard evidence for a decline in family life is hard to come by; there are no indications of a decline in the number of marriages, However, there is evidence for a steadily increasing number of citizens, all of whom had to be legitimate offspring in order to be counted, suggesting that the birthrate was not declining either.

It is easy to understand why Roman authors might have seen crisis periods, especially in the Late Republic, as a sign of a decline in family values. For the Romans, who often viewed the family as a microcosm of the Roman state, it was logical to assume that if the state was falling apart that the family must be falling apart as well. Changes in family practices are indeed likely to be tied to changes in the broader society, but the question of decline is always tied to one's perspective. Roman authors chose to use the narrative of decline to explain the challenges of the Late Republic, despite the lack of evidence that the Roman family was in fact in decline. The Romans were thus among the first to develop a rhetoric of family values, where the supposed decline of family life is cited as an explanation for societal ills, a rhetoric that is still with us today.

Discussion Questions

1. In what ways might Roman "family values" have differed from family values today (for instance, the values with which you yourself were raised)? What assumptions do you personally bring to the study of the family, and how might those assumptions distort our view of history?
2. How might family life, or even the definition of the family, have been different for members of the upper classes and members of the lower classes?
3. What strategies might wives, and to some extent daughters, have employed to assert their authority within a system designed to give males control?
4. What dangers are there in thinking that certain family relationships are "natural" simply because they existed in different times and different places?
5. What would someone trying to understand families today learn from looking at gravestones? From the letters of one or two individuals? From our legal system?

Further Reading

Dixon, Suzanne (1992). *The Roman Family*. Baltimore, MD: Johns Hopkins University Press.
    One of the first books to focus exclusively on the Roman family, Dixon shows how the evidence provided by the legal sources often does not match up with the reality of family life as seen in other materials.

Evans, John K. (1991). *War, Women, and Children in Ancient Rome*. London: Routledge.
    This book offers the best analysis of the changes in the social, economic, and legal status of Roman women that resulted from Rome's expansion from city-state to empire. Using a number of individual case studies, Evans highlights how the traditional limitations on women, and on children as well, loosened over time.

Rawson, Beryl (2005). *Children and Childhood in Roman Italy*. Oxford: Oxford University Press.
    Rawson shows how, contrary to earlier ideas about childhood in Rome, children were in general welcomed and visible as members of the family. Despite the lack of direct evidence, Rawson is able to reveal how childhood in Rome was in fact very different from the modern world, even as children formed a valued aspect of Roman society.

Saller, Richard P. (1994). *Patriarchy, Property, and Death in the Roman Family*. Cambridge: Cambridge University Press.
    This book offered a critical rethinking of the concept of *patria potestas*. It argued both the life course of Roman men limited its impact, and highlighted the different elements that shaped family bonds.

Treggiari, Susan (1991). *Roman Marriage: Iusti Coniuges from the Time of Cicero to the Time of Ulpian*. Oxford: Oxford University Press.
    This volume is a massive and complete discussion of Roman marriage practices. Treggiari demonstrated that marriage above all was an agreement between two people to be married. She also discussed how different forms of marriage and marriage at different times of life affected women's status more than men, and also discusses influences on the choice of partner and about divorce.

6
Gender and Sexuality

In Chapter 2 we touched briefly upon the story of Lucretia from Rome's mythic period as the inspiration for the Roman hatred of monarchy. The full details of that story are useful for beginning to think about Roman sexuality and gender expectations. The episode begins when Sextus, the son of King Tarquin the Proud, attended a party with his friends. At the party each man boasted of his own wife's excellence. The young men decided to sneak back to Rome and check up on their wives to see which one was truly the best of wives and best of women. Most women were found feasting with friends, but one woman, Lucretia, was found spinning wool even though it was late at night: that made her the clear winner of the contest. Unfortunately, the king's son found her beauty and evident chastity a target and formed a plan to have sex with her. The next day he returned and with his sword drawn entered her bedroom. He threatened that if she did not submit to him, he would kill her and an enslaved attendant, and so deprive her of both her life and her honor, since everyone would think that she had been killed for having sex with the enslaved person. Faced with this prospect, Lucretia gave in and Sextus rode away having satisfied his desire.

Livy does not end the story there, however. Lucretia immediately sent messages to her father and her husband. When they arrived, she explained what had happened and pulled a knife from under her dress. Crying out that no unchaste woman in the future would ever live by citing Lucretia as an example, she plunged the knife into her heart and fell dead on the ground in front of them. Her husband and father were too stunned to react, but Brutus, a family friend who had accompanied the father, grabbed the knife and swore vengeance upon the king and his entire family. The husband and father then swore vengeance as well, and together they roused the people "as was fitting for Romans" as Livy says. The Romans rose up and drove the family of the Tarquins into exile, leading to the establishment of the Roman Republic.

A Social and Cultural History of Republican Rome, First Edition. Eric M. Orlin.
© 2022 John Wiley & Sons, Inc. Published 2022 by John Wiley & Sons, Inc.

It is surely meaningful that the Romans used this story to explain the transition away from a monarchy. This is no Boston Tea Party and "taxation without representation is tyranny." For the Romans, tyranny was symbolized by the sexual assault on a married woman.

Even if we do not ask "did this really happen?", the story raises more questions than we can hope to answer. We could ask about the relationship between husbands and wives; we could ask about Roman men and warfare, or about Roman women in the economy; we could follow up on Rome's political history and talk about the hatred of kings. Our concern in this chapter is to explore what the story reveals about how the Romans viewed women's roles, men's roles, and sexuality. For example, the story reveals that chastity was one of the highest values assigned to elite women, although we of course need to ask whether the same standard held for non-elite women of free status. Even though Lucretia acquitted herself of the crime, she nonetheless applied the punishment for adultery, revealing an ideology that for Roman women there was never any excuse for sex outside of marriage. On the male side, self-control and action were the expectation: Brutus has to scold the husband and the father, who might have been expected to leap into action but were too consumed by their grief. The story thus provides an appropriate jumping off point for an exploration of Roman ideas concerning gender and sexuality.

Sex and Gender

Let us begin with another question: what do we mean by "sex" and "gender"? Most people use "gender" when they want to refer to different social and cultural expectations. These expectations may relate to roles in society, such as whether or not women are expected to work outside the home. Or they may refer to individual qualities that men and women are supposed to possess: women expected to bear primary responsibility for child-rearing may be expected to be nurturing and compassionate, while women expected to work outside the home may be praised for their strength. "Sex" on the other hand has usually been considered to be a biological term, referring to individuals with different genitalia and reproductive capacities, although there is now increasing awareness that "sex" is not a straightforward scientific term, and that "sex" and "gender" are not so easily distinguished from each other. It may therefore be more useful to think about a "sex/gender system," a term coined by Gayle Rubin to refer to "a set of arrangements by which the biological raw material of human sex and procreation is shaped by human, social intervention and satisfied in a conventional manner." While there are biological differences between human beings that relate to how they have sex, how those differences are categorized (for instance, as female or non-binary or other categories) and how sexual activity is categorized and marked with approval or disapproval is determined by each culture.

These observations suggest that one of the biggest mistakes we can make is to assume that certain gender roles and certain types of sexual behavior are "natural" and others are not. People do not automatically have certain qualities because of their biological attributes. This point has an important consequence for our consideration of the Roman sex/gender system: since this system functioned as a part of their society, their notions in these areas are different from our own, no matter what our own society may be. While there may be certain similarities, these similarities are likely due to the facts that in both ancient Rome and modern European and American societies, males have held more power than females and have shaped the sex/gender system to their own benefit. As in other spheres of society, gender roles and sexual behavior tend to reflect the power dynamics within that society. The differences between these societies are as significant as any surface similarities.

One key area of difference is that the Roman texts indicate a widespread belief that gender differences and gender roles were in fact part of the natural order of things. This ideology helped reinforce the notions of dominance and dependence: male dominance was part of the natural order and women's dependence needed no further justification. We might well question how widely the Roman sources, written almost exclusively by elite males, reflect society more broadly, and especially whether these ideas extended to the non-elite. Roman sources also tended to divide the world using the categories of male and female; the idea that some people might be non-binary or transgender was largely absent. They did, however, recognize that some people did not fit neatly into the biological categories of male and female, and their responses to these situations offers revealing glimpses into their sex/gender system and how strongly they tried to keep to a binary division.

Thinking with Sex/Gender: Hermaphrodites

Hermaphrodites, people born with the sexual organs of both females and males, offer insight into this part of the Roman sex/gender system. On several occasions, our sources tell us about the birth of hermaphrodites, and we can judge how disturbed the Romans were by their reaction. The child was placed in a wooden box, rowed out to sea, and drowned in the ocean, or in one instance a river. Hermaphrodites did not fit in the Roman sex/gender system: according to the natural order of things as the Romans understood it, they could not exist. The existence of such an individual therefore had to be caused by divine intervention. In Roman eyes such bodies were deformed and signaled a deformity in the Roman state, a signal that something was wrong in the world. For the Romans, the solution was to remove the deformity as quickly as possible, and thus to restore the "natural" order of the world. The idea itself did not disappear as easily: hermaphrodites appear with some frequency in Roman art, both painting and sculpture. These depictions often seem to be making a joke, for instance, by hiding the genitalia that reveal the hermaphroditic nature (**Figure 6.1**). These attempts at humor may have been a way of handling the discomfort around figures that did not fit neatly into Roman categories, but they also suggest that many Romans found these figures combining male and female genitalia as a useful means of thinking about sexuality.

The flip side of the Roman treatment of hermaphrodites can be seen in their treatment of the priests of the Magna Mater, the *galli*. According to the practices of this cult, the priests castrated themselves, a reflection of the myth of Attis, who

Figure 6.1 Sleeping hermaphrodite, second century CE Roman copy of a Greek original. Palazzo Massimo, Rome. Note how the male genitalia are only visible from a certain angle.

was driven mad by Cybele. As castrated males, eunuchs could not fit into the Roman sex/gender system: they are males who lack male sexual organs. However, since the Romans had decided to make the cult of the Magna Mater part of their own religious system, they could not simply eliminate the *galli* as they did with hermaphrodites. Instead they erected both physical and symbolic barriers around these priests. On one hand, the *galli* were restricted to the temple precinct, which was hidden behind a wall; on the other hand, the Romans passed a law stating that Roman citizens could not become *galli*. The *galli* thus served to reinforce the "normal" Roman categories of sex and gender, in a similar fashion to the artistic depictions of hermaphrodites. Figures that did not fit into the Roman sex/gender system could exist, but only when marked out as not Roman and, in the case of statues, not even real.

Sexuality

Female Chastity

The story of Lucretia told above reveals clearly that the primary quality valued in Roman women was chastity (**Figure 6.2**). Lucretia makes clear that even though she has committed no crime, she kills herself so that no woman after her will be able to use her as an example of adultery. This story and others like it demonstrate the importance to especially elite Roman men of controlling the sexuality of women.

Figure 6.2 Statue of the Pudicitia type, first century BCE. Walters Art Gallery, Baltimore, MD.

Roman men justified their need to control women's sexuality by claiming that women were by nature completely lacking in self-control. They reasoned that if they did not carefully control women's sexuality, women would run free with wild abandon, having sex and possibly children with strangers. Drinking wine posed a particular problem from this point of view, since even the Romans recognized that drinking wine caused one to lose self-control. Roman men therefore assumed that if a woman had been drinking, she must inevitably have had sex with someone: as Valerius Maximus (*Memorable Deeds and Sayings*, 2.1.5) wrote in the first century CE: "after Father Liber [wine] the next step in the lack of self-control is likely to be illicit sex." The supposed connection between wine and illicit sex was used by some ancient authors to explain the Roman custom of kissing their female relatives on the lips rather than on the cheek: it was a way of detecting whether the females had been drinking. It also helps explain several legendary stories told by Pliny the Elder of women who were put to death for drinking wine: the punishment was not for the drinking itself, but was based on the assumption that the woman must have committed adultery. The ideology of male dominance and control required an ideology of women's lack of control, which played out in sexual relations as elsewhere in Roman society.

Issues of control are particularly visible in the one group of women who had a public and thus more powerful role in Roman society: the Vestal Virgins. As female priestesses who managed critical aspects of the Roman religious system, the Vestal Virgins held an indispensable place in Roman society, and their legal and social position reflected their importance. Vestal Virgins were preceded in processions by a lictor, the same ceremonial guard that preceded male magistrates, and they had special seats reserved for them at the games. They were released from the authority of their fathers and they could make wills and give testimony in court without swearing an oath. To gain this status, however, a woman had to give up virtually all of her entire childbearing years: Vestal Virgins were chosen for service between 6 and 10 years of age, and had to serve for at least 30 years. The punishment for violating their oath of chastity was death: Vestals convicted of having sex were buried alive. The Vestals vividly illustrate key elements of the Roman sex/gender system: the absence of sexual activity by these females was matched by the granting of certain social, legal, and economic rights normally attached only to males. The presence of Vestal Virgins at public events and elsewhere throughout the city therefore served as a constant reminder of expectations for women and their sexual behavior.

The idea of female chastity also seems to be connected to the ideal of an *univira* (meaning "to one man"), a woman who was married to only one man in her lifetime. It is a mark of the lack of individuality of women that the good reputation she earned comes entirely from the man and is named after him; in similar fashion daughters were named just by their family name, without a personal name. The ideology can be seen clearly in Vergil's epic poem the *Aeneid*, composed at the end of the Republic. Dido, the queen of Carthage, had lost her husband many years before the start of the action. When the protagonist Aeneas reaches Carthage, she falls in love with him, and so falls away from the ideal of "one man forever." Aeneas, however, leaves her to continue his journey to Italy, making her relationship with him a short-term fling. Dido goes mad as a result and commits suicide, thus offering an example to the Romans of what happens when a woman does not stay loyal to her husband, even after he has died. This ideal of an *univira* is also visible in the gravestones of many ordinary women, signaling that in this case the ideal does seem to have extended beyond the elite. The message is clear: in the male-dominated Roman world, sex for women should ideally be confined to one man and to marriage only.

Exploring Culture: *What's in a Name?*

Roman names, like many modern names, often carried meaning beyond identifying a person. In the early period, Roman men possessed two names: a *nomen*, the family name, and the *praenomen*, the personal name. This practice already marked the Romans as different from other ancient Mediterranean societies, where individuals often had only a single personal name: "Pericles, son of Xanthippus." The Romans placed the highest value on the family name: Romans were addressed in public by their family name, while the personal name would rarely be heard outside of the house.

This lack of emphasis on personal names enabled the Romans to use a very small number of personal names. During the Republic, 99% of all known Roman names used one of only 17 personal names. Standard practice called for a son to be named after his grandfather, a situation that has caused great confusion to modern historians, and perhaps to Romans themselves, in trying to determine which Publius Cornelius (for example) was meant.

Some time in the fourth century some Roman aristocrats began adding a third name, the *cognomen*, which could then be passed through the generations. These seem to have been nicknames that highlighted an individual quality or peculiar identifying feature. One of the earliest such individuals was **Appius Claudius Caecus** (circa 340–275 BCE), the builder of the Appian Way and of Rome's first aqueduct around 300 BCE. *Caecus* is the Latin word for blind, which makes his accomplishments as one of Rome's leading statesmen in this period even more remarkable. Not all names were complimentary: *cicero* is the Latin word for chickpea, and Plutarch suggested that one of Cicero's ancestors had a cleft nose that resembled a chickpea. Modern historians are inclined to discard this story as hostile propaganda, suggesting that Cicero's ancestors made their fortune through growing and selling chickpeas. However we understand the nickname, the example certainly indicates that names could be a subject for political attack.

Names can also help us see the Roman lack of respect for women as individuals. Where men would normally have a first name as well as a family name and potentially a cognomen, by the Late Republic women used only a family name: Cornelia. More than one daughter was simply called Cornelia the second, Cornelia the third, and so on. The connection to a woman's birth family was so strong that even upon marriage she retained her father's name rather than taking her husband's. This practice also made it easy for Romans to tell at a glance which two families had contracted a marriage relationship: Cornelia and Tiberius Gracchus represented a connection between the Cornelii and the Gracchi.

By the Late Republic the system where each citizen possessed *tria nomina* ("three names": *praenomen*, *nomen*, and *cognomen*) was well established. Since Greeks and others typically only had one name, it was thus easy to see who was a citizen and who was not. Enslaved persons who were restored to free status were quick to take on three names, almost always using the *nomen* of their former owner. These practices enable Roman historians today to trace both political and social connections among individuals in the Roman world.

Male Dominance

In contrast, Roman men could have sex outside marriage with very few restrictions, as an expression of his dominance. An early play of Plautus hints at the only restrictions on male sexuality (*Curculio*, lines 35–38): "as long as you keep away from the bride, the widow, the virgin, the young man, and freeborn boys, love whom you please." Issues arise only if a man were to have sex with the wrong person: it was the status of the partner rather than whether the man was married that determined whether the act counted as adultery or not. Brides and virgins were of course connected to other men, and the ideal of the *univira* indicates that widows too were still held to be connected to a man. In Roman law, only children born within a marriage had any legal claims on the father, so a male did not even have to worry about financial issues such as child support or claims on the estate. If an enslaved person, a prostitute, or a non-citizen gave birth, the child had no legal connection to the father.

Since the Romans viewed women as lacking in self-control, it was important that men be able to demonstrate self-control: they needed to be able to dominate their own desires as well as other people. An anecdote about Cato the Elder illustrates how men should approach their sexual needs. Seeing a man exit a brothel and try to run away, Cato called him back and praised him, presumably because he had found an appropriate outlet for sexual gratification. But when Cato saw the same man exiting the brothel repeatedly he criticized him with the comment: "I praised you because I thought you visited this place, not because you lived there." The man earned a scolding not for the sex itself but for the lack of self-control that Cato felt was not appropriate for a man.

Plautus' list of forbidden sexual partners might at first sight seem surprising, but actually offers an important insight into Roman sexuality. As parallels to the three categories of women, Plautus suggests that one should avoid making approaches to young men and freeborn boys. There is no suggestion that men in general should be off limits but only these two categories, just as there were only the three categories of women. The concern with the males is their status as Roman citizens on an equal level, just as the concern with females is with those of an equal social status. Note that Plautus specifically remarks that it is "freeborn" men who are off limits, suggesting that no such concerns might prevent one from having sex with an enslaved male. The poet Horace at the end of the first century CE confirms this interpretation (*Satires* 1.14–19):

> when your groin bulges,
> if a servant-girl or estate-born boy is handy, whom you can jump on
> right away, would you prefer being ruptured by the swelling?
> Not me; I want my sex ready and accessible.

Not only does this passage reveal an expectation that enslaved persons should be sexually available to their enslavers at all times, but Horace, a good Roman male, sees little difference between using a male or a female for sex when his need arises. These passages, along with others like it, suggest that Roman sexuality operated differently from modern notions of heterosexuality and homosexuality. It was possible for Roman men to engage in male–male sexual relationships without being criticized for being unmanly.

The Penetration Model

How then might we understand Roman sexuality? Perhaps the most useful way to think about Roman sexuality uses the "penetration model." The penetration model suggests that in sexual activity, the person doing the penetrating is the one to be respected, and the person being penetrated is weaker. We can see here how Roman ideas about dominance and dependence were reflected in their sex/gender system: the person penetrating plays the dominant role. Since biologically women's bodies do not easily lend themselves to playing the penetrative role in sexual activity based on genitalia, the Romans viewed it as natural for men to be the dominant partner in a sexual relationship. Male–female couplings thus fell easily into the Roman sex/gender system, with an active penetrating male who was thereby defined as powerful and aggressive in other spheres of gender expectation, while women were defined as passive and dependent. Unlike in many societies, both ancient and modern, a penetrating partner in a male–male sexual encounter generally faced no criticism, since he was fulfilling the position of dominance that went along with being a male. The passive male partner, on the other hand, might be criticized precisely on those grounds, that it was unmanly to be the submissive partner in the relationship and have someone else express his dominance. What mattered from the Roman moral perspective was not the biological sex of one's partner, but whether one was dominant or submissive, expressing manliness in ways appropriate to a Roman.

These observations suggest that in the Roman sex/gender system, sex was not idealized as an expression of mutual intimacy between partners. Rather, it could be seen as a one-way street, from the dominant to the submissive partner. There was no expectation that a woman should derive pleasure from sex, but her sex life was supposed to be contained within marriage and be concerned with procreation. Men, on the other hand, should be concerned primarily with the demonstration of their power over others and with their own gratification. As always, however, we must question whether the reality of Roman lives matched the ideals promoted by their sex/gender system. Some literary evidence suggests that there were women who enjoyed, and expected to enjoy, sex. Wall paintings from Rome and Pompeii also suggest that Roman sexual activity took many forms, not all of which conformed in straightforward fashion to expectations. We can see some of these complexities by exploring the sexual activity of one Roman in the middle of the first century BCE.

Working with Sources:
The Explicit Paintings of Pompeii

The walls of Pompeii have proved an unexpectedly rich source of information about Roman sexuality. The uncovering of a purpose-built brothel raises few eyebrows: the exchange of sex for money has existed in most societies throughout history, and paintings depicting various sex acts on its walls are hardly surprising. The existence of explicit paintings (**Figure 6.3**) in private homes, and even in public buildings such as baths, however, may seem strange to us, a reminder of how different Roman attitudes towards sex are from our own. How can we use these paintings to learn more about the Romans and not simply be amused or appalled by them?

Context offers a crucial element in understanding paintings such as these. Archaeologists always want to know where an object was placed in the house or the city, because the location makes a significant difference in what the object can tell us (underwear on the floor of a locker room means something different than underwear

Figure 6.3 Wall-painting from the House of Iucundus, Pompeii, first century CE. Naples Archaeological Museum.

on the floor of a bedroom – or the kitchen!). The owner of this house was a businessman of modest means named Caecilius Iucundus, and Caecilius placed this painting on a wall in the peristyle courtyard of the house. Not only did he display this explicit sex scene to every guest that was invited into the house, he even spent additional money to decorate parts of it with gold leaf, including the woman's jewelry and the cloth that covers her legs. Caecilius wanted to draw everyone's eye to this painting. He knew, as scholars have learned from other houses at Pompeii, that houses of the rich frequently contained explicit paintings as a sign of their status, and he wanted everyone in Pompeii to know that he had the same good taste as his rich neighbors. Context thus helps us understand that sexually explicit paintings in Pompeii were not necessarily meant as a direct stimulus for sexual activity, but to mark the owner as a man of good taste.

The painting itself offers clues to Roman sexual behavior as well as to Roman attitudes towards sex. If you look behind the woman, you can see another figure, a servant, who approaches the bed right in the middle of the sexual activity taking place on the bed. Similar servants can be found in other explicit paintings and the literary sources also reveal their presence at the most intimate moments. The Romans simply did not have a conception of privacy anything like our own: the presence of the servant does not distract either the man or the woman from what they are doing.

Wall paintings also add complexity to our understanding of the Roman sex/gender system. Women are often depicted on top of men in a role that we would usually define as more active, suggesting that notions of active and passive may not exactly match dominant and dominated. Other paintings depict threesomes, including one where a man penetrates a woman while apparently being penetrated from behind by another man. While these paintings may represent male fantasies more than reality, the willingness to display themselves in these positions suggests that these depictions did not undermine the Roman sex/gender system.

A Late Republic Male: Catullus

In the middle of the first century BCE the poet Catullus provided some of clearest expressions of the nature of Roman sexuality. His poetry suggests that Catullus fell hopelessly in love with a woman he calls Lesbia, which is clearly a pseudonym since his girlfriend was a married woman. His poems provide a window into a Roman lover's emotions, first infatuated with his girlfriend and then infuriated with her when she dumped him. In many ways Catullus transgresses the Roman sex/gender system, for instance by having a relationship with a married woman. In violating the norms of behavior, however, he shows us clearly what those norms were: the fact that he can announce that he is having sex with a married woman but must hide her identity shows his recognition that this behavior was allowed for him and not for her.

Catullus also illustrates how Roman sexuality revolved around the poles of dominance and submission. He frequently presents himself as beholden to his girlfriend in a reversal of the normal male–female gender roles. In one poem (51), Catullus writes of his weakness when he sees Lesbia with another man: "my tongue falters, a subtle flame steals down through my limbs, my ears ring with inward humming, my eyes are shrouded in twofold night." Even more, this poem was modelled on one composed by the female poet Sappho from the island of Lesbos in sixth century BCE Greece, about a woman whom Sappho desired. Catullus' pseudonym for his girlfriend means "woman from Lesbos" and so in this poem Catullus likens himself to a woman with same-sex desires. Catullus here seems to be deliberately playing with the categories of male and female, dominant and dependent, but his choices indicate how these categories were normally constructed.

Catullus was also capable of operating within the normal Roman sex/gender system when it suited his purpose. Early in his relationship with Lesbia, Catullus responds to criticism of his poetry with the following verses (poem 16):

> I will take you from behind and force it down your throat
> *pathicus* Aurelius and *cinaedus* Furius...
> Because you've read my (poem about) countless kisses,
> do you think I am less of a man?
> I will take you from behind and force it down your throat.

Catullus here threatens forcible penetration of two men as a means of reasserting his manliness. The *pathicus* and the *cinaedus* were two figures who could be opposed to a proper man in Rome: *pathicus* refers to the man on the receiving end of anal sex, while *cinaedus* appears to have been a more general term for a man who preferred to be the passive sexual partner. Both were thus inversions of Roman manliness, so Catullus can use these terms as part of the reassertion of his manliness: in his relationship with Aurelius and Furius he will not only be the active partner, but a doubly dominant one, both penetrating them and doing so against their will.

The figure of the *cinaedus* raises further questions to consider, but because we have no texts that represent the view of the *cinaedus* some of these questions may be unanswerable. One question is raised by the very nature of this term: in a Roman world where gender revolved around dominance and submission, some men apparently made the choice to be submissive voluntarily. In so doing, they put themselves outside the bounds of manliness. We know little about why such men would have made this choice and what kind of life they might have led. It has been suggested that a subculture may have grown up around these men in Rome, centered not just on the performance of sexual deviance but also hairstyles, clothing preferences, and other markers of identity. At the very least, the existence of the *cinaedus* points us to the fact that Roman sexuality was more complex than the outline we have been able to sketch above: while *cinaedus* might have been a term of scorn for Furius, in other contexts the term might not have such a negative meaning.

The very word *cinaedus* raises a further level of complexity: it is a direct borrowing of the Greek word *kinaidos*, which was also used of men who took the passive role in a sexual relationship. It is unclear how to understand this borrowing. The sex/gender system in Greece was different than that in Rome: nudity was more widely practiced, especially in the gymnasium, and elite men were *expected* to engage in male–male relationships during a certain period of their lives. Elite Romans tended to disapprove of these Greek notions of male sexuality. Cicero, for example, criticizes as "absurd their system of exercise for young men in gymnasiums," remarking on "how free and easy are their contacts and love relations" (*On the Republic* 4.3–4). The use of the word *cinaedus* may be connected to this critique of Greek culture, although early uses of the word are more closely connected to a type of effeminate dancer rather than any sexual activity. The Romans also had a habit of adopting elements of Greek culture even while they critiqued it, so the use of a Greek term does not automatically imply disapproval. On the whole, there is little evidence that the Romans raised moral objections to male–male sexual relationships, or even that male–male relationships formed a distinct category of sexual behavior within their sex/gender system. Here, as elsewhere in his poetry, Catullus drew upon a wide variety of associations with Greece in constructing roles for himself and others within the Roman sex/gender system.

Gender Roles

Ideas about the proper roles for females and males help to organize a society. A society's notion of femininity and masculinity conditions what it expects from various people and helps it assign tasks that are considered appropriate for each, whether those tasks are political, economic, or social. They can also help us, as modern researchers, understand the principles used by a given society to organize itself. What then were Roman ideas about the proper role of women and the proper role of men? And how do these ideas help us understand Roman society?

Women

> Friend, I have not much to say; stop and read it. This tomb, which is not fair, is for a fair woman. Her parents gave her the name Claudia. She prized her husband in her heart. She bore two sons, one of whom she left on earth, the other beneath it. She was pleasant to talk with, and she walked with grace. She kept the house and worked in wool. That is all. You may go. (*CIL* 6.15346)

So reads the gravestone of a woman who lived somewhere at the end of the second or beginning of the first century BCE. We might ask questions about each of the items listed after her name. The inscription does not use the normal Latin word for "love." Is this choice of words just for poetic effect, or does it mean that she was not expected to love her husband, that "respecting" or "prizing" him was the true value? When the inscription places this fact before the children that she bore, does it mean that marital affection was more important than childbearing? The inscription mentions only her two sons: did she only bear two children, or did the person who erected this monument decide that daughters were not worthy of mention? It references her grace and easygoing manner: why did the person who erected the inscription include these two specific qualities? And finally the inscription mentions two domestic activities. The first part can just mean "to keep" or "to live in," but the Latin word can also be used in reference to protecting or guarding the state: is Claudia's role in the household supposed to be like the role of a general in protecting Rome? The second reference leaves us with a final image of Claudia working in wool: why is this one specific detail pulled out for special mention? The answers to these questions can tell us much about gender roles for women in Rome.

Claudia's primary "accomplishment" as identified by the person who erected this gravestone is that she gave birth to two boys. In the Roman context this was high praise: childbearing was often seen as women's primary function in Roman society. As in most premodern (and some modern!) societies, boys were particularly valued, because the family name and property were passed through the male line. The importance of childbearing can be seen in the two major categories that the Romans used for freeborn women: *virgines* and *matronae*. Generally speaking, the first category comprises women who had not yet reached childbearing age and the second is women who had reached that age. This expectation colored the lifecycle for Roman women of free status: they tended to marry very close to the age when they were first able to bear children, and the expectation was that they would stay married throughout their reproductive years. Without knowing anything about Claudia's lifespan or cause of death we cannot speak to her specific case; marriage and childbirth are the first two items highlighted by the person who preserved her memory for us.

Claudia's ability in wool might seem to us an odd choice for a person to single out on a tombstone, but wool-working appears over and over as the singular trait associated with a proper Roman woman. Recall that in the story of Lucretia, she won the prize in the contest among the wives because she was found late at night "given over to wool." The ideal Roman woman may have differed little from women in other ancient Mediterranean societies in this regard. Homer's *Odyssey* presents Penelope as the paragon of a good wife, waiting patiently for her husband to come home from the war without remarrying: her virtue is confirmed by the fact that she puts off her suitors by claiming the need to weave a death shroud for her father-in-law. So a claim of wool-working creates a comparison to the very best of aristocratic women.

The evidence we have for ancient Rome demonstrates clearly that wool-working as a woman's occupation reflected an ideology rather than the reality of women's lives. Women can be seen in a wide variety of respectable professions: farmers, bakers, skilled craftsmen in gold and silver, as well as with cloth manufacture (**Figure 6.4**). Of course, there was also a wide variety of what the Romans categorized as

Figure 6.4 Market scene from relief at Ostia, second century CE.

disreputable professions: prostitution is obviously a prime example, but women also served as pimps and brothel-owners, and outside the sex-work industry we find actresses, musicians, and gladiators. However, even if women participated in respectable professions, wool-working remained the ideal: it was an activity that kept women inside and connected to the activity only of their immediate household without participation in the broader economic activity of the city. Of course this ideal was developed by and for elite males, those who could afford *not* to maximize their economic activity, but Claudia's funerary inscription shows how this ideal, like other aristocratic values, had filtered down into other social classes.

Key Debates: *Why Did the Romans Object to Sex-Work?*

Prostitution, pimps, brothel-owners: it is not difficult for us to imagine that there might be some social stigma or even legal incapacity that attached to these people. As always in studying another people, however, we need to be careful about applying our own moral standards to others. It seems clear that the Romans raised some objections to these professions, but the grounds on which they objected is much less clear.

The Romans had a legal category known as *infamia* ("bad reputation") that included actors and actresses, gladiators and their trainers, and others in addition to sex workers. Persons who were assigned to this category faced varying types of legal disabilities. Cicero defends a client accused of sexually assaulting an actress by saying that such behavior was an established custom towards people of that profession. There seems to have been an assumption that being an actress was the same as being a prostitute, a fact which ought to alert us that something very different is happening in Roman society than in our own.

In addition to these legal disabilities, some social stigma seem to have attached to this class of individuals. In the first century BCE, a man named Horatius Balbus provided burial plots for people in his community except for "those who had bound themselves to serve as gladiators ... or had followed a filthy profession for profit." Some gladiators and actors might achieve a certain notoriety and be invited to mingle with the upper-classes as a type of celebrity, but even in these circumstances it was clear that they were thought to be inferior.

No clear answer has emerged that might link prostitutes and pimps to actors and gladiators. On one hand, these are all professions engaged in by the lower classes and often by enslaved persons, which might have created a class stigma. We might compare it to blue-collar workers (machinists, mechanics, etc.) today; these individuals typically are paid less and have less education, and therefore lower socioeconomic standing, than white-collar workers such as lawyers and businessmen. This explanation does not appear to be sufficient for Rome: there were other "blue-collar" jobs that were not considered disreputable, and some enslaved persons held jobs that we (though perhaps not the Romans) would consider respectable, such as doctors and teachers.

The best suggestion offered so far has to do with the use of the body for the pleasure of others. These professions – prostitutes, gladiators, actors – displayed their bodies to audiences for entertainment in exchange for money. Prostitutes of course might do this individually while actors and gladiators gave their bodies to a mass of people at the same time, but the principle seems to have been the same. Opening one's body up to others made one available for penetration, at least symbolically. Accepting money for such activity brought one closer to the status of an enslaved person: others could use your body as they wished. If this hypothesis is correct, it tells us why the Romans placed such a high value on impenetrability and using one's body according to one's own wishes: that was a sign of a free man or woman.

Men

The Latin language provides an essential clue to understanding expectations for men in Roman society. Latin has two words that can be translated as "man." *Homo* is the more generic word used to describe the species, men as opposed to animals. *Vir* is the term used specifically to define men as opposed to women, and sometimes takes on other meanings related to this gender distinction (for example, it is often used to mean husband). This word also forms the core of the word *virtus*, the source for our English word virtue and one of the highest Roman values. In light of these connections, how should we understand the meaning of **virtus**, and what does it tell us about gender expectations in Roman society?

We can start by noting that the best English translation of *virtus* is "manliness" rather than "high moral standards." That definition is helpful in one way: it clarifies that in Roman society virtue was specifically a male-gendered attribute. Males, as we have seen already, were supposed to dominate others; fundamentally *virtus* was concerned with having the power to dominate, both over others (for instance sexually, as

Political Issues: *A Woman Behaving Badly*

The Late Republican woman Fulvia provides a dramatic example of a woman who refused to accept the gender role assigned to her. She was born to an aristocratic family and married three times, to three of the leading politicians in Rome: P. Clodius Pulcher, C. Scribonius Curio, and most famously to Mark Antony, Julius Caesar's second in command and Octavian's chief rival for power in Rome. While she did not fulfill the ideal of the *univira*, each of these marriages did involve political alliances; with her first two husbands she had five children and she supported their political careers. She first came to prominence at the funeral for Clodius who was killed by a violent mob: her public grieving and testimony in court led to exile for the mob leader.

It is in her alliance with Antony that she truly broke the mold. During Antony's absence from Rome, Fulvia was acknowledged as the most powerful person in Rome, influencing decisions in the Senate. The historian Dio even claims that she was effectively the second consul in Rome along with Antony's brother. During this period, she raised armies on behalf of her husband and gave orders to the troops, even wearing a sword and giving the password to the soldiers on night patrol.

All of these were masculine activities in Rome, and the Romans knew it. Plutarch wrote that she was "a woman who took no thought for spinning or housekeeping... but wished to rule a ruler and command a commander." Cicero criticizes her in a different way. In a verbal attack on Antony he labelled Antony the passive partner in his sexual relationship with Fulvia. As the discussion of sexuality in this chapter shows, Cicero manages to hit both Fulvia and Antony at once for their unnatural behavior: Antony should be the active one and Fulvia the passive one in Roman eyes – a confirmation that Cicero both recognized Fulvia's unique power and felt threatened by it.

As well he should have: when Antony and Octavian joined forces, Cicero was one of the first targets for execution. When his head was brought to Fulvia, she is reported to have pulled out his tongue and stabbed it with her hair pins. The story may not be true, but again demonstrates how unnatural Fulvia was: she uses feminine tools not to passively make herself presentable to men, but as an active demonstration of masculine aggression. The Roman writer Velleius Paterculus perhaps summed up Fulvia the best: she had "nothing womanly about her except her body." Had she been a man, Fulvia likely would have been praised for her *virtus*, but as a woman in the Roman world, such a thing could not exist.

described above, or in battle) and over oneself (over one's desires, as Cato insisted above, or over one's fears). It has been argued that a *vir* can be seen as one who is not penetrated, and so the definition is closely linked to sexual activity. *Virtus* was not an inborn quality of all men, but must be earned through action. *Virtus* could even be earned by people other than free men, but since the Romans believed in natural differences between men and women, a woman who was seen to possess *virtus* violated the Roman sex/gender system and risked the consequences of that action.

For the Romans, the military battlefield was a primary venue for displays of *virtus*; the term can often be a synonym for "military bravery." An expectation of every Roman *vir* was to serve in the army when called, so the battlefield was the place where every Roman could try to distinguish themselves from their peers. The battlefield was one of the most public places for displays of power and so was perfectly suited for a performance of manliness that would earn one credit in Roman society. The more powerful side emerges from battle victorious, while penetration by swords, spears, or arrows demonstrates the lack of power exercised by the defeated party. The victors then gain the rewards that go with success – land, money, enslaved persons – and can live as they want as true men. On the other side, the less powerful may be forced to do things they do not want, or even become enslaved, where they have to do what others tell them to do. Those not displaying *virtus* in battle are thus assimilated to women or enslaved persons, even if not actually deprived of free status.

The tombstone of Lucius Scipio Barbatus (c. 337–270 BCE) provides a perfect example of what a Roman man should try to be (*CIL* 6.1285):

> Lucius Cornelius Scipio Barbatus born of his father Gnaeus, a brave and wise *vir* whose handsomeness equaled his *virtus*. He was consul, censor, aedile among you. He captured Taurasia, Cisauna in Samnium, he subjugated all of Lucania and he led away hostages.

The only specific accomplishments listed describe Scipio's success in battle: this is how Romans knew he was a man of *virtus* (they had to take his handsomeness on faith, but this may also speak to his sexual desirability). Barbatus provides the ideal vision for an elite Roman male, but there are reasons to believe that this value applied to all Roman men. As we will discuss in Chapter 9, Roman success in war was built more on the cohesiveness of their soldiers than on superior weaponry or tactics or even leadership, and Roman authors consistently reference the *virtus* of the common Roman soldier as the primary reason for victory in battle. Manliness for the Romans meant demonstrating dominance in as many areas of public and private life as possible.

Conclusions

Just like other elements of human behavior, sexuality cannot be separated from the society in which it exists, and we might conclude by asking about the ways in which Roman attitudes towards gender and sexuality reflect broader elements of Roman society. Some are obvious and still widespread in many parts of the world: the expectation that men should be dominant and active while women should be submissive and passive. Others are more particular to the Romans. Roman society, as we have seen in other chapters, was built on a series of hierarchies, each one based on a different type of dominance and dependence: in politics, in relationships of patronage, in the family, in relationships with foreigners. Sexuality participated in these hierarchies: those who penetrated others demonstrated their ability to dominate. Sexuality thus reinforced the high value placed by the Romans on freedom of activity and bodily integrity. The equation of manliness with freedom affected not only relationships with other free Romans that we have discussed in this chapter, but also their relationship with politics, with the economy, and even with their own households.

Discussion Questions

1. What are the defining features of the Roman sex/gender system? What would you say are the defining features of the sex/gender system of your society? In what ways are sexuality and sexual behavior linked or not linked to societal expectations for individual's behavior?
2. Consider again the Lucretia story from the opening of the chapter. In what ways does it conform to expectations in the Roman sex/gender system? In what ways does it undermine those expectations? What other Roman stories can you recall that support or undermine the system?
3. Compare Lucretia to Claudia and Scipio Barbatus to Catullus. What evidence, if any, do you see of changes in the Roman sex/gender system over time? What changes might be due to Rome's expansion? To getting our information from a literary source vs. an epigraphical source? To individual difference?
4. Toxic masculinity is a term used to describe a notion of manhood defined by violence, sex, status and aggression, with harmful effects to both men and women. Is it appropriate to define masculinity in ancient Rome as toxic? Why or why not?

Further Reading

Caldwell, Lauren (2015). *Roman Girlhood and the Fashioning of Femininity.* Cambridge: Cambridge University Press.
  This book focuses attention on girls as they transition from childhood through marriage. Caldwell investigates the reasons for certain practices, including the emphasis on premarital virginity, and how these practices created women who conformed to the demands of the Roman sex/gender system. Her analysis uses legal texts and medical treatises in addition to the more typical literary sources to provide a fuller understanding of the social forces shaping the lives of girls.

Clarke, John R. (2001). *Looking at Lovemaking Constructions of Sexuality in Roman Art, 100 B.C.–A.D. 250.* Berkeley, CA: University of California Press.
  Clarke offers a detailed study of erotic visual material including an exploration of the attitudes of women and the non-elite. He documents the range of objects with sexually explicit themes and the wide socio-economic range of consumers, as well as the range of sexual activities depicted. He focuses on the contexts in which these objects were found to demonstrate that erotic art was often proudly displayed in owner's homes, a sign of the difference between Roman culture and modern American and European cultures.

Hallett, Judith and Marilyn B. Skinner (Eds) (1997). *Roman Sexualities.* Princeton, NJ: Princeton University Press.
  This volume established Roman notions of sexuality and gender difference as an area of research in its own right, separate from work done on Greece . Essays in the collection focus on literature, history, law, medicine, and political oratory to investigate relationships of power reflected in Roman sexual relationships. Ideas about penetration are explored, both how they operated in Roman society and how they could be upended.

Masterson, Mark, Nancy Sorkin Rabinowitz, and James Robson (Eds) (2014). *Sex in Antiquity: Exploring Gender and Sexuality in the Ancient World*. New York: Routledge.

This collection of essays looks back to previous scholarship on gender and sexuality as well as pointing towards future areas of work. The collection includes essays on Greece and the ancient Near East, allowing for comparison between Roman practices and other major cultures of the Mediterranean. Essays in the collection use a variety of perspectives, both historical and theoretical, allowing readers to see how different approaches contribute to our knowledge of sex and gender.

Strong, Anise K. (2016). *Prostitutes and Matrons in the Roman World*. New York: Cambridge University Press.

Strong compares the figure of the whore to that of a proper Roman matron in order to investigate women's roles in Roman society. She explores the evolution of these stereotypes to argue that the simple binary between bad and good women is not sufficient to explain women's activity in Rome, highlighting the public roles that prostitutes could play in Roman life. She uses visual as well as literary evidence to demonstrate the different ways that erotic imagery could have functioned.

7
Outsiders

The historian Livy tells two stories about how Rome first grew in size. After the death of Remus, Romulus completed the fortifications of his new city and set his mind towards an increase in population. He opened a place of refuge – an *asylum* in Latin – in order to attract people of humble and obscure birth, and a large group of both freemen and enslaved persons "eager for change" answered the call. This step solved the problem of adding manpower to the new city, but, as Livy points out, the life of the new village threatened to be short-lived, since there were no women and therefore no possibility for future generations. The nearby villages were not thrilled by their new neighbors and so refused to allow the Romans to marry any of their women. Livy then tells the story that we discussed at the beginning of Chapter 5: Romulus invited the neighboring Sabine tribe to celebrate a festival in Rome, and then had the Romans kidnap the young women who were present in order to provide wives for themselves. When the Romans made peace both with the women and with their families, they came together with the Sabines to form a single community, with the capital in Rome.

These stories do not seem to reflect well upon the Romans: according to their own account their ancestors included a bunch of cattle thieves and enslaved persons who forced marriage on unwilling women. Like the other legendary stories of early Rome, this story can still open windows into Roman history if we ask the right questions. Why did they choose to preserve this story, and what it might suggest about Roman attitudes towards themselves and others? The story reveals that the Romans portrayed themselves as a people who lacked a common ethnic or genetic core: their origin stories about both males and females emphasized that they were a nation of immigrants, that they were willing and even needed to incorporate foreigners into their state. At the same time, the story of the Sabine women also serves as a reminder that in many instances foreigners were compelled to become part of the Roman

A Social and Cultural History of Republican Rome, First Edition. Eric M. Orlin.
© 2022 John Wiley & Sons, Inc. Published 2022 by John Wiley & Sons, Inc.

state whether they wanted to or not: the choice of incorporation might not rest with the local community. These twin components, of openness and compulsion, are threads that run through the history of the Roman Republic.

Rome and Italy: The Early Republic

Cultural Acceptance

Perhaps the first question to ask about this Roman openness is when did this behavior originate. The foundation stories just narrated and other stories from the royal period give the impression that Rome was open to outside influences from its earliest days, but these sources come from a much later period: Livy lived roughly 700 years after the foundation of Rome. Yet there are numerous other pieces of evidence that support the view that Roman openness goes back to its early history. Early artwork indicates the presence of the multiple Etruscan elements in early Rome: the *fasces*, a bundle of rods tied together and holding an axe that symbolized power, and the *sella curulis* in Rome, a special chair used by Roman magistrates. The temple of Jupiter on the Capitoline hill, the most important temple in Rome, used an Etruscan architectural design with three separate **cellas** (chambers for the gods), and was decorated with architectural terracottas according to Etruscan style. The foundation of the temple was placed in 509 BCE, the same year that the Tarquins – an Etruscan family – were supposedly driven from the city and the Republic founded.

Political change did not mark the end of Roman open-mindedness towards Etruscan culture. Etruscan elements continued to find a home in the city even after Rome had turned the tables. The Etruscans were the source of a special class of priests, known as the ***haruspices***, experts in reading lightning strikes and the entrails of animals to determine the will of the gods. In the middle Republic, the *haruspices* were one of the four main colleges of Roman priests, a remarkable testament to the openness of the Romans. They regularly consulted a group of men classed as outsiders on the most important matter: their relationship with the divine. The Roman absorption of religious practices extended to other communities in Italy besides the Etruscans: the Romans brought numerous gods and goddesses from defeated Italian towns to Rome, built them temples, and worshipped them as part of their own religious system. This feature of incorporating religious practices from defeated communities rather than destroying them has few parallels.

If we ask whether the Roman acceptance of elements from the Etruscans was simple and uncomplicated, the answer is "of course not." A story from the second century BCE demonstrates this point clearly. In 163 BCE, the Romans were conducting an election when an election official suddenly died. The Roman Senate asked the Etruscan *haruspices* for an opinion: the mere fact that the Romans asked a group of foreigners a question about their own elections is a remarkable testament to their position in the center of Roman society. However, when the *haruspices* replied that the elections were invalid, the consul Tiberius Gracchus flew into a rage, saying "shall you, who are Tuscans and barbarians, have the right of the auspices of the Roman people, and be able to be the interpreters of our assemblies?" Despite his anger, the consul was eventually forced to admit that the elections were invalid and to call for new elections: to save face he found different grounds for the do-over and assigned the matter to a group of Roman priests. Cicero, who recounted these events (*On the Nature of the Gods*, 2.4.10), concludes the story by remarking that the events proved the validity "both of our augurs and of the Etruscan *haruspices*." Even in a story where the Etruscans are challenged and identified as foreign, they are recognized as a valid and accepted part of the Roman system.

Similar conclusions emerge from reviewing the presence of Greek culture in Rome. Roman tradition placed the worship of the Greek hero Hercules even prior to the actual founding of Rome. Even if we discount this and similar stories as being legendary, several temple foundations in the early Republic confirm the presence of Greek cults in Rome. Livy records the dedication of a temple to Castor and Pollux dated to the year 484 BCE, and a temple to Apollo in the year 431 BCE in response to a plague. An inscription dating to the sixth or fifth century BCE confirms the Greek nature of Castor and Pollux. It reads *Castorei Podlouqueique qurois* ("To Castor and Pollux, the youths"); "qurois" is a transliteration from the Greek, indicating that the author was thinking in Greek terms even while using Latin letters. We will see that the Roman relationship to Greek culture was complicated, just as with the Etruscans, but the openness to outside cultures at an early date is supported both by archaeological evidence and literary texts.

Political Acceptance

On the political level the questions about openness are more complicated, as they often are when the conversation turns to the incorporation of foreign peoples and not just cultural materials. The Roman conquest of Italy, which proceeded in fits and starts as described in Chapter 2, offers a first opportunity to assess how the Romans treated conquered communities as they built their territorial empire. Over the course of the fifth and fourth centuries BCE, Rome had gradually come to be one of the leading cities in central Italy. Rome's position seems to have been recognized in a treaty between Rome and an alliance of Latin cities: Rome alone was singled out as partner to all of the other cities. In the middle of the fourth century BCE, however, a number of these cities went to war with Rome over their treatment, the so-called Latin Revolt. Rome reconquered them in a war stretching from 341–338 BCE, and needed to settle on a new treaty arrangement.

Livy's account of the settlement of 338 BCE emphasizes that "since the condition of each state was different, the treatment of each should be decided according to its own merit" (8.13–14). Accordingly four individual towns received full Roman citizenship, while a fifth town retained the citizenship status it had held prior to the war. Most of the other cities were given a status that has become known as ***civitas sine suffragio*** (citizenship without the vote). This status gave inhabitants the ability to marry and to trade with Roman citizens, but not public rights such as voting in Roman assemblies. Other cities that had strongly supported the revolt were punished: one city that revolted despite already having Roman citizenship was depopulated and Roman citizens were sent to live there instead, while others lost territory even as the town itself remained intact.

We might pay special attention to a few elements here, since they became part of a pattern repeated on multiple occasions later in Rome's history. First, the Romans did indeed share Roman citizenship with people not born in Rome or indeed living in Rome; while this might not seem unusual today, it was uncommon in the ancient world and marked the Romans as more inclusive than most other ancient states. Not only was Roman citizenship a mark of special status, but it brought practical economic and social advantages, such as the ability to use the Roman legal system if necessary. At the same time, this status might still not be satisfactory to local communities, who were required to follow the Roman lead in foreign affairs and to provide soldiers whenever Rome decided to go to war. Although specific issues might differ from city to city, it is possible to understand why local cities might feel more like oppressed subjects than trusted allies.

At the same time, conquered cities were generally allowed to remain as self-governing entities using their own customs, and they shared both directly and indirectly in Roman military success. With rare exceptions, they maintained their own local government system and their own religious system; divinities from these towns might even be worshipped in Rome, as discussed earlier. Each community, and especially the elite members of that community, was given incentives for cooperating with Rome in the future, in the hopes that they might earn future privileges. For example, a town which possessed citizenship without the vote might eventually gain full citizenship and the right to vote. Elites might earn the opportunity to become important players in Rome, individual soldiers who fought successful wars received a portion of the loot captured in the war, and the city benefited from the increased economic opportunities. The compulsion to become part of the Roman system was balanced by an openness to share its benefits.

The Romans likely employed this system more out of self-interest than benevolence, though the ideology of openness to outsiders may have been important as well. Because control of the local community rested with the local elite, Rome could avoid providing military garrisons or bureaucratic oversight. Rome's expenses for running an empire were thus much lower than other comparable empires: during the Republic only a few thousand Roman soldiers were permanently stationed outside Rome, and not until the second century BCE. This structure, in which communities were tied directly to Rome with a clear stake in her success and with obligations to provide manpower in times of war, became the blueprint for future conquests.

In the settlement of 338 BCE, the Romans also sent out Roman citizens to inhabit several cities in the area as colonies. In subsequent years sending out colonies, either with full citizen rights (the so-called **Roman colonies**) or just with the rights of intermarriage and trade (the so-called **Latin colonies**), became a regular practice. Roman colonies tended to be small in scale: 300 families is the number most often given by the ancient authors. Latin colonies were somewhat larger and families received a small plot of land in exchange for moving and giving up their full Roman citizenship. Unlike European colonial settlements, these Latin colonies were not directly controlled by Rome, but became independent towns, bound only by the same treaty obligations as other Italian towns. The explanation for distinctions between Roman and Italian colonies and the overall impact of colonization on both Romans and Italians is still a matter of discussion, but no one doubts that the presence of Roman colonies in the Italian landscape shaped the development of the peninsula for the next several hundred years.

As a result both of the granting of citizenship status to Italian towns and the founding of Roman colonies, the Romans created a situation where one could be a full Roman citizen even while living outside of Rome. The term "Roman" no longer meant someone of free status who lived in Rome, but now could be applied to numerous people living on the Italian peninsula. Just as it was possible for outsiders to come to Rome and become citizens, so it was possible for citizens to live far from Rome. There is evidence that some of these people took the several days necessary to travel to the city and vote in elections, but many others saw the value of Roman citizenship primarily in the status and privileges it conferred rather than in the ability to participate in the political process. The untethering of citizenship from the city itself is a significant development that had long-term repercussions. The notion of citizenship as a bundle of rights rather than an opportunity (or even an obligation!) to contribute to decision-making for the community is a regular feature of most democratic countries today.

A Test of the System: Hannibal and the Second Punic War

As a consequence of these arrangements, Rome had a supply of manpower both from the city itself and from the various types of citizen bodies scattered across the Italian landscape. This near continual supply of soldiers was one of the strengths of the Roman army through the subsequent years of expansion from central Italy to the rest of the peninsula, a process largely complete by 265 BCE. The real test of the system, however, lay ahead, in the Punic Wars against Carthage. A key component of the Carthaginian general Hannibal's strategy in taking his elephants and his army across the Alps was to detach Italian cities from alliance with Rome: if they saw Rome as an unfair imperial power, they might seize the opportunity to re-establish their autonomy. Hannibal did in fact achieve some success in this regard, particularly after his overwhelming victory in the battle of Cannae in 216 BCE. Several major cities in southern Italy that had only recently been conquered, especially Capua and Tarentum, came over to Hannibal's side. Yet the vast majority of cities in central Italy remained loyal, including many other recently conquered cities, perhaps realizing that they would merely be replacing domination by Rome with that of Carthage. The adherence of these cities to the Roman cause ultimately enabled the Romans to withstand Hannibal's attack, to regain control over the rebellious cities of the south, and eventually to launch a counter invasion of north Africa that brought a successful end to the war. The result of the war proved that the Roman system was

Political Issues: *Roman Colonization, the Bulwark of Empire?*

In a famous passage, Cicero refers to colonies as the *propugnacula imperii* ("bulwarks of empire") and other ancient authors describe them similarly. This interpretation has influenced many interpretations of Roman colonization, but as always we should ask what a member of the Roman elite might have left out of their story.

The evidence does indicate that many Latin colonies were planted in strategically significant locations. Latin colonies tended to be larger than Roman colonies, averaging perhaps 3000 families, enough for a fighting force, and the Latin colonies at Luceria and Venusia did play important roles in the Roman wars against the Samnites, which allowed the Romans to expand southward. Roman colonies, on the other hand, were planted along the coast and closer to Rome in less strategic positions, suggesting that other motivations may have played a larger role in their foundation. Some Latin colonies were also located along the coast, causing scholars to question whether the Romans had a clear organizational plan for determining where to plant colonies and of which type. It has even been suggested that some colonies were intended to benefit one or another Roman politician, and so reflected politics in Rome more than any coherent strategy.

Modern scholars have also suggested that socioeconomic issues played a larger role in colonization than Roman sources acknowledge. Most often it was propertyless Romans who became colonists: they would receive a small plot of land as a citizen in the new colony. Owning land was a status marker in the ancient world and for many families working a farm offered a better economic opportunity than being an unskilled laborer in the city of Rome, so this was a significant incentive. Persuading poorer inhabitants of the city to move solved a social welfare problem for the Romans, since they did not have a public system for feeding the poor until the end of the Republic. Since those who owned land made up the bulk of the Roman army, creating new landowners also facilitated military recruitment.

Recent studies have also been reassessing the impact of the Roman colonies on Italy. Despite differences between Roman colonization and European colonialism, post-colonial research has proved useful in thinking about the Roman world. At one time it was thought that colonies served to model Rome in miniature and thus functioned to spread Roman culture throughout the Italian peninsula. Archaeological research, however, has revealed that significant differences existed between the colonies and Rome and even between the colonies themselves, and also demonstrated that the interactions between colonists and local populations were considerably more complex. Certainly the original colonists had grown up in Rome and so used Roman legal, social, and economic customs, while the people living around them generally used customs that differed to varying degrees, but over time contact with each other made these differences less noticeable. Whatever the nature of the specific interactions, colonies ended up playing a central role in the exchange of ideas throughout the Italian peninsula.

working: Italian communities felt sufficiently welcome in the Roman project that they continued to support Rome even when given a real choice.

The Impact of Expansion

The Roman success in the Second Punic War, and in the multiple campaigns in the East over the first 25 years of the second century raises another set of questions: how did these conquests affect Roman attitudes about openness? These campaigns brought with them a massive increase in the territory effectively controlled by the Roman state, and thus in the peoples and cultures with whom the Romans engaged. People living in what we now call Spain, Africa, Greece, Egypt, and the Middle East became part of the regular circle of Roman concerns. Like the Italians, these people spoke a variety of languages and possessed different customs, religious and otherwise. Did the distance to these places make a difference in how the Romans perceived and treated them?

Working with Sources
The Color of Ancient Art

We might at first sight think that visual evidence provides the most helpful way to understand what Romans thought about other peoples, but when scholars explore this material, the picture turns out to be much more complicated. Part of the issue is that sculpture portraits and painted vases depend on the vision and skill of the artist and depict what the person paying for them wants, which may or may not be an accurate reflection of reality.

Most people are familiar with pristine white figures that we often see in museums, but we know that the Romans (and Greeks) used lots of color in their portraits. Marble of different colors might be used to create a dramatic look and eyes could be inlaid with gemstones; the use of precious materials also served as a demonstration of the patron's wealth. Sculptures were painted using many different colors; since many sculptures would be viewed from a distance, paint would have made details of clothing or armor more visible as well as making the sculpture more attractive (**Figure 7.1**). Skin tones were painted in a variety of colors, suggesting that Roman artists and patrons acknowledged the many different physical appearances of people in the Roman community. Although most of this paint has faded over the past 2000 years, scholars have been aware of the polychrome nature of ancient art for several hundred years. Unfortunately, the ideology of white supremacy led many scholars and others to ignore or deliberately suppress this knowledge, using the supposedly white sculptures of antiquity to reinforce the racist claim that white skin is a sign of beauty and that colored skin is inferior.

Scholars can still use these images to gain an understanding of how the Romans perceived other people. Some images present figures that are clearly intended to be foreigners, using artistic conventions related to their physical appearance or their clothing. For instance, Persians are frequently depicted wearing long pants and a distinctive style of cap, the kind of clothing that Plautus joked about in his play, while freedmen of any ethnic group wore a different style of cap as a sign that they had been restored to free status. Artists and writers developed stock depictions of foreigners, using characteristics that they decided were typical for different peoples: red-haired Gauls, curly-haired Spaniards, and dark-skinned Africans. Visual attempts to represent other people may indicate curiosity, but there is little in the ancient material to suggest that they were intended to mock the foreigners. If modern observers see these images as racist caricatures, that perhaps says more about attitudes embedded in our own society than the Romans.

Figure 7.1 Marble head of a deity wearing a Dionysiac headband. 1st c. CE. Metropolitan Museum of Art, NY. The eyes, lips, and headband show red pigment, and the hair retains traces of gilding.

The conquest may also have changed Roman attitudes towards the people living on the Italian peninsula. They had provided crucial manpower to Roman armies and deserved significant credit for the Roman success, and their greater geographical proximity may have allowed for greater cultural links. Did the conquest of distant places change the Roman attitudes towards these communities, for better or for worse? These are crucial questions to consider in the wake of Roman overseas expansion, and evidence from both texts and material cultures is helpful in thinking about the answers.

Outsiders Across the Seas

Roman involvement with Greek culture goes back to the early Republic, but the intensity of their engagement increased as they expanded their territorial holdings to include Greece. Some Romans such as Cato the Elder did express concern about the Roman relationship with Greek culture, but the Romans continued to absorb elements of Greek culture throughout this period. Several examples, however, demonstrate a slight shift as the Romans began to draw distinctions between Greek and Roman culture and to identify what they might have considered to be a Roman practice.

The most celebrated event of the early second century in Rome, a religious incident involving the Greek god of wine, offers a prime example. In 186 BCE, the Senate cracked down on the cult of Bacchus in response to rumors about the behavior of worshippers. This action has often been viewed as an early Roman example of intolerance and hostility to a foreign culture, but the official Senatorial response, preserved on a bronze inscription found in southern Italy clarifies the situation (see

Exploring Culture: *Cato the Elder*

Marcius Porcius Cato (234–149 BCE), also known as Cato the Elder to distinguish him from his great-grandson, offers us a fascinating glimpse of the Roman response to Greek culture. Cato was a man at the very heart of the Roman ruling elite: he was elected censor, Rome's highest office, in 184 BCE and continued to be one of leading men in the state for the remaining 35 years of his life. He also cultivated a public persona as a protector of traditional Roman practices, and so his behavior in the period when Rome transformed herself into the dominant Mediterranean power provides an illuminating example of Roman behavior.

In public, Cato presented himself as scornful of Greek culture. For instance, Plutarch's biography of Cato records that Cato refused to give a speech in Greek even in Athens, saying that "on the whole he thought the words of the Greeks were born on their lips, but those of the Romans in their hearts" (Ch. 12). Plutarch also noted that Cato "regarded all Greek culture and training with scorn, out of patriotic rivalry. Cato says, for instance, that Socrates was a dangerous babbler... [and] he made fun of the school of Isocrates, declaring that Isocrates' pupils kept on studying with him till they were old men..." (Ch. 23). These anecdotes suggest unease, at least, with Greek intrusions into the Roman world.

> Other anecdotes suggest an alternative view. Plutarch noted that Cato could have delivered his speech in Greek if he had wanted, and in another passage reported that Cato's writings were "moderately embellished with Greek sentiments and stories, and many literal translations from the Greek have found a place among his maxims and proverbs" (Ch. 2). Cato's willingness to include Greek in his writing suggests that he did not in fact mock *all* of Greek culture, but found many items of value that he felt worth sharing with his Roman audience. He may have genuinely found some aspects of Greek culture objectionable, but he also may have wanted to make a public scene in order to draw attention to the contrasts. For example, Romans at this time seem to have valued direct public speaking rather than the grandiose style that was associated with the Greeks: the punchline of the story about the speech in Athens is that the Athenians were "astonished" at the speed and force of his speech in Latin. Cato could thus highlight a distinction between Greek and Roman oratory, while also suggesting ways that Roman oratory might in fact be superior.
>
> Cato's attitude thus appears as more complex. Where Roman practices were more useful towards that goal, he used them, but he showed a willingness to use Greek culture wherever he found it useful. In keeping with Roman practice, he found it important to maintain publicly that the custom of the ancestors was best, but all evidence points to Cato being a change-maker as well.

Working with Sources textbox, Chapter 8). The decree placed the cult of Bacchus under governmental control, just as other Roman religious practices had to conform to Roman practice, but there was no effort to ban it. The Senate formally allowed the worship of this foreign god, but according to Roman behavioral norms, just as we saw that the worship of Castor and Pollux had been accepted in the fifth century BCE.

Romans also showed themselves willing to adapt Greek literary forms. Roman comedy performed at public religious festivals from the 190s to the 160s BCE was based on Greek models (see further in Chapter 13.) Even later in the second century BCE, an embassy of three Greek philosophers came to Rome and delivered a number of lectures to large groups of young people. While some Romans may have grumbled about their presence, the Romans made no effort to ban the teaching of philosophy in Rome, and by the middle of the first century BCE the main schools of Greek philosophy had many followers in Rome. The Romans seem to have become more aware of differences between their own culture and Greek culture throughout the second century BCE, but they also clearly continued to incorporate elements of Greek culture just as they had in earlier periods.

A similar approach can be seen elsewhere as the Romans continued to expand their empire and their contacts with other cultures. The city of Carthage in north Africa offers a good example. Hannibal's invasion of Italy in 218 BCE had brought a military enemy to the gates of Rome, so we might expect the Romans to have some resentment towards them. While the peace treaties imposed on Carthage were one-sided in Rome's favor, there are not many signs of a long-lasting hatred on the Roman side. For example, within 15 years of the end of the war with Hannibal, Plautus wrote a comedy called the *Poenulus* ("Little Carthaginian") in which the main characters are Carthaginian. These characters drive the action just as a Greek or Roman character drives the plot of other plays, and the Carthaginian characters are generally presented sympathetically. The play marks the Carthaginian characters as different from Romans: one character speaks a few lines in Carthaginian and there are some stereotyped jokes about wardrobe. Overall the play seems to humanize the Carthaginian characters rather than presenting them as caricatures or lifelong enemies of Rome. Even as Roman authors suggested differences between themselves and others, military and political rivalry does not seem to have caused a closing of the Roman mind.

The Roman reaction to other peoples in Africa mirrors their response to the people of Carthage. The comic playwright Terence was apparently born in Africa, as suggested by his cognomen *Afer*; an ancient biography reports that he had a "dark complexion" (**Figure 7.2**). Like the Greek Polybius who came to Rome at the same time, Terence was accepted into the highest circles of Roman society. The family of the Scipios, conquerors of Carthage, even gave him a commission for a performance at the funeral games of Aemilius Paullus, victor in the war over Macedonia. The Romans continued to build a multi-ethnic community even as they ventured further overseas and conquered more territory.

By the first century BCE, Rome was home to thousands of people born outside Italy, let alone the city of Rome. The term "Roman" had never comprised a single ethnic group, but now it included people from all over the Mediterranean. Some had voluntarily moved there while others had been brought forcibly as enslaved persons. As discussed elsewhere, enslaved persons became full Roman citizens if

Figure 7.2 Folio 2r, from Vat. Lat. 3868, with portrait of Terence, ninth century CE. Vatican Library, Rome.

Figure 7.3 Terracotta vase from Etruria, fourth century BCE. Metropolitan Museum of Art, NY. The short curly hair, broad nose, and fleshy lips identify him as a Black African.

restored to free status, such that people from all over the Mediterranean and of many different physical appearances were included in the Roman citizen body. It is clear that the Romans noted the physical differences between themselves and others. For instance, the Romans noted the dark skin, curly hair, and thick lips of a people they called "Aethiopians," but drinking cups with images that match this description suggest primarily a Roman fascination with bodies different from their own (**Figure 7.3**). The Romans do not seem to have singled out skin color as a reason for treating people differently, and unlike in modern racist discourse there is no indication that the Romans ascribed negative traits to these physical features. One reason for the Roman approach may be that ancient writers often associated differences among peoples with their surrounding environment: people in the north were flabby and of pale complexion because the cold and wet made them sluggish, just as people to the south had strong bodies in order to withstand the heat of their climate. The story of Rome's founding suggests an ideology that Rome built her strength by incorporating outsiders into the state, and the surviving evidence suggests that this openness extended to people living overseas as well as in Italy.

Key Debates: *Race in Ancient Rome?*

Scholars in recent years have paid increasing attention to issues of race in antiquity. One central question has been whether it is appropriate to speak of "race" as a concept in antiquity, or whether race is a modern concept that has no parallel in the ancient world. Much of the answer depends on how one defines the word "race."

Race is not a biological difference, but a category created by humans designed to create a semi-permanent hierarchy of people. The modern notion of race was created in the seventeenth century, using pseudoscience such as the shape of the brain to divide human beings into four or sometimes five groups. Although biologists today have noted that there are many legitimate ways in which one could classify people, some of which would put Swedes and Italians in the same group as Nigerians, the seventeenth century writers chose criteria that separated humans according to skin color. Conveniently for European colonialists, they deemed the other groups inferior to whites, thereby offering a justification for conquest and enslavement. Even skin color was not always sufficient: in the United States, many states had a "one-drop" rule, in which persons with one drop of Black blood would be labeled as Black for racial purposes. Thus a person could have a light skin color but if they were determined to have a Black ancestor they would be categorized as Black for the purposes of discrimination. Discrimination, not biology, lies at the heart of the choice to focus on brain shape or skin color or blood to identify one's race.

Race in this sense did not exist in the ancient world. The Romans did notice the existence of people with different appearances: a glance at Roman literary texts or Roman painted objects reveals a great variety of skin color. There are dark-skinned Aethiopians, but also neighboring Egyptians who are frequently depicted with a lighter skin tone. The Roman historian Tacitus speaks of two groups inhabiting Britain in 100 CE: red-haired Caledonians of German origin and "the colored faces of the Silures with their curly hair" that he believes come from Spain. Even in Italy our texts give evidence of a wide variety of physical characteristics. Many of these people were citizens of Rome. We cannot sort the inhabitants of the Rome into groups based on skin color alone. Any attempt to label the ancient Romans as "white" in opposition to the Aethiopians or other groups is a misguided result of applying modern notions of race into the Roman world.

While the Romans made little attempt to sort humans into categories for the purposes of oppression, Benjamin Isaac has suggested that the Romans held *proto-racist* views. He defines the term as attributing "common characteristics [to people] considered to be unalterable because they are determined by external factors or heredity" and he argues that by ascribing hereditary characteristics to groups the Romans may have contributed to the development of modern racism. For instance, Roman authors made claims that all Britons had certain qualities or all Greeks certain other qualities. The Roman attitude may not be far from the claims that all Africans, and by extension all Black people, had certain inferior qualities that justified their enslavement, the ideology that supported slavery in the United States. Even if race did not exist in the ancient world, understanding the forms of oppression from that period can help us better understand these concepts when they appear in our own world.

Outsiders at Home: The Italians

If Roman expansion saw them continue to incorporate outsiders from the broader Mediterranean into their community, it created a new set of challenges for their relationship with people living closer to home. The loyalty of Italians who did not possess full citizenship had been crucial to the Roman success in building their empire, but the inequalities in the system became much more apparent now that the scale of potential benefits had increased dramatically with the wealth now coming into Rome. A pressing question thus concerned whether the rewards of empire should be distributed differently in light of these changed circumstances.

Two incidents from the early second century BCE might lead us to question whether the Romans had truly incorporated the Italians into their enterprise. In 177 BCE, cities in Italy with the Latin status, i.e. one step below full citizenship, made an appeal to the Roman Senate: too many of their inhabitants were moving to Rome in an effort to gain full Roman citizenship. As a result, these towns were struggling and they claimed they would soon be unable to provide enough soldiers to the Roman army. In the same year Livy reports that one of the Roman generals gave victory bonuses to Italian soldiers in his army that were half as large as those to full Roman citizens. These episodes suggest that both the Romans and the Italian communities continued to see a distinction between the two. The Romans did not see the Italians as fully equal and the Latin communities did not ask for full citizen status for all of their residents.

At the same time, it is important to remember that these communities were run by local elites and these people may have been content enough with the economic benefits they received as wealth from conquest flowed into the peninsula. They may have been happier to be powerful leaders of their own smaller communities rather than minor figures in the larger Roman world: agitating for full inclusion may not have been in their personal interest. The evidence suggests that the poorer members of these communities, those who made up the bulk of the soldiers sent to Rome, felt differently. They were not receiving an equal share of the benefits, and many apparently felt that they could do better by moving to Rome, obtaining full Roman citizenship, and gaining a larger share of the pie. These episodes thus reveal divisions starting to appear, as the desires of those who wanted to move to Rome undermined the position of Italian elites and Romans alike. The unequal distribution of resources became a source of tension, and the privileges of full Roman citizenship were becoming more apparent.

By the end of the second century BCE, unequal treatment by the Romans had become a problem for Italian elites as well. In the 170s, the censor Fulvius Flaccus stole the roof tiles from the sanctuary of Hera at Croton in southern Italy, one of the most famous buildings in the region, for use in a temple in Rome. This new temple would have been the first building in Rome with a marble roof, and so would have enhanced both Rome's appearance and Fulvius' prestige. There was an outcry about the theft in the Senate in Rome and Fulvius was forced to return the tiles, but no one could be found who knew how to replace the tiles on the roof. Fulvius left the stolen tiles stacked by the side of the temple, which would have served as a constant reminder to visitors of the high-handed behavior of a Roman magistrate. Later in the century, a consul arriving in an Italian town demanded that the men's baths be cleared out and cleaned so that his wife could use them. When the wife declared that it took too long for the baths to be ready and that they still were not clean, the Roman consul had the local magistrate stripped naked, tied to a post in the middle of town, and whipped. These stories may have been merely instances of bad behavior by individual Roman magistrates, but they stood as examples of compulsion that threatened to outweigh the benefits of openness. Perhaps the Romans no longer looked at the Italians as partners, even partners on an unequal basis, and the Italian elites may similarly have no longer viewed the Romans as a reliable source of privilege.

The legal treatment of Italian cities by the Romans adds another layer to our discussion. In discussing the incident of the Bacchanalia earlier, we noted that the Romans did not actually ban the worship of this Greek god, but insisted that the worship conform to Roman customs. Significantly, the Senate's decree about the worship of Bacchus seems to have applied not only to Rome and Roman colonies, areas that were clearly subject to the Senate's jurisdiction, but they also seem to have applied to the rest of Italy. In doing so, they represented an intrusion into the self-government of local Italian towns, who were no longer allowed to worship Bacchus in the way they chose. In a similar fashion, Rome set herself up as the judge in disputes between two Italian towns on several occasions, willing to intervene in the internal affairs of Italian cities as if the people involved were Roman. It is hard to determine whether the local communities resented these intrusions or saw them as a sign of closer integration into the Roman community. Even as these incidents may have blurred the line between Roman and Italian, however, they reinforced the notion that those living in Rome were superior to those living elsewhere.

The evidence from archaeology also reveals a blurring of the lines between Roman and Italian. Excavations and finds from numerous sites have revealed the existence of common cultural elements by the second century BCE among the peoples living in Italy, whether we label a city Roman, or Italian, or Greek. At the level of daily life – food, clothing, houseware – it becomes more difficult to observe clear distinctions between these cultures, at least in the items preserved in the material record. Perhaps in response, there are some signs that the Romans made extraordinary efforts to insist upon some distinctions between themselves and the others living on the peninsula. Although stone theaters had long been known in Greece and had begun to appear in the Italian countryside in the second century BCE, the Romans actively objected to constructing a permanent stone theater in Rome. In fact, in 154 BCE Scipio actually demolished a stone theater that had already been partially completed. The reasons are not entirely clear, for the Romans had been staging theater in the city for hundreds of years, and the process of assembling and disassembling wooden theaters must have been time-consuming and expensive. The city of Rome was in fact quite late to have a permanent stone theater or amphitheater. While Pompeii had built its earliest stone theater in the early second century BCE, Rome's first stone theater was completed only in 55 BCE. Similarly, the amphitheater in Pompeii (**Figure 7.4**), the oldest surviving amphitheater in the Roman world, dates

Figure 7.4 Amphitheater, Pompeii, circa 70 BCE.

from around 70 BCE, while the Colosseum – the icon of the Roman empire – was not built for another 150 years. The fact that the buildings for which the Romans are best known actually originated elsewhere in Italy provides an important reminder that the outsiders brought as many benefits to the Romans as the Romans brought to them.

While the Romans may have been insistent on maintaining some distinction between Roman and Italian, to other people in the ancient world, this distinction mattered less, as a particularly horrifying example can illustrate. In 88 BCE the Romans had become entangled in a dispute in western Asia Minor between the kingdoms of Bithynia and Pontus. The Romans on the scene made matters worse by encouraging Bithynia to attack Pontus. Feeling that he could not get fair treatment, Mithridates, the king of Pontus, encouraged officials throughout his kingdom to orchestrate a massacre of all the Romans and Italians in their towns. On the given day at least 80 000 men, women, and children were killed throughout the kingdom. The historian Appian in recording these events mentions several times that "all who were of Italian blood" were targets of this attack, not merely the Romans. As far as Mithridates was concerned, a Roman and an Italian were the same thing and were equally guilty in his eyes.

People living in Italy at the time would have been surprised by this conclusion, because in 88 BCE a war was raging between Italian communities and Rome over this very question. The tensions had risen to the point where a significant number of Italian communities felt that their relationship with Rome was irreparably broken. The outsiders had clearly not been incorporated and they launched a war in response, the so-called **Social War** (from the Latin word *socii*, or "allies"). Scholars debate whether the aims of the Italians were to set up a federal state completely independent of Rome or whether they were simply demanding greater inclusion and greater rights within the Roman state, and different cities likely had different aims. To fight the war, a confederacy was created with a capital at Corfinium, renamed as "Italia," as indicated on the coins minted by the alliance (**Figure 7.5**). This war became more like a civil war than anything else, as soldiers who had fought alongside each other for years now found themselves on opposite sides of the battlefield. The fighting was among the most severe the Romans encountered, because the Italians had trained

Figure 7.5 Silver Denarius minted by the Marsic Confederation, 90–88 BC. The obverse presents an image of Italia, while the reverse shows eight soliders pointing swords at a pig held by a boy.

with the Romans and so their forces were similar to the Romans in most aspects. In the end, the only way the Romans were able to quell the revolt was by granting citizenship to the Italians.

While the end of the Social War marks the political acceptance of the Italian communities into the Roman state, there are still questions to be asked. After all, the Romans had only grudgingly, at the point of a sword, granted citizenship. On the one hand, by the end of the war, the vast majority of former Italian allies had been granted Roman citizenship, with full rights to vote, trade, and even run for office. On the other hand, the Romans dragged their heels in enrolling the new citizens on to the voting rolls, and even then attempted to pack the Italians into only a handful of voting groups in order to limit their influence; gerrymandering is not a modern phenomenon. It took nearly 50 years for Italians to begin to make significant inroads politically in the Roman state, suggesting that the Romans were less than open in their welcome of the new citizens. Whether from a desire not to share the increased revenues coming into the Roman state from their empire, a world-view changed by contact with a much wider world, or simply the disdain that comes from living in close proximity, the Romans treated most of Italy as foreigners and as inferior for almost all of this period.

In many ways, the "Italian question" became caught up in the conflicts of the Late Republic. Not only did Romans fight Italians during the Social War, but Sulla's forces fought first against Marius and then against Senatorial armies in the 80s: Roman fought against Roman. In the aftermath, Sulla posted names of Romans who could be killed with impunity: labelling them as "enemies" he effectively declared that those people were not Roman and thus no longer protected by the Roman legal processes. These problems recurred over the course of the next 50 years: Caesar and Pompey amassed great armies to fight each other, and in the aftermath of Caesar's assassination, the Senate and Caesar's heirs launched attacks on each other, each representing themselves as the "true Romans." In a time of civil war, the question of who counted as Roman and who did not could only be resolved through military means.

The clearest illustration of the shifting nature of the definition comes from Octavian and Antony. These two men joined forces to defeat the forces of Caesar's assassins, declaring that they were true Romans defending the state from Brutus who had committed treason by killing a legitimately elected leader. Later, when conflict arose between Octavian and Antony, Octavian devoted much of his public relations effort toward painting a picture of Antony as non-Roman, and Antony responded in kind. These efforts may have had some impact on public opinion, but in the end it was Octavian's military victory that allowed his definition to become decisive.

The Augustan Aftermath

In one of the most important studies of Roman history, Sir Ronald Syme observed that the victory of Octavian (later Augustus) in the civil wars "may, in a certain sense, be regarded as a triumph of Italy over Rome." As a result of Augustus' military conquest, leading members of the Italian municipalities – the Italian bourgeoisie as Syme calls them – became leading players in Rome. The question of whether Italian communities should be fully integrated into the Roman state was resolved decisively in favor of them. Yet local identities remained important: members of these communities could feel that they had citizenship in two places, not just one. Distinctions between different parts of Italy did not fade away: it is impossible to speak of Italy as a unified country in the modern sense of the word until the nineteenth century, and even today local identities remain strong in Italy. However, the peninsula did eventually take on a special status among the territories of the Roman empire: just as Rome was divided into 14 administrative districts for easier governance, Italy was divided into 11 regions, unlike the overseas provinces, which were ruled as a single unit by a provincial governor. The story of how both Italy and the provinces fared under the Empire belongs to a different book, but Augustus reaffirmed the Roman willingness and ability to incorporate outsiders into the state, which remained a central tenet of Roman behavior until the end of the Empire.

Conclusion

Contact with other peoples is an essential part of any community's history, and how they choose to respond to these others often reveals their core values. The Romans also held complicated feelings toward outsiders. On the one hand they often prided themselves on their openness to foreigners, and indeed their record can be compared favorably to most other ancient and some modern communities. On the other hand, they were not always fully accepting of those foreigners and could be subject to fits of xenophobia and stereotyping just as in any other society.

Perhaps the most important result of increasing encounters with these outsiders was that it helped the Romans better understand themselves. The contrasts between their own traditions and customs and those of the conquered people enabled them to see what was unique in their own behavior. States in the ancient world did not grant citizenship to other peoples and incorporate features of their culture as much as the Romans did. The prominence of the incorporated outsider image in later Roman texts suggests that the Romans began to recognize this fact and to promote it as a part of their identity. Thus, while not everyone might take pride in deriving their origins from the men of "humble and low birth" that Livy described, for the Romans it was a mark of distinction that even their ancestors came from all over central Italy. For us, as non-Romans ourselves, it might be easier than it was for the Romans to identify how they differed from other cultures, and for us just as for the Romans, it is the encounter with people unlike us – in our case perhaps the Romans themselves – that help us see ourselves more clearly.

Discussion Questions

1. What were the benefits and drawbacks to Roman society of incorporating outsiders within their society? What were the benefits and drawbacks to the Italians and other communities who were brought into the Roman system? How do these benefits and drawbacks compare to communities in our own day?
2. What unique aspects of their own society were the Romans able to see more clearly only after their encounter with other cultures? What unique aspects of your own culture (however you choose to define it) are you able to see more clearly by looking at others?
3. The Romans were able to incorporate religious elements because their system was polytheistic: they believed in more than one god. To what extent do the monotheistic religions of the modern world make the Roman style of openness more difficult?
4. In what ways, if any, did Roman conquest and the acquisition of a territorial empire change Roman attitudes towards openness on a cultural and/or political level? Does the acquisition of empire make this kind of change inevitable?

Further Reading

Dench, Emma (1995). *From Barbarians to New Men: Greek, Roman, and Modern Perceptions of Peoples of the Central Apennines*. Oxford: Oxford University Press.
   While the specific focus of this study is on the non-Roman people of central Italy, Dench's innovative study analyzes the development of a specifically Roman identity that was built out of the ideology of incorporating foreigners. She uses both literary and archaeological evidence to explore both the Roman perceptions and these communities' own perceptions of themselves.

Gruen, Erich S. (2010). *Rethinking the Other in Antiquity*. Princeton, NJ: Princeton University Press.

This book uses artwork as well as texts from the ancient world, including Jewish authors alongside Greek and Roman, to argue that people often sought connection with other cultures rather than simply drawing contrast. Gruen shows how ancient peoples often offered praise for the accomplishments of other societies and used myths and legends to connect themselves to those they admired. He thus sees the relationship between different peoples of the ancient world as more complex and intertwined rather than a simple opposition.

Kennedy, Rebecca Futo, et al. (2013). *Race and Ethnicity in the Classical World: An Anthology of Primary Sources in Translation*. Indianapolis, IN: Hackett.

This sourcebook contains translated excerpts from a wide variety of both Greek and Roman authors, illustrating differences between themselves and other cultures. Part I of the book focuses on the explanations that ancient authors offered for these differences, including genealogy and the environment (nature and nurture). Part II tours the ancient world, including northern Africa, Persia, India, Judea, Arabia, Germany, and Gaul, offering descriptions of local customs including sex and marriage, food, and clothing.

McCoskey, Denise (2012). *Race: Antiquity and Its Legacy (Ancients and Moderns)*. Oxford: Oxford University Press.

McCoskey tackles the thorny question of how different societies throughout history have thought about race. She argues that Romans did not use skin color as the basis for creating categories and that assumptions about race need to take into account factors other than physical appearance or supposed biological traits.

Padilla Peralta, Dan-el (2015). "Barbarians Inside the Gate, Parts I and II." Eidolon. https://eidolon.pub/barbarians-inside-the-gate-part-i-c175057b340f.

Padilla Peralta explicitly compares Roman attitudes towards foreigners with twenty-first century American attitudes towards immigrants. He argues that the Roman attitude was not as welcoming as many (including the author of this textbook) assume and suggests another way of using Roman history to think about the modern world.

8
Religion

Christian writers of the Roman Empire constantly poked fun at the religion of the Romans: too many gods, too many superstitions, too many stories in which the gods themselves behave in irresponsible and immoral ways. In a famous example, the Christian theologian Augustine (354–430 CE) complained that one god was not even enough for the Romans to guard a simple door, but they needed separate gods for the doors, the hinge, and the threshold. The Romans also took it as a sign of divine favor whether or not chickens ate their food greedily, or whether birds flew into a prescribed area of the sky at a certain moment. To most people today, this behavior looks superstitious rather than something we would call "religious."

The Romans, however, took their claim to be the most religious of all the peoples of the ancient Mediterranean world seriously. They did not hesitate to claim that their success in building an empire was a direct result of the favor of the gods for their religiosity. In 193 BCE, a Roman official sent a letter to the people of the Greek city of Teos stating that people can judge how much piety the Romans show to the gods from the favor that the Romans have received from them. The Romans clearly understood their behavior to be religious, and indeed they saw later Christian behavior as superstitious.

These competing views immediately present a central question: what is religion, or what does it mean to be religious? It is easy for most of us to agree with Augustine, because most Americans and Europeans were raised in traditions rooted in monotheism, the belief in only one god. A **polytheistic** tradition, one in which multiple gods are worshipped at the same time, may answer these questions differently. This

A Social and Cultural History of Republican Rome, First Edition. Eric M. Orlin.
© 2022 John Wiley & Sons, Inc. Published 2022 by John Wiley & Sons, Inc.

chapter will engage first in a consideration of what constitutes religious behavior and then explore evidence for religious behavior on the part of the Romans.

What Is Roman Religion?

Defining *Religio*

The word "religion" is surprisingly difficult to define. Though many people often associate the idea in terms of a set of beliefs and moral behavior, such a definition works best for the three best-known monotheistic traditions: Christianity, Islam, and Judaism. It fails to account for other traditions that are generally recognized as falling within the category of religion or for the varieties of religious activity across both space and time. Some scholars have therefore argued that religion should be described in psychological terms to describe actions that enable individuals to make sense of the world around them, while others have seen it as an important sociological force holding societies together. Religion functioned in all of these ways for the Romans. At the same time, these definitions often do not reveal what is distinctive about *religious* behavior in relation to other types of behavior, such as philosophical, social, or cultural.

Belief in the existence of a supranatural power seems to be the one factor common to all religious traditions. Whether this power is believed to lie in a single being or multiple entities, the existence of this power is widely accepted by the members of the society. Human beings, both as individuals and as a community, have often found it necessary to develop means of relating to this invisible, unprovable, but superpowerful reality. Indeed, the modern word religion is derived from the word *religio*, which seems to be connected to the Latin word meaning "to tie back." In its very origins the word may indicate the need for humans to tie their behavior to the extraordinarily powerful beings that are believed to exist in our world.

A definition along these lines downplays the importance of belief in a religious system: the specific beliefs people hold about their god(s) may not be as important as the simple fact of believing in a supranatural power. In many modern religions, specific beliefs *do* play a central role in defining the religious group: whether or not one believes that a carpenter from Nazareth was the son of God is a defining characteristic of a Christian. While belief was also important to the Romans, they did not have a specific dogma or creed. Rather the Romans believed that the gods were a constant presence in their daily lives and had the capability to do whatever they wanted, whenever they wanted. The story about the sacred chickens provides a good example. Although the Romans seem to have trained these chickens to eat greedily by starving them prior to the attempt to obtain a good omen, this training was irrelevant to the Romans. They believed that the gods had the ability to make the birds do as the gods wanted, including rejecting the food even if the birds were hungry. A strong belief in the power of the gods was necessary for a Roman.

Key Debate: *What Personal Religious Beliefs Did People Hold in Ancient Rome?*

Attempting to understand the mindset of people who lived two thousand years ago is an almost impossible task, one that has led most scholars to concentrate on the *behavior* involved in Roman religion as something that can be determined from the texts and remains, rather than on *belief*, which leaves few remains. Instead, scholars have attempted to develop models that might explain the visible behavior. The most prominent model for ancient Greek and Roman religion is known as the polis-religion model, derived from the work of Christiane Sourvinou-Inwood, who argued that religious activity was "embedded" in the *polis* ("city-state"). As she wrote, "the *polis* anchored, legitimated, and mediated all religious activity." In other words, religious activity can only be understood in the context of the city-state and its structures. Because Rome during the Republic shared many structural similarities with Greek city-states, this model has often been employed in regard to Roman Republican religion as well.

One of the critiques that have been raised in regard to this model is the reluctance to address matters of personal belief, and more recent work has tried to confront this issue. One study suggested that by the Late Republic there existed something like a "marketplace" in the sphere of religion, where individuals had some degree of freedom to choose the cults in which they wanted to participate. The polis-religion model has some room to accommodate this notion, for it does not assume that every individual will behave in exactly the same way towards state-sanctioned cults, but it does assume that state-sanctioned cults will provide the outlet for religious behavior.

Increasingly, attention has been paid to what has been labelled as "lived experience," where the evidence comes from votive offerings or inscriptions to divinities who are not prominent in the literary or state records. Figurines to Attis are one example, as are inscriptions to the god Faunus, which reveal a much deeper commitment to this god than the written sources would have us believe. The religious behavior of the household has become a particular focus of study; while Roman households were very much a part of the hierarchy of the state, the variance in practice among households has been seen to reveal more personal choices; the presence or absence of votives or household shrines offers clues as to what the residents of that house saw as important. While the polis-religion model has been extremely useful in clarifying many aspects of ancient religion, in other areas a new model seems necessary.

Ultimately the religious beliefs of a people long since dead are probably unrecoverable. On the one hand, it seems unlikely that people in the Roman Republic had a separate "religious identity": where people today might identify as Jewish, Muslim, or Christian, a person then might simply have identified as "Roman," simultaneously a civic and religious identity. However, the connection between these two identities should not allow us to assume that they did not have religious beliefs or to diminish those beliefs.

Because of this belief, the Romans felt it necessary to maintain proper relationships at all times with the gods, which they called the *pax deorum* ("peace with the gods"). The Romans felt that proper religious action was the key to success on this point: if they properly performed the rituals in honor of the gods, the gods would then provide them with the benefits they desired. These benefits might be victory in battle, a good harvest, a safe journey, or a return to good health. To some degree Romans believed that when they performed a rite, they were making a contract with the gods. The formula *do ut des*, "I give so that you may give," encapsulates this attitude: the Roman gave the sacrifice and the god was expected to give the requested item in exchange.

Of course, the Romans did not believe that they could control the supranatural powers: gods cannot be forced to act in certain ways. Rather, the Romans believed that if they made the proper request, the gods always responded in the affirmative. In any situation where the request was not granted, the Romans concluded that they must have made an error in performing the ceremony. Because they had not carried out their obligations properly, gods and goddesses were under no obligation to respond. Sacrifice (**Figure 8.1**) was the primary ritual that the Romans used to communicate with the divine, and great care was taken in its performance so that nothing went wrong. If there was a mistake or even the slightest interruption – a sneeze even – the entire ceremony would be repeated from the beginning. We know of instances where a sacrifice was repeated four or five times or even more, because of indications that it had not been properly performed. A defining feature of Roman religion was thus its focus on orthopraxy ("correct action") rather than orthodoxy ("correct belief"). To the extent that the Romans had a core belief, it was that proper ritual action would bring them the favor of the gods.

Figure 8.1 Marble altar depicting a sacrifice, Sanctuary of Diana at Nemi, circa 200 CE. Ny Carlsberg Glyptotek, Copenhagen. The sacrifice is being performed jointly by a male and a female, suggesting that sacrifice was not an exclusive male domain.

This observation brings up another key distinction between most modern religions and the Romans. For many people today, religion is primarily a private individual matter, while for the Romans religion was very much the business of the state. Success in war, good harvest, even the selection of competent public officials were all thought to depend on the will of the gods. The state therefore took an active role in the performance of religious rites. Magistrates performed rituals regularly throughout the year: when they took office, when they convened a public meeting, before embarking on a campaign or beginning a battle, and of course on festival days.

This difference between ancient and modern can be overstated. We shall see that private individuals did engage in religious activity in a number of different situations and clearly held their own beliefs about which gods to appease and when. Because Roman religion concerned itself more with action than belief, the Roman government did not intervene as long as these actions were not deemed harmful to the state. However, the notion of a blanket separation between church and state would have been unthinkable to the Romans: one basic function of government was to ensure that public obligations to the gods were properly fulfilled. As a result of this essential connection between religion and public life and politics, the Roman Senate exercised control over religious activity. Religion thus formed part of the structure of the Roman state, and as the state changed so did its religious practices.

Public Religion

In 217 BCE, learning that Hannibal had crossed the Alps and was descending into Italy, the Roman Senate received reports of unusual happenings all over Italy. Among these reports were: at Praeneste there was a shower of red-hot stones; at Arpi shields were seen in the sky; at Caere the waters ran mingled with blood and the spring of Hercules bubbled with drops of blood; in Rome itself the statue of Mars on the Appian Way and the images of the Wolves sweated blood. The consul therefore consulted the Senate about a religious response to these accounts. A decree was passed proclaiming a three-day period of prayer and also that the Board of Ten Men should consult the oracular Sibylline Books to learn the will of the gods. On their advice, additional sacrifices were ordered and gifts of gold and silver were presented to Jupiter, Juno, and Minerva. Only after these actions did the consul turn his attention to the military needs of the state.

This episode typifies many aspects of Roman religion already discussed. As with many people, the Romans faced a crisis by turning to the gods for support. Blood in the water or statues sweating could only be explained by divine intervention (think of the Nile turning to blood in the Bible). Such divine intervention could only indicate divine anger and a rupture in the *pax deorum*. The most important response was therefore to restore the good relationship with the gods. To rebuild that relationship, the Romans performed a number of religious rituals, specifying the types of animals to be used in order to please the gods. To ensure that they had responded appropriately, they consulted religious experts, who indicated additional rituals that needed to be performed. Only after convincing themselves that the gods were again on their side did they turn to human affairs. The episode is unusual only in the quantity of strange occurrences reported and the number of Roman actions in response. These differences are undoubtedly related to the seriousness of the crisis: Hannibal's invasion of Italy. Exploring the details of this episode in more detail can thus help us see the most important features of Roman religious practice.

The center of religious authority in the Roman Republic appears clearly in this episode: when a religious crisis occurred, the consul and the Senate took the lead in determining the religious response. There was no separate group of priests who decided upon the proper course of action or performed the ritual. In the episode above, the Senate did consult a Board of Ten Men, but these were not religious experts in our sense of the phrase. They had charge of one particular aspect of Roman religion: custody of the oracular Sibylline Books, which they consulted only upon the direction of the Senate. The Romans had several such colleges, each with specific responsibilities: for example, the **augurs** were responsible for reading the signs from the gods, while the **pontiffs** had charge of the calendar and other elements. Leading politicians were generally chosen to serve as members of these colleges for life; unlike in most modern societies, being a priest was not a job on its own. This overlap between religious authority and political authority is understandable in view of the importance of public religion to the well-being of the state. It is also another way that the Roman ruling class controlled public religion.

Political Issues: *Telling Time in Ancient Rome*

Calendars are an often unappreciated source of information and power. Structuring time structures both public and private life on a regular basis and so reveals many of a society's priorities. The Romans were no different.

To take one example, the Romans used an eight-day cycle rather than a seven-day week. Every eighth day was a "market day" on which people from outlying areas might come into the city or town to buy and sell products, ranging from food to domestic items. The eight-day cycle did not contain regular weekends, but there were festival days sprinkled throughout the year that provided citizens with a break in their daily routine. These festivals reveal priorities important to the Romans. Some were concerned with ancestors, reflecting the importance of family and of spirits of the dead to Romans. Many others reflected the agricultural origins of the city and celebrated a harvest: the Vinalia for grapes, for example, or the Cerialia for grain. Still others reflect the importance of the Roman military: the Tubilustrium, literally the cleaning of the trumpets, took place in late March prior to the start of the summer campaigning season.

Calendars can also be intensely political. Early in Rome's history, it appears that calendars were not written, providing a great advantage to the elite who might be the only ones to know which days were public hoidays and which were legal for what business. In 304 BCE,

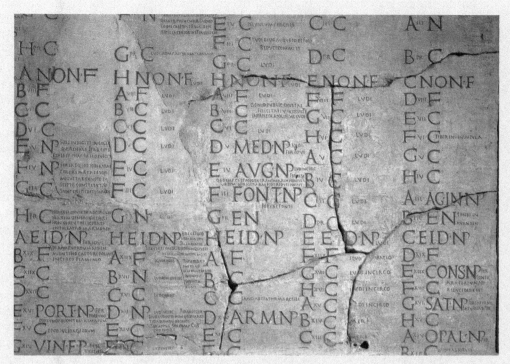

Figure 8.2 Part of the *fasti Amiterni*, indicating festivals on the Roman calendar, first century CE. Palazzo Massimo, Rome. The first capital letter indicates the day of the 8-day cycle, the second indicates whether the day was open for business (C) or a festival.

there was great opposition when a magistrate finally succeeded in publishing a calendar, but by the Late Republic we see the emergence of permanent stone calendars (**Figure 8.2**). By then another problem had arisen: because a Roman year consisted of 355 days, the priests had to add 10 days every year. Where they added these days became important: holding an election or a trial 10 days later than normal could provide a major advantage. It became impossible to agree on where to insert the extra days, with the result that the calendar was three full months out of sync: harvest festivals were falling in the middle of winter. Indeed, perhaps Julius Caesar's most long-lasting reform was to switch to a solar calendar with a leap day every four years, the same basic calendar we still use today.

We can even track changes in Roman society over time using the calendar. The Parilia on April 21 began as a ritual aimed at shepherds and their flocks; by the Late Republic, however, it had morphed into a holiday that celebrated the foundation of Rome. Such changes are not unusual: in the United States the original meaning of Memorial Day and Labor Day has been lost for many people, for whom these days serve as the unofficial start and finish of summer. Changes in the calendar, in how it is set and in how it is observed, simply reflect the broader changes going on in the larger society. Calendars thus provide a unique window into the changing values of a society.

These colleges also served to spread religious authority among many individuals: no single college possessed the capability of making unilateral pronouncements on religious matters. Individuals could only serve on one college, preventing any one person from gaining too much influence, a constant fear of the Romans. Religious authority was thus similar to political authority in its structure: just as the Romans had two consuls as a means of avoiding a single tyrant, no one person or religious body could outweigh the collective power of the ruling class as a whole.

One group, the Vestal Virgins, offers both an exception to normal Roman customs and also reinforces some of these customs. On the one hand, Vestals were typically selected only from the most distinguished families and their selection brought prestige to the family. They were required to remain chaste, since their unchastity was viewed as a public calamity: a guilty Vestal would be put to death. These elements are entirely in keeping with elite control of the state and Roman gender expectations. The Vestals were exceptional in being the only religious body comprised of women and they performed specialized tasks that no one else could. They tended the sacred hearth and they made the *mola salsa*, a special grain used in almost all sacrificial rituals. Girls between six and ten years old would be selected for this role, and they served for at least 30 years; the limited evidence suggests that most women served for life, since marriage was generally out of the question by the time they completed their service. In exchange, the Vestal Virgins received certain privileges, such as reserved seats at the games, the ability to make a will, and the ability to testify in court. As a group, the Vestals were the most visible women in their contribution to Roman public life during the Republic: their visibility was a reminder of the power of women and also of the Roman ways of controlling that power.

Domestic Religion

The Vestals point us to another aspect of Roman religion that mirrored Roman society: the way the family served as a microcosm of the Roman state. When a girl became a Vestal, legally she left her birth family and came under the supervision of the *pontifex maximus*, the head of the college of pontiffs. Symbolically, the state became her family and the rituals she performed were part of its religious system.

Families had their own religious systems, meant to guarantee the prosperity of the family just as the public religious rituals were meant to guarantee the safety of the state. The *paterfamilias* often acted in the way a consul would, pouring libations for the health of his family or for a good harvest, just as the magistrates performed rituals on behalf of the Roman state. Several Roman state festivals also involved rituals to be performed in the house, such as the Parentalia in honor of a family's ancestors. The best evidence for the religious activity of individuals, however, comes from the material remains from the Roman world. Excavated Roman houses usually contain a *lararium*, a shrine to the **Lares** or household divinities (**Figure 8.3**). Numerous

Figure 8.3 A Lares shrine, from the the House of the Vettii, Pompeii, first century CE. Naples Archaeological Museum.

ritual objects such as small statuettes have been found in the vicinity of these shrines attesting to their frequent usage. Nor was it only in the household that individual Romans could express their religiosity; various objects – lamps, anatomical figurines, or even statues – have been uncovered in a wide range of sanctuaries. These served as votive offerings, thanks to a divinity from an individual Roman for the successful fulfillment of a vow. These offerings could be made to state divinities such as Jupiter, but also to some who had not been officially "approved" by the authorities. We can conclude that alongside the publicly approved cults existed a range of cults and religious activities with which the governmental authorities did not interfere. Sometimes the existence of these cults is known only from these material remains. These individual offerings complemented the official state offerings and both operated with fundamentally the same belief: all good things came from the gods, and maintaining their support and giving them thanks through ritual action was the appropriate sphere for religious behavior.

Changes in Roman Religion

The Tradition of Absorbing Foreign Cults

From as soon as traces are visible, Roman religion was as open to external influences as the rest of Roman society. For instance, Roman myths suggest that an altar was dedicated to the Greek hero Hercules even prior to the foundation of the city. The altar, known as the *Ara Maxima* ("greatest altar"), has been identified with remains under the church of S. Maria Cosmedin in Rome. Other early sanctuaries in Rome include a shrine to Mater Matuta, a Latin goddess whose most famous sanctuary is at Satricum, and to the Greek twins Castor and Pollux, known as the Dioscuri. The earliest Roman sanctuaries also reveal foreign influences: the temple of Jupiter Optimus Maximus ("Best and Greatest") on the Capitoline hill, the most important temple of Republican Rome, shows similarities to Etruscan temples in its triple cella and in the terracotta figurines that decorated the pediment. Roman sources even describe a ceremony by which the leading divinity of an enemy town would be symbolically "called out" and brought to Rome. Any discussion of Roman religion must recognize that elements from outsider cultures changed Roman practice from its earliest days.

Exploring Culture: *"Calling out" the Gods*

Roman writers preserve stories of a ceremony known as the *evocatio*, which was used on several occasions to bring foreign gods and goddesses to Rome. *Evocatio* means a "calling out" and the idea was that Romans would invite the chief divinity of a besieged town to come to Rome, in the belief that conquest would be easier (or perhaps only possible) once the town was deprived of its supranatural protective force.

The best-known example comes from the Roman siege of Veii in 396 BCE. Just before the final attack on the city, Livy (5.21) records that the dictator Camillus prayed to Juno Regina "who now dwells in Veii that you follow us, after our victory to the City which is ours and which will soon be yours, where a temple worthy of your majesty will receive you." After this prayer, the Romans launched their final attack on the city, which included an assault from men who had dug a tunnel underneath the city and emerged into the temple of Juno Regina. After the sack of the city, a select group of men cleansed themselves, entered the temple, and asked the goddess if she was willing to go to Rome. The story goes that the goddess either nodded assent or verbally agreed to go, and the Romans placed her in a wagon, transported her ten miles to Rome, and installed her in a temple on the Aventine hill. Other Roman authors suggest that Vortumnus from Etruria and Juno Caelestis from Carthage also arrived in Rome in this fashion.

It should be immediately apparent that there are some questionable elements to Livy's story: a wooden statue should not be able to indicate assent. A broader look at the war with Veii raises further questions about the historical nature of this account: Roman writers

> made this war appear as a second Trojan war, complete with 10 years' worth of fighting. The Roman soldiers emerging into the temple of Juno might be compared to the Greeks emerging from the wooden horse. The myths surrounding the Trojan War insisted that Troy could not be captured as long as it possessed its statue of Athena, so Odysseus had to steal it before the final attack. The *evocatio* of Juno Regina might therefore be the Roman variation on this story.
>
> Whether or not the *evocatio* is an actual historical ritual, it is important to consider why the Romans would have told these stories. Few other peoples imagined that they had anything to gain by installing the gods of defeated peoples within their own religious system. After all, their own gods had just proved themselves stronger than those of the enemy. The *evocatio*, however, loomed large in the Roman imagination. They did believe that the proper worship of foreign gods and goddesses brought benefit to their city. The *evocatio* might thus be seen as symbolic of the Roman openness to foreigners: even as the Romans demonstrated their military superiority, they showed themselves willing to recognize and incorporate elements of the defeated people within their own society.

The pace of change does appear to have picked up dramatically in the late third and early second centuries BCE, the period in which Rome found herself beginning to control a Mediterranean-wide empire. Until 220 BCE only a small handful of cults with Greek connections had found a place in Rome; between 220 and 50 BCE, five more cults with eastern connections were officially welcomed into Rome, and a number of other cults made unofficial entrances. Existing cults in Rome also underwent transformation: the cult of Ceres, a Latin cult dating back to 494 BCE, added "Greek rites" during this period, administered by priestesses who were brought to the city from the culturally Greek areas of southern Italy. New rites were added to other cults as well, such as the introduction of the Saturnalia as a week-long festival of feasting and gift giving – the precursor to modern Christmas celebrations – instead of merely the sacrificial ritual.

The period from 220 onward also saw several notable controversies concerning religious practice. These controversies deserve special attention because they can tell us about the concerns of the Romans at this time. It has often been claimed that the Romans reacted strongly against the influx of Greek or eastern elements into their religious system, but a close examination will reveal that the Romans continued to be open to outside religious elements. The variety of Roman reactions to foreign cults suggests that the Romans treated each cult on its own terms and in its own particular context.

Bacchus and the Magna Mater

The affair of the **Bacchanalia** is the most famous religious incident of the Roman Republic and helps us understand Roman attitudes not just towards foreign cults but also towards religious change in general. It began in 186 BCE when Roman magistrates claimed to have suddenly discovered the existence of orgiastic rites involving both men and women being held at night in honor of the god Dionysios, or Bacchus as the Romans called him. It is difficult today to recover the true nature of this cult because Livy, our only source for the events, described the events like a melodrama for the stage: his account comes complete with wicked stepmothers, virtuous prostitutes, naïve young men, and heroic Roman magistrates (39.8–19). Yet there is no doubt that something happened that drew the concern and attention of the Senate, because they passed a decree outlining restrictions on the worship of Bacchus. In addition, Livy reports more reliably that several thousand people were put to death in the following years on charges related to the Bacchanalian affair. Clearly something had gone very wrong, at least from the standpoint of the authorities.

This incident has attracted a great deal of attention because it seems so unlike the general openness of Roman religion and because to many scholars it seems to foreshadow later persecutions of Christians in the Roman Empire. At first sight, the incident might seem to fit a narrative of the Roman government closing ranks against Greek culture. Worship of Dionysios as the god of wine was widespread in Greece and the Romans did tend to be nervous about having women and wine in close proximity to each other (see Chapter 6). Further, the unrestrained worship of Bacchus contrasts strongly with the scrupulous attention to detail of Roman ritual.

Yet there are reasons to be wary of such a simple explanation. For one, Bacchus was not a newcomer to Rome in 186 BCE; the Romans had been worshipping the god of wine for many years. Secondly, a copy of the Senate's decree was found in southern Italy and it is clear that the Senate did not actually outlaw the worship of Bacchus or even the presence of men and women worshippers together. Finally, despite Livy's overheated accusations about the cult, his account makes clear that the only people executed were those who had been found guilty of crimes such as forgery or poisoning, not merely participating in cult activities. All these points suggest that seeing the Bacchanalia as a hostile reaction against foreign cultic activities is too simple an answer.

Working with Sources
The SC de Bacchanalibus

Perhaps the most valuable source for understanding Roman religion is the *senatus consultum de Bacchanalibus* ("Senatorial opinion on the Bacchanalians"), discovered at Tiriolo in southern Italy in 1640 (*CIL* 10.104). This inscription has therefore been the subject of intense scholarly study for nearly four hundred years, and yet there are still important unanswered questions.

Some scholars have focused on the find spot of the inscription over 600 kilometers from Rome and the preamble to the Senate's decree, which specifies that the Senate's decree was directed at "those who are allied with us," to suggest that the decree represents a significant expansion of Roman legal authority over Italians who were not yet Roman citizens, and thus in theory not subject to Roman civil legislation.

> From the point of view of understanding Livy, the inscription is invaluable in confirming key points of Livy's text on the restrictions placed on the cult of Bacchus. For instance, one clause of the decree reads as follows:
>
>> No one of them shall have a place devoted to the worship of Bacchus: and if there are any who say that they have a need for such a place, they shall appear in Rome before the urban praetor; and our Senate shall make a decision regarding these matters....
>
> In his account, Livy reported that the Roman Senate had decreed that
>
>> There should be no Bacchanalian rites in Rome or in Italy. If anyone considered that this form of worship was a necessary obligation ...he was to make a declaration before the City praetor and the praetor was to consult the senate.
>
> Another set of clauses on the inscription include the following prohibitions:
>
>> No one of them shall have a common fund.... No one in a company of more than five persons altogether, men and women, shall perform such rites; nor in that company shall more than two men or three women be present, unless it is in accordance with the opinion of the urban praetor and the Senate....
>
> Compare that with Livy:
>
>> [A Roman might] observe those rites on condition that not more than five persons took part in the service, that they had no common fund, and that there was no priest or conductor of the ceremonies.
>
> Livy's text is so exact on the provisions that it seems highly likely that he or the source he was using had seen a copy of the inscription, and can give us some confidence in his account. Although our copy comes from southern Italy, it makes clear that copies had been set up in Rome and all over Italy, so viewing a copy would not have been too difficult.
>
> At the same time, the inscription can help us pierce through some of Livy's overheated rhetoric. For instance, the fact that men and women were allowed to worship Bacchus together suggests that the specter of orgies that play a prominent role in his narrative was not a major Roman concern at the time. While scholars continue to disagree about precisely which elements of Livy's account should be accepted, having the actual copy of the Senate's decree helps us clarify a central historical fact: that the worship of Bacchus was not in fact outlawed following this incident.

To understand the Roman government's reaction to the cult of Bacchus, it is instructive to compare it with their reaction to the cult of the Magna Mater ("Great Mother") 20 years earlier. In 205 BCE, at the close of the Second Punic War, the Romans had imported a black stone considered to represent this goddess from Asia

Minor in the East, where she was more commonly known as Cybele. The Romans installed this stone in the temple of Victory on the Palatine hill, and shortly afterward built a temple for her also on the Palatine. Like the cult of Bacchus, this cult hailed from the Hellenized eastern part of the Mediterranean, and like Bacchus it contained many elements foreign to normal Roman sensibilities. The festival of the Magna Mater involved celebrations by priests dressed in bright colors who danced wildly through the streets accompanied by the clashing of cymbals – hardly a Roman style mode of worship (**Figure 8.4**). More shockingly for the Romans, the priests of the Magna Mater were eunuchs, a category of person totally despised by the Romans for lacking the manliness of men. Yet the Roman government still brought this cult to Rome after a long invitation process in which they surely learned some of these details about the cult's practices. Even more, they found a home for it on the oldest and most prestigious hill of the city. If fear of strange religious customs did not prevent the Romans from welcoming the Magna Mater to Rome, it can hardly be an overall explanation for Roman behavior during this period.

If we look for consistent elements in the Roman behavior in an effort to find explanations for it, one characteristic that stands out is the control exercised by the Roman elite over Roman religion. The Magna Mater was brought to Rome through all the mechanisms by which the elite retained their authority. First an omen occurred for which the Senate decided to seek a remedy. Then the members of the elite who

Figure 8.4 Silver plate known as the Parabiago plate, with an image of Cybele and Attis, second to fourth centuries CE. Milan Archaeological Museum.

composed the college in charge of the oracular Sibylline Books identified a solution for the Senate. The Senate followed by sending an embassy to make a diplomatic request in Asia Minor for assistance. When the goddess came to Rome, the noblest male and female were selected to welcome her, and a temple was constructed in the most aristocratic quarter of the city. At every stage along the way the ruling elite made their approval known and placed themselves at the front of each activity.

The situation with Bacchus demonstrates the same elite control but with opposite results. The cult was not openly welcomed by the elite, but increasing numbers of non-elite Romans were apparently attracted to the cult. Eventually the Senate felt the need to act, and did so not to eliminate worship of this cult, but to control the manner in which worship was conducted. In taking this action, the Senate asserted its traditional prerogative to make decisions about Roman religion. The Roman elite thus gave its stamp of approval to both the Magna Mater and to Bacchus, and its actions show a continuity with practices from earlier periods, including the willingness to accept foreign religious traditions.

Continuity and Change

The similarities in the Roman treatment of the Magna Mater and Bacchus highlight several aspects of religious change following the Roman conquest of the Mediterranean. Two that we have already discussed are the continued openness to foreign religions and the efforts of the Roman elite to control the process of change. A third seems to be a growing Roman concern to identify elements that they wanted to see as distinctive of their own practices. For instance, Romans seem to have ordinarily performed sacrifices with their head covered, unlike the Greeks who sacrificed bare-headed: the Romans began to label this practice as celebrating according to the "Greek rite" (**Figure 8.5**). The practices associated with Bacchus and the Magna Mater after their acceptance in Rome point in the same direction. The restrictions on Bacchus placed limits on the number of male and female worshippers in any one place and on private ownership of cult sites, in keeping with Roman behavior. The limitations on the Magna Mater are even more revealing: no native-born Roman was allowed to walk in the procession that celebrated her festival and no Roman could perform any of the Phrygian-style ceremonies. Instead, Romans worshipped the Magna Mater according to their own practices: Roman magistrates performed sacrifices and held games in honor of the goddess and the Roman elite invited each other over for feasts. The Roman Senate used its control of religious and political authority to decide what counted as "Roman."

As much as the Senate tried to control the direction of Roman religion, we can also detect ways in which the non-elite of Rome practiced in ways of their own choosing. It is important to remember that the incident of the Bacchanalia began because some part of the population began to worship Bacchus in ways that made the elite uncomfortable. The elite thus felt they had to step in and reassert the "proper" ways to worship the god. In regard to the Magna Mater, the elite tried to organize the festivities so that they might enjoy feasting at each other's houses while

Figure 8.5 Detail from the so-called Via Labicana Augustus, c. 20 BCE. Rome. Palazzo Massimo, Rome. The toga hem pulled over his head indicates that the emperor is participating in a sacrifice according to Roman practice.

the rest of Roman society was supposed to be satisfied with games and processions. The non-elite actually found their own ways to express devotion to the Magna Mater: scores of figurines of Attis, the consort of the Magna Mater, have been discovered in the vicinity of her temple. Without these figurines, we would have no idea that Attis was even worshipped in Rome at this time; the elite literary sources make no mention of him. The archaeological data here as elsewhere are crucial in reminding us that there is a strata of Roman society not represented in the literary sources that was every bit as important to the development of Roman religion.

These observations help us see what may have changed in Roman religious behavior during the second century BCE. In the fifth and fourth centuries BCE the Roman elite was happy to welcome foreign religious elements into their system and in general does not seem to have been concerned to put a "Roman" stamp on them. Etruscan style architecture, Latin gods, and Greek gods came to Rome and became part of the system without much drama. As the Romans came to find themselves in charge of a Mediterranean-wide empire with increasing numbers of immigrants finding a home in Rome, it became more of an issue for the Romans to define for themselves what being a Roman meant. Their treatment of the Magna Mater may be representative of this change: foreign elements continued to be welcome in Rome, but the Roman elite now attempted to define what was typical Roman practice.

Indeed they may even have used these opportunities as the means for making these statements: that is, the Magna Mater was particularly useful *precisely* because her celebrations were so unRoman. Over the next several hundred years, Jews and other easterners came to play this role as well: at most times Jews were allowed to practice their own customs without any problems, but on occasion they were temporarily banished from Rome as a reminder of their unRoman status. The growing interest in Egyptian cults met with a similar response in the Late Republic: Isis appears to have become popular and increasingly accepted, even as Romans were reminded of her foreignness. In this regard, religious developments during the last phase of the Roman Republic showed continuity with earlier traditions.

The Late Republic

The fundamental connection between politics and religion that we have witnessed suggests that political changes should be reflected in the religious system as well. For example, in the 30 years after the tribunate of Tiberius Gracchus, the lower classes continued to chip away at the power wielded by the elites. In 104 BCE, right in the middle of this period, a law was passed placing the selection of pontiffs in the hands of the tribal assembly rather than the elite, chipping away at their religious authority as well. The connection between religion and politics made itself felt in many other ways during the Late Republic, and all of them demonstrate how important religion continued to be in the life of the Romans.

The rise of the individual as opposed to the collective ruling elite probably represents the most fundamental change in Roman religion during the Late Republic. This phenomenon began before Julius Caesar. At first we see prophets or soothsayers directly connected to an individual. The first known example is Marius, who is said to have kept a prophetess named Martha on his staff to foresee his victories. The attempt by individuals to access prophecies or mark themselves as destined by the gods to rule grew more frequent over the next 50 years. As we saw above, the Romans preferred to rely on group consensus in order to prevent any one individual from claiming power, so this new phenomenon undermined that system. As the structures of the Roman Republic came under increasing stress, it is hardly surprising to see religious practice exhibit the same forms of stress.

If Marius started a trend towards having access to a personal seer, the following generation of Romans engaged in conflict took the next logical step: they connected themselves directly to divinities. Marius' rival Sulla might be considered the first Roman leader to assert this connection. Sulla's nickname, *felix*, implies the sense of being blessed by the gods, and in the course of his campaigns he claimed the special favor of the Cappadocian goddess Ma. The phenomenon reached a peak with Pompey and Caesar, the great rivals of the civil wars. These two men competed to claim the mantle of the favorite of Venus, ancestress of the Roman people. In 55 BCE, Pompey built a temple to Venus, the bringer of Victory, at the top of his massive building complex that included the first stone temple in Rome. Caesar, however, had an advantage over Pompey in this contest: his family traced their descent from the goddess and he was thus able to claim a direct inheritance of her favor. Caesar's temple, vowed during the climactic battle at Pharsalus and built in the following years, was dedicated to Venus Genetrix, the ancestress of the Roman people. In making this claim to be the direct descendant of a divinity, Caesar set the stage for the imperial period. His nephew Octavian would claim descent both from Venus and from Caesar himself, who was deified after his death. Octavian thus placed himself on an elevated religious plane, and this status eventually became a key plank in the Roman imperial ideology of the next four hundred years.

Conclusion

The developments of the Late Republic have often been viewed as a sign of decline, just as the narrative of the Late Republic is often presented as one of disintegration (see Chapter 1). It is easy to claim that the behavior of the Roman elites at this time reveals a shocking lack of belief and a willingness to use religion to manipulate the unsuspecting masses. One can point to the story of Bibulus, Julius Caesar's colleague in the consulate, claiming to see adverse signs in the heavens in order to obstruct Caesar's legislative activity, or Caesar trying to lock Bibulus in his house in response. In another famous story, the consul Metellus ran through the forum to evade the tribune Milo in order to avoid hearing that the omens were unfavorable for holding elections. To modern eyes, either Milo was manipulating the omens or Metellus was manipulating the notification, or both. Cicero's writings also reveal doubts held by at least one highly educated member of the Roman elite about the effectiveness of religious actions and the reliability of omens. All of these pieces of evidence might suggest that Roman religion was no longer what it once was.

Yet the picture, as always, is not so simple. On the one hand, it is clear that Cicero did not completely disregard belief in Roman religion, and we should not let the thoughts of one man shape our understanding, no matter how much he wrote. In fact, the very fights that took place over religion indicate how seriously many Romans continued to take their religion. Caesar and Pompey would not have battled to claim support from the gods if they did not think that there was an advantage in doing so. On the other hand, evidence from archaeology and from other stories indicates that much religious activity carried on without much change; shrines continued to attract worshippers and defenders, and individuals continued to make dedications as thanks for personal benefits. Rather than viewing Roman religion in a state of decline, we might observe that the terrain of Roman religion was shifting. It was being transformed in ways that enabled it to stay relevant in the lives of Roman citizens. Actions that earlier generations of Romans would not have dreamed of taking now became acceptable; beliefs that Romans of earlier generations would not have imagined now became commonplace. Ultimately these changes culminated in the creation of a new style of Roman religion, one that included practices linked to the imperial family among other developments, but that is a story that belongs to the era of the Roman Empire.

Discussion Questions

1. How would you define "religion" and should Roman behavior described in this chapter fall within the sphere of "religion"?
2. How do the basic characteristics of Roman religion differ from modern religions?
3. How was the Roman religious system intertwined with their social and political system during the Republic? A good exercise is to choose a major festival from the Roman holiday calendar and analyze how those factors interacted in that single example.
4. Did the basic characteristics of Roman religion change as a result of Roman expansion, and if so, how?
5. In what ways is it fair to speak of a "decline" in religion during the Late Republic, and in what ways is using such a term misleading?

Further Reading

Beard, Mary, John North, and Simon Price (1998). *Religions of Rome*. 2 vols. Cambridge: Cambridge University Press.
Intended for use as a textbook for Roman religion, Volume 1 is a "history" of Roman religion while Volume 2 collects sources (both literary and material) relating to the study of Roman religion. Although the authors have a particular take on Roman religion, this book is thought-provoking throughout and provides an essential starting point for any further reading.

Flower, Harriet I. (2017). *The Dancing Lares and the Serpent in the Garden: Religion at the Roman Street Corner*. Princeton, NJ: Princeton University Press.
This well-illustrated book focuses on gods who were central to the everyday lives of both elite and non-elite Romans: the Lares. Flower argues that these gods were benevolent protectors of place, with numerous local shrines often tended by ordinary Romans including enslaved persons and freedmen. She examines both rituals and festivals to explore connections with politics as well as with household life.

Padilla Peralta, Dan-el (2020). *Divine Institutions: Religions and Community in the Middle Roman Republic*. Princeton, NJ: Princeton University Press.
This book focuses on the crucial period from 396 to 202 BCE when Rome expanded from a small city to the dominant power in the western Mediterranean. Padilla Peralta uses archaeology and insights from sociology and anthropology to argue that religion, in the form of pilgrimage to the city of Rome and the construction of new temples in the city, held the new community together.

Scheid, John (2003). *An Introduction to Roman Religion*. (Trans. Janet Lloyd). Edinburgh: Edinburgh University Press.
Perhaps the best short synchronic introduction to the subject. Scheid is an expert on Roman ritual and on Roman priests, and his book focuses on the behavior of the Romans, with very clear explanations of practices such as sacrifice. Subdivisions within chapters make it easy to follow the main outlines.

Staples, Ariadne (1998). *From Good Goddess to Vestal Virgins: Sex and Category in Roman Religion*. London and New York: Routledge.

Staples explores questions of religion and women, since religion was the rare place where women played an important public role in Rome. She is concerned both with how women perceived their own participation in religion and how men perceived it. By exploring myths and rituals including the Vestals Virgins, she argues that religion helped define women sexually and that this definition affected other aspects of Roman culture.

9
Law

In the year 456 BCE according to Livy (3.31–34), the patricians of Rome finally agreed, after years of badgering by the plebeians, to create a commission "to propose measures which should be useful to both sides, and for the purpose of making liberty equal." A commission of three men was sent to Athens to study Greek legal systems. After the commissioners gave their report, the Romans set aside their usual political system and gave all power into the hands of 10 men (*decemviri*), charged with drawing up a set of laws for the emerging Roman state. After a year of work and public review, the assembly met and approved the 10 tables in 451 BCE. Immediately a general feeling arose that two additional tables were needed. A new set of *decemviri* was elected and gave the Twelve Tables their final form. These laws served as the basis of all succeeding Roman law, so that over 400 years later Livy could remark that "even now, in this great welter of laws piled one upon another, [they] are the fountain-head of all public and private law."

Parts of this origin story ought to seem suspicious. The embassy to Greece at a time when Rome was still a small farming village seems unlikely and the need to revise a law code immediately after a long process to compose it seems odd. The last might be explainable: Americans might remember that the first 10 amendments to the United States Constitution were passed within three years of the ratification of the Constitution itself. In regard to the Twelve Tables, the immediate revision to the law code turns out to be suggestive of a particular feature of the Roman legal system. Unlike many other legal systems, the Romans rarely repealed or overturned laws that they no longer desired: instead they added to them or interpreted them in new ways. This practice might best be understood as an illustration of the Roman notion of *mos maiorum*, the custom of the ancestors: the Romans preferred to justify behaviors by claiming that they were just doing what Romans had always done. Repealing a law acknowledges that the original law was a mistake and it is time to do something differently. The Romans chose to reinterpret their laws or to add to them in a way that enabled them to claim that the old laws were still in force.

We might also question the very framework of Livy's story as an element in the Struggle of the Orders, the conflict between the elite and lower classes. In Chapter 2 it was suggested that the Struggle was more of a Roman myth than reality, so we need to consider how the Twelve Tables might fit into the myth and history of early Rome. Of course, we will also need to consider how Roman law changed over time, and especially after Rome's conquest of the Mediterranean, if only to examine Livy's claim that the Twelve Tables were the "fountainhead" of all Roman law. Even when the Roman stories are not literally true, they help us to frame the questions that we need to explore. In the case of Roman law we are especially fortunate, because we can begin with the Twelve Tables themselves.

The Twelve Tables

We are fortunate to possess many provisions of the Twelve Tables preserved in later sources to help us assess these questions. We do not possess the full text of the law code and it can be difficult to be certain of the exact order of the tables and even the meaning of some of the provisions. For example, one provision indicates that on the 17th day after a successful judgment the creditors could "cut shares." Ancient Roman authors took this to mean that the creditor could literally cut pieces of the debtor's body, but modern scholars have usually interpreted this phrase as a reference to the creditor's property. The archaic language used on the surviving tables is thus part of the problem, even though it serves as good evidence for the early date of the Tables.

The surviving provisions of the Twelve Tables deal with three areas that were a concern of the Romans not only early in the Republic but all the way through the Empire: legal procedure, status, and property. The provisions often remind us of the distance between ourselves and the Romans.

For example, little of the Twelve Tables deals with criminal law, and some of the prohibited actions seem unusual. For example, death was the penalty for anyone who sang an "evil song." The Romans themselves were not sure what to make of this provision: it may have referred to magical spells that aimed to harm another person – what we might call black magic – or simply to words that dishonored another Roman. Not only did they have a different view of free speech, but also a wholly different view of what crimes might be worthy of capital punishment. It is a remarkable fact that the Romans had no statute against murder, though they clearly recognized that murder was wrong. These observations should help us see that a law code does not only reflect the values of a community, but that the specific provisions reflect specific needs of the people who wrote the laws. Exploring the ways in which the Twelve Tables approach their key concerns can help us understand what those needs were for the Roman elite.

Exploring Culture: *Getting Away with Murder?*

Murder is typically defined in modern legal systems as the killing of another human being with malice aforethought, a technical legal term that refers to causing intentional harm. The surviving text of the Twelve Tables does not include any provision outlawing killing defined in this way. It is of course possible that there was a provision against murder that was not preserved in our sources, but it seems unlikely that such an important law would not be mentioned in any source for hundreds of years. Furthermore, classical Latin has many words for killing, but no word equivalent to the English "murder." Does that mean that the Romans let people get away with murder?

It is clear that the Romans recognized the killing of another human being as something worthy of punishment. A provision of the Twelve Tables appears to deal with *unintentional* killing, what we might define as manslaughter: "If a weapon has sped accidentally from one's hand, rather than if one has aimed and hurled it, to atone for the deed a ram is substituted as a peace offering to prevent blood revenge." This clause does not specifically state that the accidental discharge of a weapon killed a person, but that is the clear implication of noting that the punishment is intended to prevent blood revenge. Other portions of the Twelve Tables indicate that the Romans employed a version of *talio*: an eye for an eye, tooth for a tooth, life for a life. This provision, therefore, seems to be trying to avoid the life for a life situation when the killing was accidental. If accidental killing merited punishment, we can be sure that intentional killing was not acceptable either. Why, then, is it not mentioned in the law code?

Judy Gaughan suggested that we can approach an answer by exploring who in Rome was legally empowered to put citizens to death. On the one hand this right was granted to the oldest male in the family: *patria potestas* gave the father the power of life and death over his children and indeed anyone in his *familia*. On the other hand, the highest magistrates of the state were empowered to carry out executions, but a law passed in the second year of the Republic gave citizens the right to appeal a capital sentence to the assembly. This law limited the power of the magistrate while keeping the power intact. In other words, the state had very limited ability to put people to death, but this power was instead invested in the individual families, even if they rarely exercised it.

Several conclusions might flow from this observation. It reveals a fear of centralized state authority: killing citizens with impunity is a central feature of autocratic systems. A key feature of Roman ideology was the hatred of kings, and the absence of a specific murder law is another reflection of that ideology. The absence of a specific murder law also underscores the self-help nature of the Roman legal system, which depended on the power of individual elite families to police themselves alongside the rest of Roman society.

Procedure

"If the plaintiff summons the defendant to court the defendant shall go. If the defendant does not go the plaintiff shall call a witness thereto. Only then the plaintiff shall seize the defendant."

This clause is generally agreed to be the first provision of the first table, and so possibly reflects the issue that was most important to address. It demonstrates that one of the highest concerns in the Roman legal system was correct procedure: this clause lays out the process by which a defendant shall appear in court. His attendance is required, and he can in fact be forced into court, but only if the proper procedure was followed. The first three tables all concern themselves with these types of procedural issues, and together they point toward a fundamental feature of the Roman legal system.

Like other early law codes, the Romans utilized a self-help system: there was no public authority such as police officers to enforce the law or public prosecutors to present your case. If you wanted to bring a suit against someone, it was your responsibility to make sure they appeared in court. If you succeeded in court, it was your responsibility to ensure that the other party paid up; under certain circumstances you might hold the debtor in chains in your own house, provided that you fed him enough to keep him alive. It hardly needs to be said that this system benefits the powerful: a non-elite would have great difficulty forcing a member of the elite to appear in court or to execute judgment against them, while the elite could more easily gather supporters to force a poorer citizen into court. Indeed, the challenges poorer persons faced were so substantial that we might doubt how often they actually filed lawsuits. We will return to the question of social class and the law shortly, after considering the other main concerns of the Twelve Tables.

Status

Several of the tables concern family relationships, and some of the individual provisions and their implications (such as *patria potestas*) have been noted in earlier chapters. Another provision in that table states that "a child born within ten months of the father's death shall enter into the inheritance." A child is assumed to belong to the deceased father as long as it was possible that they could have been conceived by the deceased, and the child would then be considered part of the family for purposes of the family name and inheritance. Clarity about who belonged to the family thus had both symbolic and practical importance. These provisions speak to the Roman desire for clarity about status, resolving potential questions before they arose.

The Twelve Tables contain several provisions relating to the status of females within the family. Legally a woman tended to come under the control of their husbands when they married, but the law provided that "if any woman is unwilling to be subjected in this manner to her husband's marital control she shall absent herself for three consecutive nights in every year." The legal system here reveals with stark clarity the Roman ideology around women: in Roman law, possessing an item for one full year gave one legal title to it. Roman law thus categorized women as a type of "movable possession:" only by interrupting the possession of their husband each year were they able to remain legally outside of their husband's control.

While the Twelve Tables helped to shape the Roman ideology about women and children, we must be careful not to confuse ideology with practice. We noted in Chapter 5 that children were not in fact regularly killed by their fathers and that women exercised considerable authority within the household and could own property in their own name. Most of us can think of behaviors in our own society that do not conform to legal expectations, whether driving over the speed limit or downloading copyrighted music and books from the internet. The Romans were particularly good at finding loopholes to use the law as they wished. Roman women, for example, seem to have capitalized on the three day's absence each year to give themselves a break from the household. Concerns with status were important for the legal system, but such concerns likely did not affect daily existence for the vast majority of Romans.

Property

Legal definitions are important for a third element of Roman law illustrated in the Twelve Tables: property. A significant portion of the Twelve Tables is concerned with issues of ownership and possession, both larger issues such as how one established ownership of an object or piece of land or smaller matters, such as that "branches of a tree shall be pruned all around to a height of fifteen feet" or whether individuals are allowed to keep the fruit from a neighbor's tree that falls on one's own property. Many issues that people today might see as a criminal law are connected to property as well: theft and fraud fall into this category. On the whole, these provisions give the appearance of a small society heavily dependent on agriculture. Protection of private property – whether that property is land, animals, or movable possessions – is built into the very heart of the Roman legal system. These protections naturally benefit those who already own property, i.e. the wealthy. Like the provisions about procedure and the concerns about status, the laws on property illustrate how the Twelve Tables skewed towards the interests of the elite.

The Twelve Tables in Context

The fact that the Twelve Tables were designed to benefit the powerful should not be surprising in itself; the same is true for many legal codes in many times and places. It does, however, raise specific questions about Roman society worth considering. For one, it does not square well with the Roman tradition as expressed by Livy that the Twelve Tables were drafted in response to complaints by the poor about the power wielded by the rich. On the face of it, the Twelve Tables do not seem to have addressed this problem. If we ask how the Roman tradition arose, we could answer simply by suggesting that the tradition is incorrect, that Roman historians wrongly assumed that every significant domestic action needed to be understood through the lens of the rich/poor dynamic like the Struggle of the Orders. We can certainly solve the problem in this way, but it is often more productive to search for an answer to a paradox rather than just discarding it.

The impact of a having a written code of law may be hard for people living in the digital age to imagine. In a society with no written laws, the non-elite had very little access to the rules of the game: they could not simply run an internet search for the full text of any law they needed to know. Engaging in a legal dispute about possessions or power with a member of the elite would be all but impossible for such people. Unless they had a friend or relative with knowledge of the law – or a patron willing to support their cause – they probably lacked even a basic knowledge of their rights, such as the rules of ownership. A member of the elite could pretend that a particular law gave him rights to repossess a piece of property or to raise the interest rate on a loan, and the non-elite would find it difficult to know whether that was true.

In these circumstances, the mere existence of the laws on a public monument represented a step forward for the poor. If a member of the elite attempted to bully his way into a settlement, the weaker party could now consult the publicly available laws and know his rights. Even for members of the society who were illiterate, it would have been much easier to find someone who knew how to read than someone who knew the contents of the law code. We should take seriously the possibility that the content of the Twelve Tables was less important to the non-elite than the mere fact of their compilation and publication.

This observation might lead us to a further conclusion. The legal system did not need to be weighted towards the wealthy in order to reinforce aristocratic control. In the early and middle Roman Republic the challenges to the elite came primarily from individuals who wanted acceptance into the ruling class, rather than challenges to the ruling class as a whole. It seems unlikely that non-elites tried to use the law to challenge the power of the elite. Conversely, the elite might not file suits against the non-elite: it could be seen as "punching down" and cause more harm than good. More importantly, since the elite had greater political, economic, and social resources they could often, within reason, take what they wanted without resorting to the legal system: occupying land for instance. The little evidence that we have supports this conclusion: the vast majority of legal disputes that we know involved people of roughly equal status.

This discussion suggests that we ought to see the one-sided provisions of the Twelve Tables in a different way: to resolve disputes among members of the elite. Each litigant would have had full access to the legal recourses provided in the law code. In such cases, the legal system provided a way of establishing superiority among the elite. Resolution of a conflict by the legal system avoided resorting to violence or another tactic that might have threatened overall elite control of the state. Thus, the provisions of the Roman legal system may have been aimed as much at restraining members of the elite themselves as at controlling the non-elite. As we proceed to explore the further development of Roman law, we should be alert to this aspect of Roman law.

> **Political Issues:** *Character Matters*
>
> People approaching the speeches delivered in the course of Roman legal proceedings of the last phase of the Roman Republic are frequently surprised by what they find. The vast majority of these speeches barely mention evidence that might be used to support the case that they are trying to make, and even more rarely do they mention the laws that supposedly govern the case. These speeches come almost entirely from the stylus of Cicero, so it is possible that this oddity is merely a feature of his style. Cicero was known among the Romans as among the most successful litigators of his day, so it is unlikely his behavior violated the expected norms of a Roman court. If we accept that what Cicero did was accepted practice in Rome, we have to ask why. What might his method tell us about Roman legal proceedings?
>
> The speech he delivered on behalf of Aulus Cluentius in 66 BCE offers a good illustration. Cluentius was accused by his mother Sassia of poisoning his stepfather Oppianicus; eight years earlier Cluentius had accused Oppianicus of attempting to poison him as a means of gaining control of the family's property. In the earlier case, both sides had apparently attempted to bribe the jury, and the case resulted in the exile of Oppianicus, who died shortly afterward. In the period between the two cases, the accusations of bribery became broadly known, and public opinion began to turn against Cluentius, leading to the second trial.
>
> Although Cluentius had been charged under a law on poisoning, Cicero devotes little attention to the legal issues or to evidence that might exonerate his client. Instead Cicero devotes about three-quarters of his speech to establishing the evil nature of Oppianicus and Sassia, and the good character of his own client. He dwells at length on other crimes supposedly committed by Oppianicus in pursuit of the family estate, even though Oppianicus was dead by this time. Even in the short section of the speech notionally devoted to presenting evidence supporting his client's innocence, he devotes a significant section to an attack on Sassia's character.
>
> These choices are revealing. To a modern observer, the legal issues appear substantial, as the law in question may not have applied to Cluentius, but Cicero spends only the barest minimum of his speech here. It suggests that legal issues and evidence often were not the decisive factors in the courts of the late Republic. Rather, it was character that counted: destroying your opponent's reputation made a more significant impact upon a jury (assuming no bribes were involved!). While this case had only limited political significance – the parties lived in a small hilltown over 250 km from Rome – the same principle is visible in more celebrated cases in Rome: character attacks in the courtroom had visible impacts on political careers. The case of Cluentius helps us see how criminal trials in Rome could serve as a venue for political maneuvering in Rome just as much as the Senate.

The Early Development of Roman Law

Legal procedures in Rome were marked by a strict attention to detail that looks similar to Roman religion (see Chapter 8). A connection between the legal system and religion is actually quite common; even in the United States today, witnesses swear to tell the whole truth "so help me God." In the Roman system, the *legis actio* ("action of law") involved the exchange of formulaic words by both parties and the judge before the case could proceed to the second phase. These formulas were important: Roman jurists preserved the story of a man who lost a lawsuit against a neighbor who chopped down his vines because he needed to use the word "trees" in the formula rather than vines, since trees was the word that appeared in the law code.

The use of the *legis actio* further demonstrates that the legal system was for the use of the elite. The non-elite would have less knowledge of these formulas and less experience using them properly. Even the publication of the *legis actio* in 304 BCE did not help the non-elite as a class as much as it helped those individuals who had newly become part of the elite. Publication of the *legis actio*, however, does point to some early changes in the Roman legal system. We should recall that the fourth century BCE saw Rome extend her territorial control over the Italian peninsula, and that during this period some Romans of plebeian birth successfully made their way into the Roman ruling class. Roman tradition might have seen the publication of legal formulae as a triumph for the plebeians, but it more likely reflects the shifting composition of the elite.

Another development of this period is the creation of the office of praetor and its increasing importance for Roman law. The office was created in 367 BCE to take on some of the responsibilities of the consuls, who previously had been the only magistrates with *imperium*. Over time the praetors assumed oversight of the legal system, which led to significant changes in the administration of law in Rome. At the beginning of his term, the praetor would post an edict in public, listing the types of cases he would accept, and would provide the formulas for these cases. This system allowed for greater flexibility: the praetor could, for example, accept the word "vine" as part of the suit rather than insisting that the plaintiff stick to the old formula. As a result of this flexibility, this formulary procedure became the more common form of litigation in Rome and the praetor's court in the Roman Forum became the most common place where claims were contested. Praetors tended to abide by the edicts laid down by earlier holders of the office and add to them when appropriate, in keeping with the Roman desire not to repeal outdated laws. This respect for precedent has had a powerful influence on legal procedures in the European world and is one of the most lasting impacts of Roman society.

Key Debates: *Who Lay Down the Law in Rome?*

Outlining the laws for his ideal state, Cicero wrote the following in the middle of the first century BCE:

The administrator of justice, who shall decide or direct the decision of civil cases, shall be called praetor; he shall be the guardian of the civil law. There shall be as many praetors, with equal powers, as the Senate shall decree, or the people command (*De Legibus* 3.8).

Livy, writing perhaps 25 years later, claims that the praetor was created in 367 BCE "to administer justice in the City" (6.42). This assignment of legal responsibilities to the praetor has been accepted as a standard part in most discussions of the Roman system of government. Some scholars, however, have suggested that this picture may not necessarily have been true when the office of praetor was created. As often in Roman history, the challenge is with our sources: do Cicero and Livy relay accurate information about early Roman history or do they simply reflect the situation of their own day?

One of the few facts about the early praetor that seems certain is that he possessed *imperium*, the supreme power of the state that was invested in certain magistrates. It allowed individuals to give orders and demand obedience to them, most visible in commanding soldiers but also in dispensing justice within the city. In Roman thought it had belonged to the kings and was then transferred to the consuls, and eventually to the praetors when they were created. The *imperium* of the consuls was always greater than the praetor, but the grant of *imperium* to the praetor suggests that his original duties were military. Every magistrate with *imperium* prior to 367 BCE had served in a military capacity, so we might expect the same for the praetor.

If the praetor initially had military responsibilities, it raises the question of why and when he became associated with judicial matters as Cicero and Livy know him. One argument has seen this development in the 240s BCE with the creation of a second praetor. The full title of this magistrate in the Republic was "he who speaks the law *inter peregrinos*." The last phrase can either mean "between foreigners" or "among foreigners" and here the translation matters. The first phrase implies a judicial position, while the second phrase could still cover a military role (we still speak of "laying down the law" in a way that implies force rather than legal proceedings). In the 240s Rome was engaged in the First Punic War in Sicily, which could provide a military context for a new commander, but Rome's territory had also expanded enough by the third century BCE where they might have needed a special legal setting for cases involving non-Romans.

The Romans added two additional praetors around 225 BCE and an additional two in 198 BCE, for a total of six throughout the second century. Since the other praetors could handle most additional military needs, the *praetor peregrinus* became more attached to the city of Rome, and at this time, if not earlier, his focus likely shifted more to the administration of the city and its judicial needs.

The Effects of Expansion on Roman Law

We have already seen one example of how Roman expansion impacted Roman law in the use of the praetor's edict as a response to growth in Italy. The extension of Roman hegemony over the Mediterranean naturally led to additional changes. In part these changes responded to the increasing complexity of the Roman world: the conquest of the Mediterranean led to significant changes in the Roman family, the Roman economy, Roman politics, and elsewhere, as detailed in other chapters, and the legal system needed to adapt in order to handle these changes. A law code that imagines its citizens living in close proximity to each other is of limited use when many male citizens are fighting on overseas campaigns for years at a time. A code created for a predominantly agricultural society is similarly of limited use when that society becomes more heavily involved with overseas trade. We might well ask whether the basic principles of Roman law discussed earlier – concerns with procedure, status, and property – continue to be important in the Late Republic and, if so, how might those principles have been applied in a changed environment.

One place to start is to note the increasing number of laws passed in the aftermath of the Roman conquest of the Mediterranean. It is difficult to quantify this element precisely because our sources come from this period and so may simply be recording more laws from their own time than earlier days. Nevertheless, there does appear to be an overall increase in legislation: we know the names of twice as many laws passed between 200 and 75 BCE as from the entire period from 500 to 200 BCE. On the one hand, it is not surprising that a larger and more complex world should require more laws. We can think about the expansion of laws in our own societies and the response to the digital world and so the implications of having more laws are likely to be different in the context of Roman society and need to be considered.

The increasing number of laws might, for example, be seen as one indication of the breakdown or at least the dramatic transformation of Roman society. Laws tend to arise to solve a particular problem, especially when the social relationships are no longer sufficient to manage the situation. We saw this phenomenon with the Twelve Tables: the Roman tradition about their origins indicates that the plebs no longer felt that they had a sufficient relationship with the patricians to trust them, but also that the elite needed to manage the hierarchical relationships among themselves without violence. Thinking about laws in this way suggests that laws are a weaker and less desirable means of solving disputes than social relationships. If a conflict can be resolved without using the court system, both parties are more likely to go away from the encounter at least partially satisfied. This solution is also better from a societal perspective: the more that citizens find common ground with each other, the stronger the society will be. The increasing number of laws thus offers evidence not just that the world has become increasingly complex, but that citizens increasingly were not able to find common ground or that they lacked sufficient social connections to do so. Roman expansion brought challenges to their traditional societal rules, and the increasing number of laws may be seen as an attempt to stabilize the system.

Laws concerned with status, one of the prime concerns of the Romans as outlined above, show these changes clearly. As Roman territory expanded, questions of citizenship became increasingly important. Some Romans might find themselves living outside the city of Rome, and inhabitants of allied towns in Italy might be granted either Roman citizenship or a lesser status known as Latin citizenship. As these numbers grew and as people moved from one status to another, it became increasingly important both to define who held what type of citizenship and what specific privileges belonged to each type. The dramatic increase in the number of enslaved persons also raised issues of status: when an enslaved person returned to free status in Rome they also gained the status of a citizen. Clarifying the status of free, freed, and enslaved, and especially of children born to parents of differing status, became an important concern of the legal system.

Regulating Wealth

One particular group of laws responded more directly to the Roman conquest of the Mediterranean and the resulting influx of money: laws limiting the purchase or use of luxury items. It is worth noting that **sumptuary legislation**, as these types of laws are known, deals with issues of property, but in a different way than we might normally imagine: it limits how individuals can use their own property. For instance, one early law limited the number of guests that could be invited to a dinner party. The *lex Fannia* of 161 BCE offers a prime example that can help us understand the role of sumptuary laws. It allowed a maximum expenditure of 100 *asses* per day for dinner on major holidays, 30 *asses* on 10 lesser occasions each month, and 10 *asses* on all other days (10 *asses* were likely enough to feed a few friends, but not more). Homegrown food, such as leafy vegetables, grains, and domestic wine, was exempted from these limits. Only one chicken could be served, and only as long as it had not been specially fattened for eating. In addition, hosts were not allowed to use more than 100 pounds of silver, which seems to be a reference to tableware: plates, cups, knives, and the like.

The variety of provisions forces us to question what they had in common and what the true purpose of the legislation was. On the surface, it seems like an effort to control spending on luxury items in Rome, but a moment's reflection might suggest that is not the case. These provisions only deal with hosting a dinner party. Gaudy clothing or luxury houses were not touched by the law, and indeed a rich Roman could purchase as much silver tableware as he wanted; he was just not able to use more than 100 pounds of it at one dinner (**Figure 9.1**). The exemption on foods grown by the household also provided a giant loophole. Indeed, that provision has led some scholars to suggest that the target of the spending cap was not all luxury items, but imported ones: exotic animals, spices, imported wines. We might also ask how enforceable these limits were: in the absence of a police force, it would be difficult to learn about violations of the law, and an invited guest who had enjoyed a lavish meal was unlikely to spill the beans! There were thus many ways for a Roman to throw an extravagant dinner even after the law was passed.

The fact that these sumptuary provisions only applied to dinner parties is suggestive of another explanation. While in theory the law applied to everyone, only members of the elite were likely to invite upwards of 30 people to their house on major holidays and as many as 10 people 10 other times each month. Non-elites were not feeding over 100 guests every month! The behavior being regulated here is clearly the behavior of the upper classes, suggesting a new application of a principle visible in the Twelve Tables discussed above. The purpose of the legislation was to keep the competition and potential conflict among members of the elite at a manageable level. Dinner parties were perhaps the important aspect of socializing for the Roman elite, and no doubt a certain amount of political work was done in these informal surroundings, even if only to build one's network of supporters. Allowing for some extravagance, and even showing off the produce of one's own estate, provided some opportunity for elites to capitalize on these occasions. The

Figure 9.1 Fresco of banqueting, from the Casa dei Amanti, Pompeii, first century CE.

cap on luxury spending embodied in the *lex Fannia*, limits which were reinforced on multiple occasions over the course of the next hundred years, served as a reminder not to disrupt the system entirely. Even as Roman society underwent dramatic changes as a result of its imperial conquests, this fundamental feature of Roman law remained unchanged: a primary function was to manage relationships among the elite in a non-violent manner.

The Rise of Specialists

The increase in legal activity created a need for increased understanding of the law. Most aristocrats were able to comprehend and offer advice to others on the Twelve Tables, but the flexibility of the system based on the praetor's edict required more knowledge of precedent and more interpretation. Some individuals began to write commentaries that explained the connection between these edicts and the existing code of law, and to organize the existing legal materials (**Figure 9.2**). While such jurists existed as early as the fourth century BCE, the territorial expansion of the second century BCE brought Roman jurisprudence into the mainstream. Roman comedy uses both legal language and procedures for humorous purposes, jokes that

Figure 9.2 Marble altar known as the Altar of the Scribes, first century CE. Terme di Diocleziano, Rome.

would only be funny if the mostly non-elite audience was sufficiently familiar with the legal system.

Perhaps the most interesting figure in the development of Roman legal analysis is Q. Mucius Scaevola (140–82 BCE). Mucius served as consul in 92 BCE and was elected *pontifex maximus*, the state's highest religious office, in 89 BCE. His family had long been involved with both the legal and religious systems: numerous relatives had served in religious offices prior to him, and many had specialized in legal interpretations; the connection between the religious and legal spheres had a long history in Rome. Mucius does not seem to have provided answers to individual questions about the law, but wrote a commentary in 18 books following in the tradition of earlier jurists. He incorporated new law that had been created by the praetor's edict into the existing body of the law, drawing on a wide variety of analytical techniques. Most importantly for the future of legal analysis, he used hypothetical cases to explore legal concepts: because these cases generally lack specific details, they illustrate more clearly the underlying legal principle. This type of practice became standard in Roman law, eventually affecting the practice of law throughout all of Europe. The theoretical approach to law and the increasing professionalization of the legal system can be seen as a direct result of Roman territorial expansion.

The Late Republic

Despite the efforts of the legal system, by the beginning of the first century BCE it had become increasingly difficult to contain conflict among members of the elite. Recall that this is the period when violence became a regular part of the dispute resolution process in Rome, first with the killings of the Gracchi and later with the military ventures of Sulla and Caesar. The Roman legal system, just as other areas of Roman society that we have explored, reflects the changed dynamic of this period. The system repeatedly attempted to come to grips with the new situation and to find new solutions to the problems that were being posed. The extraordinary nature of the attempted solutions offers an indication that the legal system itself was not up to the task.

The Introduction of Permanent Courts

One attempt to handle the challenges of the period was the institution of permanent criminal courts in Rome in 149 BCE. The *lex Calpurnia* established the first permanent court to handle cases of extortion involving Roman provincial governors. Members of the Roman elite tried to enrich themselves individually from governing territories recently conquered by the state, another outcome of Roman imperial expansion. The legal system never succeeded in controlling this problem, as similar laws were passed several times over the next 50 years, expanding the court system, changing the procedures, and/or making the penalties for extortion more severe. Many members of the Roman elite wanted their chance to get rich quick, either by taking a bribe or getting their turn as a governor. The very fact that the law needed to be repeatedly updated is a good sign that the law was not working. The very need for a permanent court system to resolve disputes gives a clear indication that the Roman elite were becoming unable to manage conflict agreeably.

The appearance of permanent courts marked a change in how the Romans dealt with criminal law. As we saw earlier, the Twelve Tables created a system of civil law for resolving disputes between citizens, including many actions that we would identify as crimes: theft, for example. Almost the only crime prosecuted by the state was treason, and the seriousness of this charge meant that only a handful of cases are known. The creation of a court to deal with extortion – a crime against the state rather than a crime against an individual – led to the creation of further courts, each focused on a different crime. By 80 BCE, the Romans had separate courts for extortion, embezzlement, electoral misbehavior (often bribery), and treason, all of which might be seen as crimes against the state. However, there were also courts on "dagger-bearers and poisoners," on violence, and on falsehoods, which often included acts committed against individuals; for examples, forged wills came under the heading of falsehoods. We should not automatically assume simply that these types of criminal activities became more frequent in the Late Republic. It is more likely that the changed social and political situation made it difficult for the Roman elite to resolve disputes as they once had, requiring more legal mechanisms in an effort to keep them in check.

Working with Sources:
The lex Cornelia on Counterfeiting

The Cornelian law on testaments holds as follows: Anyone who knowingly and maliciously writes or reads publicly, substitutes, suppresses, removes, re-seals, or erases a will, or any other written instrument; and anyone who engraves a false seal, or makes one, or impresses it, or exhibits it; and anyone who counterfeits gold or silver money, or washes, melts, scrapes, spoils, or adulterates any coin bearing the impression of the face of the emperor, or refuses to accept it, unless it is counterfeit, shall, if of superior rank, be deported to an island, and if of inferior station, be sentenced to the mines, or punished capitally (Paul, *Sententiae*, 5.25).

So reads one of our best sources on a late Republican law identifying crimes to be tried in a public court. The text presents an immediate problem: since the law was named for L. Cornelius Sulla, it was passed in the 80s BCE, but the reference to the emperor cannot date earlier than 27 BCE. Some time between 27 BCE and the lifetime of the author Julius Paulus in the third century CE, the law must have been modified. Since legal sources generally date from the third to the sixth centuries CE, Roman legal historians are often faced with this type of challenge.

We can gain additional information on our law from the *Digest* of Justinian, a collection of the writings of Roman jurists published in 529 CE by the eastern Roman emperor Justinian (**Figure 9.3**). The *Digest* quotes Marcian, another third century CE

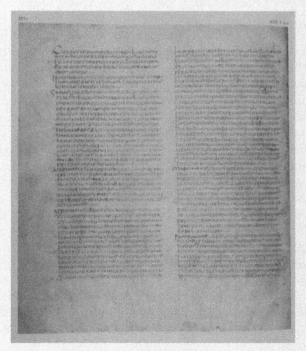

Figure 9.3 Page from the *Pandectarum codex Florentinus*, otherwise known as the *Littera Florentina*, a copy of the *Digest* of Justinian made within 20 years of its publication, sixth century CE. Biblioteca Medicea Laurenziana, Florence.

jurist, as noting that "the penalty of the *lex Cornelia* is imposed on a person who with malicious intent conspires for the giving of false witness or the delivering one after another of false evidence" (48.10.1). His testimony allows us to see that the Cornelian law dealt with fraud more broadly: giving false testimony and falsifying financial records were included along with forging wills and counterfeiting money.

On occasion our sources provide enough information to trace the development of a law. Callistratus indicates that the emperor Claudius (41–54 CE) has "added to the *lex Cornelia* that anyone who, in writing another's will or codicils, writes in a legacy to himself in his own hand is then liable" (*Dig.* 48.10.15). Similarly the historian Tacitus (*Annals* 14.41) reports a conspiracy to forge a will in 61 CE where someone colluded in an attempt to avoid justice by indicting the defendants before the wrong court. The Senate added a clause to affirm that such actions were equivalent to bringing a false accusation and so were subject to the *lex Cornelia*.

These last examples offer a good illustration of the evolution of Roman law. In both cases there was some question whether a particular activity was covered under the terms of a law. A decision was then made on the specifics of the case, and the precedent set by that decision became part of the law going forward; the *Digest* is filled with examples of these precedents. This notion of precedent has become central to American and European notions of law and represents one of the most significant legacies of ancient Rome.

The Breakdown of Public Law

Turning our attention away from criminal law and towards the laws that governed the Roman state reveals further ways that the legal system was unable to cope with the disruptions that erupted during the Late Republic. The death of a citizen such as Tiberius Gracchus at the hands of another citizen needed to be justified legally: otherwise it would be considered murder. The first mechanism employed was the passage of a Senatorial decree that told the consuls to take any steps necessary to ensure that no harm came to the state. We might think of this decree as a form of martial law, and a later Roman historian called it the *senatus consultum ultimum* (often abbreviated *SCU*: "the final decree of the Senate"). It was first passed against Gaius Gracchus in 121 BCE as part of the Senatorial campaign against him. The supporters of Gracchus were so incensed at this effective declaration of martial law that they brought criminal charges against the consul Opimius. His acquittal in the trial made clear that the court system did not necessarily offer protection against violence, but that the *SCU* could be used as a legal justification against political opponents.

An alternative means of justifying violence against one's opponents was to have them declared a *hostis* ("enemy"). This declaration not only stripped the individual of Roman citizenship and thus the protection of Roman laws but turned them into an active enemy of Rome. Romans now had a duty to kill this person. A further advantage of declaring an opponent to be a *hostis* was that it could only be done through legislation and therefore with the support of the people, rather than only the narrower group of Senators. More significantly, both the *SCU* and the *hostis* declaration fall well outside the normal operations of the Roman legal system. The first declares itself to be the "final" word and authorizes the overriding of all normal laws, while the second uses the legal system only to change the status of an individual to "non-Roman." Procedure and status continue to be the focus of Roman legal activity, but by the end of the Republic they are used to condone violence rather than prevent it. Not only could the legal system no longer contain violence, but we might say that it had almost ceased to be a functional system.

Conclusion

The extent of the problems can be seen most easily in the reforms of the dictator Sulla and their aftermath. After Sulla marched on Rome he had himself declared dictator for reforming the state and passed a series of laws intended to stabilize the government. Within 10 years, however, all of these reforms had been undone through the threat or actual use of military force: the example he had set through the use of force proved more powerful than his laws. Ultimately Sulla pointed the way to the future: the Roman system began to function well again when the emperor Augustus took power. His personal military superiority served as the final arbiter for debates over status, but he was scrupulous in following procedure and in showing respect for private property, even altering the design for his new forum when the owner of an adjacent piece of land refused to sell. These actions set the tone for the Empire: as an autocrat, the Emperor managed questions of status, while Roman law continued to concern itself with property and procedure. The concern with these last two issues in Western countries today is a direct legacy of these developments.

Discussion Questions

1. What do the elements of the Roman legal system tell us about their values? In what ways does the legal system of your own country reflect its values?
2. What benefits do elite members of society gain from having a clearly defined legal system? What benefits, if any, do non-elite members of society gain? How do these apply to your own country?
3. What are some of the principal ways in which the ideal of Rome as imagined by the law code differed from reality? How do they differ in your own world?
4. In what ways did Roman law change following the conquest of the Mediterranean basin? To what degree were those changes a direct result of imperial expansion?

Further Reading

Crook, John A. (1967). *Law and Life of Rome*. Ithaca, NY: Cornell University Press.

This book focuses on Roman law in its social context, showing how the provisions of the legal code affected Romans in their daily activities. Crook goes into great detail with primary sources to discuss issues such as inheritance and its impact on family relationships, contracts, and relationships between enslavers and the enslaved.

Frier, Bruce W. (1985). *The Rise of the Roman Jurists: Studies in Cicero's Pro Caecina*. Princeton, NJ: Princeton University Press.

This book uses a single speech from Cicero to explore the reasons why law emerged as a distinct profession in the later Roman Republic. Frier combines both historical and legal perspectives to argue that the political instability of the period created a desired for stability in other areas and led to an effort to clarify and regularize the laws of the state.

Gardner, Jane F. (1986). *Women in Roman Law & Society*. Bloomington, IN: Indiana University Press.

Using both literary and inscriptional evidence, this book investigates the legal position of women in ancient Rome. Gardner describes how laws affected women throughout their lives: as daughters, wives, and mothers; as heiresses and testators; as owners and controllers of property; and as workers. The book is especially valuable for exploring the ways in which the strict letter of the law was circumvented and changed, and for analyzing what the laws themselves tell us much about the situation of Roman women.

Gaughan, Judy E. (2010). *Murder Was Not a Crime: Homicide and Power in the Roman Republic*. Austin, TX: University of Texas Press.

This book builds from the observation that the Roman Republic had no specific law against murder to argue that private acts of violence were not considered a threat to the state in Rome. Gaughan emphasizes that individual families maintained the ability to carry out punishments for unlawful killings, further evidence of the decentralized Republican system of power, and the self-help nature of the legal system.

Meyer, Elizabeth (2004). *Legitimacy and Law in the Roman World: Tabulae in Roman Belief and Practice*. Cambridge: Cambridge University Press.

This fascinating study concerns itself with the wooden tablets on which the Romans wrote not only legal documents, but public and religious ones as well. Meyer suggests that the use of writing helped bring order to both the human and divine worlds and highlights how Roman law gained authority from this connection. These tablets then became the ancestors to legal documents that are so common today.

Riggsby, Andrew M. (1999). *Crime and Community in Ciceronian Rome*. Austin, TX: University of Texas Press.

This book uses the speeches of Cicero to illustrate the political nature of the public court system of Rome. Riggsby examines four major charges: bribery, poisoning and assassination, extortion, and public violence. He suggests that the Roman court system aimed at supporting the public good rather than pursuing abstract notions of justice.

10
The Military

In 29 BCE, at the very end of the Roman Republic, when Octavian (soon to be Augustus) returned to Rome after the final defeat of Antony and Cleopatra in Egypt, he closed the doors of the temple of Janus. According to Roman tradition, the doors to this temple remained open whenever the Roman state was at war, and were closed when the state was at peace. Octavian proudly recounts this moment in the autobiographical summary of his accomplishments written at the end of his life:

> Before my birth, it is recorded that the temple was closed twice in the entire time since the founding of the city, but while I was the leading man the Senate voted that it should be closed three times (*Res Gestae*, 13).

While Octavian wants to draw our attention to his own deed, our attention should also be drawn to the remarkable fact that prior to him the doors had been closed only twice. Only twice in the previous 500 years were the Romans NOT engaged in a war somewhere! Even if Octavian's claim is not 100% accurate, Rome existed in a nearly constant state of war for nearly the entire Republic. The need to have an army was a central feature of their society, and military matters must have played a significant role in almost every aspect of Roman life. We need to ask what impact this situation had on Roman society on a day-to-day basis, and on both elite and non-elite individual Romans. In other chapters we have discussed the impact of Roman expansion achieved through victory in war, but in this chapter we will explore what made that expansion possible and how the military needs of Rome affected their society.

A Social and Cultural History of Republican Rome, First Edition. Eric M. Orlin.
© 2022 John Wiley & Sons, Inc. Published 2022 by John Wiley & Sons, Inc.

The Army in Early Rome

Warfare in the Early Republic

We have had occasion already to talk about the difficulty in reconstructing elements of fifth century Roman history, and warfare is no different. Livy's narrative presents a series of continuous wars, where Roman armies took the field year after year. Many of these narratives are almost carbon copies of each other, suggesting that Livy did not really know what was happening and so just used a basic model that may have been based on his own experiences more than actual knowledge. Let us take a look at one of these episodes.

Livy (2.43–52) reports that in the 480s BCE, one consul was sent to fight the Aequi east of Rome, while the other was sent to Veii about 10 miles north of Rome. In the first campaign, Livy merely writes "nothing happened worth recording." In the other, one of the Roman generals was killed and the Roman line nearly gave way. The battle looked bleak for the Romans until the consul Fabius, a relative of the dead general, rode up to the line, shouted words of encouragement and dove back into battle. His bravery won the day for the Romans, though he too was mortally wounded. The army then returned to Rome in triumph, with the war apparently won. In the very next year, however, Livy reports a renewed battle with the people from Veii: "from that time, there was neither peace nor war with the Veientines, whose methods closely resembled those of brigands." The family of Fabius offered to fight this war on their own at their own cost. Livy gives the number of soldiers in this band as 306, all members of the same clan. This force set out to the north, but after some initial success, they were completely wiped out by an ambush. The Romans were thus forced to regroup and send out a regular army in the following year.

What can we make of an account such as this? There are hints in the text that offer clues to a clearer picture of Roman warfare at this time. For one, Livy's text reveals the small scale of fighting at this time: the force of the Fabii was a mere 300 men, which was enough to fight the Veientines to a standstill. We should also note the often indecisive nature of the fighting: a great triumph is followed by more fighting and then a significant defeat for the Romans that required a change in tactics. This episode does not fit the all-powerful Roman army of popular imagination, or even of Livy's imagination for that matter. Indeed, it seems to have something in common with undeveloped nations, since developed states do not ordinarily turn their military affairs over to private armies.

Comparison with other undeveloped agricultural societies suggests they engage primarily in two kinds of conflict: cattle raiding and border skirmishes to establish boundaries. The first may not involve formal armies, but simply bands of individuals seeking personal benefit. Livy's narrative might be interpreted in this light: the Fabii were perhaps not a public army, but one family involved in trying to steal cattle from a neighboring town, and they were caught red-handed. Border skirmishes can often be a consequence of these cattle raids. A state might send out a small force to protect the cattle of its citizens and to put an end to cross-border raids. Livy's account of these early battles with Veii fits neatly into this pattern. Constant yearly fighting is certainly consistent with the attempt of two communities to establish boundaries. Victory of one side in one year leads to an attempt by the other side to reset the boundary in the following year: these were not long-lasting triumphs, but minor victories. While the Roman historical tradition may have turned these events into heroic tales, a careful reading helps us recognize that the pattern of fighting looks more like an undeveloped state.

Organization of the Roman Army

If such border skirmishes represent the typical fighting in this period, it raises questions about the organization of the Roman army at this time. Livy describes a reorganization of the Roman army, in which Roman citizens were slotted into classes based on their wealth. Since citizens were expected to provide their own military equipment, one's census class determined one's role in the military. The wealthiest, who could therefore afford to own horses, served as the cavalry, while next group served as the heavy-armed infantry and made up the bulk of the army. The remaining classes were progressively less well-armed, and the last class served in a variety of non-combat roles (**Figure 10.1**). Each class was expected to contribute a set number of fighting units of 100 men each, and thus was known as a **century**, and each century was led by its own **centurion**. This system provided the organizational basis for the Roman army from the time of the reform forward.

Roman Centuriate Organization

Class	Census (= wealth)	Military Role	Total Centuries
1	400,000(?) *asses**	*equites* = cavalry	18
	100,000 *asses*	*pedites* = foot-soldiers	80
2	75, 000 *asses*	lightly-armed foot-soldiers	20
3	50, 000 *asses*	lightly-armed foot-soldiers	20
4	25, 000 *asses*	lightly-armed foot-soldiers	20
5	11, 000 *asses*	armed with slings	30
	<11,000 *asses*	Engineers	2
	<11,000 *asses*	Musicians	2
	<11,000 *asses*	*capite censi* = noncombatants	1

* an *as* is a weight of uncoined copper

Figure 10.1 Roman centuriate organization.

One way to understand how the Roman army was embedded in Roman society is to remember that centuries as described above served as the organizational basis for the *comitia centuriata*, where decisions on declaring war and elections for magistrates with *imperium* – the ability to command troops – took place.

Although Livy places this reform in the middle of the sixth century BCE, such a well-developed system is completely inconsistent with the type of fighting seen in the fifth century. Among the most obvious problems, it would yield armies larger than 300 soldiers. Most scholars therefore believe that at first the Romans did just draw on small groups for their military needs. The new system then developed as Roman warfare developed from border skirmishes into campaigns that occurred at a further distance from Rome. Rome began to embark on larger-scale campaigns in the fourth century BCE, and this period is more likely to provide the context for these shifts in the Roman military.

The first major step in Rome's expansion was an organized attack on Veii, the stronghold of the Etruscan league, and this campaign may have provided the impetus to reorganize army recruitment. The Romans claim to have besieged the town for 10 years, a number that seems suspicious since the Trojan War also lasted 10 years and the Romans believed they were descended from the Trojans. While we should not take the details of the historical accounts at face value, the campaign did require a permanent force to surround Veii. After their success at Veii, the Romans ventured further away from Rome and subdued many of the cities of central Italy by 338 BCE, which would have required larger armies and more regular recruitment. The fourth century thus seems the most reasonable period for the reorganization of the Roman army.

In his account of the fourth century campaigns, Livy describes another reform that can give us a sense of both of the fighting techniques the Romans used prior to this moment and the one that would become standard from this point forward. The changes he describes involved using the *scutum*, a smallish oblong shield, rather than the *clipeus*, a large round shield. This shift enabled the Romans to move away from a formation as a single mass of soldiers pushing forward all at once to the composition into **maniples**. Each maniple was composed of three lines of companies: the front line were the *hastati*, armed with spears, followed by the heavy-armed *principes* and *triarii*. *Velites*, loosely-armored soldiers from the lower classes armed with javelins, would be stationed in front of the maniple to provide cover. Our sources suggest that a Roman **legion** consisted of thirty maniples, 10 of each type, for an overall fighting force of perhaps 3000 men per legion in the fourth century. The fact that Livy places the introduction of the maniple in the fourth century offers another reason to believe that the centuriate organization described above dates to this period as well. This arrangement of forces became the backbone of the Roman army, since it proved successful time and again. As army service became more regular, its impact on the rest of Roman society was bound to increase.

Army and Society: The Elite

Military service was embedded in the careers of Roman politicians. The two highest magistrates in Rome held military as well as civilian duties. Consuls and praetors did spend some of their term in office administering the city, but they spent the majority of their time on military service, especially from the third century BCE onward. Military service was so important to members of the Roman elite that they could not even embark on a political career until they had amassed 10 years under arms. To ensure that members of the elite continued to engage in warfare, the Roman system also made it as risk-free as possible. If a campaign proved unsuccessful, the Romans blamed religious omens or other factors rather than the commanding general. In this way, the political system generated constant support for additional warfare among the elite.

A successful military career was one of the surest ways to political success. It brought fame to the successful general, especially if he were successful enough to be awarded a triumph. This ceremony allowed him to parade through the streets of Rome with his entire army as well as all the plunder he had captured; many triumphs also contained wagons with representations of cities captured or the decisive battle so that he could tell the story of his campaign. He could thus leave an impression in the minds of the population to increase his name recognition and his stature among them. A successful campaign also put money into his pocket: generals had nearly complete control over the plunder from the campaign. Some of this would be distributed to his soldiers as a bonus, but some could be kept for his own purposes. Many generals created monuments of one sort or another to remind people of their victory. Triumphal arches are mostly a feature of the later Imperial period, but many generals vowed temples to the gods while on campaign, while others created non-religious monuments. These buildings all contained inscriptions reminding people of the general's successful campaign. All of these means provided Roman politicians with ample motivation to fight aggressive military campaigns in the hopes of victories that would further their career.

Political Issues: *The Roman Triumph*

The Roman triumph brought together the Roman military, politics, and religion in one celebration. A triumph was the only time a general was allowed to march his troops through the city, in celebration of the great victory. The most complete description comes from Plutarch describing the triumph of Aemilius Paullus in 167 BCE (*Aemilius Paullus* 32–34):

> The people erected scaffolds where they could best behold the show. This triumph lasted three days. On the first were seen the statues, pictures, and colossal images taken from the enemy, drawn in 250 chariots. On the second was carried the finest and richest armor of the Macedonians, both of brass and steel, all newly polished and glittering. After these wagons there followed 3000 men who carried the silver that was coined. On the third day was brought the gold coin and all the gold plate that was used at Perseus's table. After a little intermission, the king's children were led as captives, and then came Perseus himself, clad all in black. Finally Aemilius himself came, seated on a chariot magnificently adorned, dressed in a robe of purple interwoven with gold and holding a laurel branch in his right hand.

The 10-minute long scene in the 1963 movie *Cleopatra* in which Elizabeth Taylor enters Rome, while not actually a triumph, gives a good sense of the spectacle (**Figure 10.2**). A well-executed triumph allowed a Roman politician to make a lasting impression upon the populace.

Figure 10.2 Still photo from Cleopatra (1963) starring Elizabeth Taylor, depicting Cleopatra's fictionalized entrance into Rome.

The triumph could be political in other ways as well. The right to celebrate a triumph could be a hotly contested matter. Commanding officers who had finished a successful campaign needed to ask the Senate to grant them a triumph. The grounds for granting a triumph were flexible and depended on the politics of the moment as much as on the general's accomplishments. Victory in battle was no guarantee of a triumph, since political opponents might try to deny a returning general his moment in the sun. Even Aemilius Paullus, mentioned above, was almost denied his triumph: it was granted only after one of his soldiers stood up and revealed his battle scars in order to shame the opposition.

At its heart, however, the triumph was a religious procession. It started outside the religious boundary of the city and took a roundabout route past many of the city's altars, temples, and other monuments before ending at the temple of Capitoline Jupiter. There the general climbed the steps of the temple and offered a sacrifice to thank the gods for his victory. The end of the ceremony reminded both the Romans and the general himself that they owed their success to powers beyond their control. During the procession, an enslaved person even rode in the chariot with the general constantly repeating the phrase "Remember you are only a man." The ceremony thus elevated one man above the crowd while also reminding him that he was still a part of the crowd. The triumph may thus be the best representation of the Roman connection between military success, political success, and religious success.

Army and Society: Ordinary Citizens

The life of an ordinary Roman citizen was also bound up with the military, and ordinary Romans also benefited from Rome's near constant warfare. All Roman citizens were expected to serve in the military. The procedure for recruiting troops was straightforward: on a given day, all citizens of military age were required to appear in Rome, and the military tribunes would select those who were to serve in the coming year. Fighting in the army began as a seasonal occupation: until the Romans began to embark on overseas campaigns, soldiers would be dismissed at the end of the year and a new army drafted in the following year. When campaigns were short and close to Rome, no payment was offered to the soldiers. As campaigns began to stretch out during the fourth century BCE, soldiers did receive a daily allowance to compensate for expenses, similar to jury duty today. This practice may have been intended to prevent poorer citizens from falling into poverty and thus becoming ineligible for service in the heavy infantry.

While Roman soldiers were not paid for their service, they did have a financial incentive for fighting, in the form of a share in the spoils of war. When the Romans captured a city, the soldiers were often allowed to roam the city and take whatever they could back to their camp. The officers would then make an equal distribution among the soldiers. It was also common for a general who celebrated a triumph to give his troops a bonus, and to give centurions and other officers a double bonus. Thus, Roman citizens might volunteer for military service beyond what was required, in the hopes of a financial windfall if the war should be quickly successful. The average Roman citizen might thus spend most of his adult life under arms.

By examining the career of one Roman soldier, we can get a clearer vision of a Roman soldier's career. In a discussion about military service dated to 171 BCE, Livy (42.34) reports that a man named **Spurius Ligustinus** stepped forward from the crowd and spoke as follows:

> I joined the army in 200 BCE, and I served two years in the ranks in the army which was taken across to Macedonia, in the campaign against King Philip. In the third year T. Flamininus promoted me, for my bravery, to be centurion of the 10th maniple of *hastati*. After the defeat of King Philip and the Macedonians, when we had been brought back to Italy and demobilized, I immediately left for Spain as a volunteer with the consul M. Porcius Cato (195 BCE). ...This general judged me worthy to be appointed centurion of the first century of *hastati*. I enlisted for the third time, again as a volunteer, in the army sent against the Aetolians and King Antiochus. M'. Acilius Glabrio appointed me centurion of the first century of the *principes* (191 BCE). When King Antiochus had been driven out and the Aetolians had been crushed, we were brought back to Italy. Thereafter I saw two campaigns in Spain, one with Q. Fulvius Flaccus as praetor (182 BCE), the other with T. Sempronius Gracchus in command (180 BCE). I was brought back home by Flaccus with the others whom he brought back with him from the province for his triumph, on account of their bravery. And I returned to Spain because I was asked to do so by Tiberius Gracchus. Four times I held the rank of Chief Centurion. Thirty-four times I was rewarded for bravery by the generals. I have been given six civic crowns. I have completed 22 years of service in the army, and I am now over 50 years old.

Note the longevity of Ligustinus' career: there were only seven years between age 22 and 50 when he did not participate in a military campaign, and all of the campaigns he mentions took place overseas. In each of these campaigns Ligustinus was directly involved in combat action; centurions were not safely stationed in the back with the commanding general and his staff, and the casualty rate for these officers was high. Ligustinus specifically mentions volunteering on three occasions and some of his fighting involved wealthy Greek kingdoms. Since he had achieved several promotions, he likely accumulated a decent nest egg. Even if the spoils of war were not equally distributed, his account suggests that the average Roman citizen was more than willing to go to war for many years at a time.

The question arises: how typical was Ligustinus? On the one hand, Ligustinus must have been an outstanding soldier to have survived so many campaigns and to have been promoted so many times. Since there were a limited number of centurions, not every Roman can have been as successful. We might also question the truthfulness of his account: Ligustinus himself may have exaggerated his accomplishments, or Livy may have got the details wrong. On the other hand it is unlikely that the claims were so extraordinary that no one could imagine a career like it: Livy and his audience must have believed that a career like this was in the range of the ordinary. It thus provides a good sense of the overwhelming dominance of military service in the life of a Roman citizen: a Roman might spend up to 70% of his adult life on military service.

Ligustinus can also help us think more broadly about the social impact of the constant Roman warfare. Ligustinus presumably left a wife and perhaps children behind in Italy for the long periods of time that he was away on campaign. Roman family life and women's roles were shaped by the absence of 15% of Rome's adult male population for long stretches of time. As discussed in Chapter 5, the Roman *familia* technically consisted of multiple generations, so members of the household living elsewhere might have been able to provide some assistance. Indeed, the need for such assistance may have contributed to the notion that the *familia* extended beyond the nuclear unit. In many families teenage boys would have to assume the role as the leading man of the house, or wives with smaller children would have had to fend for themselves. The eulogy of a woman from the very end of the Republic gives some sense of what this life might have been like: she had to move houses several times, eventually staying with her mother-in-law, and she had to fight for her property rights when her father's will was challenged. The story of constant warfare is thus not limited merely to the series of military victories or the men on campaign, but affected every member of Roman society.

Working with Sources
The Life of Turia

Late in the first century BCE, an unknown Roman man erected a large tombstone for his deceased wife and inscribed a eulogy for her on it. This remarkable document (*CIL* 6.41062) is known as the *laudatio Turiae* ("praise for Turia"), because at one time the unnamed wife was identified with a woman named Turia. Despite not knowing the identity of the woman and other challenges of interpretation, it offers us an unparalleled record of one Roman woman's life in the late Roman Republic.

> The inscription falls into the genre of a funeral oration, and so one task is therefore to consider how the text may have been shaped by this context. A speaker at a funeral was expected to praise the virtues of the deceased. Perhaps the deceased did not possess all those qualities, but the virtues stressed can tell us which qualities were valued by that society. We might also compare it to other eulogies, although we must adjust our expectations: men were often praised for service to the state, not a role expected of women.
>
> Parts of the speech seem concerned to display qualities that might be expected of a devoted wife by the Romans. The husband touches dramatically on these points:
>
> > Why should I mention your domestic virtues: your chastity, obedience, affability, reasonableness, industry in working wool, religion without superstition, sobriety of attire, modesty of appearance? Why dwell on your love for your relatives, your devotion to your family? You have shown the same attention to my mother as you did to your own parents, ... and you have innumerable other merits in common with all married women who care for their good name.
>
> The wife's chastity (*pudicitia*) and devotion (*pietas*) may be conventional words of praise for women, but the detail that she honored her in-laws on a par with her own parents suggests that her husband saw this as exceptional.
>
> Other sections of the speech display the wife taking a public role to protect the interests of the family. When her husband had been forced into exile, she defended the validity of her father's will against those who sought to overturn it. She also sent money and supplies, including her own jewelry, to support her husband. Most notably her husband noted that when a gang of men attempted to "break into our house to plunder, you beat them back successfully and defended our home." The language used carries a military overtone and qualities that the Romans normally associated with men, as does language describing her actions in helping her husband devise an appropriate strategy when he was able to return. The wife's service to her family seems to be equated to a man's service to the state.
>
> If this unknown woman was unique in some ways, her actions were not: we know of other women who similarly took independent action in the interests of their families. The *Laudatio Turiae* is valuable precisely because it opens a clearer window on to the challenges faced by Roman women and their ability to overcome them.

Explanations for Success

As we have seen in other chapters, the fourth and third centuries BCE proved to be the pivotal moments in Roman history, when the Roman successes in war set them on the path to empire. Now that we have looked at the key elements of the Roman army up to this point, we can try to answer the question most often asked about the Roman military: why were the Romans so successful in war? Why were they able to conquer the entire Mediterranean?

One practical answer emerges from a discussion of Roman roads. We tend to think of roads as a way to get from one place to another or else, but for the Romans they were less about moving people than about moving goods, and especially military supplies. An army setting out from Rome could walk across hillsides as easily as it could walk on a path paved with stones, but food and other supplies needed to be loaded onto carts. Most armies in the ancient world did not have the ability to feed themselves for an extended period of time. Individual soldiers might bring several days rations, but after that the army would have to purchase or forage for food, and supplying thousands of men with the necessary calories could become a serious issue. Attacking armies thus needed to engage the enemy as quickly as possible, a fact which gave the defenders a significant advantage. They could delay the battle and begin to create problems for the invaders, or they could choose their best position for the battle, knowing the attackers would be forced to give battle even from a disadvantage. By creating supply lines for their armies, the Romans avoided these problems and could wait for their opponents to make a mistake, or even for defenders' supply issues to force them into battle. The Romans had an organizational ability rarely paralleled in the ancient world, perhaps only exceeded by Alexander the Great – and of course Alexander was the most successful general the ancient world knew.

Exploring Culture: *All Roads Lead to Rome*

Roman roads and aqueducts are among the most visible legacies of the Romans, constructed not only in Italy but all around the Mediterranean. Two of the best preserved aqueducts are the Aqueduct of Segovia (Spain) and the Pont du Gard outside Nimes (France), while Roman roads, arches, and bridges can be found nearly everywhere. As noted, these are also among the earliest public construction projects undertaken by the Roman state. It is worth considering why these types of projects commanded so much interest from the Romans for such a long period.

Aqueducts and roads held practical value of course. As the population of the city grew, an increase in the water supply was necessary. Aqueducts served in effect as artificial rivers, bringing a continuous supply of fresh water into the city; the improved drainage system that began with the *cloaca maxima* enabled the excess water from these "rivers" to make its way into the Tiber and then into the sea. The operation of the water supply system also reinforced existing hierarchies in the Roman state: wealthier families might be able to tap directly into the aqueduct, while poorer residents would have to access water at a fountain or other common location. Aqueducts, like roads, were often named for the person who built them, so that in addition to these tangible benefits, the aqueduct brought political capital to an individual for providing a public service.

Roads also created value in multiple ways. Movement by land was always slower and more expensive in the ancient world, and roads eased this challenge to some degree. Most scholars believe that roads were originally constructed for military purposes, to enable the quicker movement of troops from the capital to wherever the next campaign happened

Figure 10.3 The Via Appia (Appian Way), begun in 312 BCE and completed in 264 BCE.

to be. The history of road building lends some support to this notion. The first road, the Via Appia, led south towards the Samnites, and was extended to Brindisi in 264 BCE, just after Rome's campaigns against Pyrrhus had led to significant fighting in the boot of Italy (**Figure 10.3**). The Via Aurelia and Via Flaminia, both constructed in the middle of the third century BCE, headed northeast and northwest respectively, in a period when Rome's attention was drawn to the Gauls and Ligurians in the northern part of the peninsula. Once built, of course, roads were available to all residents of Italy: merchants, farmers, and craftsmen. The ease of travel thus also facilitated migration and movement around a peninsula now increasingly under Roman control.

The symbolic function of these projects must have been equally important. As the Romans expanded the territory under their control, these signature building projects served to announce visibly the Roman domination of the countryside, and their power over the land's inhabitants. They might be seen as a way for the Romans to demonstrate their dominance over nature as well, reshaping the landscape routing water courses to suit their own needs. These projects left an indelible mark on the landscape, reminding everyone who saw them of the power of Rome, and, indeed, following a road would lead one, inevitably, to the city of Rome.

Another explanation looks to the Roman response to military defeat. Any country that fights as many wars as the Romans did is bound to suffer a certain number of losses. As a rule, the Romans chose not to acknowledge military defeat, but instead saw defeat as a prelude to a greater victory. For instance, Livy can skim over the destruction of the Fabii to report on the Romans' eventual victory over Veii. The same pattern repeats itself in more historical periods: the massive defeats they suffered at the hands of Hannibal at the beginning of the Second Punic War became merely the prelude to their eventual victory. The Roman sense that the gods were on their side, or could be brought to their side, gave them a sense that ultimate victory lay within their grasp. These factors may have contributed to the Romans' willingness to continue fighting at a point when others might have sought peace.

The Greek historian Polybius cited Roman discipline as a reason for the success of their armies (**Figure 10.4**). He describes the severity of punishment for soldiers who failed to carry out basic duties: for example, failing to properly carry out the night watch was punished by having the other soldiers beat him to death. Whole units could even be punished in this way, with a small percentage of soldiers chosen at random for death at the hands of their fellow soldiers. Polybius noted that Romans as a result chose to face death in battle, knowing that a certain death awaited them if they were to flee.

The Romans balanced this brutality with positive reinforcements both for those who were on campaign and also to those who remained at home. Soldiers displaying special bravery were honored not only among other soldiers, but among the entire population in Rome. Returning soldiers wore decorations that marked their military honors in religious processions, and often placed the spoils captured in war in the

Figure 10.4 Scene from the Column of Trajan depicting the testudo, or "turtle" formation. Rome, early second century CE.

most conspicuous places in their houses as a visible sign of their bravery. For Polybius (6.39), these practices explained Roman success: "By such incentives those who stay at home are stirred up to a noble rivalry and emulation in confronting danger, no less than those who actually hear and see what takes place.... considering all this attention given to the matter of punishments and rewards in the army and the importance attached to both, it is no wonder that the wars in which the Romans engage end so successfully and brilliantly."

While all of these factors may have played a role in the Roman success, perhaps the most significant contributor to Roman success was simply their ability to draw on greater reserves of manpower than any other state. Polybius reports that at the beginning of the Second Punic War in 218 BCE, the Romans could draw on 700 000 infantry soldiers and 70 000 cavalry. These numbers may perhaps be exaggerated, but they are likely to give a good sense of scale. Many Roman opponents found these reserves of manpower to be their undoing. In Rome's first major international war, King Pyrrhus found that the Romans could afford to lose a greater number of troops than he could (hence the phrase a "Pyrrhic victory": he won the battles but lost the war because his casualties in war could not be replaced as easily). In the Second Punic War, the Romans are said to have lost 100 000 men in three battles early in the war. These losses would have led most states to collapse or at least to surrender, but the Romans were able to keep going: by some estimates as much as 30% of the Roman male citizenry were serving in the legions during the war. For comparison, at the end of World War II, only about 20% of the adult male population of the United States were engaged in combat duty.

This data, as so often in historical research, raises a new question: Why were the Romans able to draw on a greater supply of manpower than other states? The answer lies in two factors. On the one hand, the Romans had a much lower property qualification for serving in the military than other ancient cities. Polybius reports the minimum as 400 Greek *drachma* (equal to 4000 Roman *asses*), a very modest amount, probably just above what we might call the poverty line. Ligustinus whom we discussed above had only ½ an acre to his name and he served in the army for 22 years. Thus, nearly every adult male citizen served in the army. Just as importantly, the Romans drew on manpower from all over Italy. As discussed in Chapter 7, conquered Italian cities were required to send military contingents to Rome when asked. Because Roman society was more egalitarian than any of their neighbors – they distributed power more widely than anyone else and allowed foreigners to become citizens – they developed strength that no one else could match. One might even suggest that increased manpower was part of the purpose of this openness, another way in which the Roman need for a powerful military decisively shaped their society.

The Beginnings of an Imperial Army

As we have seen, for the first four hundred years of the Republic, the Romans relied on a citizen army. Volunteers were welcomed, but the Romans also had a process for filling out the ranks when needed, and serving in the army was both a civic duty and a way to improve one's lot in life, assuming one survived the campaign. The Roman conquest of the Mediterranean brought deep changes to the Roman military just as to other areas of society. The campaigns of the early second century BCE were fought overseas against the wealthy kingdoms of the eastern Mediterranean, but after the destruction of Corinth and Carthage in 146 BCE, there were few such kingdoms left to conquer. This may have made recruitment of troops more difficult. It has also been suggested that these wars of the second century BCE resulted in a greater number of casualties than earlier campaigns, a demographic issue with trickle-down effects on the military, on family life, on politics, and elsewhere. The changes in Rome's standing forced the Romans to change the way they went about their campaigns, resulting in even further changes to Roman society.

Professionalization of the Roman Army

Over the course of the second century BCE several changes in Roman military practice can be observed. While the wars of the fourth and third centuries may have relied on superior manpower and the strength of the battle line, in the second century Roman commanders recognized the advantages of the division of the army into maniples. The tactical flexibility provided by these units or by cohorts (two maniples) meant that they could respond to events during a battle by sending a cohort to reinforce a weak spot, or that they could launch attacks mid-battle on the enemy flanks. The superiority of this system became evident in the series of battles with the Greek phalanx beginning in 197 BCE. The phalanx was a rectangular mass formation that had to move as a single unit where any break in the line was often fatal, and the Roman flexibility allowed them to emerge undefeated from these wars. Wars in Spain confirmed the value of the cohort: maniples were too large to handle the guerrilla warfare the Romans faced.

At the end of the second century, Marius standardized the use of cohorts and the weapons they used. Romans began to use a type of javelin instead of a spear, and all soldiers were also equipped with a short sword. Techniques from gladiatorial training were adapted so that his soldiers might be proficient with these weapons. Marius also introduced the eagle as a legionary standard for soldiers to rally around. These changes improved the effectiveness of the Roman army: Marius was able to bring challenging campaigns in northern Africa and in southern Gaul to successful conclusions.

Over the course of the second century BCE, the property qualification to serve in the army steadily dropped, a change with significant if unforeseen repercussions on Roman society. Somewhere in the middle of the century the minimum property amount to register for the infantry was lowered from 4000 *asses* to 1500. This number likely lies below the poverty line: it might equate to enough money to buy 2–3 loaves of bread per day and nothing else. At the end of the century, Marius is reported to have eliminated the property requirement entirely, and accepted volunteers for his army in Africa from anyone who wished to serve. These individuals generally viewed service in the army as a way to improve their lot in life. This change is thus frequently viewed as the first step in the professionalization of the Roman army: service in the army, and the rewards that came with it, could be a career chosen by the poor for economic reasons, rather than a civic obligation for landowning citizens.

A primary question for both ancient and modern historians has been why exactly the property qualification disappeared. The Roman historian Sallust (86–35 BCE) suggested two reasons. The first was that Marius wanted to curry political favor with the poor who had just voted him into office; this explanation has generally been discarded, especially since the lowering of the property qualification began before Marius was even born. Sallust also suggested that a shortage of manpower required the property qualification to be lowered or dropped in order to maintain the supply of troops. This hypothesis seems more reasonable, but simply pushes the question to a different place: what had happened in the second century BCE to cause a shortage of manpower? Answers have ranged from a decline in the overall population to a decline in the number of landowning citizens or a decline in people willing to serve in the army, and it may not be possible to answer this question beyond a reasonable doubt.

Key Debates: *Roman Manpower in the Second Century*

For a long time it was assumed that manpower shortages lay behind the decision to recruit troops from the lowest census classes in the second century BCE. The argument was that only an inability to recruit troops in the usual manner could have forced a change in this long-standing tradition. The narrative concerning the Gracchi brothers, which emphasizes the absence of free farmers in Italy, seemed to strengthen the hypothesis. Tiberius' own reforms could thus be explained by the need to restore small property owners to their farms in order to create a pool of manpower. Since the Gracchi served as tribunes in 133 and 122 BCE, Marius' final elimination of the property qualification somewhere around 105 BCE fits conveniently into this narrative. Because the Senate had thwarted the reforms of the Gracchi, the number of propertyless Roman citizens continued to increase, creating the crisis which Marius' reforms were intended to address. The narrative derived from the literary sources is both consistent and logical.

In theory the Romans conducted a census every five years, and it might be thought that these census figures could shed further light on the manpower issue, but they turn out to be complicated. The figures show the Roman population hovering around 300 000 for most of the second century BCE, rising to 900 000 in 70 BCE, and then exploding to over 4 million in 28 BCE, the first census of the emperor Augustus. The increase in these last two numbers has seemed so large that many scholars argue a change in procedure must have taken place, and that the large figures must reflect men, women, and children combined, not just adult men. If this hypothesis is correct, the count in 70 BCE would represent 225 000 adult males, a significant decline in population.

Yet the theory of manpower shortages has been challenged on several grounds. Scholars who work more closely with comparative data have pointed out that no other society in history has experienced a population decline similar to what the census hypothesis requires. Since the evidence suggests that the city of Rome itself was home to around one million people in the time of Augustus, it seems impossible to accept this steep decline. If so, the figures of 900 000 and 4 million must also represent adult males only, and those figures give no reason to believe in a declining manpower.

Archaeological surveys of Italy in this period also fail to support the hypothesis of manpower decline due to the absence of small farms. While some areas do seem to show a lack of small farms, others show many small farms. These differences seem to be regional rather than spread uniformly across Italy, but the manpower shortage thesis implies a widespread change. It is possible that some farms were less prosperous than in previous years; archaeology is not equipped to answer questions of that nature. The current arguments around Marius' reforms therefore revolve around the degree of poverty in the Roman countryside and the possibility of an unwillingness to serve in the army rather than a straightforward decline in the population numbers.

We might instead turn our attention to a question we can try to answer on the impact of the changes to military recruitment: how did they impact Roman society in the late Republic?

The Army and Politics in the Late Republic

Since the military was tightly connected with other spheres of Roman society, the change in recruitment strategies had an almost immediate impact on Roman life in the Late Republic.

The composition of the Roman army from a largely landowning class to a largely propertyless class represents a massive change. As we saw in the earlier period, ordinary Romans such as Ligustinus were willing to volunteer for army service in exchange for portable wealth: they would gain a share in the plunder from the campaign. Because they already owned land, the money provided them with stability and the ability to improve their position. Soldiers who owned no property, however, faced a different situation: returning to Italy with money but no land provided them with fewer benefits. They may actually have volunteered for service in the hope that they would get some land as a consequence of their service, but there was no land in Italy available for distribution. Thus soldiers returning from the wars at this time faced economic challenges that previous generations of soldiers had not.

The Senate did not recognize this changed situation; the state was not accustomed to making land grants to soldiers upon their return from campaigning. Indeed, the Senate had not needed to make any provisions for such soldiers, since the distribution of plunder by the commanding general had generally been sufficient to satisfy their needs. Thus, when soldiers who completed their service in the army needed land on which to settle down, it fell to generals to take care of them. In order to do so, generals had to push legislation through the political system. This necessity strengthened the political bond between commander and soldier: the stronger the general was in the political arena, the better deals he could negotiate for his soldiers. In addition, the creation of military eagles and longer terms of service generated a sense of identity among the troops. As a result, even when released back into civilian life, soldiers began to retain loyalty to their commanders as political leaders and not just as military leaders. These consequences seem obvious in hindsight but were likely not to be evident at the time.

While Marius was the first to arrange land grants for his soldiers, the impact of this shift was fully realized under Lucius Cornelius Sulla. Sulla was elected consul in 88 BCE and drafted an army to fight against King Mithridates in Asia Minor. As he was preparing to depart, Marius convinced the assembly to pass a law transferring the command to himself. Marius' action was beyond the norms of ordinary behavior, but not technically illegal; the assembly had the right to confer command on whomever it wanted. Sulla, however, refused to be deprived of the opportunity for military glory. He turned to the troops that he had recruited for support. The troops, fearing that Marius would replace them with his own soldiers and thus deprive them of the economic opportunity offered by the war, agreed to march against Rome and reinstall Sulla as their commander.

This moment marks a watershed in the Late Republic. In the previous section, we noted the close connections between the military and the civilian aspects of the Roman state during the previous 400 years of the Republic. Despite these connections, the Romans had created structural barriers to ensure that civilian decision-making always preceded military power. For example, the legal power to command troops only existed outside the religious boundary of Rome: as soon as the general crossed into Rome, his troops were no longer bound to obey his commands. Sulla's example demonstrated that this obstacle no longer existed. Though the troops were not bound to obey Sulla's commands, they saw it as in their personal interest to follow him. His legal authority was thus irrelevant. Sulla's successful march on Rome made clear that a general with military troops under his command could dictate political outcomes.

On the one hand, Sulla is an extreme case, but, on the other, his example demonstrated that soldiers had become a political force that needed to be taken into account. On most occasions, they simply became part of a network that a skilled politician could try to activate in pursuit of his own political interests, but the knowledge that soldiers might support an individual who sought to impose his political will by violent means conditioned Roman politics for much of the period. When Pompey returned from his multi-year and highly successful campaigns in Asia, people in Rome waited nervously until he disbanded his army. The changed nature of military service had changed the nature of Roman politics; even when armies were not directly involved, violence in the form of street gangs often dictated political results. When in 49 BCE Julius Caesar followed Sulla's example and convinced his troops to march against Rome, he set off a chain of events that led to the transformation from republican to imperial rule.

Conclusion

In some respects, the Late Republic demonstrates a principle similar to that seen in earlier periods of Roman history: military success was a central means to political power. In the earlier period, this principle played out indirectly: a successful general earned name recognition and was valued for his leadership, and these traits could earn him election to higher political offices. Citizen-soldiers obtained a share of the plunder, enough to satisfy their needs on their return home. The structure of the army and the unwritten rules of political behavior allowed the military and civilian spheres to overlap without the one dominating the other.

In the Late Republic, the rewards for overseas service, both for generals and their troops, became increasingly greater. An increasingly professional army was still treated as if it were comprised of volunteers, so that soldiers came to rely upon their leaders for the rewards they felt they had earned through their military services. Many generals, swayed by the scale of money and glory to be won, began to stretch the limits of the system rather than accepting certain unspoken limits.

The Roman Republican system for managing its military was unprepared for the kind of army it needed to manage an empire. The Senate proved unwilling to take the steps needed in order to complete the professionalization of the army, enabling charismatic leaders to take advantage of the situation. It was only under the Roman emperors that the process was completed, a key part of the story of the Empire.

Discussion Questions

1. In what ways are the structural factors that led the Romans to war similar to and different from the factors that have led modern nations to war?
2. Are the benefits and drawbacks that the Romans encountered using a citizen volunteer army (as opposed to a professional army) similar to those that modern nations face? Are the tradeoffs of a professional army worth it?
3. Which explanation for Roman military success makes the most sense to you? What are modern explanations and in what ways do they parallel the explanations given for the Romans (allowing for technological changes)?
4. Was it inevitable that a state that depended so much on violence directed towards foreign opponents should end up with violence directed inward towards political opponents?

Further Reading

Armstrong, Jeremy (2016). *War and Society in Early Rome: From Warlords to Generals*. Cambridge: Cambridge University Press.
    This book focuses on the Early Republic to the conquest of central Italy, focusing on changes to the Roman army and the changes they brought to Roman society. Armstrong suggests that Rome transformed from dependence on "warlords" who operated outside of state authority to the use of a civic army controlled by state authors. He draws on recent archaeological work as well as the literary accounts to reconstruct the shape of early Roman civilization.

Brice, Lee L. (2019). *New Approaches to Greek and Roman Warfare*. Malden, MA: Wiley.
    A great collection of essays that covers issues such as the economics of paying for warfare, the role of women in families and as victims of war, and the psychological components of

military service such as morale, panic, recovery, and trauma. Chapters on Greece and on the Roman Empire allow for useful comparisons to the Roman Republic.

Clark, Jessica H. (2014). *Triumph in Defeat: Military Loss and the Roman Republic*. Oxford: Oxford University Press.

This book takes an unusual perspective focusing on Rome's military defeats during the Roman Republic. Clark argues that in the wake of the defeats of the Second Punic War, the Romans had to develop means of seeing these as part of a larger narrative of victory, which could include redefining victory objectives. The book thus provides good material for thinking about war stories in general and not just in Rome.

Milne, Kathryn H. (2020). "The Middle Republican Soldier and Systems of Social Distinction." In *Romans at War: Soldiers, Citizens and Society in the Roman Republic* (Jeremy Armstrong, and Michael P. Fronda, Eds.). London: Routledge, Taylor & Francis Group, pp. 134–153.

Milne focuses on the role of the ordinary soldier in upholding the Roman system, highlighting how triumphs and awards ennobled the activity of these soliders as a means of reinforcing the importance of certain types of military actions. She argues that these soldiers in turn reinforced the importance of the military to Roman society in order to ensure that the benefits conferred on them continued to have value.

Östenberg, Ida (2009). *Staging the World: Spoils, Captives, and Representations in the Roman Triumphal Procession*. Oxford: Oxford University Press.

Östenberg offers a comprehensive discussion of the Roman triumph, utilizing a wide variety of written sources as well as evidence from material culture and epigraphy. She focuses both on historical details of the celebration as well as the significance of the triumph within Roman culture. The three central chapters on the display of spoils, captives, and figural representations of the campaign demonstrate how triumphs depicted the city of Rome as a dominant world power.

Rosenstein, Nathan (2004). *Rome at War: Farms, Families, and Death in the Middle Republic*. Chapel Hill, NC: University of North Carolina Press.

Rosenstein offers a careful analysis of the impact of the Roman conquest of the Mediterranean on Roman families and the traditions of Roman farming. His first chapter provides an excellent summary of the debates over military recruitment and small farmers, highlighting many places where previous ideas have been shown to be unsatisfactory. The remainder of the book is a rethinking of these ideas and a suggestion of new ways to view farming and warfare in the Roman Republic.

11
The Economy

Somewhere around 160 BCE, Marcus Porcius Cato (Cato the Elder), former consul and censor and still a leader in the Roman Senate, wrote a handbook on agriculture. He began with the following words:

> It is true that to obtain money by trade is sometimes more profitable, were it not so risky; and likewise money-lending, were it respectable. Our ancestors held this view and embodied it in their laws … When they wanted to praise a worthy man their praise took this form: "a good husbandman" or "a good farmer." Someone praised in this way was thought to have received the highest accolade. I consider a trader to be an energetic man, and also one bent on making money, but as I said above, it is a dangerous career and one subject to disaster. On the other hand, it is from the farming class that the bravest men and the sturdiest soldiers come, their calling is most highly respected, their livelihood is most assured and is looked on with the least hostility, and those who are engaged in that pursuit are least inclined to be disaffected.

The text that follows is a hodgepodge of information, more like a notebook than a polished book. It includes suggestions on purchasing and managing a farm, but also inventory lists of needed equipment, instructions on how to build a mill or an olive or wine press, recipes for food but also for medicine, sample contracts, religious rituals, and more. While it offers some broad observations such as "building requires long thought but planting requires not thought but action," most of the handbook is filled with advice on smaller details: "Be sure to have a big manure heap and keep every piece of dung." It is also, coincidentally, the first surviving work of Roman prose.

A number of questions arise even just from this short passage. For one, what is a leading Roman statesman doing writing a handbook on agricultural techniques

A Social and Cultural History of Republican Rome, First Edition. Eric M. Orlin.
© 2022 John Wiley & Sons, Inc. Published 2022 by John Wiley & Sons, Inc.

filled with such ordinary information? It is not the kind of thing we might expect from someone at the very top of the Roman political order. We discussed in Chapter 3 how the ideology of farming as the noblest profession that creates the bravest and sturdiest men helped maintain elite social status. So we should be wary of accepting Cato's praise for farming and disrespect for trade and banking at face value, especially since we know that Cato himself engaged in merchant shipping. Reality does not always match the ideology, and both the Roman economy and the values associated with making money changed over time. Cato's handbook, however, points us to some crucial questions: what exactly was the role of agriculture in the Roman economy and how did its role change over time?

Cato's handbook also includes information on enslaved persons: when to buy and sell them, and how to get the most out of their labor. These sections remind us of the existence of slavery in the Roman Republic. Ancient Rome has long been considered to be one of the five known slave societies. Questions arise here as well: was Rome always a slave society, or was there a time when it might be better described as a "society with enslaved persons?" Is there even a meaningful difference between a "slave society" and a "society with enslaved persons?"

All of these questions will be explored in this chapter, beginning with the role of agriculture and the different types of farming in the early Roman Republic. As with other topics considered so far, the development of Rome's Mediterranean empire caused dramatic changes to the Roman economy, and so we will have to examine the impact of Rome's conquests upon the economy, and then the impact of these economic changes on other aspects of Roman society.

The Agricultural Basis of the Early Roman Economy

The Position of Farmers

To the Romans, having the leader of the Roman Senate writing a handbook on agriculture would have seemed perfectly normal: leading Roman politicians were almost always landowners. Cato's introduction above makes the ideological reasoning explicit: farming created the sturdiest soldiers. The high social status attached to farming explains in part why land was always the most valuable resource in Roman society, more than gold or silver (though Romans liked those too!). We should, however, press this point further: why did the Romans think that farming was a more honorable way to make a living? Cato's introduction again gives us the clue we need: their livelihood is "most assured" and "least subject to disaster." Farmers are capable (in theory at least) of producing the food they need to survive. The ideal of self-sufficiency was particularly emphasized in ancient Greece, but this idea was widespread across the Mediterranean. In the ancient world, food scarcity was an ever-present problem for many individuals: a single year's bad harvest could create significant hardship. The writings of Roman historians are filled with mentions of droughts or crop failures, and these were a concern requiring state attention as much as warfare.

Agriculture thus lay at the heart of ancient economic systems, and farmers provided its backbone. All other professions needed to produce something else (clothing, furniture, foreign luxury items) in order to trade for food, but only farmers could feed themselves. These conditions also explain why money-lending (or banking) ranked so low on the social scale: bankers did not produce a single tangible item that they could trade for food. They might be able to stockpile gold, silver, and bronze, but in a drought year those lumps of metal might be harder to trade than a new pair of shoes or a yoke for the oxen. It is no wonder Cato considered farming the safest way of earning a living.

Settling on a piece of property and trying to grow crops was not the only option for those working the land. Animal husbandry also produced food, especially cheese products, which could be traded for agricultural produce. It also produced wool, which as we have noted formed a key part of Roman society. On the other hand, meat was only a small part of the ancient Roman diet, primarily on festival celebrations; killing an animal deprived one of future benefits from it, so killing one was a real sacrifice. As a rule, the Romans did not have large ranches for sheep, goats, and pigs. Instead, many of those engaged in raising animals practiced transhumance. In the winter months, they would keep their animals at lower elevations, perhaps using one property as a base or perhaps moving from one place to another, but in all cases avoiding the bad weather at higher elevations. In summer, some of the men would take the flocks to other locations, especially at higher altitudes, allowing the animals to graze on the new spring grasses. Archaeological traces of transhumance paths suggest that the distances travelled could be significant, and some transhumance patterns can still be seen today in parts of Italy, such as the Molise. Because transhumance involved moving from place to place and living the summer months away from home, it was generally seen as a less desirable form of farming, but it also required less equipment and thus less money, and so was attractive to those who lacked the resources to manage a farm.

Not only did farming enable one to feed one's own family, but it could also provide an income. Excess produce was sold at markets, and in exploring the Roman economy we will need to distinguish between two types of farms. In the ancient Italian countryside we can find **subsistence farms**, where a small farmer might raise a number of different crops for his own family's subsistence and then sell the excess at market. We can also find small-scale commercial farms that aimed to produce cash crops; these specialized in a smaller number of agricultural items (typically grain, olives, or grapes) with the intent to sell these at a profit and then purchase other necessary foodstuffs. Let us explore these two models in more detail, which will lead us to further questions about the nature of farms devoted to one style of farming or the other.

Subsistence Farming in Ancient Italy

Subsistence farming means that the landowner is concerned primarily to plant and harvest crops to feed his family. He is not concerned with market fluctuations that might make one crop or another more valuable to sell, since he expects to have little or no excess crops that he might sell. Other items that his family might need, such as clothing, might be produced on his own farm by the women of the family using the wool from the family's flock: we can think back to the discussion of wool-working as the feminine ideal (see Chapter 5). Thus a subsistence farmer might have little contact with the market and could live wherever he wants. If there were a few items that he could not produce on his farm, such as iron tools, he might acquire these through barter for a small portion of his crops.

Historians have several reasons for believing that subsistence farming was the dominant method in the fifth and fourth centuries BCE, the first two hundred years of the Roman Republic. For one reason, there is little evidence from archaeology for the acquisition of significant wealth at this time. A second compelling reason is the absence of coinage as a means of exchange at this time. Towards the end of this period we do see lumps of bronze and other metals being used in the barter system. These lumps could then be used in an exchange for another good, or saved and melted down for use as a farm implement. Unfortunately for the purposes of exchange, these lumps came in a number of shapes and sizes; the lack of standardization meant that for each usage the two parties would have to agree on the value of the metal in the exchange. One conclusion we can draw from these conditions is that trade was only a limited element of the Roman economy at this time, because it would be a nightmare trying to run a market where one had to negotiate the value of the currency in each transaction.

Coinage and the Beginning of a Market Economy

The early third century BCE saw the introduction of Roman currency, generally known as *aes signatum* (**Figure 11.1**), or coined bronze. These pieces of bronze were cast in a standard size and stamped with a design, indicating that a government authority guaranteed the weight, and thus the value, of the metal. This was a significant step towards making market transactions easier, as both parties would know the value of the currency in advance. At the same time, the *aes signatum* was a crude currency: each "coin" weighed 3.5 pounds and making change was all but impossible since this was the only size. Its value to trade was therefore limited: traders had to find a way to clip off fragments of the bronze or else revert to the barter system in order to make up the difference. The next generation of currency, the *aes grave*, appeared in the middle of the third century BCE and attempted to address this problem. It came in multiple denominations and so made coinage more functional and trading easier than before. In the same period Rome saw the appearance of its first silver coinage, the *denarius*, first minted in 211 BCE. Silver coinage had been used in Greece since the seventh century BCE, so the Romans were late to the party.

While these experimentations with currency are interesting in their own right, they are particularly useful for what they tell us about the Roman economy: they suggest that in this period we see the transition of Rome into a market economy. The development of a standardized currency indicates an increase in trade and a desire to make trading easier. The adoption of silver coinage in particular shows the desire to trade with the Greek cities of southern Italy and also with cities in Greece proper.

Figure 11.1 Aes Signatum ("stamped bronze"), Rome, third century BCE.

The appearance of this currency roughly corresponds to the time when Rome expanded its domination over all of peninsular Italy. The defeat of Pyrrhus in 270 BCE led to Rome's undisputed control of southern Italy at precisely the moment when we see the emergence of silver coinage. We should be careful in drawing conclusions, since two things happening at about the same time does not mean that one caused the other: correlation does not equal causation is a common phrase among historians. In this case, however, there are good reasons, as well as other examples of how imperial conquest impacts trade, to believe that the conquest of Italy was a major spur to increased trade. We will see the impact of Roman military success on the Roman economy again and again.

How does this discussion of coinage affect our understanding of Roman farming practices? The increase in trade suggests an increasing use of markets, and thus ought to mean an increasing production of crops for sale in a market rather than just consumption at home. Cato's handbook shows clear signs of this transformation. Remember that this handbook was written around 160 BCE, or about 50 years after the introduction of the *denarius* as the dominant silver coinage in Rome. The transformation of the economy may have proceeded further by the time this text was written, but the text also suggests that Roman farmers must have been engaged in market practices already in the third century BCE.

Cato indicates his awareness of planning for market in a number of different ways, beginning with the first suggestions he makes in the text. He starts by noting that one ought to purchase a property with a sizeable town nearby, and/or a good road or river nearby for transportation. In the very next section he notes that one should check to make sure the property comes with "plenty of presses and vats: remember that the lack of them means a lack of produce." An owner needed to be able to press his own olive oil and wine, because it would cost him money to have his olives and grapes pressed elsewhere, and the olives and grapes on their own have a limited retail value. Cato shows a keen awareness of the market in another section: he recommends building extra vats for storage so that an owner "is free to wait for prices to rise, which will be better for income, better for self-esteem, better for reputation."

The system described by Cato has often been called the villa system of agriculture: small estates, clearly producing a number of products with an eye towards the market. One significant element of villa-style agriculture is the increased use of the stolen labor of enslaved persons, and this requires us to ask questions about the nature of slavery in the Roman Republic. The use of servile labor also displaced the free laborers from agricultural work, and the question of how many free farmers were displaced and what happened to them is crucial to understanding the Roman economy. When we look at slavery, we should ask not only about the impact of unfree labor on the Roman state, but also about its impact on these unfree individuals. Understanding slavery in the Roman Republic is vital to understanding their economic system.

Slavery in the Roman Republic

Enslaved persons existed in substantial numbers during the early centuries of the Roman Republic. They are mentioned in the Twelve Tables in several places, including that the monetary punishment for injuring an enslaved person is half of that for injuring a free person. Calculations suggest that there were over 50 000 enslaved persons in Rome during the fourth century BCE, primarily as a result of campaigns in Italy against the Samnites and other foes. The presence of significant numbers of enslaved persons in the late third century BCE is suggested by the fact that the Romans freed 8000 enslaved persons to replenish their manpower against Hannibal. The total number of enslaved persons must have been much higher, because even in a crisis the Romans would only have freed a portion of them.

The truly massive increase in the number of enslaved persons followed the conclusion of the war against Hannibal in 202 BCE. Roman sources report that over 500 000 individuals were captured and enslaved from that time until the final conquest of Macedonia in 167 BCE. The Romans, like many other societies of the ancient Mediterranean, used what we might call the ideology of victory to justify slavery: enslaving enemy combatants was a natural result of a successful military campaign. Unlike the modern USA, the Romans did not develop an ideology of racial superiority, since it was understood that anyone could suffer the misfortune of being enslaved. In Roman society it was often difficult to distinguish an enslaved person from a free person from their physical appearance, so clothing or other means had to be used to indicate enslaved status.

In fact, one of the key moments in the history of Roman slavery may have been an attempt to address this issue of identifying enslaved persons. In 326 BCE the *Lex Poetelia Papiria* outlawed the practice of **nexum**, or debt bondage. Up to this point, a free Roman could become enslaved if they were unable to pay off a loan: they would become the property of the creditor until they could pay off their debt. Nexum slavery differed from chattel slavery because the former allowed individuals to retain their Roman citizenship while the latter treated enslaved persons entirely as property. Chattel slavery individuals could be killed or, more often, sexually abused by the owner at will, while in theory a *nexum* enslaved person could not. Indeed, the Roman myth that led to the abolition of *nexum* revolved around the chastity of a young boy who had been placed in *nexum* by his father; the enslaver's attempt to sexually assault the boy led to a public outcry and eventually to the ban on *nexum*. The story, which has clear overtones to the sexual assaults of Lucretia and Verginia used to explain other significant legal changes, revolves around the inability to recognize a Roman enslaved on account of *nexum* from a non-Roman chattel.

The passage of the law, however, likely had more to do with the changing Roman economy than with sexual morality. As noted above, the first significant increase in chattel slavery of 50 000 individuals occurred during the fourth century BCE during the conquest of Italy. It became important for the Romans to be able to distinguish between Roman debt-enslaved persons and foreign-born chattel enslaved persons. This change also caused a significant shift in the Roman economy: the unpaid labor of those whose rights were completely held by the enslaver replaced the labor previously provided through *nexum*. The *Lex Poetelia Papiria* might thus mark the beginning of the transition of Rome from a society with enslaved persons into a slave society that was dependent on the exploitation of other human beings.

Key Debates: *What Is a Slave Society?*

Ancient Rome has traditionally been labelled as one of the five known "slave societies" in world history, along with ancient Greece, and the southern United States, the Caribbean, and Brazil in the eighteenth and nineteenth centuries. Of course the institution of slavery has existed in many times and places outside of these five, but scholars have tried to distinguish between slave societies and societies with enslaved persons. A society with enslaved persons is one in which slavery exists, but is only one of a number of different systems of labor, alongside systems such as family labor or wage labor. In a slave society, by contrast, unpaid labor from enslaved persons is the principal form of labor, and the effects of slavery are reflected not just in the economic system, but in social relationships, political structures, philosophical ideas, and more. Moses Finley, the originator of the distinction, suggested in a slave society enslaved persons comprised at least 20% of the total population (including women and children) and were responsible for the surplus production that is sold on the market, rather than just production necessary for survival. In the southern United States, for example, census data indicate that enslaved persons made up over 30% of the total population between 1790 and 1860. While we lack census data for Rome – no one ever bothered

> to count the number of the enslaved – the variety of literary, archaeological, and legal evidence makes clear that Rome exceeded this threshold by the first century BCE.
>
> Recently this distinction has been challenged on several grounds. To be sure, no one has argued that Rome was not a slave society, but the 20% threshold has been criticized as an arbitrary number plucked out of thin air. Slavery affects every society in which it exists: at what level are its effects significant enough that one should label it a slave society? Scholars have further suggested that even under this arbitrary definition there may have been other societies that should be considered as slave societies, including additional societies from the ancient world, some Native American societies, and certain African kingdoms. It is noteworthy that the original group of five slave societies are all Western societies, suggesting a bias and narrowness of focus on the part of scholars who created this list.
>
> Some scholars have even pushed back against the model itself, arguing that scholars have relied upon assumptions derived from European civilizations to create a binary opposition between slave and non-slave societies where the reality was much more fluid. For instance, ideas of political freedom and participatory government have shaped a conception that freedom and slavery are key opposites; the presence of political freedom as a core philosophical idea in the European world has led scholars to focus studies of slavery on the European world as well. Similarly, European ideas of private property have created notions of enslaved persons as property that may not be applicable in all societies. Enslavers in the southern United States clearly drew upon the models of Greece and Rome to support their own system, but the differences between the southern US and the ancient world are as significant as the similarities. Limiting ourselves to narrow notions of slave societies may thus be to accept and to reproduce their mindset, and a broader approach to the topic is necessary.

Many Romans were brutally calculating in their use of enslaved persons. The Romans, following Greek thinkers, likened enslaved persons to "talking animals," and their treatment of enslaved persons shows how they put this principle into practice. Cato's handbook provides good examples. He carefully prescribes how much bread, salt, and olive oil should be rationed to each enslaved person, even noting differences between farm laborers, the farm manager, and the "chain gang." While he does allow that enslaved persons should get a ration of wine, he offers the following as the recipe for them:

> Mix ten parts grape juice with two parts sharp vinegar. Add two parts of boiled wine and fifty parts of sweet water. After mixing, add one forty-eighth of seawater (!) and let ferment for ten days.

It is no wonder that Cato concludes: "If any remains after the solstice, it will make very sharp excellent vinegar."

Manumission, the practice of restoring enslaved persons to free status, and other apparently generous moments of Roman slave-owning likely grew out of a desire to exploit enslaved persons as efficiently as possible. Cato advised that one should sell enslaved persons when they grew old as one would an old ox or wagon, presumably to avoid paying for the upkeep of an unproductive worker. Columella (4–70 CE), author of another handbook on farming, recommends that the enslaved person in charge of managing the farm be allowed to have a female companion "to keep him content." From a legal perspective enslaved persons could not marry, so such relationships could be broken at any time by the enslaver. Columella further discusses the role of female enslaved persons in producing new people of servile status, noting that he sometimes restored freedom to women who were "unusually prolific."

Other Roman authors encourage enslavers to talk with their enslaved persons and use words rather than whips to motivate them. These statements unintentionally reveal that beating was standard practice for motivating enslaved persons. Columella also makes clear that he uses these gentler techniques not out of any moral objection to beating another human, because "I observe that they (the enslaved persons) are more willing to set about a piece of work" when they think their advice is sought. Some enslaved persons, particularly those who had been well-educated prior to the capture of their home city, had more day to day autonomy and might even live in the relative comfort of the owner's house. These persons often served as teachers or tutors to elite Roman youth, or as business agents for a wealthy owner, or even as doctors; the most famous doctors in Rome were all enslaved persons. Roman texts, however, contain several stories of enslaved persons in the *familia* suffering extreme punishments by disappointing their enslaver: beatings and executions were common, especially for enslaved persons who tried to escape. For the Romans, as for other slave societies, the most efficient exploitation of a particular enslaved person governed their treatment.

Exploring Culture: *The Reality of Slavery*

In the National Museum in Rome one can see the slave collar illustrated in **Figure 11.2**. This example is one of about 45 examples that we have found to date. Although these collars with inscriptions all date to the fourth and fifth centuries CE – the Late Imperial period and not the Republic – we do have slave collars from the Republican period. These later collars give us a clearer visual image of Roman slavery that help us see the realities of Roman practices.

The inscription attached to this collar uses a shorthand that would have been familiar to any Latin speaker. The text when expanded reads as follows: "I have run away; seize me. When you have brought me back to my master Zoninus, you will receive a gold coin."

Figure 11.2 Slave collar for Zoninos, fourth century CE. Terme di Diocleziano, Rome.

Other texts use similar language: almost all indicate that the person has attempted to escaped from their enslaved status and that the finder should restrain the wearer. Many indicate the person to whom the fugitive should be returned, though not all promise a reward.

A key question concerns how widespread was the use of these collars. Forty-five collars is a fairly small number, considering the hundreds of thousands, or perhaps millions, of enslaved persons in Roman Italy. It is thus unlikely that all enslaved persons were forced to wear a collar. Those who performed skilled labor or were considered part of the *familia* – doctors, wet-nurses, teachers – seem unlikely candidates for this treatment. Enslaved persons put to work on farms are more likely to be have been treated in this fashion, but there is some debate as to whether all such persons were forced to wear these collars, or perhaps only those who were being punished or who had tried to flee their status in the past. One Roman practice regarding enslaved persons who had tried to flee was to tattoo them on the face as a permanent visible mark of their enslaved status. It is possible that these collars provided an alternative to that practice.

It is difficult to see these slave collars as somehow marking an improvement in the lives of enslaved persons. The Zoninus collar is made of bronze and iron, and the collar was riveted shut after the tag was attached, making its removal, if the enslaved person was ever restored to freedom, a challenging proposition. It thus served as a semi-permanent marker of inferior status, a visual sign not just to the enslaved person but to all who encountered them of Roman dominance over the bodies of other human beings.

Changes in the Roman Economy

The conquest of the Mediterranean basin caused change throughout the Roman economy as in so many of the other areas of Roman life. At the most basic level, these conquests brought massive amounts of wealth into Rome, in two forms. Defeated countries were often required to pay large war indemnities, in theory to compensate the Romans for the costs of the war. The capture of major cities also allowed Roman generals to seize property, including enslaved persons. Typically he distributed some of these proceeds to his soldiers while keeping a significant portion for himself. In addition to this direct income, the territory conquered often held significant natural resources: the conquest of Spain allowed the Romans to begin intensive silver mining and expand the silver coinage in circulation. In turn, that money coming into Rome allowed the government to abolish the direct taxation of land in Italy in 167 BCE. From that point forward, taxation was primarily levied on the subject peoples of the Roman world, and the impact of this arrangement raises a series of questions that will need to be addressed elsewhere in this chapter.

Agricultural Changes?

Writing in the second century CE, the Greek biographer Plutarch described the situation in Italy in the second century BCE prior to the reforms of Tiberius Gracchus. He claimed that "all Italy was conscious of a scarcity of freemen, but was filled with workhouses of foreign enslaved persons. The rich worked the land using these enslaved persons, after they had driven away the free citizens." Writing in the first century CE, the natural historian Pliny the Elder similarly described the presence of *latifundia*, large estates specializing in single products such as wine or olives and worked primarily by servile labor. In his account, half of Africa was owned by six landlords; this number is likely an exaggeration, but it gives a sense of the size of estates that could be imagined.

The question of when these large estates worked with enslaved persons came into existence is a crucial one for an understanding of Roman history, since changes in the agricultural landscape of Italy would have had impacts throughout the Roman state. Farmers moving off their property would need to relocate, probably to a city, and would create an unskilled workforce that needed to be employed. Many scholars have questioned the accounts given by Plutarch and Pliny: since both wrote their texts over 200 years after the events in question, there is a suspicion that their accounts reflect the economy of their own day, in the more settled conditions of the Roman empire, and Plutarch's account is clearly intended as an explanation for the actions of Tiberius Gracchus. A decline in the number of free farmers would certainly have implications for military recruitment but as we saw in Chapter 9 the issues with military recruitment may not be related to population decline.

Other scholars have turned to archaeology for answers, especially by analyzing the results of large-scale surveys. These studies have found evidence for continued villa-size farms in the third and second centuries BCE, but very little evidence for large estates at this time. Archaeology often cannot tell us whether a farm was worked by enslaved persons or by free men, so it is possible that wealthy Romans used their share of war profits to acquire estates in many different places rather than just one large estate. Cicero tells us about one ordinary member of the Roman elite who owned 13 separate estates worth a combined 6 million *sesterces*. Individually these estates might not appear as large estates in the archaeological record, and whether enslaved persons or free tenants working this land is a critical unanswered question. However, the survey evidence suggests that we should see more continuity than a sudden change in farming during the second century BCE: *latifundia* worked by enslaved persons had not yet crowded out "family farms."

Working with Sources
Surveying the Land

Survey archaeology has emerged in the past 50 years as a vital tool for trying to understand broader questions about earlier society. The practice of survey archaeology involves a team of researchers who spread out at an equal distance from each other and walk across a set piece of land (**Figure 11.3**). As they walk, they examine

Figure 11.3 Individuals walking a field doing survey archaeology.

the ground in front of them for variations and artifacts, and they record their observations: the number of pottery fragments, the type of pottery to assist in dating, architectural or sculptural fragments, remains of walls, and more. Survey archaeologists do not remove anything from the land and they do not dig beneath the survey, although a survey project can be followed by excavation.

Survey archaeology offers multiple benefits relative to excavation projects. It is non-destructive. An excavation can only be done once; after the soil has been removed, it cannot be replaced in the same way. Survey archaeology can be repeated so that its results can be replicated by others or so that new information can be sought on a second pass. It is significantly faster. Depending on the amount of details recorded, a team of survey archaeologists can cover 100 acres or more in a single day. It is also significantly less expensive. The only equipment needed is notebooks for recording the information. The team does not have to make arrangements for the safe handling of artifacts recovered, since all materials are left in the ground, or replaced in the ground if a piece if lifted up for photography or closer examination.

Survey archaeology is important because it attempts to answer different types of questions than traditional excavation methods. Rather than focusing on the architectural remains of a single site or the quest for museum-quality artworks, survey attempts to understand patterns of land use across a region. Such regions can be narrowly defined, such as the habitation in the suburbs of a known city, or broader, such as a rural landscape. Survey archaeology thus provides information about a range of human uses, from pastoral camps for herdsmen to rural villas to smaller agricultural villages.

Survey archaeology is thus particularly vital for studying questions about the Roman economic system and its land use patterns. In Italy, projects such as the Tiber River Valley or Sangro River Valley project have added invaluable context to the information from literary sources, while projects in southern Italy, such as Metapontum and Croton, have provided information on areas where the literary sources offer very few tools. Survey archaeology, now conducted with GPS data and analyzed using GIS software, has become one of the primary sources of new information about the ancient world.

Other archaeological evidence helps us to see that a transition in Roman agriculture was underway at the end of the second century. This evidence comes in the form of large amphorae for the transportation of liquids, known as Dressel 2–4 amphorae after the scholar who made the first classification (Figure 11.4). These amphorae could hold about 25 liters of liquid each, and their primary function was for transportation of wine or olive oil to the market over long distances. A transition to a plantation economy would have required greater numbers of these amphorae, since the intent was to sell virtually all of the produce in major cities. Smaller estates would use smaller vessels for any produce they intended to sell on local markets. The Dressel amphorae begin to appear in large numbers during the early first century BCE, suggesting again that the agricultural transformation occurred after the period of the Gracchi.

Figure 11.4 Amphorae, as they might have been stacked for shipping, first century BCE. Museum of Underwater Archaeology, Bodrum, Turkey.

It is likely that commercial farming had been on the rise for several decades prior to the appearance of these amphorae. They must must have developed in response to a need. We might see Cato as the beginning of this trend as early as the 160s BCE: it is not far from his awareness of how to maximize profits in the local market to an understanding that producing items for sale further away might bring even greater profits. It is possible or even likely that commercial estates with enslaved labor emerged alongside subsistence farms: free farmers might have worked on commercial estates at harvest time when there was a need for additional workers. The extra cash they made could then have helped them manage the financial challenges of running their own farms, and the evidence indicates that smaller farms continued to play a major role in the economy in ancient Italy for many years to come.

Some families, however, may not have been able to keep their farm going. We saw in our discussion of the Roman army that more and more Roman men found themselves on extended overseas campaigns during the second century BCE. The females and young children, especially those without the support of extended family, might have had difficulties managing the labor necessary to make the farm sustainable. As a result, they may have moved to cities in search of retail or other work. The evidence for urban population growth of the first century BCE seems to be well established; by the time of the first emperor, Rome was a city of a million people. The demand created by a city that size would have encouraged increased specialization of produce, which in turn would have contributed to a cycle of farm consolidation. While it seems clear that agricultural practices in Italy did change, they seem to have been more of a long-term result of conquest rather than an immediate disruption.

It is notable that Roman ideals did not change even as this transformation was underway. Cato continued to trumpet the value of farmers even as he himself increasingly engaged in other forms of economic activity. Plutarch reports that Cato "came to regard agriculture as more entertaining than profitable" and that he "used to loan money also in the most disreputable of all ways, namely, on ships." To avoid the bad reputation of earning money the wrong way, Cato formed a partnership with many others and had himself represented by Quintio, one of his freedmen. Freedmen already possessed low social status, so the stigma would not attach to him in the same way. Cato thus foreshadows another of the major changes in the Roman economy: the use of partnerships as a means to engage in trade and similar activities.

The Rise of Business Partnerships

As noted above, the conquest of the Mediterranean opened up possibilities for trade on a much grander scale, and the increased population in Rome created demand. Resources were needed to supply the food needs of both wealthy and poor, and the wealthy increasingly sought luxury items as a way to distinguish themselves from others. Large-scale trade, especially in the ancient world, was not for everyone. On the one hand, to acquire a large ship and the goods to be sold back in Rome required a significant amount of capital. On the other hand, long-range trade carried the risk of piracy or shipwreck, which meant the loss of the entire investment. While the social stigma against trade reflected by Cato and Cicero may have kept some Romans out of the trade business, it seems more likely that the risky nature of trade was the primary deterrent for most of the elite. At the same time, it is clear that many Romans did engage in trade: *negotiatores* ("traders" or "businessmen") were active all over the Mediterranean in the second century BCE. Over 750 Italian names attesting to their involvement in trade have been found in inscriptions on the island of Delos, a duty-free port in the Aegean Sea, and parallel developments with Italians deeply involved in trade can be seen elsewhere in the Mediterranean. So how did the Romans overcome these challenges to encouraging trade?

The solution was to create a partnership that was in some ways similar to a modern corporation, the *societas publicanorum*. A **societas** (plural *societates*) was a partnership formed for a legal common interest, where individuals each contributed funds to a common pool. They could then use the joint funds to purchase transport ships or goods. The partners would share both the profits and the risks. Roman law even allowed the individuals to structure the partnership so that one person could be exempted from the risks while still allowing them to share in the profits. The existence of these partnerships was critical to the growth of the Roman economy, but the primary drawback of these partnerships was that they were dissolved if even a single member withdrew or died.

These partnerships are actually known from earlier periods in Roman history, where they engaged in public works: the word *publicani* means "relating to public revenue." For example, early *societates* were formed to build and restore temples or even to provide horses for the races in the circus. Livy reports that these groups had enough political clout in the Second Punic War to convince the government officials to continue making contracts even when faced with a wartime financial crisis. It was natural for these *societates* to expand into overseas trade during the second and first centuries BCE. A *societas* allowed a Roman not only to hedge his bets financially, but also to lessen the appearance of engaging in a less honorable profession, just as Cato did. Most Senators still invested the majority of their wealth in land, and they often reinvested the proceeds from the *societas* in the acquisition of new property.

If the *societates* played an important role in the expansion of trade, they played an absolutely crucial role in another area: tax-farming, i.e. the collection of taxes from the provinces. Because the Romans chose not to develop administrative structures during the Republic, they needed another method of collecting taxes. The *societas* provided a solution at hand. The government put the contract for collecting taxes up for auction, just as they did for other public contracts such as rebuilding temples or roads. The *societas* with the highest bid would win the right to collect taxes in the province, and whatever they collected in excess of their bid was profit for the partners. Because tax collection was so important to the operation of the state, these *societates* were given certain advantages; in particular a *societas* for the collection of taxes continued in existence even if a member died or withdrew. The Romans saw two distinct advantages in this system of tax-collecting: first, it guaranteed a certain level of income from tax revenue and, second, it kept bureaucratic infrastructure to a minimum.

However, the system had one significant drawback: it was open for corruption on a massive scale. Because tax-farmers were allowed to keep anything in excess of the amount owed to the Roman government, they used a variety of methods to try to collect *more* than the actual amount owed. The only recourse for provincial citizens was to appeal to the Roman governor, charged with enforcing Roman law in the province. Frequently, however, these governors participated in the corruption, either by stealing directly from wealthy individuals or by accepting bribes from the tax-collectors to look the other way – or both. A Roman proverb held that a governor needed to make three fortunes during his term in office: one to pay off the debt incurred in running for office and obtaining the governorship, one to bribe the jury to acquit him when he returned, and the third for his personal use in retirement. As a rule governors did escape conviction upon their return to Rome: Gaius Verres, governor of Sicily, is one of the few who was held accountable, and Cicero's successful prosecution of Verres is what turbocharged the orator's political career. The challenge of properly collecting revenue from overseas possessions is an indication that the Roman economy, now increasingly globalized, had outgrown the ability of a local government to manage it.

Political Issues: *A Rare Roman Case of Fighting Corruption*

In 73 BCE, Gaius Verres was sent as governor to Sicily, one of the richest Roman provinces because of its abundant grain production. Over the next three years, Verres extorted as much money from the province as he could. He accepted bribes from the tax-collectors. He made legal claims on artwork in private houses or even in temples. He arrested enslaved persons on false charges, and then demanded money before he gave them back to their owners. He even demanded that an enslaver produce a non-existent enslaved person whom he accused of plotting rebellion; when the person could not be produced for questioning, Verres threw the owner in jail until his family ransomed him. Verres thus disregarded the rights of citizens, non-citizens, and even the gods all at once, trusting in his money and his friends at Rome to protect him from retribution.

When he finally left Sicily for Rome, a delegation from Sicily asked Cicero to help them obtain justice. The defense hired the most famous lawyer in Rome to lead their side, and tried a number of tactics, including manipulating the calendar, to postpone the trial in order to get a more friendly judge and jury. Cicero responded by changing his own tactics: instead of the usual short introductory speech, he delivered a blistering accusation. To modern eyes, this first speech seems curious, because it does not focus much attention on Verres himself:

> The thing to be desired the most, and which ... would have the greatest influence in quieting the unpopularity of your order and the bad reputation of your judicial decisions has fallen into your lap. For the belief has become established, destructive to the state and dangerous to you ...that in these courts no wealthy man, no matter how guilty, can possibly be convicted (*Against Verres*, 1.1).

Cicero tried to make the case that the reputation of the state and the Senate was at stake rather than the reputation of Verres.

Cicero's tactics were very much in keeping with traditions of the Roman law-court, where jury verdicts were conditioned as much – perhaps more – by personal and political consideration rather than the bare facts of the case. This particular attack was so successful that the defense recognized the futility of their efforts and Verres went into exile even before the completion of the trial. Cicero eventually published the speech he would have given at the trial itself, and it is this speech that provides the details of Verres' abuses. It is unclear how typical Verres was; it is certainly possible he was worse than a normal governor. Yet even if not every governor committed all the crimes that Verres did, this speech offers the best glimpse into the types of corruption that seem to have been common in a Roman province.

In the aftermath of the speeches, Cicero agreed to a settlement with a low assessment of damages to the people of Sicily. The ultimate resolution of the case shows that at heart Cicero remained a Roman politician: he was more interested in advancing his own career than in obtaining justice for the residents of a Roman province.

Conclusion

By the end of the Republic, the Roman economy had been thoroughly transformed. While land ownership still brought prestige, involvement in trade and tax-farming brought more wealth, and increasingly brought political power. As the *publicani* gained in wealth, they were able to develop their networks of patronage to avoid conviction and to lobby for policies favorable to them, sometimes tax-related but sometimes on foreign policy. The impact of the *societates* on the Late Roman Republic might be compared to the influence of modern corporations on politics today, despite some differences between the two: powerful but not accountable within the political system. The power of the *societates* diminished only when the emperors were able to centralize control of public contracts and the legal system, dramatically reducing the opportunities for fraud and corruption.

At the same time, agriculture continued to be a significant element of the economy throughout Rome's history. Most estimates suggest that by the end of the first century BCE Rome was a city with a million inhabitants, partly as a result of the displacement of small farmers but partly because of the trade opportunities in the city. All these people needed to eat and drink, and Rome needed to import huge amounts of grain in order to keep its inhabitants fed: grain shortages are a recurring theme of the Late Republic and early imperial period. From an economic standpoint, Rome and other urban concentrations of people have been considered "consumer cities." That is, there was minimal production of goods and services in the city that could be exchanged for the production of the countryside. Instead, Rome offered military protection and some administration, and extracted produce from the countryside through taxes. Similarly, the wealthy members of society tended to live mostly in the city even while owning land, and extracted produce through rent and then servile labor. While some aspects of the Roman economy may seem familiar or modern, these elements, and of course the extensive use of enslaved persons, reminds us how different the ancient city was from our own. Perhaps it is time to take a closer look at the development of Rome as a city.

Discussion Questions

1. How might the need to feed one's family – or the memory of such a need – have affected the way individual Romans answered questions about their economic future?
2. How do you think questions of wealth inequality played out differently in the Roman world than they do in our own day?
3. What factors that we today might consider "non-economic" shaped the Roman approach to economic issues? What non-economic factors, if any, shape our own approach?

4. What are the advantages and disadvantages of the Roman approach to the economy – minimal bureaucracy and minimal oversight? Did it work for the Romans, and could a similar system work in our own day with more cash and more trade?
5. How might the fact that Roman slavery was not based on racialized categories and that Romans often restored enslaved persons to free status have affected how Roman society developed over time?

Further Reading

Hopkins, Keith (1978). *Conquerors and Slaves*. Cambridge: Cambridge University Press.
   Hopkins focused on the impact of conquering an empire on Rome's economy, with a special focus on the development of Rome's system of slavery. Hopkins demonstrated how continuous warfare and the influx of plunder from warfare were interrelated with changes in landholding patterns and with the growth of urban markets in the Roman world.

Kay, Philip (2014). *Rome's Economic Revolution*. Oxford: Oxford University Press.
   Kay focuses on the economic change in Italy between the Second Punic War and the time of Cicero. Kay argues that the increased availability of cash, in the form of silver that could be turned into coins, fundamentally altered the Roman economy, stimulating development in investments, farming, trade, construction, and manufacturing.

Lenski, Noel, and Catherine Cameron (2018). *What Is a Slave Society? The Practice of Slavery in Global Perspective*. Cambridge: Cambridge University Press.
   The collection of Lenski and Cameron reconsiders the question of how to categorize slave societies. Some articles challenge the conventional definition of a slave society, while others present arguments for including other societies including Native Americans, West Africans, or the Ottoman Empire. The broader consideration of slavery provides a better understanding of Roman practices.

Roselaar, Saskia T. (2010). *Public Land in the Roman Republic: A Social and Economic History of Ager Publicus in Italy, 396–89 B.C.* Oxford: Oxford University Press.
   Roselaar focuses on Roman state-owned land of Rome from the fourth to the first centuries BCE. She argues that as pressure on land available for public farming increased, there was a growing demand for privatization of this land, as producers wished to safeguard the rights they had to use the land. This forced the Roman state to develop new legal solutions for land use. Her argument challenges traditional views of late Roman Republican history about the decline of the Roman peasantry.

Tan, James (2017). *Power and Public Finance at Rome, 264–49 BCE. Oxford Studies in Early Empires*. Oxford: Oxford University Press.
   Tan explores how the influx of money from Rome's imperial conquests upset the balance between the state, the aristocratic elite, and the people. He argues that the elimination of taxation on the Roman people ended up depriving them of a crucial lever of power and enabled the elite to pursue policies that enriched themselves at the expense of the state.

12
The City of Rome

The Roman biographer Suetonius (c. 69–125 CE), writing in the early Roman Empire, made the following remarks about the city of Rome during the time of the first emperor Augustus:

> Augustus improved the city, which had not been decorated in a manner fitting for the majesty of the empire, and was also liable to flooding from the Tiber and to fires, so that he boasted with some justification that he had "found it a city of brick, but left it a city of marble" (*Life of Augustus*, 29).

This statement has often been cited by historians discussing the urban development of the city of Rome. Although it comes from the period of the Empire, it provides a good starting point for an exploration of Rome during the Republic. Suetonius implies that at the end of the Republic, the city of Rome was not a suitable capital for the Roman Empire and that Augustus transformed the city during his reign. These are obvious questions to explore: what did the city look like at the end of the Republic, and what kinds of changes had already taken place? There is more to unpack: Suetonius notes that during the Republic the city was liable to frequent flooding and fires: what might that information tell us about the nature of life in the ancient city?

As always, we need to think about the nature of our sources for this question. Augustus, as the first emperor, had a vested interest in claiming to have improved life in the city of Rome for all of the inhabitants he now controlled. Roman authors including Suetonius may have been taken in by his claim, or they may have had their own reasons for accepting this narrative about the nature of the city, including comparing Rome to the other great cities of the ancient Mediterranean, such as Alexandria, Carthage, and Athens. The archaeological remains of the city of Rome thus provide crucial information: the actual remains of the city from its different periods will give us the most accurate picture of the city, even if there are still gaps needing to be filled in. As we explore the city, we should bear in mind questions we have confronted in other aspects of Roman social and cultural life, such as the relationship between Romans and foreigners, between men and women, and between elite and non-elite. The development of the urban fabric of Rome has much to reveal about those relationships.

The Beginnings of the City

In Chapter 1 we briefly touched on the story of Romulus' foundation of Rome, dated by Roman tradition to 753 BCE. In that chapter we noted that the legendary stories of early Rome may offer better information about the character of individuals and the values of the community than about specific historical details. It turns out that while there is some evidence for scattered habitation on the site of Rome as far back as the tenth century BCE, the middle of the eighth century BCE does in fact provide the first evidence for significant urban settlement. Excavations have revealed a number of post holes on the Palatine hill that served as the primary supports for a series of thatched roof huts (**Figure 12.1**). From the same period comes evidence that may indicate an earthen wall around the Palatine as well as a number of burials in the area that would become the Roman Forum. The existence of walls and a cemetery in regular use suggests the presence of a

Figure 12.1 Reconstruction of eighth century BCE village on Palatine hill, Rome. Museo della Civiltà Romana, Rome.

settled community, so a mid-eighth century date for the foundation of Rome is now broadly accepted. This early community, however, seems little more than a loose collection of simple houses.

The first major constructions in the city were temples for the gods. A sanctuary on the site of the later church to Sant'Omobono included two temples that are dated to the early part of the sixth century BCE, and there may be another earlier temple beneath them. The first truly monumental building in the city appears to have been the temple of Jupiter Optimus Maximus on the Capitoline hill, whose foundations can still be seen today in the Capitoline Museum, going deep into the hillside. Roman tradition dated the dedication of the temple to 509 BCE, likely an attempt to match the date to the first year of the Roman Republic; the archaeological evidence suggests a sixth-century date for the structure, which makes the traditional date at least plausible. It is hardly surprising that the first major public building in Rome was a temple: the same is true in many ancient societies, where the beginnings of excess wealth were devoted to honoring the god(s) who had brought them prosperity. This practice is especially evident in Rome, a natural result of the way they constructed their relationship with the divine, and temples continued to form a significant part of the urban landscape as the city grew.

These temples provide further indication of the openness of early Roman society. The Sant' Omobono temples were dedicated to Fortuna and Mater Matuta; the latter had an important sanctuary 30 miles away at Satricum, and the terracotta cult objects from the Roman temples find their best parallels in a major Etruscan sanctuary. The temple of Capitoline Jupiter also reveals Etruscan influence in its design (see Chapter 7) and with its decoration: the terracotta rooftiles, the decoration running around the upper edge of the building, and the cult statue all show Etruscan style. Despite the expulsion of the Etruscan Tarquins, the Etruscan cultural influence continued to be felt in Rome.

Perhaps more significant to the urban development of Rome was the Etruscan knowledge of hydraulic engineering, or drainage. In the earliest periods of Rome's history, the low-lying area that became the Roman Forum was little more than a marshy swamp that flooded repeatedly when the winter rains swelled the flow of the Tiber River. Beginning in the seventh century BCE, a network of channels was dug into the area around the Forum that all drained into a single channel known as the *Cloaca Maxima*, or Greatest Drain, and then into the Tiber (**Figure 12.2**). By means of this system, the land between the Palatine, Capitoline, and Esquiline hills was effectively reclaimed for development. Recall that Suetonius cited the frequent floods that limited Rome's development, even after the construction of the Cloaca. His report should remind us that when we imagine life in the city of Rome in its earliest period, we should remember how fragile and tenuous life in the low-lying areas must have been. It's impossible to imagine any urban development at all without the drainage of this central area. It is no wonder that the Palatine hill was long the favored address for the elite: not only did it have a mythological connection to Rome's founder, but its inhabitants were safe from the periodic flooding that plagued those not fortunate enough to live on its slopes.

Figure 12.2 Cloaca Maxima ("Greatest Drain"), Rome. Originally constructed in fifth century BCE and still in use.

Archaic Rome

Suetonius' claim that the Republican city lacked the grandeur of a world capital likely derives not so much from the origins of the city as from the manner in which it grew. Perhaps the most important event in the early development of Rome was not its growth, but its destruction. As discussed in Chapter 2, Rome was sacked by the Gauls in 390 BCE, and Livy suggests that the damage was significant enough that it even prompted consideration of moving the entire population to another location rather than rebuilding. His account continues as follows (5.55):

> Once the bill was rejected, the City began to be rebuilt in a random fashion. Roof tiles were supplied at public cost, and a law allowed everyone to quarry stone and to hew timber wherever they liked, after providing a bond that the building would be completed within that year. In their haste they paid no attention to making straight streets and they built on any vacant space, paying no attention to their own and others' property rights.... For this reason the appearance of the City is more like one where the land has been occupied rather than formally divided.

Of course, this account needs to be questioned. Livy himself suggests that records of this period were difficult to obtain and scholars working with the material remains of Rome have begun to question whether the destruction was as complete as Livy suggests.

What is clear from this account, however, is that in Livy's own day – the very end of the Republic – the city had few straight streets and was felt to lack a sense of city planning. Indeed, the historical center of Rome today still maintains a feel of haphazardness, despite the many arterial streets that have been built over the past century. At the same time, we might ask whether an ordered appearance is the proper way to judge whether a city is "properly developed." Rome's aqueducts and sewage systems provided better living conditions than most cities of the ancient world and these may have been appreciated by its citizens more than having straight streets. Furthermore, there was no shortage of monuments throughout the city. An alternative perspective, one that emphasizes how the city was used by its residents rather than the topographical or architectural history of building forms, might reach a different conclusion. The emphasis on Rome's supposed disordered appearance might reflect an inferiority complex relative to Greek or Egyptian cities and/or the desire of Augustus to present himself as the creator of a properly ordered city rather than an accurate judgment.

Key Debates: *The Spatial Turn*

Much recent work on Roman urbanism has revolved around what scholars have labelled the "spatial turn." In broad terms, this phrase is used to cover analyses that focus on how space is used within a city or how people move through the spaces in a city, rather than focusing solely on the development of new architectural forms or the use of new building materials. Those discussions, some of which have been included in this chapter, still possess importance: understanding how people move through a space is dependent on knowing what the space looked like. The spatial turn thus builds on earlier work and attempts to offer a new way of understanding the lived experience of the city of Rome.

One way to understand the spatial turn may be to consider the Roman triumph (see Textbox on Political Issues in Chapter 10). One approach to studying the triumph has been to try to identify its route. Our ancient texts mention several landmarks such as the fact that it entered the city through the *porta Triumphalis* (Triumphal Gate) and passed by the Circus Flaminius and the Circus Maximus on its way to the Forum and the Capitoline hill. The route connecting these monuments is not specified and some scholars have devoted energy to working out the route. The spatial turn focuses attention on how generals and their troops moved through the city, for example how the surrounding monuments may have impacted the viewer's experience of the triumph. This perspective might lead to the suggestion that perhaps there was no single established route but that generals might alter the route in order to pass (or avoid) certain monuments. Doing so might allow a general to imprint his own experience on the viewers rather than appearing as merely one in a long series of undifferentiated parades.

The spatial turn can also be applied to larger questions about what it meant to live in a city during the Roman Republic. Most urban centers prior to Rome's growth were relatively small with moderate populations, and could easily be crossed in a few minutes. Navigating the metropolis that Rome became over the course of its history required a greater investment of energy and created a new image of what a city should be. It seems to have led to new ideas of what a neighborhood might be, as a smaller constituent part of a larger urban mass. It also led to new regulations about the use of space as well as new technologies for managing traffic through the city. These types of observations depend primarily on thinking about how the one million people experienced the city of Rome, and provide some of the key insights of the spatial turn for understanding life not just in Rome, but in ancient cities more generally.

However, one views the city after the Gallic sack, the defeat galvanized the Romans into constructing better defensive fortifications. The literary sources suggest that the sixth king of Rome, Servius Tullius, built the city's first wall, but as noted above there is archaeological evidence for an earthen wall already in the eighth century BCE. There appears to have been a stone wall built in the sixth century BCE that would match the supposed date for the reign of Servius, but this wall was proven insufficient by the Gallic sack. In the years following that defeat the Romans undertook the construction of a massive wall, which is conventionally (if incorrectly) known as the Servian wall (**Figure 12.3**). The surviving sections of this wall, on the Aventine hill and near the Termini train station, indicate that the wall must have been at least 6 miles long, at least 20 feet high, and 11 feet wide at the base, a height and thickness that compares favorably with other major fortified sites. This wall proved more than adequate for Rome's defensive needs: the city was not conquered again until Alaric's attack in 410 CE.

Walls are among the most common remains from the Roman world, and the more different questions we ask about them the more we learn about that world. In most cases, Rome's superior military was sufficient to protect the city and the Servian wall was only needed on a few occasions, such as when Hannibal invaded Italy in 217 BCE. The wall thus came to play a more important role in marking space, separating the urban from the suburban and rural. City walls served as the most visible, though not always the most important, boundary of the city. Building the Servian wall also required a tremendous amount of labor, so its construction offers insights into Roman economic practices. Further, archaeologists have noted that this wall

Figure 12.3 Remains of the "Servian" Wall, Rome, fourth century BCE.

was built from grotta oscura tufa, a stone from Etruscan quarries that was different from those used in earlier Roman constructions. The use of this stone thus reflects Rome's growing control over Italy. The connection between Rome's military expansion and architectural developments is a recurring theme in the growth of the city.

Censorial Building and the Growth of Rome

In exploring the development of Rome over the years following the Gallic sack, we need to consider why the city developed in the haphazard fashion that it apparently did. Orderly street planning was known in Magna Graecia and Sicily in this period, but was not utilized in Rome despite their familiarity with those places. One explanation for this difference may lie in the manner in which important public works were constructed in Rome. Beginning in the late fourth century BCE, it became an accepted part of the censors' responsibility to undertake public building projects to benefit the city. Like other magistrates, the censors generally had a free range of action to choose the projects they wished to undertake. There was no central organizing authority, nor did they receive direction from the Senate. As a result of this practice, public construction in Rome lacked a master plan, but depended on the sensibilities of individual Roman politicians working within the *mos maiorum*. Public building in Rome thus reflects broader Roman attitudes about how to order their society.

The censorship of Appius Claudius Caecus (circa 340–275 BCE) offers a good illustration of this approach to construction. Appius served as censor in 312 BCE and is best known for two projects that still bear his name: the *Via Appia* (Appian Way), which stretched for over 130 miles from Rome to Capua, and the *Aqua Appia*, Rome's first aqueduct, extending 10 miles out from the city to a spring east of Rome. The *Via Appia* would eventually extend all the way to the port of Brindisium, the launching port for voyages to Greece. Appius encountered significant opposition to his plans from other members of the leading elite who did not feel that this type of building activity was appropriate. Perhaps they feared it might bring too much glory to the single individual responsible for such beneficial public works, or perhaps they simply objected to the fact that Appius extended his term in office from 18 months to 5 years in order to complete his projects. Appius was a shrewd politician, however. He either earned the support of the poor because he created the jobs for them or had developed sufficient allies among the elite, but either way he was able to pursue both projects. Even in antiquity they were included among his chief accomplishments. Appius thus paved the way for individuals to gain political credit for building projects, and his activity seems have set the precedent for the censorship as the magistracy responsible for such projects.

The projects of Appius illustrate several critical features of the urban development of Rome. Roads and aqueducts are among the most well-known Roman construction projects, and here we see that they were among the earliest public building projects of the city. These building projects exist largely outside the city; an aqueduct, for example, comes into the city only at its tail end, and so its physical appearance would have a significant impact on the countryside, but less on the city itself (**Figure 12.4**). Nevertheless roads and aqueducts had a significant impact on the

Figure 12.4 The Aqua Marcia. Rome. Constructed 144–140 BCE.

lives of the urban residents: roads enabled easy transport for the majority of citizens who served as soldiers as well as for goods coming into the city, and aqueducts of course brought fresh water into the city. Rome indeed was, and still is, known for its plentiful water supply and fountains, and in this regard Rome might be seen as superior to other cities in the ancient world.

The construction of the *Aqua Appia* also suggests a degree of growth in Rome during the last part of the fourth century BCE: the need for more water means the existing supply must have been inadequate, indicating that there were now more people attempting to live in the city. That growth can be seen in other ways as well. The Forum continued its transformation into a commercial center. After the draining of the marshland, archaeological exploration has indicated that butcher shops and other enterprises sprang up in the area. In the late fourth century BCE, these shops seem to have turned more towards financial matters such as money-changing: moving the smell and the mess created by butchering meat out of the immediate center of the city must have marked a dramatic improvement. The consul Maenius in 338 BCE is also said to have attached the prows (*rostra*) from ships captured in a sea battle to the speaker's platform, giving it a new name but also creating one of the first public monuments to Rome's military success.

Temples and Other Military Monuments

Rome's military success and prosperity can be seen in another set of buildings that contributed to the haphazard growth of the city. In the 50 years from roughly 300 to 250 BCE, 20 new public temples (**Figure 12.5**) were erected in Rome. This total represents one-fourth of all the new temples built during the 450 years of the Republic, and so it is noteworthy for the tremendous impact it must have had on the cityscape of Rome. The majority of these temples came about as a result of a vow that a general had made in the midst of a battle: when the Romans emerged victorious, the general gained the approval of the Senate to fulfill his vow by building a temple to the divinity he had invoked in the heat of battle. The procedure thus demonstrated similarities with construction projects undertaken by the censors: there was no master plan and individual magistrates took the initiative. Not every general built a temple or even a victory monument, but many did. Those who did were responsible for locating a piece of land for the building on their own, as in the temples of the Largo Argentina. Beginning in the late fourth century BCE, therefore, Rome began to acquire public buildings and public spaces that might be associated with a major city, but the growth was unplanned thanks to the characteristically Roman mechanisms for construction.

This method for constructing new buildings not only provided an urban core for the city of Rome, but also served to help the Romans create a sense of historical identity. Roman buildings frequently served as places of memory: sites where important events were felt to have occurred became part of the city's landscape and thus

Figure 12.5 Republican Temple, usually identified as the Temple of Portunus, Rome, second century BCE.

Working with Sources
Identifying Temples in the City of Rome

In the center of modern Rome lies the Area Sacra di Largo Argentina. The site includes four small temples built during the Republican era, labelled A, B, C, and D because we have no identifying information for any of the buildings (Figure 12.6). They thus provide a great opportunity to understand the development of the city as well as how scholars try to understand the topography of the city.

Dating a building is essential if we are to understand the growth of the city, and is also often the best place to start in an attempt to identify it. Temple C uses large blocks of tufa stone similar to buildings of the early third century BCE. Temple A was built on the same ground level also with tufa stone, and so these two buildings were likely to have been built in the same period. The entire area was paved at the end of the second century BCE, putting Temples A and C on the same level as Temple D, which must therefore have been constructed after A and C. Temple B was built on top

Figure 12.6 Remains of Republican Temples in the Largo Argentina, Rome, fourth–second century BCE.

of this pavement in the space between Temples A and C, indicating that it was the latest of the four temples. We can therefore determine the order of construction – C, A, D, B – and the approximate dates.

Identifying temples tends to be more problematic in cases like the Largo Argentina, where we have no epigraphic evidence. Remains of a colossal female figure were found in Temple B, the last one built, that have led to a consensus that this temple was dedicated to "Fortune of this Day" built in 101 BCE. Scholars also feel confident that Temple C, the oldest, should be identified with the temple of Feronia that was built in the Campus Martius in 290 BCE. The other temples are more challenging. A brief reference in a much later author that the temple of Juturna was located near an aqueduct has led some to identify Temple A as Juturna. While the dating fits – the temple of Juturna was built in 242 BCE – the evidence is completely circumstantial. Similarly, Temple D has often been identified as the temple of the Lares Permarini, but its identification depends on a connection to another building whose own location is not certain. Reconstructing the precise topography of ancient Rome sometimes involves too many moving parts.

Even without knowing the precise identity of the buildings, the progression of temples in the Largo Argentina helps us see the growth of the Republican city. These temples were fairly small monuments that lined an important street, near places

> where Romans went to vote and also to train for military service, and so were placed for maximum visibility. It is understandable that later temples would have tried to fit in the available spaces. The renovations, such as paving the area and repairs to the temples, remind us of the importance and necessity of regular upkeep. They also suggest how both existing buildings might be modified to form a unit with newer buildings. The Largo Argentina thus vividly demonstrates both how Rome grew haphazardly at first, dependent on individual initiative, but eventually formed into an urban landscape.

fed into the Romans' narrative about who they were and how they had come to be in the position they were in. For example, the Romans carefully preserved the "hut of Romulus" on the Palatine hill, even rebuilding it when periodic fires burned it to the ground. Preserving it provided a visible reminder of the origins of the city. Temples might serve this same function: the temple to Castor and Pollux in the Roman Forum was built at the site of a spring where two mysterious horsemen (Castor and Pollux were known as great horsemen) watered their horses after leading the Romans to a critical military victory. Roman generals took advantage of this practice to promote themselves and their accomplishments when they undertook to complete a building project on behalf of the state. As individual Romans went about the city on their daily business, they would encounter these various buildings and be reminded of the deeds, both bad and good, of their ancestors. The growth of the city in the fourth century BCE is therefore also important in providing Romans with a clearer sense of their identity as a defined people.

New Directions in the Middle Republic

The successful conclusion to the Punic Wars and the expansion of Roman hegemony into the Greek East led to next major phase of urban development in Rome in

Political Issues: Publica Magnificentia:
Public Building and Fame

In 190 BCE, Lucius Aemilius Regillus faced off against Antiochus III of Syria in a naval battle in the Aegean Sea. Following in a tradition that the Romans stretched back to Romulus, Regillus vowed a temple to the gods if he should prove victorious in battle. On his return to Rome, work began on the temple, which was dedicated in 179 BCE by M. Aemilius Lepidus, a relative of Regillus who was serving as censor in that year. Livy (40.52) reports that above the folding-doors of the temple a tablet was affixed with this inscription:

> When Lucius the son of Marcus Aemilius went out to battle to put an end to a great war and to subdue kings ... under his auspicious command and fortunate leadership the fleet of Antiochus, ever before invincible, was defeated, shattered and put to flight between Ephesus, Samos and Chios, before the very eyes of Antiochus and of his whole army, his cavalry and elephants. On that day forty-two ships of war were captured there, with all their crews; and after that battle had been fought, King Antiochus and his kingdom [surrendered?] ... Wherefore, because of this action he vowed a temple to the Lares Permarini.
>
> As short as it is, the text provides insight into how a Roman general might memorialize his accomplishments. It emphasized that the fleet of Antiochus had previously been undefeated in battle, so that Lepidus had done something no other person had done before; he makes sure to emphasize this point by using three different words to describe what happened to his fleet. It was also important for him to highlight the fact that Antiochus himself watched the battle from the shore, a witness to Lepidus' grand accomplishment. Even more, Lepidus mentioned not only that Antiochus' army watched the defeat, but also his cavalry and his elephants! Of course, elephants had no role to play in a sea battle, but Lepidus wanted everyone to know about their presence in the army of Antiochus. They helped him mark how extraordinary an opponent Lepidus had defeated and thus how much credit he should receive for his accomplishment.
>
> Curiously, the temple itself seems to have been a rather ordinary building. Many scholars identify it as Temple D in the Largo Argentina (see Textbox on Working with Sources in this chapter). The surviving foundations of the temple indicate that it was modest in size, as were the other temples built as a result of military victory here and elsewhere in the city. The combination of building and inscription suggests the limits of self-glorification: the building itself was dedicated to the gods and was not intended to glorify human beings. The general was allowed to leave a record of his accomplishments at the same time as he indicated his piety towards the gods. A successful public image for a Roman statesman always included this combination of the religious and the political.

the early second century BCE. These conquests brought significant financial resources into Rome, and also brought a range of new architectural ideas and styles to the city. Considering the changes we have seen throughout Roman society as a result of these military conquests, we should not be surprised at the transformation of the city at this time. Indeed, we would be more surprised if these military successes had failed to leave their mark on the city. The appropriate question to ask is therefore not whether the Roman conquest of the Mediterranean led to changes in the city, but how the urban development of Rome compares to changes in other aspects of Roman society.

One area in which the development of the city parallels developments in other areas lies in a continued openness to outside culture. This period reveals the increasing presence of Greek elements in the city to complement or even replace the previously existing Etruscan elements. One small example that may by symbolic comes from the early third century BCE: the Etruscan terracotta statues that had decorated the Temple of Jupiter on the Capitoline were replaced with bronze statues, bronze being a popular medium for Greek statues. The presence of Greek elements in the architecture of the city increased dramatically at the end of the third and beginning of the second centuries BCE, just as it did in other areas of Roman life.

The arrival of a new style of building in Rome, the basilica, offers another illustration of Greek cultural influence. The basilica was essentially a large covered space to provide shelter from the elements (both sun and rain) for public activities such as markets and courts. In form it was a long rectangular building with a central aisle, often flanked by two small aisles with lower roofs; windows in the sides of a higher central aisle could then provide light for the interior (**Figure 12.7**). The form is clearly drawn from the Greek East: *basilica* is derived from the Greek word *basileus* ("king"), and the form imitates that of the Greek *stoa*, known from Athens, Pergamon, Alexandria, and other great cities of the Mediterranean. The earliest excavated basilica in Rome is the basilica Porcia, erected by the famous Roman statesman Cato the Elder after the end of the Second Punic War in 202 BCE, another sign that Cato was not an enemy of Greek culture. Basilicas had apparently been constructed elsewhere in the city even before this time; they are mentioned in the plays of Plautus that predate Cato. This new architectural style would go on to have a long and productive life throughout the Roman Empire: the presence of a basilica was one of the markers of a "properly Romanized" city. The form was adopted by the early Christian

Figure 12.7 Reconstruction of Basilica Fulvia, Rome. Originally constructed 179 BCE. Digitales Forum Romanum.

church and persists to this day: a modern church basilica has the same basic structure, with perpendicular aisles added at one end to create a cross.

The addition of the basilica to the Roman Forum assisted in the transformation of that space from a primarily commercial to a political space. We discussed earlier how the earlier Roman conquests had caused a transformation from service industries such as butcher shops to a focus on trade with its need for money-changing. In the third century BCE the Forum began to assume a more political aspect. That period saw a complete rebuilding of the **comitium**, the political center of the city where magistrates and others gathered to make speeches to the people on matters of public policy. The new design provided a focal point for political activity at one end of the Forum and just next to the **curia**, or Senate house. The design of the third-century *comitium* shows significant similarities to the places of assembly used by Greek city-states, suggesting that once again the Romans borrowed an architectural form from the eastern Mediterranean and put it to good use in their own city.

The use of marble as a building material marks one other Greek architectural fashion visible in Rome beginning in the second century BCE. The earliest temples in Rome had been built from a local volcanic rock known as tufa, and subsequent temples used other inexpensive stones, in part because there were no convenient local sources for marble. The first attempt to use marble came in 179 BCE, when Fulvius Nobilior used marble tiles taken from a famous temple of Hera in southern Italy to roof the temple of Hercules Musarum that he was building in Rome. Fulvius thus attempted to solve the supply problem by using marble that had been pre-cut for another building. Unfortunately for his plans, he was forced to return the tiles to Croton following opposition from the Senate, whether because of religious scruples about looting another temple, concern about increasing luxury in the city, or simply political opposition to Fulvius.

Whatever the reason for the delay in using marble as a building material, it did not last long. Thirty years later, in 146 BCE, Quintus Caecilius Metellus celebrated his role in the final subjugation of Greece by building or perhaps rebuilding temples to Jupiter Stator and Juno Regina; Roman sources indicate that this temple of Jupiter was the first in Rome to be constructed entirely of marble, followed by two others in the next decade. Just as we saw earlier with the use of tufa from Veii, the Roman military victory led to the exploitation of new building materials and thus a physical reminder of that victory. Indeed, Metellus' entire project had a Greek feel: in addition to the Greek building material, Metellus used a Greek architect and surrounded his temples with a *porticus*, a structure that directly imitates the Greek stoa with one side open to provide more access to the outside. The porticus of Metellus was not the first in Rome; his porticus actually replaced an earlier porticus on the same site. However, his complex – porticus plus an all-marble temple – popularized both the use of marble and this Greek architectural style, and so made a greater impact.

Foreign cultural features appear in private housing as well as major public buildings. Not surprisingly, they are most evident in the houses of the elite. A typical Roman *domus* ("house") was built around an *atrium*, a courtyard open to the sky with the roof sloping in to collect rainwater (**Figure 12.8**). The Romans believed

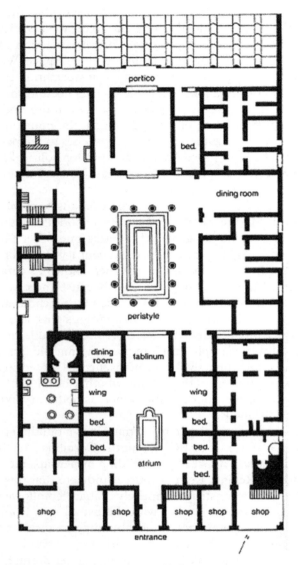

Figure 12.8 Plan of the House of Pansa, Pompeii, first century CE.

that the atrium derived from the Etruscans, and they used it as a public space: visitors could come directly into the atrium and wait for the owner there. In the third century BCE as Greek elements became increasingly known and visible in Rome, many elite Romans added a peristyle garden, based on Hellenistic Greek models, to their atrium houses. The few elite houses excavated in Rome (more are known from Pompeii during the empire) show the Romans adapting both Greek cultural elements and more local elements for their own purposes.

Exploring Culture: *Home Is Where the Public Is*

Roman notions of privacy differed greatly from those of the modern Western world, from abstract ideas such as the composition of the family to more intimate items such as bathing and sex. Exploring a Roman house provides one of the easiest ways to grasp some of the differences.

The Roman house was a critical place where the elite conducted public business: men of lower status would go around to the houses of the elite to consult on public or private business, or simply to build good relationships for the future. The architectural writer Vitruvius (c. 75–15 BCE) identifies multiples spaces of a Roman's house according to public or private use:

> Private rooms are those into which nobody has the right to enter without an invitation, such as bedrooms, dining rooms, bathrooms, and all others used for the like purposes. The common are those which any of the people have a perfect right to enter, even without an invitation: that is, entrance courts, *cavaedia*, peristyles, and all intended for the like purpose (*On Architecture*, 6.5).

Even the private rooms were semi-public: the distinction made by Vitruvius is that no one could enter without an invitation. In practice we know that elite Romans often invited important visitors into these spaces either for individual discussions or as a way to show deference to a guest. The idea that "a man's home is his castle" was completely foreign to the Romans.

The architecture of the Roman *domus* (house) helps us see how this concept might work in practice. The House of Pansa might be considered "typical," though of course every house was slightly different. Here we might focus on just two elements. First, the public areas as described by Vitruvius are evident: visitors would enter through the *fauces* ("throat") and step into the broad atrium, the "common" spaces according to the architect. Second, the architecture of the house was such that a visitor in the atrium had visual access to most of the rest of the house, because of the axial organization. From the atrium a visitor could look through the wooden partition to the *tablinum*, a large open room that led to the garden beyond, meaning that even these "private" spaces could be observed and would contribute to the impression made upon the visitor. Important visitors or close friends might also be invited into those spaces, in full view of those in the atrium. In this way even the "private" parts of house played an important role in contributing to the public standing of the owner.

Vitruvius indicated that the non-elite might not need grand public spaces in their houses, but he noted that their houses might have public elements in different ways. He wrote: "Those who do business in country produce must have stalls and shops in their entrance courts, with crypts, granaries, store-rooms, and so forth in their houses." Again, archaeology bears out this statement, as many houses devoted space to business interests, whether

Figure 12.9 House of the Thermopolion, Ostia, third century CE.

a room in front as a shop for commercial transactions or at the back for production, of grain or olive oil for instance (**Figure 12.9**). We might think of families today who live above or behind a small convenience store. Thus, even for the non-elite, the line between public and private in their houses was never, and perhaps could never, be clearly drawn.

The non-elite of course lived in very different surroundings. A single-family home might consist of one or two rooms facing the street, and the remains found in these rooms indicate they were often used as shops as well as living quarters. As the population of Rome increased over the course of the second and first centuries, more people lived in apartment blocks known as *insulae* (literally "islands"). Early buildings were often built cheaply from wood: the use of charcoal for cooking and heating meant that fire was an ever-present danger, and air quality in these dwellings must have been poor. The discovery of concrete allowed for more stability and safety, but *insulae* were often overcrowded and afforded little space for privacy, even among family members. Over the course of the Republic, such housing covered the Aventine hill south of the city center and spread across the Tiber River, so that by the Late Republic the proverbial seven hills of Rome and the valleys between them had been largely filled in.

The Late Republican Transformation

In other chapters we have observed how changes in other aspects of Roman society reflected the political upheavals of the Late Republic, and in particular changes caused by the increasing competition between leading members of the elite that often violated the norms of earlier behavior. The urban fabric of the city of Rome was impacted by these upheavals in much the same way. For instance, it became more difficult to manage the regular upkeep of the city. While the population of the city continued to increase and created the need for more infrastructure, such building projects, let alone the repair of existing structures, were less attractive as a means of making a name for oneself. The competition for glory and the breakdown of normal civic processes are in fact visible in what services were provided. Despite these conditions – or rather because of them – the Late Republican city underwent a significant transformation.

The creation of Rome's first ever fire-fighting brigade provides one example of how the dynamics of Late Republican politics affected what today would be considered public services. As noted in the earlier section, fire constantly threatened the lives and houses of non-elite citizens, living in densely-packed wooden houses and using fire for heating and cooking. In the early first century BCE, the politician Marcus Licinius Crassus had the idea to form a fire brigade from the enslaved men in his household as a means of increasing his wealth. When a fire broke out in the city, he would take these enslaved men to the site of the fire and negotiate a price with the owner. If the owner was willing to sell at "pennies on the dollar," Crassus had his men extinguish the fire through a bucket brigade and thus added the now-surviving building to his real estate empire. If not, Crassus would let the fire burn and the owner would be left with nothing. While Crassus is sometimes credited with creating the first fire brigade in European history, the enslaved men who were forced into this dangerous work and the property owners who likely felt cheated of their property must have viewed the situation differently. While the total number of fires in the city certainly decreased, the willingness to place personal advantage over the needs of the state – something we have seen in other aspects of Late Republican life –also appears here.

Similar motivations also appear in the major architectural changes to the city during this period, although they were perhaps not as brazenly displayed. The largest and probably most significant building project in Rome in the first half of the first century BCE was the complex constructed by Pompey the Great in the Campus Martius. It included the first stone theater in Rome, large porticos that extended in front of the theater surrounding a garden filled with fountains and statues, and ending in a *curia* that was used for meetings of the Senate (**Figure 12.10**). Historically this had been an underdeveloped area since it lay outside the walls of the city, and Pompey's project marked the beginning of the transformation of this area into urban space. As we discussed in Chapter 3, Pompey formed part of the First Triumvirate with Crassus and Julius Caesar. We therefore need to ask questions not just about how this project changed the city of Rome but how it fits into the competition between these three men.

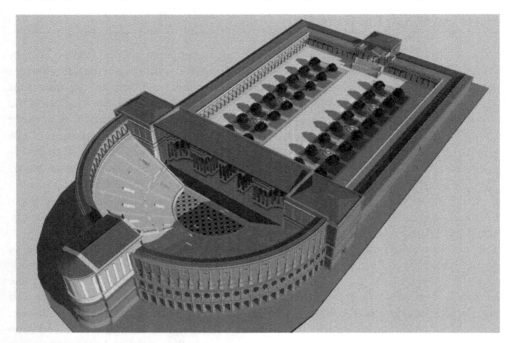

Figure 12.10 Reconstruction of Theater of Pompey, Rome. Dedicated 55 BCE.

From one perspective, Pompey's project might appear normal in the context of Roman traditions. He had spent many years campaigning in the Greek East, and on his return he commemorated his successful conquests with a monumental building project. The project included a temple to Venus that sat at the top of the theater, as well as a new comfortable *curia* that provided a public service to his fellow Senators. Pompey's time in the East had exposed him to new ideas in Greek architecture and these are visible in several aspects of the project, especially in the lavish gardens and fountains that filled the space as well as a hundred-column porticus. Marble pavements and large Hellenistic sculptures decorated the space, making Pompey's gardens one of the favored public spaces in Rome. Many of these individual ideas may have been new, but by this time, nearly one hundred years after the first marble temple in Rome, Greek architectural ideas had long been part of the Roman tradition.

Viewed in another way, however, Pompey broke with Roman norms in an effort to distinguish himself from his competition. At one end, the complex incorporated four temples built by earlier generals, and then extended in the other direction for four times the length of those temples, making it more than 20 times larger than previous projects. Pompey's architects also made use of new technologies, such as the concrete we have encountered in the *insulae*. Pompey combined concrete and stone to form vaulted supports that allowed the complex to be built up high even though it was constructed on flat ground. One hundred years later the temple to Venus remained one of the highest and most visible buildings in Rome. In size alone, the project was unrivalled in Rome, and far above the scale of monuments traditionally erected by Roman generals.

Pompey broke precedent in another significant manner, and one that did not escape the notice of his peers: the first permanent stone theater in Rome. Previously, theatrical performances in Rome had been staged either in temporary wooden theaters or on the plaza in front of a temple, using the temple's steps for seating. The Romans were thus intentionally late to the notion of having a stone theater in the city; a previous attempt to build a permanent theater in Rome in 155 BCE had been unsuccessful, when the Senate declared the construction to be a violation and ordered it destroyed after it was nearly completed. The reasons offered for the objections are either moral – theaters would lead to decadence – or political – theaters would provide a convenient meeting place for a mob, something we know happened under the emperors. Pompey maneuvered around these objections by claiming that his theater was merely just the front steps of the temple of Venus. It is unlikely that anyone was fooled by this claim, but Pompey was able to overpower the objections. While Pompey was eventually defeated by Julius Caesar in their conflict, there is no small irony in the fact that Caesar's assassination occurred in the new *curia* of Pompey. While use of the *curia* was abandoned after this point, the rest of the complex remained in use all the way until the sixth century CE when Rome had fallen under the control of the Gothic kingdoms.

Julius Caesar, quite naturally, had no intention of allowing Pompey to be the only one to reshape Rome and he initiated his own building program. Some of his projects, such as changing the course of the Tiber, had to be abandoned as impractical, while Caesar's premature death halted others. Indeed, Caesar's most significant project had to be completed by his adopted son and successor Octavian/Augustus. By the middle of the first century BCE, the central part of the Roman Forum had become extremely congested with monuments and buildings constructed by earlier generations of Roman politicians. The lack of planning left little open space for people to conduct their daily business, and the continued growth of Rome to a population of nearly one million people presented a further problem. Caesar thus began construction of a new forum just off the northwest corner of the traditional center of the city. Caesar's forum included a porticus on three sides of an open rectangle, with a temple at one end. The temple, eventually completed by Octavian, was dedicated to Venus Genetrix, Venus the Ancestress of the Roman people – and also claimed as a personal ancestor by the Julian family. Caesar thus competed with Pompey in creating a large public space that attempted to win the support of both gods and men. Like Pompey, his efforts also created a lasting precedent. For the 150 years after his death, emperors continued to add new projects adjacent to the old Forum that simultaneously created new public spaces for Rome's urban population and advertised the virtues of the project's sponsor.

Conclusion

We began this chapter with the testimony of Suetonius that Augustus claimed to have found Rome a city of brick and left it a city of marble, transforming it into a city that was worthy of serving as the capital of a Mediterranean empire. Our exploration has revealed that there may have been some truth to this statement: as a city Rome did lack an orderly grid plan and its streets and buildings had been erected in a haphazard fashion. By the time of Caesar's death in 44 BCE, however, one might legitimately question the truth of this claim. The projects of both Pompey and Caesar created new and needed public space for Rome both inside and outside of the city wall and, significantly, both used marble in their construction, to go along with the handful of other buildings in Rome constructed with marble. The transformation of Rome into a city worthy of its empire had begun well before the time of Augustus. Recent studies have even suggested that marble would have been most visible in the Augustan era either as a pavement or as it was transported through the city to one of a handful of high profile building sites. We should not be surprised to learn that a politician exaggerated his own accomplishments or took credit for completing the work that others had started. Augustus' claim simply provides us with another reminder of the need to check the claims of our sources against the available evidence.

Perhaps more interesting than Augustus' claim is what the transformation of Rome meant for the development of urban life throughout the Roman Empire. We have seen that the Romans remained willing to incorporate elements from foreign cultures, whether Etruscan, Greek, or otherwise, into their urban fabric, just as they incorporated these elements into other aspects of their life. Sometimes they were slow to adopt an idea for one reason or another. We have seen that it took them a long time to build a stone theater in Rome, and the first amphitheater in Rome, the Colosseum, was not completed until 80 CE; the amphitheater in Pompeii was built 150 years earlier. Once an idea had been adopted in Rome, it began to be exported all over the Roman Empire: having a theater and an amphitheater, basilicas and temples and porticos, formed an essential part of being considered a real city, or at least a "civilized" Roman city. While the form of the elements might have changed for us today – we have music arenas and sports stadiums, temples and churches and mosques, city hall and libraries – the idea remains the same. The city of Rome thus served as a filter and a shaper, an importer and an exporter, and continues to shape notions of the city even today.

Discussion Questions

1. In what ways is the militarism of the Roman state visible in the development of the city of Rome? In what ways is this similar to or different from the visibility of militarism in other areas of Roman life?
2. In what ways are foreign influences visible in the development of the city of Rome? Is there a distinctive "Roman" architecture that can be distinguished?

3. In what ways are differences between elites and non-elites visible in the structures of the city of Rome?
4. How does thinking about a city as a place where people live rather than as a collection of monuments change the way one views it?
5. In what ways does the architecture of a city, whether Rome or your own, reveal the values of the people who live there? In what ways does it shape those values?

Further Reading

Bernard, Seth (2018). *Building Mid-Republican Rome: Labor, Architecture, and the Urban Economy*. New York: Oxford University Press.
   This study utilizes coins, epigraphy, and especially archaeological remains in addition to literary sources to understand the transformation of the city. It uses quantitative models to highlight the emerging frameworks that shaped the organization of public construction in Rome, including the increasing reliance on slavery and an urban labor market. Bernard thus offers a new perspective on the development of Rome in the Middle Republic, from 396 to 168 BCE.

Claridge, Amanda (2010). *Rome: An Oxford Archaeological Guide*. Oxford: Oxford University Press.
   This book is the most indispensable guide to the monuments of Rome. Claridge has provided essential archaeological information as well as maps, plans, and photographs, all organized by neighborhood. A glossary of terms and suggestions for further reading make this book essential reading for anyone traveling to Rome and interested in exploring the ancient city.

Dyson, Stephen L. (2010). *Rome: A Living Portrait of an Ancient City*. Baltimore, MD: Johns Hopkins University Press.
   Dyson offers a readable narrative of Rome as it grew between the third century BCE and the fourth century CE. Dyson looks beyond the physical development to explore the social, economic, and cultural history of the city, dividing it into neighborhoods, each with its own distinct character. His approach utilizes comparative urban history and theory, allowing him to reconstruct the society that thrived among the monuments.

Russell, Amy (2016). *The Politics of Public Space in Republican Rome*. Cambridge: Cambridge University Press.
   This study offers a new analysis of the issue of public and private space in ancient Rome, focused on the "private" aspects of supposedly public spaces such as the Forum. By combining textual and archaeological evidence, and by focusing attention on how women, enslaved persons, and non-citizens interacted with these spaces, Russell illustrates how space functioned as a part of political culture in Rome.

Vout, Caroline (2012). *The Hills of Rome: Signature of an Eternal City*. Cambridge: Cambridge University Press.
   Vout explores how Rome came to be known as the city of seven hills through an analysis of art, literature, and politics from the earliest periods of Rome into the twentieth century. Her study goes well beyond the ancient city to offer a fantastic introduction to the rich history of Rome on multiple levels.

13
Roman Arts and Letters

"Captured Greece conquered her fierce conqueror." These are the most famous and often quoted words when it comes to addressing questions of the development of the arts in Rome, both visual and literary, in the Roman Republic. The poet Horace wrote these words in his second *Epistle*, offering his interpretation of the development of Latin literature. One question we might ask is exactly what Horace meant by these words, which appear to acknowledge Rome's military superiority but also suggest that Greece in some way had proven stronger than Roman military power. His contemporary Vergil expressed a sentiment that appears to be somewhat similar in his *Aeneid*, often considered the crowning glory of Latin literature (6.847–850):

> Others will hammer out bronze that breathes with a softer touch
> Others will draw a living face out of the marble
> Others will plead cases in court better, trace the movements
> Of the sky with instruments or describe the rising of the stars.

While Vergil does not name the Greeks explicitly, the references to sculptures in bronze and marble and to forensic oratory, areas where Greeks were acknowledged to be masters, suggests that he had them in mind. An exploration of the arts in Rome must therefore confront a question we have confronted many times already: what is the relationship of Roman practice to outside influences? As we proceed we should again consider some of the elements we have observed elsewhere in Roman society – questions about receptiveness and appropriation – and see how they apply in the artistic realm. Again we should consider other themes we have encountered: distinctions between elite and non-elite, gendered elements, and the importance of the military to the Roman elite. As always we must start with earlier Roman practices in order to assess that degree of change in the later period.

A Social and Cultural History of Republican Rome, First Edition. Eric M. Orlin.
© 2022 John Wiley & Sons, Inc. Published 2022 by John Wiley & Sons, Inc.

The Early and Middle Republic

Early Roman Art

We should begin by reminding ourselves of the development of the city of Rome, which we examined in the previous chapter. We noted numerous instances where early Roman architecture, and especially the construction of temples, reveals the importance of the military and the incorporation of foreign ideas. The Romans themselves acknowledged their dependence on foreign artists: the earliest artists named in Roman texts as working in Rome are all foreigners, including an Etruscan man named Vulca who was initially placed in charge of the cult statue for the temple of Jupiter. While the statue does not survive, we can gain a sense of its appearance from a statue of Apollo found at Veii dated to the same period (**Figure 13.1**). Identifying a foreigner as the creative mind behind the most important cult statue in Rome seems a remarkable acknowledgement of dependence on outside influences, and Roman temples continued to be decorated with terracotta statues for several hundred years.

Figure 13.1 Etruscan Terracotta statue, known as the Apollo of Veii, c. 500 BCE. Villa Giulia, Rome.

In the area of painting we can observe a similar story of sharing in local artistic traditions. In one of the oldest burial areas of ancient Rome on the Esquiline hill, a fourth century BCE tomb was uncovered with a small fragment of a dramatic painting preserved on the walls (**Figure 13.2**). Painted inscriptions identify the two men depicted in the two scenes as Fannius and Fabius. Fabius is thought to be Q. Fabius Maximus (c. 350–280 BCE), victor in the battle of Sentinum in the Second Samnite War and honored with a triumph; Fannius is therefore assumed to be the Samnite commander and the second scene his surrender to Fabius. The centrality of the

Figure 13.2 Wall painting from tomb on Esquiline Hill, Rome, third century BCE. Musei Capitolini, Rome.

military to Roman identity makes it hardly surprising to see military scenes depicted in a Roman tomb. The technique of showing the same figures in multiple scenes may in fact derive from paintings shown in the triumphal procession itself, suggesting that military practices may even have driven artistic techniques. The painting also bears similarities to the Lucanian tomb paintings found south of Rome in the static composition of the scene and the style of the figures. The earliest Roman painting we have thus shared in broader central Italian artistic styles just as early Roman architecture and sculpture did.

The Beginnings of Roman Literature

Claims about early Roman literature are more difficult to make, for the simple reason that our earliest surviving Latin texts come from the third century BCE. It is often thought that written literature does not seem to have developed in Rome until this period, although there is evidence for a lively oral culture in Rome and some texts may have found their way into written form. Nonetheless, Rome clearly did not emphasize written literature in the same fashion as the Greeks. To provide some comparison, the great Athenian playwrights Sophocles and Euripides, and historians Herodotus and Thucydides come from the fifth century BCE, roughly the period immediately after the foundation of the Republic. While some elements of Greek culture did find their way into Rome at this time, particularly in the religious sphere (see Chapter 8), written culture emerged in Rome only during the more extended encounter with Greek culture that began in the third century BCE.

This direct nature of Greek impact on Roman written culture is visible at the very outset of Roman literature. The first known literary work written in Latin was a translation of Homer's *Odyssey* by Livius Andronicus (c. 284–204 BCE). Livius was apparently an enslaved person who became a teacher in a Roman household and eventually regained status as a free person. We should pause for a moment to note the extraordinariness of this set of facts. For one, the first person to write a text in Latin was not actually a Roman, but a formerly enslaved person captured during a difficult war against Tarentum, a powerful Greek colony in southern Italy. Two, the first text was not an original Latin composition, but a translation of a great Greek epic, which made the Greek tradition accessible to a Roman audience and thus influenced generations of Roman authors. The development of Latin literature is thus connected to war and to Greek culture from the very beginnings of the Roman written tradition. From this point forward, Roman authors of all genres engaged with Greek authors and models as part of their creative enterprise.

Comedy, another genre popular in Greece, also emerged in Rome at the end of the third century BCE. Livius and his contemporary Gnaeus Naevius (c. 270–200 BCE) wrote comedies known as *fabula palliata* ("plays in a Greek cloak"), apparently based on the model of Greek new comedy popularized by Menander (late fourth century BCE) and others. Naevius is better known as the author of the *Bellum Punicum* ("The Punic War"), the first epic poem we know composed in Latin. This poem combined mythological background with a recent historical event, and in many ways laid the foundations for a specifically Roman style of epic poetry. War again figures prominently in the development of Roman literature: Naevius was a Roman citizen who had fought in the Punic Wars, and made that war the focus of his epic poem. He also developed a new genre of tragedy known as *fabula praetexta* that focused on Roman historical subjects, often involving the military; the name derives from the *toga praetexta* that was the special garment of Roman magistrates. Unfortunately, we have only fragments of all of these works.

For the first surviving Roman comedies we must look to the 20 plays (out of over 100 written) from Plautus (c. 250–184 BCE) and six more from Terence (c. 190–160 BCE). Both men wrote *fabula palliata*, utilizing plots, scenes, and characters that are well known in Greek New Comedy. The origins of these authors are noteworthy: like Livius they were not Roman. Plautus seems to have grown up in a town in Umbria that had been captured by the Romans and then moved to Rome at some point. Terence seems to have been born in north Africa, enslaved, and then regained his freedom only after coming to Rome, perhaps in a manner similar to Livius. While successful writing careers brought all these men into contact with the leading members of Roman society, the prominence of non-Romans and non-elites among the earliest writers of Roman literature is remarkable. It might attest to the openness of Roman society, but it might also be a sign of the general lack of respect given to writing at this period in Rome's history: "real" Romans fought wars, they did not write comedy.

Enslaved persons appear throughout these plays, part of the evidence suggesting that slavery was well known in Rome prior to the end of the third century BCE. Enslaved persons in Roman comedy often behave with a freedom and a willful disobedience that seems unlikely to represent the behavior of actual enslaved persons in Roman society. It is not entirely clear why the authors chose this portrayal and whether the plays should be seen as speaking for or against Roman power dynamics. On the one hand, Roman comedy does not seem to offer a direct critique of slavery as an institution, even if some individuals and behaviors are singled out as cruel. On the other hand, the authors came from the ranks of the non-elite and even formerly enslaved, and the jokes and behavior of the non-elites in the plays may have been intended to speak to the experiences of the non-elite and enslaved persons in the audience. One result, whether intended or not, of the portrayal of the "happy slave" may have been to help the Romans become more comfortable subjugating other human beings and claiming their unpaid labor. Certainly later slave-owning societies including the United States found the notion of the "happy slave" to be a handy image for justifying the practice of slavery.

In addition to providing a window into Roman society, these two playwrights offer an opportunity to observe the Romans' literary engagement with Greek culture. Readers might ask how far the plays adapted the originals for a Roman audience as opposed to merely presenting Greek ideas. Plautus in particular seems to have been comfortable making significant alterations. He made little attempt to make the settings seem "authentically Greek," his metaphors frequently make use of Roman rather than Greek practices, and his plays have a constant backdrop of war. Sometimes his plays provide some social commentary by critiquing a Roman value, such as doing one's duty to other members of the family or to the gods. Perhaps Plautus as a non-Roman was more comfortable making these critiques or better able to observe them. The notion that literature can both reflect and critique elements of one's own society is visible in Latin literature from its earliest days.

The Romans actually developed an entirely new genre of poetry devoted to such reflections and critiques. The genre is known as satire, from the Latin word *satura*, meaning a mixed dish, and its invention is generally ascribed to Gaius Lucilius (c. 180–100 BCE). His poems only survive in brief quotations from later writers, but as the term *satura* suggests, they do not seem to have taken a single form or to focus on a single subject. His subjects apparently covered all aspects of daily life, from the military and public service to marriage, business, and other aspects of private life. What distinguished his work was his fearlessness in critiquing practices both of the elite and of ordinary people with a biting wit; this feature of his work is what today we associate with the word satire. Lucilius' connections to powerful patrons, unusual for a poet in Rome at this time, no doubt provided him with the freedom to explore these topics, and the fact that elite Romans were beginning to write poetry might be a sign of literature's changing status in Rome. Lucilius clearly set the stage for the satirists who would follow him.

Roman historical writing also seems to have begun in this period, looking backwards to Rome's origins rather than to its own day. The Roman arrival as a world power as a result of their military conquests seems to have raised questions for the Romans about who they were and how they got there. Fabius Pictor (c. 260–190 BCE), a member of the Roman elite active in both politics and war, composed the earliest Roman historical text that we know. Although Fabius is usually considered the father of Roman history writing, it is noteworthy that he used Greek as the language for his text. Perhaps he made this choice because the tradition of history writing up to this point was in Greek, or because his audience was Greek, or because Greek had become the fashionable language in Rome, but the choice shows the continuing importance of Greek culture.

Some elements of Fabius' text seem distinctively Roman, however. It is probable, though not certain, that he wrote in the annalistic style that became the hallmark of writing Roman history. The nature of this style was to record the events of Roman history on a year by year basis, noting the most important events of each year. This style may have derived from the *annales maximi*, a semi-official record kept by the chief priest of Rome that catalogued victories and losses in battle, names of magistrates, as well as famines, plagues, and other noteworthy events. The earliest annalists like Fabius seem to have adopted this minimalist style, but by the middle of the second century BCE annalists were employing rhetorical flourishes in their glorification of Rome's past.

Fabius seems to have sparked an interest in the history of Rome and the Italian peninsula, for we know of several other texts on these subjects in the next few decades. The poet Ennius (c. 240–170 BCE), who also wrote tragedies and comedies, is most famous for his *Annals*, a narrative poem in Latin recounting the history of Rome from the fall of Troy to his own day. Ennius was born in the heel of the Italian peninsula and seems to have come to Rome as a result of a connection he developed with Cato the Elder near the end of the Second Punic War. Ennius narrated a Roman story in a Greek form: he set an important precedent by adopting dactylic hexameter, the meter used by Homer, for his poem, but titled his poem the *Annales* and so made an explicit reference to the Roman *annales maximi*. With Ennius we again see a non-Roman who came to Rome as a result of warfare making a lasting impact on Roman literature through his engagement with Greek culture.

Another Roman likely inspired by Fabius Pictor is Cato the Elder (234–149 BCE) whom we have already met several times. Cato's only surviving work is a treatise on agriculture (see Chapter 11), but his most important work was the *Origines*, the first known prose history in Latin. Cato avoided the annalistic tradition of recording events year by year to describe the history not just of Rome but of many Italian towns from their legendary foundation to his own day. Many of the surviving stories from Cato's *Origines* illustrate important Roman, and sometimes Italian, virtues, which suggests that part of his purpose was to place Rome and Italy on a par with Greek culture by showing their deep roots and glorious history.

Before we turn to the Late Republic, it may be worth pausing to consider some key differences in the writing of history and the writing of fiction in Rome. With some exceptions, the early poets and playwrights were men of lesser social status, while Roman historians tended to come from the Senatorial class: Fabius Pictor and Cato are obvious examples, but many annalists of the second century also fall into this category. One observation that might be drawn from this phenomenon is that the writing of history was an elite activity and a highly valued activity while literature was viewed with skepticism, as entertainment for the masses. Recall in our discussion of sources in Chapter 1 that history for the Romans was not merely about recounting what happened in the past. It was supposed to provide uplifting moral examples of behavior that had made the Romans great, or occasionally moralizing stories of Romans who had erred and so brought harm to the state. In this way they were expected to benefit future statesmen and continue elite control of the state, which may explain why Roman statesmen felt the writing of history was a suitable occupation for their leisure time. Certainly this argument about the utility of history was made by Roman historians such as Sallust in the first century BCE.

On the World Stage

The Roman conquest of the Mediterranean basin in the second century BCE led Roman artists and authors to grapple with a new set of issues. During the sack of the Greek city of Syracuse on the island of Sicily in 212 BCE, large amounts of Greek statuary were carried off to Rome. As Plutarch reports, the Roman commander Marcellus

> carried back with him the greater part and the most beautiful of the dedicatory offerings in Syracuse, in order to grace his triumph and adorn his city. For before this time Rome neither possessed nor knew about such elegant and exquisite productions, nor was there any love there for such graceful and subtle art, but it was filled full of barbaric arms and bloody spoils (Plut., Ch. 21).

This is a rare case where the surviving archaeological evidence lines up perfectly with the literary evidence. In the following decades, Rome began a deep and extended exposure to Greek visual and literary styles. Continuous Roman campaigns in Greece brought numerous members of the Roman elite in contact with Greek writers, and Greek intellectuals visited Rome with increasing regularity in the second century. Roman authors began looking not just to the great Greek authors of the distant past such as Homer, but to a new generation of Hellenistic Greek poets based in Alexandria. In both visual and written arts, Roman authors became more comfortable not just with absorbing Greek models, but with reusing them and reinterpreting them for a Roman context.

Key Debates: *What's Roman about a Greek Statue?*

The notion that Roman statues are mere copies of Greek originals has been around almost as long as Roman statues have existed. In part this opinion reflects the attitude of Roman writers themselves that the Greeks were better at sculpture; consider the words of Horace and Vergil at the start of this chapter. Even more, it has reflected the judgment of art historians since the rediscovery of ancient Roman statuary in the eighteenthth century. Johann Winckelmann, whose *History of Ancient Art* was published in 1764 and laid the foundations for modern art historical study, set Greek art as the ideal on account of its harmony and beauty, and the Romans as imitators of these forms. This judgment influenced countless generations of scholars, who spent their time in a search for the Greek originals that served as the supposed models for the Roman copies.

It is only within the last generation that this notion has begun to be discarded, as scholars have recognized that most Roman statues are not exact replicas of Greek originals. In many cases Roman sculptors had to develop their own vision for the statue, because they were working in marble while the Greek originals were often in bronze. Since the weight of a stone statue often required extra support in order to not topple over, many artists found ways to incorporate narrative objects such as a tree trunk to support the statue's leg or torso. Artists, or perhaps their patrons, also decided whether to model their statue closely after the original or to take elements from the original and reconfigure them; some sculptures even borrowed from two or three different originals. Making allusions to an earlier Greek version is now seen as part of the creative process: think of writers in every society who reference earlier texts, or authors of memes who build on existing images. Roman artists thus had to be creative in their own ways.

Another approach has been to consider the role that statues played in their new Roman contexts. Several scholars have suggested that Romans did not purchase copies simply to have a copy of a famous artwork in their house, much in the way that many people now buy museum prints. Rather Romans selected images that fit the visual narrative of the space in which they were placed: for example, nymphs and animals might be placed in gardens, busts of philosophers in libraries, and so forth.

These processes raise a new set of questions. Are there patterns, perhaps by region or by a particular workshop, to the types of features that might be added to a particular statue type? Was there value to owning an "original" as opposed to a replica? Did the elite and non-elite approach the acquisition of art in the same way? In the end, it may turn out that the Roman art market was not so different from our own.

Late Republican Art

Many of the statues carried off to Rome were displayed in the new temples built as a result of victory in war, and thus served as a constant reminder of Rome's military prowess. Over the following centuries, numerous marble copies of Greek original statues appeared in Rome; many of these copies have survived to our own day and have often been used to raise the issue of Roman originality in art, or the lack thereof. Certainly the Greek statues often present a different visual image than Roman ones. Classical Greek statues (fifth–fourth century BCE) often aimed for an idealized depiction, most frequently showing a youthful nude male in a naturalistic pose. Hellenistic statues (third–second century BCE) often engaged with higher degrees of emotion, showing the nude figures in moments of stress, exertion, or terror, such as the famous Laocoön showing a father and his sons entangled by monstrous snakes. Even Romans who had not participated in the military conquest were able to show their familiarity with Greek art.

The Romans did have their own style of sculpture, best known for its portrait heads of wrinkled old men, complete with scars, warts, balding hair, and sunken cheeks (**Figure 13.3**). This style of portraiture seems to have been influenced by

Figure 13.3 Head of a Roman Patrician from Otricoli in the veristic style, first century BCE. Museo Torlonia, Rome.

Roman funerary practices, where Roman aristocrats were allowed to display *imagines* in the burial procession. These *imagines* seem to have derived from death masks and so were portraits of noble ancestors who had served the state valiantly in earlier generations. Art historians have termed this style of portraiture **verism**, from the Latin word *verus* ("true"): not realism, but hyperrealism almost to an absurd level to create an impression of realism.

Figure 13.4　Portrait of Roman General, Tivoli, 80–60 BCE. Palazzo Massimo, Rome.

It might seem surprising that the subject would not have asked the sculptor to smooth out some of the wrinkles and ignore some of their less attractive features, to airbrush them a little as it were. After all, if someone was paying good money for a sculpture, we might expect them to put their best face forward. The answer seems to be, in large part, that this is how the Roman elite wanted to be portrayed. In essence, this WAS their best face. To appear as a serious person with many years of service to the state was an important part of the public image of any Roman elite male. The depiction of scars earned in battle thus served as a physical sign of one's devotion to the state, rather than as a physical imperfection that needed to be hidden away. Particularly for Roman politicians who lacked distinguished ancestors, a portrait in this manner was one way to compensate for that weakness and to increase their chances for political success in Rome. These portraits could offer a visual testimony of the Roman notion of *pietas*: obligation not just to the gods, but to the state and to the family. Verism may have become popular as a counter to the more idealizing style of Greek sculpture. Certainly this type of portraiture became so influential that middle-aged men might have themselves portrayed in this fashion, exaggerating their features to make them look more aged and worn down by cares than was really the case.

At the same time Romans seem to have been comfortable creating sculptures that combined both Greek and Roman elements. An outstanding example of a Roman portrait mixed with the idealizing Greek style is provided by a statue known as the general from Tivoli, dated to around 75 BCE (**Figure 13.4**). In this sculpture we see a Greek style body: a youthful nude torso rippling with naturalistic muscles. Roman sensibilities insisted that the lower part of his body be covered, however, so a military cloak was added. The military nature of this garment is no accident, but the more significant Roman element of the statue is its head. By itself, there is nothing unusual about the portrait head. It fits easily into the veristic style described above, a middle-aged man expressing his experience in leading the Roman state, but the combination with the youthful Greek body tends to be jarring to our eyes. This aesthetic strangeness does not seem to have bothered the Romans; it is visible on other monuments as well. Torsos seem to have been sculpted in advance, so that a wealthy patron could then pay to have his portrait head inserted on the statue. In doing so he could use Greek artistic styles to create a portrait of himself as he never existed, but one that offered the best of both worlds: an eternally youthful and powerful body but with the wisdom and knowledge that experience can bring. This example shows again the willingness and ability to adopt Greek artistic styles in ways that demonstrated Roman control over them.

Late Republican Literature

The literature of the Late Republic reveals many of the same themes as the visual arts. Poets continued to build from Greek models, but began to use different models and to turn in new directions. During the third and second centuries BCE the intellectual center of the Greek world had shifted from Athens to Alexandria in Egypt.

Exploring Culture: *An Odd Coupling: The "Altar of Domitius Ahenobarbus"*

The monument known as the Altar of Domitius Ahenobarbus offers a tantalizing glimpse at how Romans might combine Hellenistic art with their own styles. The monument is now thought to be a statue base erected in the late second century BCE in a temple of Neptune in Rome. Three of the panels were carved in a marble from Asia Minor and depict a scene from Greek mythology, the wedding of Neptune and the nymph Amphitrite (Figure 13.5). The panels are fully Greek in their design and execution. The wedding couple is shown in a chariot pulled by two tritons, perhaps best described as mermen. They are surrounded by fantastic sea creatures, including sea nymphs, sea horses, and even sea bulls. The other two panels are similarly filled with creatures. All of the carving is done in high relief, making the figures stand out from the stone, and the scene swirls with activity: horse and bull bodies rise up everywhere, and tails of sea creatures swirl in the space between figures. These elements are absolutely typical in Hellenistic Greek art, with its interest in action, expression, and drama created by the use of dynamic forms and diagonal lines in the carved figures.

Figure 13.5 Statue base of Monument of Domitius Ahenobarbus, Rome, 122–115 BCE. Glyptothek, Munich.

Figure 13.6 Statue base of Monument of Domitius Ahenobarbus, Rome, 122–115 BCE. Louvre, Paris.

Almost everything on the fourth side is completely the opposite (Figure 13.6). The figures are static, more vertical and individually smaller than on the Greek sides, and they are recognizably Roman in togas, Roman military dress, and Roman religious garb. The scene depicts the Roman ceremony of the census, in three parts. On the left people line up while a magistrate records something on a tablet, in the center Mars stands next to an altar awaiting a sacrifice, and on the right the animals for the *suovetaurilia* sacrifice are brought forward by attendants, who may include enslaved persons. The *suovetaurilia*, consisting of a pig, a bull, and a ram, was one of the most traditional Roman sacrifices, performed as part of a purification ceremony that marked the end of the census. The scene is one of the

> earliest surviving Roman historical reliefs and offers a glimpse into Roman representational styles as well as the ceremony of the census itself.
>
> To modern eyes, the strong contrast between the static nature of the "Roman" side and the fluidity of the Greek panels is jarring, but the choice must be intentional. The Roman scene is deliberately formal and dignified, perhaps because the scene represents one of the most significant ceremonies in Roman public life. The contrast also highlights differences between Roman and Greek culture more broadly, conveying a sense of solemn duty performed on behalf of the public as opposed to the frivolity and wildness of private celebration. The very liveliness of the Greek panels serves to emphasize the seriousness with which the Romans approached the world, perhaps suggesting an explanation from the Roman viewpoints for their success. The monument reveals both the Romans' comfort with integrating Greek artistic styles into their world, but also utilizing them creatively to express their own ideas and attitudes about the world.

While some Greek poets continued to work in established genres such as epic poetry, others rejected such long poems in favor of short epigrams and poems that focused on more personal themes. In today's language we might label these poets as *avant-garde*, deliberately turning their backs on tradition in order to play with different forms and different subject matter that had not been traditionally thought worthy of poetic attention. In the early period Ennius incorporated some Alexandrian elements into his work, but the style seems to have become more popular in the Late Republic. A group of Latin authors took up this mantle, ostentatiously claiming to be the first to engage with Greek literature in this way, and so they became known as the **neoterics,** from a Greek word meaning "new poets." This self-conscious posturing as innovators left its own mark on Roman literature.

The most famous Roman neoteric poet, and really the only one whose poetry survives in any quantity, is Gaius Valerius Catullus (c. 84–54 BCE) from Verona in northern Italy, another poet from outside Rome. Catullus' poems range across multiple genres and topics, allowing him to show off his versatility as an author. Some are simple, such as dinner invitations to his friends, while others are intensely personal, including poems to a woman he calls Lesbia that register either his intense desire for her or his intense distaste for her after they have broken up. There are brutal attacks against opponents, either political or personal, which often include crude language and imagery (see Chapter 6), but also a poem mourning the loss of his brother on campaign in the Roman province of Bithynia in Asia Minor. The poems make readers feel that we know something about Catullus and his life, but as with many poets it is never absolutely clear where the line between the poet and the person begins and ends. For instance, many scholars have connected the Lesbia of the poems with Clodia, a prominent married woman, but others have doubted this identification. Either way, Catullus exemplifies the characteristics of neoteric poets: a lack of respect for anything seen as old-fashioned, a focus on the intimate and personal, and technical virtuosity. Catullus undercut certain traditions of Roman poetry through his lack of respect for marriage and his lack of moderation in language in ways similar to Roman politicians undercutting traditions of the state. In that way Catullus can thus be viewed as a representation in literary terms of developments elsewhere in Roman society during his lifetime.

The poetry of Catullus in fact serves in some places as a forerunner for a genre known as Roman love elegy that became popular at the very end of the Republic and beginning of the Empire. Propertius (c. 50–15 BCE) and his contemporaries Tibullus and Ovid are the best known of these poets. Elegy as a poetic form based on couplets had been practiced in Greece, but in Rome it emerges as the form for poets to indulge in a first-person discussion of his romantic entanglements, much as Catullus had described his relationship with Lesbia. A key feature of this genre is how the poet depicts himself as unbound by his public obligations in the pursuit of his erotic fantasies. Often the poets portrayed themselves as enslaved by the female in an inversion of normal class and gender roles as a way of illustrating their own alienation from Roman upper class society. As with Catullus, it difficult to separate reality from the poet's persona, and this is particularly true for the small number of elegies written by Sulpicia, the only surviving Roman poetry written by a female. The balance of Greek and Roman material is often difficult to separate: the Roman poets often claimed to be drawing inspiration from Greek sources, but this claim may merely have been part of the self-presentation. The later Roman scholar Quintilian asserted that "we challenge the supremacy of the Greeks in elegy" and the specifically erotic aspect of the poetry and challenges to traditional morals does not have many parallels in the Greek world.

Catullus' contemporary poet Lucretius (c. 99–55 BCE) displayed a different type of maturity in his poetry. The Late Republic saw an increasing acceptance of Greek philosophical ideas in Roman society. After the deaths of Plato and Aristotle, Greek philosophy had developed along multiple lines, with two major schools emerging: the Stoics, whose ideas can be seen in the works of Cicero, discussed below, and the Epicureans. Lucretius took the essential tenets of Epicureanism and presented them in an epic poem titled the *De Rerum Natura* ("On the Nature of Things"), one of the most remarkable poems of this period. While the Roman epic poets of the third century BCE had used this form to narrate legendary elements of Rome's founding, Lucretius used this form of poetry – complete with a wide variety of imagery and metaphors – to present the principles of atomism: that the world was formed of atoms and that celestial and earthly phenomena should be explained by the movement of these atoms rather than the actions of divine beings. The Epicureans therefore placed pleasure, or more accurately the absence of pain, at the center of their belief; bodily pleasures were placed second to intellectual pleasure because the pleasures of the body often lead to pain. For an Epicurean it was therefore irrational to fear the gods or the prospect of death, and while the work does not appear to have been a direct attack on the Roman practice of religion, it does express a skepticism about traditional practices. Such skepticism about the gods did not sit comfortably with Christian authorities, and Lucretius' text almost disappeared through lack of attention in the Middle Ages, with a single text discovered in 1417 bringing atomism back into scientific discourse. The attempt to explain complicated philosophical ideas in epic poetry marks Lucretius

Working with Sources
A Woman's Voice

"At last love has come, the kind of love that to veil it rather than to reveal it naked might give me a reputation." These words are among the few words from the Roman world written by a female poet. Six love elegies from the hand of Sulpicia have survived within the collection of poems written by her contemporary Tibullus, one of the leading elegists of this period. Indeed, for a long time stretching back to the Renaissance her poems were attributed to Tibullus, as male scholars simply could not believe that a woman could have written poetry like this.

Sulpicia's family was part of the Roman elite and her family benefited from Augustus' triumph in the Roman civil wars. As a member of an aristocratic household, Sulpicia would likely have received an excellent education, and we should not be surprised that she became acquainted with the elegiac poetry that was the fashion in Rome at the time. Her poems show a mastery of the form, with technical skills equal to that of the male poets for whom she was mistaken: Poem 4, which expresses anger and jealousy that her lover may have hooked up with another woman, plays on the letter S in her name to hiss at him, while Poem 6, perhaps trying to make up after a fight, is a single sentence spread over six lines. These poems show definitively the education and ability that an elite woman in Rome might possess.

Equally valuable is the way that Sulpicia's poems shine a light into female identity, since her poems offer the only glimpse through the eyes of an actual female. They show us where she might be powerless and lack agency, as when she complains that her uncle is forcing her to leave Rome on her birthday rather than spending it with her lover as she desired. Another poem celebrates that the trip was in fact cancelled, though it does not seem that Sulpicia's wishes had anything to do with it.

But Sulpicia clearly chose her lover and recognized both the thrill and risks she was undertaking:

> Venus has fulfilled her promise: now she will tell my joys,
> In case anyone says that women do not have their own joys.
> I almost don't want to commit anything to these signed letters,
> So that no one might read it before my lover.
> But sometimes going astray is pleasurable; it's tiresome to make one's appearance match
> One's reputation: May I be said to be a worthy lover for a worthy love.

Sulpicia recognizes the role she was supposed to play as an elite female, but she has enough privilege to seek her own joy in a way that other women may not have. She can make the deliberate choice to "go astray" and not to worry about her reputation, even as her family expressed concerns about her, as we learn in Poem 5. While Sulpicia cannot be considered a typical female, her poems are invaluable for showing that women might think deeply about their expected roles in society and were capable of agency in deciding how much of those roles to play.

as a singular genius, uniquely able to use a poetic form to express Greek ideas for a Roman audience.

Other Romans responded in less unusual ways to the elements of Greek culture that found their way to the capital, of whom the orator Cicero (106–43 BCE) may be the best example. Cicero's texts have survived better than any other ancient author and include 58 speeches as well as works on philosophy and rhetoric. While Cicero's style showed off his ability to harness the flexibility of Latin, he clearly studied and drew from Greek texts. In his philosophical works it is clear that Cicero was drawn to two strands of Greek philosophy: Stoicism and Skepticism. The Stoics believed that the world was governed by natural laws, and that a proper life was lived by understanding and living in accord with these laws. The ideas of the Skeptics grew out of Plato's presentation of Socrates: they did not offer a coherent system, but argued that nothing could be known for certain, and that people should not stick dogmatically to any position. Cicero shows a deep familiarity with Plato: his philosophical writings often take the form of fictional conversations, in which Cicero has different figures present the views of a different philosophical school.

Yet Cicero was interested in more than simply translating Greek ideas into the Latin language; his texts frequently adapted those ideas to Roman circumstances, presenting different answers to some of these recurring philosophical questions. For instance, Cicero's *de Re Publica* ("On the Republic") is clearly modeled after Plato's *Republic* and attempts to describe the ideal state. Unlike Plato's utopian thought exercise, however, Cicero's republic is firmly grounded in the real world of Roman civilization. His primary speaker, corresponding to Socrates, is the Roman statesman Scipio Aemilianus, the conqueror of Carthage, and the ideal republic looks remarkably similar to the best version of existing Roman institutions. Scipio suggests that a mixed constitution (like Rome's of course) was the best form of government and that the primary threat to this government is the moral decay of the ruling elite. It is surely no coincidence that Cicero composed this treatise between 54 and 51 BCE, just when the in-fighting between Julius Caesar and Pompey jeopardized the harmony of the different parts of the Roman state, what Cicero called the *concordia ordinum*. Cicero's other philosophical treatises often reveal the same grounding in the Greek philosophical doctrines and their application to the Roman world in an effort to preserve traditional Roman values. Cicero obviously had his own spin on what constituted Roman values, but his integration of Greek ideas into his arguments resembles other Roman writers and artists we have seen.

Conclusion

We began this chapter with the famous line from Horace: "Captured Greece conquered her fierce conqueror." Perhaps at this point we are better positioned to explore the significance of these words. Horace appears to imply that Greece ultimately triumphed over Rome, and certainly Greek ideas and practices were

Political Issues: *A Voice Crying in the Desert?*

It might fairly be said that all philosophers are deeply influenced by the time in which they live, and that their ideas are shaped by their surroundings, but few people exemplify this point as clearly as Cicero. Virtually all of his surviving philosophical works emerge from the period following the triumph of Julius Caesar over Pompey, a result that Cicero among others was inclined to view as the death of the Roman Republic. Several of these texts explicitly take on the challenge of proper behavior in the light of the changed Roman world and seem clearly positioned to provide a philosophical basis for political positions taken by him and others both before and during Caesar's rule.

His dialogue *On Friendship* provides one example. The dialogue is actually named after Gaius Laelius, a staunch friend of Scipio Aemilianus who remained loyal to him in the 140s BCE despite intense political pressures to move forward with a reform program. On the one hand, centering the dialogue around Laelius, an opponent of political reform, highlights Cicero's conservative politics. On the other hand, the main argument of the dialogue is that true friendship is possible only between virtuous men and does not seek material advantage, even if such advantages might flow from the relationship. Cicero's point is to emphasize the difficulty of staying true to one's friends, especially in times of political adversity, something that might be useful for members of the Roman elite to consider at a time when all benefits in the state flowed from one man.

One of Cicero's final works, his *On Duties*, can be seen in the same light. On the one hand the text is deeply invested in the privileges of the Roman elite. Cicero argues that "vulgar are the means of livelihood of all hired workmen whom we pay for manual labor... vulgar we must consider those also who buy from wholesale merchants to retail immediately... and all craftsmen are engaged in vulgar trades." Even after the end of the Republic, Cicero is determined to uphold the traditional concerns of the Roman aristocracy, where owning property was the proper way for a gentleman to earn a living. On the other hand, Cicero makes a passionate case not only that one should do the honorable thing rather than the advantageous thing, but that the honorable thing is in fact always the advantageous thing. This idea is not new to Cicero: Plato has Socrates offer much the same idea, so this marks another adoption of a Greek idea. Cicero's version might seem more personal, since it is framed as a letter of advice to his son at a time when Caesar controlled the state: the honorable and the advantageous might no longer have appeared to be the same. Even if Cicero's advice was written with his political moment in mind, it is nonetheless worthwhile to consider whether it is good advice. It has seemed so to the Christian church and has had a lasting impact on European moral thinking: after the Bible, *On Duties* was the second text printed after the invention of the printing press.

observable almost everywhere in Rome. In crucial ways, however, Horace's judgment is also misleading. The Romans were always incorporating elements from foreign cultures into their own society, not just after the capture of Greece, and many cultures other than Greek. More significantly, in almost every case the Romans adapted what they took from other cultures for their own uses. They exercised control over foreign cultures rather than being overwhelmed or awed by them. A judgment that the Romans were "conquered" by Greek culture seems to fundamentally, or perhaps intentionally, misunderstand the nature of the relationship.

What might have led Horace to represent the relationship in this mistaken way? Part of the answer must be that the Roman conquest of the Mediterranean and the deeper encounter with Greek and numerous other cultures raised questions for the Romans about their own identity. Stories about the adoption of foreign literary and artistic traditions alongside Horace's quip suggests that the Romans came to see certain activities as not part of what it meant to be a "real" Roman. Horace's contemporary Vergil confirms this point and provides insight into what the Romans did consider to be the distinctive aspect of their culture. Immediately after Vergil provides a list of ways that foreign cultures might be superior to Rome (sculpture, oratory, science), he spotlights the particular area in which Rome was superior:

> Remember, Roman, to rule with power over people.
> These are your arts: to impose the custom of peace,
> to spare the defeated, and to beat down the proud.

There is no sense that the Romans are captured here, but that they have the power to do what they will with other cultures.

Throughout this book we have been concerned with questions about power and about the relationship between Romans and other cultures. The Romans began absorbing elements from outside cultures even before they acquired significant power; indeed one might argue that the absorption of foreign elements was critical to the growth of Roman power, and the presence of outsider elements in Rome continued to grow as they extended their control over the Mediterranean basin. Imperialism and contact with other cultures goes hand in hand. At this point we might be in a position to consider whether cultural appropriation or cultural exchange is the best way to view Roman behavior. "Cultural appropriation" has been defined in many different ways, but broadly speaking it refers to a process where one culture adopts or adapts aspects of another culture without invitation and without sufficient regard for the original cultural context. It often reflects the power imbalance between the two cultures and some scholars have argued it is intended to reinforce that imbalance. The Roman response to Greek culture that we have traced not just in this chapter but throughout this book could be seen to fall into this category. From Greek statues taken from temples and re-used as models for statues in private houses to repurposing Greek literature and philosophy in support of Roman institutions, the Romans took elements from Greek culture and built them into their own society. They could be viewed as using Greek culture to build up their own place in the world without regard for the Greeks: indeed reshaping these elements could be seen as a sign that Rome was now the center of culture.

On the other hand, Roman society was deeply changed by its encounter with Greek culture and indeed by all the cultures encountered as the Romans expanded.

Cultural exchange, finding inspiration from other people and cultures for new practices that can improve one's own society, ought to be counted as a positive. Roman accomplishments in the arts and literature can scarcely be imagined without the contributions of other cultures, from the poetry of the African Terence modelled on Greek originals to Etruscan sculptors to Egyptian painting. One of the enduring qualities of the Roman behavior is how they consciously engaged with other cultures and how frequently they accepted others into their own society. By the end of the Republic, Rome was self-consciously a multi-ethnic society, as Horace and Vergil both knew. Whether through processes of appropriation or exchange, the very definition of "Roman" had changed. This chapter and this book have merely scratched the surface of what it might mean to be Roman, a category that would continue to develop in different ways during the Roman Empire.

Discussion Questions

1. What might the identity and social status of artists in Rome tell us? Is this an important factor in determining the value or importance of the arts in any given community?
2. In what ways can we use individual pieces of artistic output, whether literary or visual, as historical sources?
3. In what ways did developments in Roman visual arts parallel developments in Roman literature? What might account for the differences?
4. How might one apply the concept of cultural appropriation or exchange to specific objects discussed in this chapter (Roman comedy, the "Altar of Domitius Ahenobarbus")? How might one apply this concept to elements of your own society? Does your specific example fit into the category of appropriation or exchange?

Further Reading

Feeney, Denis (2016). *Beyond Greek: The Beginnings of Latin Literature*. Cambridge, MA and London: Harvard University Press.
    This book asks questions about the unusual features of the development of Latin literature, and especially its attempt to present itself as a continuation of Greek literature. Feeney emphasizes the historical context of this development that coincided with Rome's growth into an imperial power. The book reconsiders what it means for Rome to have "translated" Greek literary practices into their own society, using comparative examples from the ancient Mediterranean to highlight key points.

Loar, Matthew, Carolyn MacDonald, and Dan-el Padilla Peralta (2018). *Rome, Empire of Plunder: The Dynamics of Cultural Appropriation*. Cambridge and New York: Cambridge University Press.

This recent collection of essays brings together historians, archaeologists, and literary analysts to examine questions of cultural appropriation in Rome. The goal is less to arrive at a single definition or model, but to explore the many ways in which Rome made and remade its own culture. Examples are drawn from Roman comedy, Egyptian obelisks in Rome, and Roman provinces, both east and west. The volume thus offers a wide range of interpretations on imperial power and Roman cultural appropriation.

Marvin, Miranda (2008). *The Language of the Muses: The Dialogue between Roman and Greek Sculpture*. Los Angeles, CA: J. Paul Getty Museum.

This brilliant book, written in an easy to follow style, is the best current guide to the issue of copying in the Roman world. Marvin begins with a careful discussion of where the notion of Roman copying was born, including both ancient and Renaissance scholars and up until recent times. Then she offers suggestions for better ways of understanding Roman sculpture and directions for current and future research.

Morton Braund, Susanna (2017). *Understanding Latin Literature*. 2nd edition. London: Routledge.

This book succeeds in presenting a clear introduction to the most important elements of Roman literature in an accessible format. Some chapters focus on individual authors while others focus on themes such as Roman identity, gender, and power. Throughout the book Braund shows how issues of Roman literature are fundamentally connected to Roman elite male culture.

Richlin, Amy (2017). *Slave Theater in the Roman Republic: Plautus and Popular Comedy*. Cambridge: Cambridge University Press.

This book focuses on the central figure of the enslaved person in the comedies of Plautus. Richlin uses theoretical models about transgressive humor combined with a deep understanding of slavery to identify both what people feared and what people desired. Her work explores how these plays might have conveyed different meanings to the elite who commissioned the plays and to the non-elite who comprised much of the audience.

Stewart, Peter (2004). *Roman Art*. Oxford: Oxford University Press.

This volume provides a brief illustrated overview of the history of Roman art. The book is organized around several loose categories such as portraiture, public monuments, funerary art, domestic art, and late antiquity, and included representative monuments and problems in Roman art. It also offers a survey of the range of approaches adopted by scholars in analyzing Roman art, and so serves as an accessible introduction to the field.

Ancient Authors

The following list provides the names of the ancient authors whose surviving texts provide the primary literary sources for the Roman Republic. Authors are listed alphabetically by the name with which they are generally known in English; their full name is given in parentheses. Translations of these authors are widely available; the Loeb Classical Library includes the original language and English on facing pages.

Cato the Elder (Marcus Porcius Cato)	234–149 BCE	Latin author and statesman; first surviving Latin prose author; surviving work includes a treatise *On Agriculture*; also author of a work on the origins of Italian towns (including Rome)
Catullus (Gaius Valerius Catullus)	84–54 BCE	Latin neoteric poet of the Late Republic; surviving poems include both short and longer works
Cicero (Marcus Tullius Cicero)	106–43 BCE	Latin orator and statesman; surviving works include 58 speeches, 20 philosophical works, and a large collection of private letters
Horace (Quintus Horatius Flaccus)	65–27 BCE	Latin lyric poet of the Late Republic and early Empire; surviving poems include *Satires* and *Odes* along with a number of other poems
Livy (Titus Livius)	59 BCE–17 CE	Latin historian, author of a history from the founding of Rome to his own day; surviving books cover the years 753–293 and 218–167 BCE
Lucretius (Titus Lucretius Carus)	c. 99–55 BCE	Latin poet and philosopher; surviving work is the philosophical poem *On the Nature of Things*

A Social and Cultural History of Republican Rome, First Edition. Eric M. Orlin.
© 2022 John Wiley & Sons, Inc. Published 2022 by John Wiley & Sons, Inc.

Ovid (Publius Ovidius Naso)	43 BCE–17 CE	Latin lyric poet of the early Empire; surviving poems include love elegy, the epic poem *Metamorphoses*, a poetic Roman calendar, and poems from exile
Plautus (Titus Maccius Plautus)	c. 250–184 BCE	Latin comic playwright; author of the first Latin literary works to survive in their entirety
Plutarch (Ploutarchos)	46–120 CE	Greek biographer and moralist; most famous for his *Parallel Lives*, matching biographies of Greek and Roman leaders
Polybius (Polybios)	c. 200–120 BCE	Greek historian brought to Rome in 167 BCE; surviving *Histories* focus on the rise of Rome from 264 to 146 BCE
Propertius (Sextus Propertius)	c. 50–16 BCE	Latin elegiac poet of the early Empire; surviving work includes four books of love elegy
Sulpicia (Sulpicia)	Late first c. BCE	Latin poet, author of six surviving elegies published in the collection attributed to Tibullus, an elegiac poet of the early Empire
Terence (Publius Terentius Afer)	c. 190–160 BCE	Latin comic playwright, probably born in Africa; author of six surviving comedies
Vergil (Publius Vergilius Maro)	70–19 BCE	Latin poet; surviving works include the *Aeneid*, an epic poem, plus two shorter works related to rural life; often considered the greatest of the Latin poets

Notable Figures from Roman History

The following list of notable persons is not meant to be exhaustive, but to provide a reference for significant individuals mentioned in the text. Romans who are mostly famous as authors are not listed here, but on the separate authors list. Individuals are listed alphabetically by the name with which they are generally known in English; their full name is given in parentheses.

Appius Claudius Caecus	c. 340–280 BCE	Consul in 307 and 296 BCE, builder of the Appian Way and the Aqua Appia, Rome's first long distance road and first aqueduct
Brutus (Lucius Junius Brutus)	Sixth century BCE	Legendary founder and first consul of Roman Republic; not to be confused with his descendant Marcus Junius Brutus, one of the assassins of Caesar, who took the earlier Brutus as his model
Cato the Elder (Marcus Porcius Cato)	234–149 BCE	Roman soldier and statesman; censor in 184 BCE; famous for cultivating an image as a stern traditionalist and for demanding the destruction of Carthage
Cincinnatus (Lucius Quinctius Cincinnatus)	c. 519–430 BCE	Dictator in 458 BCE; model of a Roman farmer willing to accept duty and power on behalf of the state for only as long as needed
Cornelia	195–115 BCE	Daughter of Scipio Africanus (victor in the Second Punic War) and Aemilia Paulla; mother of the Gracchi brothers; an example of a virtuous and educated Roman woman involved in the political careers of her sons

A Social and Cultural History of Republican Rome, First Edition. Eric M. Orlin.
© 2022 John Wiley & Sons, Inc. Published 2022 by John Wiley & Sons, Inc.

Crassus (Marcus Licinius Crassus)	115–53 BCE	Roman politician, part of the informal First Triumvirate; known as the richest man in Rome; killed on campaign in Parthia
Hannibal (Hannibal Barca)	247–181 BCE	Carthaginian general against Rome during the secnd Punic War; led troops across Alps and won three major victories in Italy before being defeated by Scipio Africanus
Julius Caesar (Gaius Julius Caesar)	100–44 BCE	Roman statesman and general; defeated Pompey in the Roman civil war and contributed to the end of the Republican system of government
Lucretia	Died 510 BCE	Legendary figure; wife of Collatinus; her rape and subsequent suicide is the Roman origin story for their revolution to a Republican form of government
Marius (Gaius Marius)	157–86 BCE	Roman statesman and general; consul five times in a row; rivalry with Sulla contributed to Sulla's march on Rome
Mark Antony (Marcus Antonius)	83–30 BCE	Roman statesman and general; Caesar's second in command; part of the Second Triumvirate with Octavian; allied with Cleopatra and was defeated at Actium
Octavian (Gaius Julius Caesar Octavianus)	63 BCE–14 CE	Roman statesman and general; Caesar's grand-nephew and heir; part of the Second Triumvirate with Mark Antony; defeated Antony and Cleopatra at Actium; became the first Roman emperor and changed his name to Augustus in 27 BCE
Pompey the Great (Gnaeus Pompeius Magnus)	106–48 BCE	Roman statesman and general; added the eastern Mediterranean to Roman territory; rivalry with Caesar contributed to the end of the Republican system of government
Romulus	Eighth century BCE	Legendary founder of Rome in 753 BCE; killed his brother Remus in a dispute over the naming of the city
Scipio Africanus (Publius Cornelius Scipio Africanus)	236–183 BCE	Consul in 205 BCE, victor over Hannibal at the battle of Zama 202 BCE that ended the Second Punic War
Spurius Ligustinus	c. 220–160 BCE	Roman soldier; centurion; fought multiple campaigns in Spain and Greece; rewarded with six civic crowns
Sulla (Lucius Cornelius Sulla)	138–78 BCE	Roman statesman and general; first to march Roman troops on Rome; became dictator for reforming the state, but reforms were discarded after his death

Tarquin (Sextus Tarquinius)	Sixth century BCE	Son of legendary seventh and last king of Rome, Tarquinius Superbus (Tarquin the Proud); Etruscan family; his rape of Lucretia led to the overthrow of the Monarchy
Terentia	98 BCE–6 CE	Wife of Marcus Tullius Cicero, mother of Tullia; known from Cicero's letters; played an active role in Cicero's political life
Tiberius Gracchus (Tiberius Sempronius Gracchus)	c. 170–133 BCE	Roman politician; known for passing an agrarian reform proposal against the wishes of the Senate; killed in riot instigated by the Senate, ushering in a violent period in Roman politics
Tiro (Marcus Tullius Tiro)	103–4 BCE	Enslaved person who subsequently (re)gained free status; personal secretary to Cicero and responsible for publishing his writings; invented a popular form of shorthand

Glossary

Actium site of a naval battle in 31 BCE pitting Octavian against Cleopatra and Antony; Octavian's victory is usually taken to mark the end of the Republic and the beginning of the Roman Empire

aedile a lower-ranking Roman magistrate, with responsibility for the maintenance of the city, such as public buildings

archaeology the systematic uncovering of ancient remains in the earth, including both private houses and large public structures, as well as cemeteries and roads

augurs one of the Roman priestly colleges; their primary responsibility was reading signs from the gods through the flight of birds

Bacchanalia a famous religious incident of 186 BCE when Roman magistrates reacted to the worship of Bacchus (Dionysios)

cella the interior chamber of a Roman temple, where the cult statue was located

century a subdivision of the Roman army, notionally of 100 men, commanded by a centurion; also a voting unit in the *comitia centuriata*

civitas sine suffragio literally "citizenship without the vote," a status that gave individuals the ability to marry and to trade with Roman citizens

client the weaker party in a relationship of mutual dependence with a patron; clients offered loyalty and support in exchange for protection and assistance

collegia the Roman term for associations or clubs, often organized by trade and providing benefits, especially funerary, to members

Comitia Centuriata the Centuriate Assembly, the Roman voting body in charge of elections as well as votes on war and peace, in addition to other legislation; divided into voting groups according to wealth

Comitia Tributa the Tribal Assembly, a Roman voting body for legislation other than war and peace, organized by geographical distribution

comitium the singular form of *comitia*; a spot in the center of the Roman forum where magistrates and others gathered to make speeches to the people on matters of public policy

A Social and Cultural History of Republican Rome, First Edition. Eric M. Orlin.
© 2022 John Wiley & Sons, Inc. Published 2022 by John Wiley & Sons, Inc.

Concilium Plebis the Plebeian Council; organized by geography like the *Comitia Tributa*, but consisting only of plebeians; in theory its legislation was binding only on plebeians, but by the Late Republic could pass legislation for the entire state

consul the highest Roman magistrate, invested with *imperium*; two elected annually; major responsibilities included leading armies outside of Rome

curia a building specially built to house meetings of the Senate

epigraphy the analysis of inscribed material, usually stone but also bronze or painted on walls

Etruscan from the territory of Etruria, a powerful civilization just north of Rome

familia the Latin term for a household; included all members subject to the authority of the head of the household (children whether grown or not, wives in certain types of marriages, enslaved persons)

fasces a bundle of rods tied together and holding an axe; the symbol of a magistrate's authority in Rome; taken over as a symbol by Mussolini and other fascists

fides the Latin word for trust; the basis for the patron–client and other relationships

First Triumvirate a modern term describing the informal alliance between Julius Caesar, Pompey the Great, and Marcus Crassus that dominated Roman politics between 60 and 49 BCE

freedperson an enslaved person who regained (or obtained for the first time) free status

Gaul territory today comprising northern Italy and France; a constant concern of the Romans after 390 BCE when Gauls sacked Rome

haruspices one of the Roman priestly colleges; comprised of Etruscans; primary responsibility included interpreting lightning strikes and the entrails of animals

imperium a quasi-religious authority invested in certain magistrates that gave them the authority to command other Romans, especially in the army

Lares divinities often associated with the household, but expanding into public areas; generally served as guardians (of the house, of roads and crossroads, of the state)

Latin colonies generally speaking, colonies where the citizens possessed *civitas sine suffragio* (the rights to intermarriage and trade, but not to vote)

legion the largest unit of the Roman army, consisting of roughly 4000 men during the Republic

Magna Graecia the area of southern Italy inhabited by Greek colonists from roughly 700 BCE

maniple tactical unit of the Roman army, in theory consisting of 120 men

manumission the act of emancipating enslaved persons to free status

material culture the physical artifacts produced by humans, including pottery, artwork, architecture, tools, tombs, and more

mos maiorum literally "custom of the ancestors;" the Roman way of referring to the unwritten rules supposedly approved by past experience that governed their behavior

neoterics a group of Latin poets who regarded themselves as *avant-garde*, deliberately turning their backs on older Greek traditions to experiment with different forms and subject matter

nexum debt slavery, where individuals become enslaved for failure to pay off a debt, and are restored to free status upon payment

novus homo literally a "new man;" a reference to a Roman politician who lacked ancestors among the ruling class in Rome

numismatics the study of ancient coinage

Optimates those politicians in the Late Republic who believed that authority should be invested in the Senate and the traditional aristocracy

Paterfamilias literally the "father of the family," the head of the Roman household

patria potestas literally "paternal power," the control that the *paterfamilias* exercised over his *familia*, including the power to put any members of the *familia* to death

patricians originally the ruling elite of Rome; a hereditary status that was maintained throughout the Republic even as the ruling elite expanded

patron the stronger party in a relationship of mutual dependence with a client, patrons offered protection and assistance in exchange for loyalty and support

pax deorum literally "peace with the gods," the state of affairs that the Romans believed they needed to maintain in order to obtain any good result on earth

plebeians non-patricians in Rome who comprised the majority of the population; generally less wealthy and originally excluded from full participation in the Roman political and religious systems, though later some plebeians were accepted into the ruling elite

polytheism a religious system in which many gods and goddesses are worshipped at the same time

Pompeii the city on the bay of Naples destroyed in the eruption of Mt. Vesuvius in 79 CE

pontifex maximus the head of the college of pontiffs; served as administrative head of the Roman religion but with no additional authority to make decisions

pontiffs one of the priestly colleges in Rome; it had general responsibility for religion, including setting the calendar and overseeing ritual practices

Populares Roman politicians in the Late Republic who courted support of the people even though they themselves were aristocrats; relied on assemblies for their power

praetor the second highest Roman magistrate, also invested with *imperium*; originally a military function but became associated with administering the legal system

Punic Wars a series of three wars against Carthage (264–241; 218–202; 149–146 BCE) that resulted in Rome acquiring control of the western Mediterranean basin

res publica Latin for "public thing," the standard Roman phrase for the state

Roman colonies generally speaking, colonies whose inhabitants possessed full citizen rights in Rome, including the right to vote

Secession of the Plebs a legendary technique used by the plebeians, in which they temporarily removed themselves from the city of Rome and left the city without manpower to defend itself in order to force concessions from the patricians

Second Triumvirate a formal political structure that controlled Rome from 42 to 32 BCE, consisting of Mark Antony, Gaius Octavianus, and Marcus Lepidus

Senate the body of former magistrates that met to discuss business facing the Roman state; technically the Senate had no authority to make laws, but its advice was decisive in the Early and Middle Republic

Social War the war between Rome and her former Italian allies ("*socii*") fought from 91 to 88 BCE

societas a partnership formed for a common legal interest, where individuals each contributed funds to a common pool

Struggle of the Orders the term for the legendary early conflicts between the plebeians and patricians of Rome

subsistence farming a style where the primary aim is to provide food for the farmer's own family, with any excess sold at market

sumptuary legislation laws that limit the purchase or use of luxury items

survey archaeology an archaeological method that relies on careful observation of remains on the surface rather than on digging through the soil

Tribunes of the Plebs plebeian magistrates charged to defend the interests of the plebeians through their veto power

Twelve Tables Rome's first written legal code, enacted in 451/450 BCE

Veii one of the leading Etruscan towns; its capture by Rome in 396 BCE is often taken to mark Rome's first real territorial expansion

verism a hyperrealistic style of portraiture whose aim is to create the impression of realism

Vestal Virgins one of Rome's priestly colleges, comprised entirely of females who had to maintain their chastity for their entire service in office (at least 30 years) and received special privileges in exchange for their special protective role

vir The Roman word for "man;" also an ideological term referring to the proper sort of man as the Romans saw it

virtus the Roman term for "manliness," mostly displayed in battle or other places where specifically male qualities could be displayed

Index

Note: Romans are listed according to their most recognizable English name, not their family name. Thus Mark Antony is listed under **M**, but Julius Caesar is listed under **C**. Other individuals are listed by last name.

abortion, 96–7
Actium, battle of, 41–43, 45
adultery, 107, 109–10, 112
Aemilius Paullus, L. 103, 135, 187, 188
Aeneid 111, 244
Aethiopians, 136–37
Africa, 34, 38–39, 129, 131–32, 134–35, 196, 212, 248
agrarian societies, 89, 150, 173, 184, 212
agriculture *See also farming*
   as basis for Roman economy 12, 169, 203, 207, 219
   as noble profession, 54, 202
   Cato the Elder and, 202, 250
   changes in Roman practice, 214, 216
   enslaved persons and, 200–207
   survey archaeology and, 214
Alexander the Great, 31, 38, 192
Alexandria (Egypt), 34, 41, 222, 234, 251, 254
amphitheater, 18, 139, 242
ancestors, 165
   importance of, 150, 152, 202, 232, 241, 253
   political significance of, 52, 74, 254
Apollo, 127, 245
Appius Claudius Caecus, 112, 228
   Appian Way, 193, 228
aqueducts, 112, 192, 225, 228, 231
arch, 187, 192
archaeological evidence, 9, 16–18, 27, 93, 130, 139, 162, 198, 204–5, 212, 214, 222–3, 226, 229
   as source for non-elite, 16–17, 88, 160, 237
aristocracy, 81, 82, 83
   as form of government, 69–70, 72
   as ruling elite, 31, 38, 39, 44, 50, 52, 62, 78, 85, 102, 121, 258, 260
   as web of relationships, 52–3, 62
   control of state by, 29, 39, 52, 170
   loss of authority by, 82–83
   values of, 118–9, 253
army, Ch.10 *passim*
   as means to political advancement, 52
   composition of, 29, 71, 80, 130, 184–5, 196, 198, 200
   length of service in, 195

A Social and Cultural History of Republican Rome, First Edition. Eric M. Orlin.
© 2022 John Wiley & Sons, Inc. Published 2022 by John Wiley & Sons, Inc.

manpower as strength of, 31, 129
organization of, 185–6, 196
Polybius on, 195
recruitment for, 79–80, 98, 138, 186, 189, 195, 196, 200, 212
reforms, 196–8
Athens (Greece), 9, 133, 134, 165, 222, 234, 247, 254
atrium, 235, 237
Attis, 108, 147, 160
augurs, 127, 150
Augustus, 8, 22, 41, 43, 44, 142, 181, 183, 197, 198, 221, 225, 241, 242, 258
Aventine, 29, 154, 226, 238

Bacchanalia, 19, 133, 139, 155, 156, 157, 159
Bacchus, 134, 139, 155, 156, 157, 159
bribery
accusations of, 52, 83, 171
as part of politics, 74, 85, 171, 217
bronze, 27
as medium for coinage, 204–205
as medium for inscription, 16, 18, 133
as medium for sculpture, 26–7, 234, 244, 251
Brutus, M. Junius 21–2, 25–7, 41, 106–7, 142

Caesar, G. Julius 7, 15, 19, 21–2, 40–4, 65, 76, 81, 82, 84, 85, 91, 93, 101–2, 121, 141–2, 151, 161–2, 178, 199, 239, 241–2, 259–60
calendar, 28, 40, 150–51, 218
Camillus, M. Furius15, 154
Campus Martius, 37, 231, 239
Cannae, battle of 129
Capitoline hill, 14, 27, 126, 154, 188, 223, 225, 234
Carthage (Africa), 20, 33, 34, 36, 38, 43, 92, 100, 111, 129, 134, 135, 154, 196, 222, 259
Castor and Pollux, 127, 134, 154, 232
Cato the Elder (M. Porcius Cato), 34, 62, 103–4, 113, 121, 133–4, 189, 202–4, 206–7, 209–10, 215–7, 234, 249–50
Catullus, C. Valerius, 13, 104, 116–7, 256–7
cavalry, 34, 50, 71, 185, 195, 232–3

censors, 227, 229
census, 99, 185, 197–8, 208, 255
Centuriate Assembly, 67, 71, 186
centurion, 185, 189
century (army unit), 185, 189, 223, 226, 241, 247
chastity, 28, 106, 107, 109, 111, 191, 208
children
adoption of, 103
as part of family, 54, 88–90, 92, 94, 112
enslaved from birth, 60
high mortality rate of, 56, 91, 96, 103
legal status of, 174
of freedpersons, 61
of non-elite, 92, 97
relationship to parents, 89–90, 94–99, 103
societal need for, 57, 91
Christians, 145–7, 156, 234, 257, 260
Cicero, M. Tullius, 12, 23, 41, 51–2, 54–5, 57, 64–5, 73–4, 76, 82, 91, 93–5, 99, 100, 102–3, 105, 112, 117, 120–1, 127, 130, 162, 171–3, 182, 213, 216–8, 257, 259–60
cinaedus, 116–7
Cincinnatus, L. Quinctius, 36–7
citizenship
army service and, 71, 173, 185, 189, 195, 197
as marker of status, 56, 112–3, 128–9, 174, 208
freedpersons and, 60, 64, 135
generosity with, 28, 64, 128, 137, 143, 195
Italian communities and, 31, 39, 60, 127–9, 138, 141, 142, 156
legal system and, 167–8, 174, 178, 180
voting and, 71, 73, 128
civil war, 22, 43–4, 62, 76, 104, 140–2, 161, 258
civitas sine suffragio, 127, 128, 174, *See also* citizenship
Cleopatra, 41, 183, 187
client, 50–54, 60, 74, 120, 171
cloaca maxima, 192, 223
Clodius, P., 49, 82, 121
coinage, 16, 20–22, 205–6, 212
collegiality, 36, 82

colonies
    Latin colonies, 128–130
    Roman colonies, 128–30, 139
Colosseum, 16, 140, 242
comedy, 134, 176, 247, 248
comitia centuriata, See Centuriate Assembly
concrete, 238, 240
consul, 25, 29, 38, 67, 69–71, 82, 90, 101, 121–2, 126, 139, 149–50, 152, 162, 172–3, 177, 180, 184, 186, 189, 199, 202, 229
contraceptives, 96
Cornelia (mother of the Gracchi), 63, 92, 99, 112
Crassus, M. Licinius 40, 57, 82, 85, 239
Cronon, William 8
Cybele. *See Magna Mater*

democracy, 69–73
demographics, 50, 90, 94, 196
denarius, 205–6
dependence, 47, 50–2, 55, 57, 60, 62, 65, 70, 90, 92, 99, 108, 113, 122
dictator, 7, 15, 36–7, 40, 101, 154, 181
Digest of Justinian, 179, 180
divorce, 57, 90, 92, 101–3, 105
dominance, 47, 50, 52, 56–60, 62–5, 70, 90, 92, 99, 108, 110, 112–3, 116, 122, 193, 211
domus, 235, 237
dowry, 57, 63, 92, 98

economy, Ch. 11 *passim*
    slavery and, 207–8
    gendered roles, 117
    coinage and, 16, 20, 205
    impact of conquest, 38, 62, 64, 81, 198, 205–7, 208, 212
    warfare and, 33, 197
    family and, 57, 93, 119, 130
    women and, 92
education, 57, 64, 77, 162
Egypt, 34, 36, 41, 131, 183, 254
Egyptians, 137, 161, 225, 262
elections, 38, 52, 53, 57, 71, 72, 73, 74, 81, 83, 126, 129, 162, 186
elite
    balance within, 170, 172, 174, 228
    behavior of, 53, 80, 158–60, 237
    competition among, 74, 79, 178, 239
    composition of, 31, 54, 60
    depictions in art, 254
    families, 97, 101–3
    houses of, 235, 237
    loss of political control by, 83, 161, 170, 178
    military and, 183, 187
    of Italian towns, 128
    sources by, 45, 76, 88, 108, 130, 203, 249, 250
    sources for, 20, 119
    tools of dominance, 52–3, 150, 166–70, 260
    values of, 27, 33, 43, 54, 55, 95, 107, 109, 119, 122, 152, 203, 259
    women and, 12, 57, 63, 98–9, 102, 258
enslaved persons, *See also familia, slavery*
    agriculture and, 203, 207, 209–113, 215, 219
    as authors, 247–8
    as doctors, 210–1
    as fire *brigade*, 239
    as gladiators or prostitutes, 120
    as legendary Roman ancestors, 125
    as Roman citizens, 135
    as teachers, 97, 100, 210–11
    familia and, 64, 88–9, 100, 210
    increase of, 62–3, 100, 174, 207
    law and, 64, 89, 113, 207–10
    manumission and, 21, 60, 210
    numbers of, 207–8
    religious rituals and, 255
    represented on stage, 13, 248
    sexual exploitation of, 113, 120
    tombstones, 55–6
    treatment of, 209–11
equality, 27, 47, 59, 69, 138, 165
equestrian, 50, 52
Etruscan, 16, 25, 26, 42, 126, 154, 160, 186, 223, 227, 234, 242, 245, 262
eunuchs, 109, 158
excavation, 27, 214. *See also archaeological evidence*

Fabii (family), 184, 194, 246
Fabius Pictor, Q., 249, 250
familia, Ch, 5 *passim*
    as microcosm of state, 152

definition of, 88–92, 103
economic needs of, 130, 190, 204
enslaved persons in, 64, 88–9, 100–101, 210–11
impact of war on, 190, 196, 216
importance of, 7, 56, 57, 82, 104, 118, 248, 254
legal position, 89, 92, 168
non-elite, 50, 59, 92, 97, 238
political importance of, 31, 49, 52, 74, 82, 84, 121, 161, 241
religion of, 150, 152
social status and, 52, 54, 152, 258
sources for, 12, 16, 20, 22
women's role in, 28, 118, 191

family-planning. *See contraceptives*
farming, *See also agriculture, economy*
changes in, 197, 213, 219
commercial, 204, 215–6
legends about, 5, 37
slave labor and, 100, 197, 219
subsistence, 204, 215
villa style of, 207, 214
warfare and, 80, 202–3, 212
fasces, 37, 126
Faunus, 19, 147
female, *See women*
festival, 19, 87, 134, 150, 152, 204
fides, 51
Finley, Moses 208
First Triumvirate, 40, 85, 102, 239
foreign customs, Roman response to, 16, 28, 126, 133, 155–6, 158–60, 235, 242, 245, 260, 261
foreigners, Ch. 7 *passim*
artistic depictions of, 132
as enslaved persons, 208, 212
attitudes towards, 87, 125, 127, 141, 142, 195
government, *See also res publica, Senate*
formal mechanisms, 62, 67–8, 70–3, 75–6, 78–9, 97
informal structures, 67–69
formulary procedure. *See praetor's edict*
Forum,
Roman, 16, 39, 53, 73–74, 76, 80, 162, 172, 181, 222–23, 225, 229, 232, 235, 241

of Caesar, 241
foundation of Rome, 6, 96, 126, 151, 154, 222, 223, 250
freedom
as slogan, 21, 34, 36, 46, 85, 209
equated with manliness, 122
of women, 59
restored to enslaved persons, 64, 210, 248
freedpersons, 56, 60, 63–4, 101, 112, 132, 216
duties to former enslaver, 60, 64
and names, 112
Fulvia, 121

Gaius (jurist), 99–100
Gauls, 10, 14, 15, 28, 33, 40, 76, 85, 132, 193, 196, 224
gender, Ch. 6 *passim*
definition of, 107
expectations, 106, 114, 119, 152
roles, 100, 107–8, 116, 118–9, 121–2, 257
generals, 33, 36, 38, 62, 79, 138, 184, 187, 189, 198, 200, 212, 226, 232, 240
gladiators, 119–20, 196
gods, 22, 133, 139, 145–8, 156, 159, 223; Ch.8, *passim*
gold
as form of money, 14, 179, 187, 204, 210
as luxury item, 75, 115, 118, 204
offered to the gods, 149
Gracchus, Gaius 39, 63, 79, 180
Gracchus, Tiberius 38, 43, 44, 79, 80–81, 83, 99, 101, 112, 161, 178–180, 197, 212, 214
Greece
as slave society, 208–9
coinage in, 205
military engagement with, 31, 36, 43, 67, 131, 133, 244, 259
Greek culture
literary, 116, 247, 257
mythology, 7, 255
philosophical thought, 68, 259
presence in Rome, 31, 117, 127, 134, 233, 234–6, 247, 254–5
religion, 155–6, 159–60

Roman critiques of, 117, 133, 156
Roman response to, 13, 133, 134, 247–251, 256, 259, 261
sex/gender system, 117

Hannibal, 34, 38, 67, 129, 134, 149–50, 194, 207, 226
Harris, William 33
haruspices, 126
Hercules, 127, 154
  Hercules Musarum, 235
hereditary privileges, 29, 48–9, 51–2, 54
hermaphrodites, 108
historians, *See also sources*
  Roman 7–10, 12, 16, 22, 29, 33, 41–5, 56, 68, 72, 80, 100, 112, 179, 197, 206, 221, 225
  modern, 5–6, 13, 17–18, 27, 42, 175, 205, 258
history as morals, 7, 14, 29, 250
Homer, 9, 118
homosexuality, *See same-sex relationships*
honor
  among elite, 7, 28, 54, 106, 194
  among non-elite, 55
  as Roman value, 260
Horace (Q. Horatius Flaccus), 104, 113, 244, 251, 259, 261–2
households, *See also familia*
  changes in, 100
  divinities of, 147, 152
  enslaved persons in, 60, 64, 97, 100
  non-elite, 59
  women's power in, 92, 98, 119

identity
  distinctive Roman, 143, 229, 232, 247, 261
  female, 258
  markers of, 117, 199
  plebeian, 48
  religious, 147
ideology, 87
  of superiority, 60, 137, 207
  on agriculture, 203, 216, 260
  on family, 103
  on money, 202
  on women, 87, 99, 100, 107–8, 110–11, 118, 168–9

openness as, 128, 136
immigrants, 125, 160
Imperial period, 45, 162, 187, 199, 210, 219
imperialism, 15, 33, 43, 242
imperium, 69, 172, 173, 186
inequality
  of Italians, 138
  political, 47
  wealth, 44, 80
infantry, 34, 71, 185, 189, 195–96
inscriptions, 16, 18–20, 23, 63, 118–9, 147, 156, 187, 191
insulae, 16, 238
Italian communities
  as dependent allies of Rome, 39, 140, 195
  distinctive culture of, 126, 139–40, 247, 250
  extension of Roman law to, 129, 156
  inequality of, 60, 138–41

Jews, 147, 161
Julia (daughter of Caesar), 40, 93, 101, 102
Juno, 149, 155, 235
  Juno Regina, 154
Jupiter, 38, 126, 149, 153–4, 188, 223, 234–5, 245
jurists, 172, 176, 177, 179
kings, Roman hatred of, 27, 36, 41, 70, 80, 106, 167

Laelius, C. 78, 81, 260
Lares (hearth god), 152
  Lares Permarini, 231, 233
Largo Argentina, temples of, 229–30, 233
Late Republic, 12, 42–3, 48, 52, 62–3, 73, 76, 79, 81, 82–3, 85–6, 98, 104, 112, 116, 141, 147, 151, 161–2, 171, 174, 178, 180, 198–9, 200, 219, 238
latifundia, 212–3
Latin citizenship. *See civitas sine suffragio*
Latin Revolt, 31, 127
Law, Ch. 9 *passim*
  access to, 31, 51, 128, 141, 170, 172, 173, 217
  as reflection of ideology, 89, 99–100, 168, 175

categories in, 120, 169
changes in, 172, 173, 176, 178, 180, 181, 208
creation of, 29, 165
criminal, 166–7, 169, 171, 178, 180
economy and, 217
family and, 89, 92, 112
Italian cities and, 130, 139, 156
nature of, 165, 167–71, 177, 218
patrons and, 51, 53
use of precedent in, 172, 176, 180
publication of, 47, 170, 172
reasons for, 31, 170
sources for, 96, 100, 179
women and, 62, 63, 75, 89, 92, 99, 100, 111, 168
written, 10, 29
legendary stories, 5, 25, 87, 90, 96, 106, 110, 125, 127, 154, 165, 166, 208, 222, 250, 257
legis actio, 171, 172
Lesbia, 116, 256, 257
Lex See also law
  Calpurnia, 178
  Cornelia, 179–80
  Fannia, 175–6
  Hortensia, 29, 42
  Oppia, 62, 75
  Poetelia Papiria, 207–8
  Villia, 79
  Voconia, 99–100, 103
Livius Andronicus, 247
Livy, 5–9, 11, 14–15, 25, 34, 37, 43, 47, 67, 70, 72, 76, 87, 90, 92, 106, 125–7, 138, 143, 154, 156–7, 165, 166, 169, 172–3, 184–6, 189–90, 194, 217, 224–5, 232
Lucilius, 249
Lucretia, 25, 27, 29, 38, 106–7, 109, 118, 208

Macedonia, 34, 67, 135, 189, 207
Magna Graecia, 31, 34, 227
Magna Mater, 108, 155, 157, 158, 159, 160
male, *See men*
maniple, 186, 189, 196
manliness, 54, 114, 116, 117, 119, 121, 122, 158

manumission, 60, 64, 210
marble
  as building material, 8, 138, 235, 240, 242
  in sculpture, 131, 244, 251–2, 255
Marius, G. 39, 43, 62, 81–2, 101, 102, 141, 161, 196–9
markets, 54, 150, 204–8, 214–5, 229
marriage
  affection within, 93, 101–2
  age at, 91–3
  arranged, 63, 92–3, 99, 101
  financial aspects of, 57, 92, 98
  legendary first in Rome, 87, 125
  of enslaved persons not permitted, 210
  political, 92, 101–2, 112, 121
  sex outside of, 107, 111, 112, 114
  sine manu, 98–99
material culture, 9, 15, 18, 22, 133
men *See also manliness*
  as gender category, 108–9
  attitudes towards women, 76, 91, 100, 109
  dominance of, 58–9, 65, 99, 108–11, 114, 116, 167
  expectations for, 28, 54, 107, 113, 114, 116, 119, 121, 122, 191, 254
  role in family, 57, 89
  sources by, 77, 113
military Ch. 10, *passim. See also army, generals, warfare*
  as central feature of Roman society, 33, 150, 183, 186, 189–90, 198, 199, 245, 247
  avenue to politics, 187, 199
  impact of, 190, 206
  importance to male identity, 28, 54, 121
  individual use of, 40, 43, 78, 142, 178
  monuments to success, 229, 232–3
  plebeians as source of, 48
  rewards of, 33, 187, 189, 194, 198, 200
Millar, Fergus 73
Mithridates of Pontus, 39, 62, 140, 199
modern world
  comparison of slavery to, 60, 137, 208, 248
  cultural comparison, to, 108, 151, 237
  economic comparison to, 54, 57, 120, 216, 219

family comparison to, 93, 94
  impact on 155, 172, 180–1, 192, 209, 235
  law comparison to, 171, 174
  notions of race compared to, 137, 207, 209
  political comparison to, 44, 68, 71–2, 81, 141–2, 165, 195
  religious comparison to, 146–7, 149–150
moral decay, notions of, 8, 259
mortality rate, 12, 56, 91, 94, 103
mos maiorum, 68, 78, 134, 165, 227
Mucius Scaevola, Q.101, 177
murder, 21, 41, 85, 166, 167, 180

Naevius, Gn. 247
names, 49, 63–4, 111–2
Napoleon, 27
networks, 52–3, 56, 68, 74, 78, 92, 175, 199, 219
nexum, See slavery
non-elite, 50
  access to law, 168, 170, 172
  housing, 237–9
  lives of, 97, 237, 248
  military and, 183, 189
  professions, 55
  prominence as authors, 248, 250
  religious practices of, 159–60
  role in political life, 79, 138
  sources for, 12, 16, 19, 56, 160
  sources for, 20, 88
  women in, 59, 107–8
novus homo, 52, 74, 84

Octavian (G. Julius Caesar Octavianus), 22, 41, 43, 44, 76, 121, 142, 162, 183, 241, *See also Augustus*
Odyssey, 9, 118, 247
olives, 97, 204, 207, 209, 212, 214, 238
openness *See ideology*
  cultural, 28, 126–7, 154–6, 159, 223, 233, 248
  challenges to, 139
  political, 127–8, 136, 195
Oppian Law, *See lex Oppia*
optimates, 40, 41, 44, 81
Ostia, 16
Ovid (P. Ovidius Naso), 13, 96, 97, 257

Palatine, 158, 222, 223, 232
paterfamilias, 89, 152
patria potestas, 89, 90, 94, 167, 168
patricians, 29, 31, 42–3, 47–52, 165, 174
patrons, 50–3, 60, 62, 74, 122, 170, 219
pax deorum, 148, 149
penetration model, 113, 116, 120, 122
pietas, 191, 254
pileus, 21, 132
Plato, 259–60
Plautus, T. Maccius 13, 23, 104, 112–3, 132, 134, 234, 248
plebeians, 29, 31, 42–3, 47–51, 54, 72, 165, 172
Plutarch, 14, 23, 38, 59, 63, 79, 80, 112, 121, 133, 134, 187, 212, 216, 250
Polybius, 13, 15, 33, 34, 69, 70, 71, 72, 135, 194, 195
Pompeii, 10, 16, 17, 19, 23, 114, 115, 139, 236, 242
Pompey the Great (Gn. Pompeius Magnus), 40–4, 81–2, 85, 93, 101–3, 141, 161–2, 199, 239–42, 259–60
pontifex maximus, 40, 59, 84, 152, 177
populares, 81, 83
porticus, 235, 239, 240, 241
power, *See also patriapotestas, imperium*
  formal, 70, 71, 72, 73, 90, 173
  informal, 68, 70, 73, 76
  shared among elite, 36, 43, 47, 78, 152, 161, 195
  women and, 75–6, 121, 152
praetor's edict, 172, 176, 177
praetors, 69, 157, 172–3, 186
priest, 40, 108, 126–7, 150–1, 158, 161
priestess, 57, 111, 152, 155
privacy, 83, 115, 235, 237, 238
Propertius, Sextus, 13, 257
property
  concern with transmission of, 59, 92, 103, 118, 171, 181
  law's concern with, 29, 166, 169, 170, 174, 175
  qualification to serve in army, 195–97
  women and, 57, 63, 76, 98, 100, 169, 190
prostitutes, 59, 113, 119–120, 156
publicani, 217, 219

Punic Wars, 33–4, 42, 67, 75, 103, 129, 131, 157, 173, 194–5, 217, 232, 234, 247–9
Pyrrhus, 31, 34, 193, 195, 206

Quintilian (M. Fabius Quintilianus), 77, 257

race, 60, 137, 207
racists, 131–32, 136–37
Mussolini, Benito 50
religion, Ch. 8 *passim*
  sources for, 19–20
  in public life, 57, 110, 112, 127–29, 134–5, 150–53, 177, 187, 234
  belief and, 146
  ritual and, 91, 148–49, 152
  superstition and, 145
roads, 191–2, 217, 229
Romulus, 5, 6, 7, 9, 11, 14, 22, 42, 47, 48, 51, 52, 87, 96, 125, 222–3, 232
Rubicon, 40, 85
Rubin, Gayle 107

Sabines, 87, 125
sacrifice, 148, 155, 159, 188, 204, 255
Sallust (G. Sallustius Crispus), 197, 250
same-sex relationships, 113, 116–7
Sant'Omobono, 223
Sappho, 116
Scipio Africanus, P., 34, 38, 39, 63, 92, 103, 135
sculpture, 247, 252, 254
Secession of the Plebs, 29, 48
Second Triumvirate, 41, 76
secret ballot, 53, 79, 83
Senate, 5, 7, 10, 19, 29, 34, 37, 40–1, 47–50, 67, 70–2, 78, 79–82, 126, 133, 138–41, 149–50, 156–59, 171–2, 188, 197–8, 200, 218, 227, 229, 235, 241
Servian wall, 226
sex/gender system, 107, 108, 109, 111, 113, 114, 115, 116, 117, 121
sexual activity, 25, 97, 106–7, 110–16, 119–20, 237 *See also marriage, sex outside of*
sexual morality, 208
sexuality, 106–17, 12–22
Sibylline Books, 149, 150, 159

Sicily, 34, 42, 173, 217–8, 227, 250
silver
  as luxury item, 118, 149, 175, 203
  as money, 21, 175, 179, 187, 204–6, 212
skin color, 60, 131, 136–7
slave society, 203, 208–9
slavery, 203–12 *See also enslaved persons*
  and literature, 248
  as metaphor, 27, 257
  chattel (ownership), 208
  result of conquest, 60, 100, 122, 137, 207
  nexum (debt-slavery) 207–8
Social War, 39, 43, 140, 141
sources *See also Cicero, Livy, Polybius*
  Greek, 13–15, 257
  legal, 89, 90, 179
  literary, 9, 12, 22, 73, 88, 115, 160, 197, 214, 226
  non literary, 15–16, 18, 20, 114, 147, 150, 156, 214
  Roman, 14, 15, 21, 29, 53, 97, 104, 108, 130, 154, 156, 169, 185, 207, 235
  using, 6, 9, 12, 15–16, 19–20, 22, 28, 54–56, 74, 89, 94, 167, 173, 214, 221, 242, 250
Sourvinou-Inwood, Christiane, 147
Spain, 34, 38, 43, 131, 132, 137, 212
SPQR, 10, 48
Spurius Ligustinus, 189–90, 195, 198
Struggle of the Orders, 29, 42, 47, 49, 166, 169
Suetonius (G. Suetonius Tranquillus), 221, 223, 224, 242
Sulla, L. Cornelius, 39, 40, 43, 44, 62, 81, 82, 101, 102, 103, 141, 161, 178, 179, 181, 199
Sulpicia, 257, 258
survey archaeology, 212, 213, 214
Syme, Ronald, 142

Tacitus, P. Cornelius, 137, 180
Tarentum, 129, 247
Tarquin the Proud, 25, 42, 106, 126, 223
tax-farming, 217–19
temples, 16, 159–61, 223, 229, 231–35, 240, 241, 255
  of Castor and Pollux, 127, 232
  of Juno Regina, 154–5

of Jupiter on Capitoline, 38, 126, 154, 188, 223, 245
of Magna Mater, 158–60
of Venus, 161, 240–41
of Vesta, 57
as monuments to military victory, 223, 229, 232–3
Terence (P. Terentius Afer), 13, 23, 135, 248, 262
Terentia, 93, 99
theater, 139, 239, 240, 241, 242
Tiber River, 5, 96, 192, 214, 221, 223, 238, 241
Tibullus, Albius 257–58
Tiro, M. Tullius 64, 65
tombstones, 20, 55, 56, 93, 94, 97, 118, 122
trade, 203, 205, 215, 216, 219, 238
Tribunes of the Plebs, 29, 47. 72, 75, 80, 189, 197
triumphs, 187, 225
Trojan War, 28, 155, 186
tufa, 227, 230, 235
Tullia, 91, 95, 99, 102
Twelve Tables, 29, 51, 60, 165–70, 174–78, 207

univira, 11–12, 121

Valerius Maximus, 110
values, Roman, 7, 50, 51, 114, 117, 241
Veii, 28, 154, 184, 185, 186, 194, 235, 245
Venus, 96, 161, 258
    Venus Genetrix, 162, 241
Vergil (P. Vergilius Maro), 111, 244, 251, 261, 262
verism, 253–54
Verres, G. 217–18
Vestal Virgins, 5, 57, 59, 110, 152
villa, 57, 207, 212
violence
    as tool in Roman politics, 39, 43, 79, 81, 82, 178, 180, 199

use of legal system to avoid, 170, 174
virtus, 119, 121, 122
Vitruvius (M. Vitruvius Pollio), 237

walls, 7, 10, 14, 19, 114, 214, 222, 226
warfare, *See also army, generals, military*
    centrality of, 103, 187, 250
    constant, 28–29, 189–90
    in early Republic, 184, 186
Washington, George 37
wealth
    basis of, 40, 48, 50, 54, 55, 63, 71
    impact of, 8, 31, 44, 56, 71, 98, 169, 219
    influx of, 38, 61–3, 98–100, 138, 175, 212, 233
    land as expression of, 54, 217
white supremacy, 50, 131
Winckelmann, Johann 251
wine, 110, 133, 156, 175, 202, 207, 209, 212, 214
women
    agency of, 59, 63, 77, 102, 258
    as gender category, 108
    as writers, 116, 257–8
    changing roles of, 63, 98–100
    childbearing role, 57, 118, 210
    economic power of, 57, 63
    education of, 77, 258
    expectations for, 107, 116, 118, 191, 257, 258
    ideology towards, 28, 87, 91, 106, 109–14, 118, 122, 156, 191, 254
    influence of, 92, 99, 100, 191
    legal status of, 168
    limitations on, 57, 62, 65, 72, 99, 100, 108, 110
    limited information on, 12, 77, 93
    political influence of, 75–76
    professions, 59, 118, 205
    roles, 57, 59, 92, 152, 190
wool, 97, 106, 117–18, 191, 204–5

xenophobia, 28, 142